Complete Conditioning for the Female Athlete

Bob O'Connor, Kari Fasting,
Diane Dahm and Christine Wells

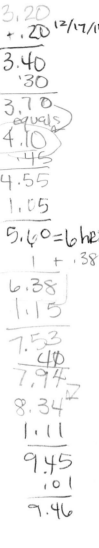

Wish Publishing
Terre Haute, Indiana
www.wishpublishing.com

LCCN: 2001086538

The author and the publisher assume no responsibility for any injury that may occur as a result of attempting to do any of the movements, techniques or exercises described in this book. These activities require strenuous physical activity and a physical examination is advisable before starting this or any other exercise activity.

Cover designed by Phil Velikan
Edited by Heather Lowhorn
Interior photography by Bob O'Connor
Proofread by Ken Samelson

Printed in the United States of America
10 9 8 7 6 5 4 3 2 1

Published in the United States by
Wish Publishing
P.O. Box 10337
Terre Haute, IN 47801, USA
www.wishpublishing.com

Distributed in the United States by
Cardinal Publishers Group
7301 Georgetown Road, Suite 118
Indianapolis, Indiana 46268

Acknowledgments

*T*hanks to Tom Laursen the sports photographer at the Norwegian University for Sport for his outstanding camera work. Tom, as always, has been a great help in capturing just what is needed in a sport photo.

Thanks also to our models Kristine Walseth and Hanne Øverlier who are athletes as well as graduate students at the Norwegian University for Sport.

Contents

Preface

What we think we "know" is often either incomplete or wrong. In the sports sciences, a great deal of research has been done during the last few years, but it has not reached the athletes or the coaches. What modern sport science is finding is often counter to what we have traditionally known. For example, there is strong evidence that stretching as part of your warm up may set you up for injury. Runners who stretch before competition have more leg injuries. Stretching may reduce your speed and power. Swimmers who stretch reduce their speed. Weight lifters who stretch reduce the load they can lift. We will look into the "whys" later. These examples are certainly against what we all thought we knew. As a coach, one of the authors has been involved in playing or coaching for 55 years. He has always stretched when competing and has always stretched his teams in their warm up – not any more.

This book is designed for the female athlete, from high school through the masters level, and for their coaches. We reference the research in case you want to read the original sources for the scientific findings, but we have tried to simplify the findings so that you as a female athlete can utilize what is known at this time.

There seems to be a nearly universal interest in developed countries to become fit. This desire for fitness may be due to a concern for living longer, for becoming more attractive as the media seems to dictate, or to just feel better. Whether the exercise is done in a physical education class, on the field of competition, in a health studio, or on one's own, the activities we do should be understood.

Many of us choose sport as a recreational or a professional activity. Sport fitness is more specific than general fitness. In sport we are usually competing. We may compete with ourselves, attempting to lower our 10K times or improving our golf scores, or we may compete against others. But the competitive nature of sport pushes us to go beyond the average and venture into the realm where superiority is required.

While the general fitness advocate can get by with little more knowledge than was gained in school — such as counting one's pulse rate — the competitive nature of the athlete pushes her toward excellence. She wants to know how to be the best.

There are also psychological and sociological effects of sport. The Women's Sport Foundation has found that young women who are athletes have fewer pregnancies. They feel better about themselves. They feel empowered by their quest and their achievements.

But not all is rosy! As in most forms of endeavor, from school to work, sport is sometimes a sphere which offers predators, both male and female, an opportunity for sexual harassment or sexual abuse. While this seems to happen less in sport than in other areas, athletes need to be aware of what can happen and must be prepared to counter any negative advances. Sexual harassment and sexual abuse, no matter where they are encountered, must be stopped for the sake of both the individual and the society.

So fitness for sport is more encompassing than just running faster, jumping higher or being stronger — it requires a strong mind in a strong body. Properly done, sport is probably our best avenue for developing our physical and psychological selves. And it may well be the most effective and visible method for achieving full equality in our society. But it must be planned for — it doesn't happen automatically.

As the Irish proverb says, "If you don't know where you're going, you'll end up someplace else."

1

Introduction

*T*he differences between men and women are not nearly as great as people commonly think. This is particularly true of trained athletes. When comparing trained men with trained women, we find that pound for pound the strength of the lower body and endurance capacity are quite similar.

Choosing Your Sport or Sports

You have probably already chosen a sport or two for your competitive nature, but there may be other options for competition. For example many people run 10-kilometer races a couple of times a month, but how many have thought about orienteering? Although practiced around the world, many Americans haven't heard about this sport. In orienteering you walk or run with a compass and map. The goal is to find every marked spot on the map as quickly as possible, so quickness is combined with intelligent map reading. The combination of skills is highly intriguing. Dr. Peter Snell, Olympic 800-meter gold medal winner in the1960s, is now the American age group champion in running orienteering. Orienteering is also done on cross country skis and in canoes.

Swimming is an outstanding conditioner. You can compete from about age 8 to age 90 in age group competitions. Or maybe you would like to play while you swim. Women's water polo has become a worldwide game. Scuba is also an interesting option for the aqua-interested woman.

Maybe you would like to combine your running and swimming with cycling in a triathlon. You can participate in all three events yourself or you can find relay events where three people perform the three different sports as a relay.

Of course there is volleyball (6 person, mixed, or doubles), basketball, tennis, rugby, ice hockey, field hockey and any number of other traditional sports. If you like combatives you can find wrestling, boxing, kick boxing, judo, karate and the other martial arts. There are some negatives with boxing, kick boxing and full contact karate. Microscopic brain injuries occur just about every time your head is punched. There are several skull bones encircling the brain. Where these bones come together there is often a rough edge. It is at these rough spots that the bouncing brain picks up small "pin point" hemorrhages. Enough of these small injuries and the brain scars. This makes it impossible for the electrical impulses in the nerves of the brain to be transmitted. (Large boxing gloves or head gear do not protect against these injuries.) The kicking sports are more likely to injure the kidneys. Professional kick boxers in Thailand seldom live to see 40.

Sports Conditioning Needs Are Specific

As we move deeper into the book we will discuss these points in much more detail. But here are some points to ponder:

1. Doing squats doesn't necessarily help your running – especially distance running.
2. You want your workouts to be as sport specific as possible. Swimming doesn't help your legs for running and running doesn't help your arms for swimming. Distance running doesn't help your sprinting and sprinting doesn't help your distance running.
3. If you are working with weights, the posture you use should be as close to your sport posture as possible.
4. Your sport fitness needs are specific:
   - How much cardiopulmonary fitness do you need for your sport?
   - How much flexibility do you need for your sport?
   - How much strength or power do you need for your sport?
   - How much strength-endurance or sprint-endurance do you need?
   - How much sprinting speed do you need for your sport?
   - How you can achieve these needs will be covered in the opening chapters of the book.

Flexibility

When we are young we tend to be quite flexible. Remember how easy it was to touch your toes when you were ten? Our ligaments, tendons and other connective tissues will tend to shrink as we age. They therefore must be stretched throughout our lives in order to keep our youthful abilities to move painlessly. If you are an athlete, a dancer or someone who needs more flexibility because of leisure time pursuits or work—you may need extra stretching to achieve your desired goals.

If you want to be more flexible, there is a best way to accomplish it.

Other reasons why people do flexibility or stretching exercises are:

- to reduce muscle tension;
- to obtain low back pain relief;
- to promote muscular relaxation;
- to develop a better posture;
- to find relief from cramps in the muscles

Strength

In our modern world most of us need less and less strength to live our daily lives. We no longer must saddle the horses, beat the rugs or churn the butter. In spite of this, athletes need more strength today because we compete with higher levels of goals than ever before. You may want more strength to serve the tennis ball harder, to ski more aggressively or to kick a soccer ball harder.

A major reason for wanting strength as you grow older is to reduce the chances of developing osteoporosis (weakened bones) which can result in a severely hunched back (a "widow's hump") or easily broken hips.

If you want strength there is a "best" way to gain it.

Developing Aerobic Conditioning

Stamina, endurance or aerobic fitness are just a few of the terms which are used to describe the adjustment of the body's heart, blood circulation system, and lungs when greater demands are placed on the body to work longer and harder. There are a number of ways to achieve this "aerobic" fitness. But whichever you choose, you will be making the best contribution you can to a longer life. Exercising to develop stamina not only reduces body fat while it makes the body more effective, but it reduces stresses, blood pressure and harmful fats in the blood.

Eating Nutritiously for Improved Performance

Effective and adequate nutrition not only helps us to live longer, but it also aids us in developing muscle strength or in gaining more aerobic fitness. After all, we are what we eat! Most people are actually undernourished. It is quite common to take in too few of certain vitamins and minerals. At the same time we often take in too much fat and sugar, and sometimes we take in too much of certain vitamins or minerals.

Injuries and Other Problems from Exercise

Some people train so hard that they injure their health. Overtraining can not only increase your chances for injury and illness, it can actually reduce your performance. Excessive training can increase the likelihood of the female athlete triad occurring – eating disorders, severe menstrual problems and bone loss (osteoporosis). We must guard against these problems for both our general health and our sport performance.

Many sport injuries can be prevented or reduced through proper exercise, clothing, shoes, orthotics, braces, taping and conditioning. Women have more knee injuries than men because of both the angle of the thigh bone and the smaller ligaments. Correct strengthening exercises, proper playing techniques, braces or orthotics may reduce the risk. Shin splints can be increased by improper shoes, poor techniques or by ignoring the need for proper orthotics.

Mental Conditioning

Your mental conditioning will determine how effectively you practice. Then when in competition it can give you the edge over your opponent. In many sports the mental edge can be the margin of victory. Your goal setting, your mental practice, your ability to relax under pressure, your ability to peak when it is needed – are all essential elements for a successful athlete.

The Completely Conditioned Athlete

All of the above factors (strength, endurance, flexibility, nutrition and mental preparation) are essential for the athlete to function at her highest level. Coaches must be aware of how to work to help the athlete develop to her fullest in each of these areas and in each sport that she chooses for participation. There are "best" ways to accomplish these tasks. Competitive female athletes are every bit as motivated for success as are male athletes. They seek success just as much. They work just as hard. And they will profit by training using the best information that modern sport science has offered.

2

Coaching Women and Girls

*I*t is often said that sport is a male world. Until recently sports have been heavily dominated by boys and men, but there have been great changes over the last 20 years. Girls and women participate more often and in a wider range of sporting activities than ever before. In most countries, however, boys and young men are still more active in sports than girls and young women. Why is that, and what are the consequences for the female athletes? Perhaps if both coaches and female athletes better understand the male hegemony in sport and its consequences, more women will participate in and enjoy sports.

Coaching Styles

A study of elite level female soccer players in the USA, Germany, Sweden and Norway found that many of the players preferred female coaches because they liked the female style of communication, which was described as understanding and caring. While many players had positive experiences with male coaches, there was also the belief that many female coaches were better psychologists.

Women may be better coaches of girls and women than many men simply because women and men have different backgrounds and experiences. A man's understanding of the way to coach sport is usually associated with the way it has been coached to boys and men. But girls and women have often been brought up in a different environment. Consequently, a different approach to coaching girls and women may be more successful. This approach, of course, also can be learned by men.

Understanding the Implication of Gender Socialization

Girls and boys are socialized differently. This obvious fact has often been used as an explanation for the lower number of girls interested and involved in sports. The values dominant in most sports are closely connected to a traditional definition of masculinity—toughness, competitiveness and aggressiveness. Boys learn this at an early age. The values that dominate women's lives have not fit into the world of sport very well. For example, women often are better caretakers than men. Many women have a great capacity for empathy, and they are often concerned with the overall aspect of what they do. The values imbedded in this are often contradictory to those central in sport and in a traditional culture of masculinity. We therefore agree with the American sport sociologist Jay Coackley when he writes that "The dominant forms of sports in most cultures are played and organized in ways that work to the advantage of most men and to the disadvantage of women."[1] He writes about "the gender logic of sport" and says that if sport had been created by and for women, the Olympic Games motto would have been "balance, flexibility and ultra-endurance," instead of "faster, higher and stronger."

In this connection is it important to know that what we define or look upon as masculine or feminine differs among cultures and also inside a culture depending on the environment. Another way of expressing this is to say that gender, and what is feminine and masculine are social constructions as opposed to sex and primary and secondary sex characteristics which are biological. As will be shown later in the book, these sex differences must be taken into account when coaching women and men. Men have more testosterone, women menstruate and get pregnant, men are relatively stronger in their upper bodies, women have more fat stores which aid in ultra-endurance races, etc. There are sex advantages for each sex. But these biological sex differences are quite different from the psychological, social and cultural factors which form the gender differences which each society creates. So both male and female coaches must be aware of both the biological (sex) differences and the psycho-social (gender) differences in their athletes. Understanding these will help you to condition them more effectively, both physically and mentally, and to reduce their chances of injuries.

It is important to know that the American College of Sports Medicine stated in 1964 that there are no biological or physiological reasons for women not participating in the same sports as men. There are no reasons based on sex that girls and women cannot box or wrestle, play tackle football or run marathons. Obviously effective padding may be required for women, as it is for men, to protect heads, genitals or shins.

The major challenge for teachers and coaches is to understand that what we often look upon as "typically feminine" or "typically masculine" behavior or personality traits, can be learned, unlearned and relearned. In practice this may sometimes be difficult first because this learning of what is appropriate behavior for girls and boys starts so early, and we as adults are often strong carriers of these gender stereotypes. How would you, for example, look at 8-year-old boys fighting or boys playing with Barbie dolls. Would your evaluation be the same if they were 8-year-old girls fighting or playing with Barbies? "Infants have a biological sex when they are born, but no 'masculine' or 'feminine' identity."[2]. Girls and boys are socialized differently. They are not treated in the same way at home, by friends, or at school. They learn very early what is appropriate for girls and boys, what it is to be "feminine" or "masculine" in that particular culture in which they live. Girls and boys are exposed to all kinds of influences. One arena is the power of girls' magazines on their behavior. Hargreaves has referred to two popular weekly magazines in the United Kingdom. "Jackie" (average reader is 10-14) and "Just Seventeen" (readers over 15 years). Sport in these magazines is associated with adventure, sweat, and masculinity, and is not a part of the feminine culture. Exercise is synonymous with aerobics and keep-fit activities, presented as part of a "caring for the body" package aimed at making girls attractive to boys.

The society and culture sometimes force different pressures on girls and women — just as they do on boys and men. Canadian Margaret MacNeill said that children, even without being taught or told, learn that certain activities are more appropriate for girls than for boys. The example she uses is the common practice in Canada of sending girls to figure-skating classes while boys play ice-hockey.[3] The Miller Lite Report on Women in Sports in the USA also showed that strong differences in gender-role perceptions emerged early in life and influenced later activity selection and participation.[4] Children learn different skills by participating in different activities. The typical male stereotyped activities are believed to encourage the development of strength, speed, analytical thinking etc., while the female stereotyped activities like dance and gymnastics are believed to encourage body awareness, fine motor and empathetic skills etc. Girls are disadvantaged here because many of the male stereotyped activities are believed necessary for success in what our society considers high status careers. [5]

Choosing Sports

Both boys and girls may limit their future professional success and life options by limiting their participation to exclusively male or female stereotyped activities. The Pellett and Harrison study showed that as females got older their perceptions of what was male or female changed and they saw less reason for a line dividing the gender activities, while males' stereotypical perceptions of female-appropriate activities increased as a function of age.[6] So girls and women look more for equality of opportunity as they matured but boys and men were likely to allow for less equality of opportunity as they grew older. It is also worth mentioning that girls and women in some countries seem to invade traditional male sport, without the opposite taking place. Girls play soccer, rugby and box and wrestle, but boys are not entering rhythmic gymnastics or synchronized swimming.

By puberty more girls drop out of sport than do boys. Is this because they really don't like to exercise or they don't enjoy competition or is it because they don't like the way the sport is coached? Or do they experience a so called role -conflict between being an athlete and being a female?

why girls drop out of sports

What are Girls Learning from Sport as It Exists Today?

How does the female culture fit the culture of sport? What kinds of experiences do young girls get through sport today? Studies from different industrialized countries show that girls get many messages with a contradictory content. There seems to exist a double standard concerning girls sport participation, and perhaps even a hidden agenda.

While most Western countries are encouraging girls to participate in sports, what do they experience? Do they experience equity, equal worth, do young women for example experience that their sport participation is as valuable as those of young men? Or do girls learn through sport that they are of less worth than boys? Certainly female top level athletes are paid less than men, they get less attention from the media, and it is more difficult for them to get sponsorships. On a lower level, boys often get better coaches and facilities.

But when girls and women first enter the world of sport, what kinds of experiences do they have? What does sport mean for them? George Sage found that winning was more important for boys in sport, while girls thought it was more important to have a good time together socially.[7] They did put weight upon the playing aspect of sport and emphasized more justness (fairness) and fair play. The fact that women put great emphasis on the relational aspect does not necessarily mean that they don't bother about their performance. Diane Gill found that girls were not as competitively oriented as boys, but it was very important for them to perform well.[8]

Coaching Can be More "Woman Friendly"

Many athletes believe that sports should be organized in a more "woman friendly" way. Companionship and caring, as well as empowerment, often emerge as major reasons for playing a sport. Carol Gilligan has said that the female experience in gendered culture produces distinctively feminine qualities that are essentially different from those of males.[9] These qualities emphasize caring, social responsibility, democratic problem solving for team problems, and adaptability.

Generally speaking, we may say that social relations seem to be of greater importance for women than for men. This is especially obvious among youth.

In coaching we often use the sport to reinforce the sexual stereotypes rather than trying to change them. Sheila Scraton found that even in coed physical education classes women teachers reinforced the traditional values.[11] So it is not just male coaches who may be guilty of expecting less from girls. Sheila's findings were that both women and men were condescending to the girls. A typical teacher's remark might be, "Well it's harder for you because you are a girl."

Qualities that adult women seem to possess are:

- A great capacity for empathy. They dare to show caring and humanity
- They gain strength from working together. They participate as a team without exaggerated emphasis on their own careers.
- They are socially responsible.
- They are adaptable and are geared to solving team problems as a group.
- They have an eye for detail. [10]

Perhaps even more than female coaches, male coaches may have to be aware of their male orientation when coaching girls and women. We must remember that "girls and women—can and do." This doesn't mean that every girl on a junior high school softball squad has the motivation of an Olympian but it does mean that girls and women can be serious about developing sports skills — and winning. But it may mean that one's teaching and motivational techniques may have to take the gender into consideration.

Political Ideologies and Coaching Styles

In coaching you must take into account that girls and boys often have developed different values and interests and that these are socially acquired. Female athletes think that coaches who scream at them are using a male-authoritative coaching style. Putting down the athletes may work for men, they say, but it is counterproductive for women and girls. Of course boys and men don't like it either — they have just become more used to being yelled at.

Being yelled at by a coach

9

As any sport psychologist or athlete knows, people respond best to praise and poorest to criticism. When that praise is yelled, it may be more positive. But when the criticism, especially a personal insult, is yelled, it becomes embarrassing and can take the athlete's attention from proper performance.

The oldest and easiest method for controlling a group is through autocratic methods. "Do what the king commands." In coaching the coach is the king. Does he or she rule with an iron hand or function as a benevolent dictator? Certainly it is unlikely that a 9-year-old age group swimmer can determine how many yards she should swim in a day for her workout, or a 10-year-old basketball player how she should shoot a jump shot, or a 12-year-old softball player how she should pitch a changeup. On the other hand if coaching an experienced high school, college or other elite athlete perhaps the athlete will have some valuable input into how the workouts can be better conducted.

Eventually at the elite level we might even find that a democratic coaching style will be best. The most successful national approach using a democratic coaching style is that of the Swedish golf program. Former LPGA golfer Pia Nielsen developed an entire golf development program from children through the pros. Her success internationally at the professional level has been astounding. For a country with 8 million people she has consistently had the Swedish women ranked high in the LPGA and the Swedish men are also highly successful.

Probably no sport has been more autocratically controlled than American tackle football. One highly successful and nationally known high school and college coach, Jim Brownfield, allowed his players to study the films and develop the best ways to beat opponents in the kicking aspect of the game (punt blocking and kickoff returns). Don't you think that his players were motivated to perform those strategic skills on Friday nights? Effective democratic techniques can be highly motivating for the players involved in the planning. It might also be mentioned that Jim won several California championships in girls track and field while coaching in Pasadena. It should follow from what has been said earlier about gender differences that a democratic coaching style definitely will fit many girls and women. The examples above may also demonstrate that it is probably effective for both women and men.

Coaching is Teaching

Most effective coaches realize that coaching is teaching. An effective coach must understand how the body works and how to make the body perform more efficiently. But more. The coach needs to understand how to teach the sport and the sport skills as effectively as possible. Poor coaches often yell at their athletes because the coaches haven't done a good job of teaching and motivating. It is hard to imagine that these same coaches like to be yelled at by their bosses, so why would they use this demeaning psychological method to attempt to get their team more motivated?

An international study of elite female soccer players and their perceptions of coaches found that the women involved in the study did not like being yelled at. They thought that yelling worked on men, but not on women.[12] They also often wanted to be pushed harder for success by their coaches. Many also believed that some male coaches didn't take the coaching job seriously enough because they were women.

yelling

"We got the feeling that he did not put in 100% for the job and that he did not understand how serious we were, I thought it was irritating. It was just as if we had to tell him, OK we are women, but we can also do our sport seriously. And it was just as if he had not expected it."

Coaching and Motivating Athletes

As a male or female coach of girls and women you should be aware that there is more than one way to coach. There is more than one major outcome possible. And what your athletes want from the sport may be different than what you want from your coaching. In fact your athletes may very well be divided as to what each thinks most important as outcomes of their sport participation.

A coach must first determine what goals should be pursued. At the youth and high school levels the development of the individual's total personality should be primary. This is true also in college. But as the athletes work toward the elite national or Olympic levels the goals may become much more performance oriented.

If you are coaching youth sports you should understand the relationship between a girl's body image, self-esteem, and the development of her own identity. This is very important for girls, because girls often have lower self-esteem than boys, and less favorable body images than males.[13]

Later in the book we will discuss in greater depth how athletes are motivated. Both sexes prefer not to be yelled at. Both sexes expect to be taught how to be better at their sports. And both sexes expect to be taught how to win. Most boys and girls, as well as men and women, want to play within the rules and with a strong concept of fair play.

what a player wants from playing

It has been found that women who were active in sports and recreational activities as girls felt greater confidence, self-esteem and pride in their physical and social selves than those who were sedentary as children. With refer-

11

ence to this Donna A. Lopiano, Executive Director of The Women's Sport Foundation in USA stated that: ". . . Adolescents who feel strong and good about themselves are more likely to be in control of their lives."[14]

A "better sport for girls" should therefore take girls lives, experiences, and wishes more into account.

Notes:

1. Coakley, J. *Sport in Æsociety: Issues and Controversies* (5th Ed.) St Louis: Mosby. 1994.
2. J. Hargreaves, "Women and Sport: Alternative Values and Practices," Paper presented to the Olympic Scientific Congress, Sport and Quality of Life, Malaga, Spain, July 14-19, 1992.
3. M. MacNeill, "Active Women, Media Representations, and Ideology," *Not Just a Game: Essays in Canadian Sport Sociology*, eds. J. Harvey and H. Cantelon (Ottawa: University of Ottawa, 1988) 195-213.
4. Miller Brewing Co., "Miller Lite Report on Women's Sports," Milwaukee, 1985
5. T.L. Pellett and J.M. Harrison, "Children's Perceptions of the Gender Appropriateness of Physical Activities: A Further Analysis," *Play and Culture* 5 (1992): 305-313.
6. ibid.
7. G. Sage, "Orientation Toward Sport of Male and Female Inter-collegiate Athletes," *Journal of Sport Psychology* 2 (1980): 355-362.
8. D.L. Gill, "Gender Differences in Competitive Orientation and Sport Participation," *International Journal of Sport Psychology* 2 (1988): 145-159.
9. *Mapping the Moral Domain*, eds. C. Gilligan, J.V. Ward and J.M. Taylor (Cambridge, MA: Harvard University Press, 1988).
10. K. Fasting, "Setting the Scene: The New Europe and Future Sports Cooperation," In: *Report X European Sports Conference 1991*: Oslo, Norway, June 3-6, Oslo, NIF, (1991): 135-147.
11. S. Scraton, "Images of Femininity and the Teaching of Girls' Physical Education," *Physical Education, Sport and Schooling*, ed. J. Evans (Lewes: Falmer Press, 1986).
12. K. Fasting and G. Pfister, "Female and Male Coaches in the Eyes of Female Elite Soccer Players," *European Physical Education Review* 6.1 (2000).

13. S.M. Shaw, "Fitness and Wellness for Young Women: The Image Paradox," *Recreation Canada* May/June 1989, 33-38.
14. Donna A. Lopiano, "An Interesting Time for Women in Sport and Fitness," Paper presented at Ascent for Women, Denver, Colorado, April 26, 1992.

3

Connective Tissues and Muscles

*D*ifferent types of exercise require varying amounts of flexibility in the joints and varying amounts of muscle stiffness (tension in the individual muscle fibers). Flexibility increases the range of motion (ROM) in a joint by stretching the connective tissue around the joint; however, it may also stretch connective tissue around the muscle and the muscle itself. Most of us have taken for granted that being flexible is always good and that stretching before a practice or a competition is a sacred duty. We may have been wrong! Walking and distance running are more efficient if the muscles are stiffer and if the person's flexibility is not excessive. Gymnastics, on the other hand, requires great flexibility in the joints, while still requiring stiff muscles.

In this chapter we will look at why stretching in sport is being reevaluated. The fact that many north European track and field coaches have stopped stretching their sprinters gives us pause to think that perhaps the traditions with which we have been raised, both in physical education classes and athletic teams, may be in error.

We will begin our exploration of the body's movement potentials by looking at the bones, joints and connective tissues. Then we will look at the effect on the muscle fibers.

Connective Tissues — Ligaments

The skeletal system is made up of over 200 bones, each connected to adjacent bones by connective tissue we call ligaments. Nearly all bones are attached to other bones by ligaments. Each joining of bones is a joint. Some joints are very mobile, such as the wrist or shoulder joints which allow many types of motion. Other joints are immobile or nearly immobile, such as the joints of the ribs with the sternum (breastbone) or the joints of the fibula and tibia in the lower leg.

It is in joints that your range of motion is determined. If your elbow joint is too loose or if there is an unusual shape at the end of the bones, the arm may be able to be bent backward past the normal straight position. If you have normally tight ligaments in the hip joint, but you wanted to be a ballet dancer who could lift your leg forward at a 120-degree angle, you would need to stretch the ligaments in the back of the joint capsule to allow for such a movement. The same would be true if you wanted to do the splits for dancing, cheerleading, or gymnastics. You would need stretched ligaments in both the front and the rear of your hip joint.

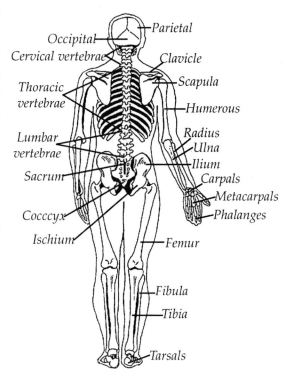

Increases in flexibility, however, do not always aid an athlete's performance. In one of the earliest studies in this area, Herb DeVries found that great increases in flexibility did not improve 100 yard running time.[1] Also, tighter subjects are more efficient in walking than the looser subjects.[2]

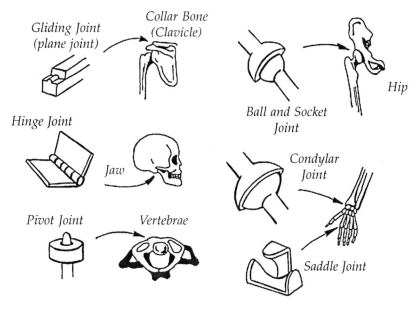

Connective Tissues — Tendons

Tendons are another type of connective tissues. Tendons connect muscle to bone. It is the function of a tendon to transfer all of the force generated by a muscle to the bone into which it connects. Obviously, if the tendon stretched, it would not be able to transfer the force effectively. It would be like trying to tow a car with a rubber band rather than with a chain. If a tendon is stretched over 4%, it is likely to be injured.

A lack of flexibility commonly appears when the connective tissues in the muscles or the tendons shorten, as happens when we age or are inactive. In the "olden days" of weight lifting and body building, it was common. It was described as being muscle bound. Now we know that it was not the muscles that were bound but that inflexibility came from not having the connective tissue stretched. The problem with the old-time body builders was that they did not do their exercises through a full range of motion. Consequently, the connective tissue in their bicep muscles was shortened by bicep curls in which they did not fully extend their arms. The connective tissues in their chests were shortened from bench presses in which they did not allow the bar to drop to the chest.

Connective Tissue — Fascia

Fascia is a term applied to connective tissue that is not otherwise identifiable as ligaments, tendons, or other common types of collagen. A few examples would be: fascia that binds the muscle fibers and that encases the muscle belly, fascia that binds our organs and holds them in place, and fascia under the skin.

When we contract a muscle in order to move something, some of the muscle's power is used to overcome internal friction and tension. The fascia between and around the muscle fibers provide over 40% of the internal resistance that the muscle encounters in developing its force. The joint capsule (the friction of one bone moving against another plus the tightness of the connective tissue in and around the joint) provides about 47% of the internal resistance. The muscle's tendon accounts for about 10% of the internal resistance, and the skin adds another 2% to the total resistance.

With these resistance factors in mind, if you are interested in efficiency of movement, stretching the connective tissues in the areas in which you need extra efficiency should be of value. Such stretching can not only increase your range of motion but can also reduce your chances of injury due to making a movement which could overly stretch the connective tissue.

The Effect of Heat and Cold on Stretching

Most studies indicate that connective tissues can be more effectively stretched if they are heated, so a warm up or warm water may allow for greater stretching. Laboratories often use ultrasound waves to warm the tissues. Additionally, cooling the muscles in cool water after stretching can help to set the stretched condition. This cooling must be done before the stretch is relaxed.[3] But because the muscle should be heated deeply, the effect of applying warm compresses to the muscle may not always help, and the results may be similar to stretching a muscle which has not been warmed.[4] However, a study at Baylor University indicated that the amount of flexibility gained was about the same whether the muscles were heated, cooled or not treated.[5]

Types of Joint Movements

There are commonly used terms that identify the various types of joint movement. Each of these could be an objective for a stretching program. The terms are also used to describe many strength development movements. We will use these terms in many of the upcoming chapters.

Flexion is generally considered to be the action of a joint which decreases the angle of the joint. Bending the arm at the elbow, bringing your lower leg backward, or bending your neck forward would all be examples of flexing the joint. Bringing your arm forward from the shoulder joint is also flexion but does not fit the general definition of the term. If you are doing a biceps curl or lifting a package to your chest, you are flexing your elbows.

Extension is generally the action which increases the angle of the joint. Straightening your arm or knee or moving your head from a forward position to a straight up position would be examples of extension. Bringing the arm back to the side from a flexed position would also be extension — even though the angle of the joint is actually being reduced. If you are getting up from a chair, your knees and hips are extending.

Hyperextension is bringing the joint past what would be the normally extended position. The elbow and knee will not normally hyperextend, but if the head is moved past the vertical so that you are looking upward, your neck has been hyperextended. Similarly, if your arm is brought backward at the shoulder joint so that it is now past the point where it was hanging at the side, it is hyperextended. If you are swimming the crawl stroke and are pulling your arm out of the water in its recovery, your shoulder is hyperextended. If you bend your back past the vertical, as in an advanced high jumping technique, your spine is hyperextended.

17

Abduction is taking away your arm or leg from the mid-line of your body. Raising your arm out to the side or lifting your leg to the side would be examples of abduction. In doing a jumping jack both your arms and legs are abducted at the beginning of the movement.

Adduction is the returning of your arm or leg to the midline of the body from an abducted position. So in your jumping jack exercise, when your arms come back to your sides and your legs are together, they have been adducted.

Rotation is the pivoting of a body part around its own axis. Twisting your head to the side (as in "no"), twisting your torso, or rotating your arm or leg would be rotation.

Circumduction occurs when the end of your arm, leg or head describes a circle. Swimming the butterfly stroke would be an example of the arms circumducting. If you were to draw circles in the sand with your toes, your leg would be circumducting.

Other Specific Movements

For the forearm and hands, supination is an outward rotation of the forearm. If your arm was flexed at the elbow and you had a bowl of soup in your hand, your hands would be supinated. If your hand is then turned back inward and downward it would be pronated.

For the ankles, if you turn the sole of your foot inward, it is called inversion; if you turn them outward, it is called eversion.

For the shoulders, protraction occurs when your shoulders are pushed forward, such as when doing a pushup or reaching forward with an oar while rowing. Retraction occurs when you pull your shoulder girdle backward such as when standing at attention or pulling backward on an oar while rowing.

Range of Motion

Your range of motion is the measure of flexibility for each joint or combination of joints. That range of motion is determined by the ligaments and tendons and by the tension in the muscle fibers. When the muscle tension is very high, the muscle is said to be in a state of contracture. The contactures can generally be reduced by effective stretching exercises within a few weeks. Movement restriction caused by tight ligaments will generally take much longer.

Some people are highly concerned with increasing their range of motion. Many athletes need flexibility that is beyond what is normally needed for day to day living. Hurdlers, divers, high jumpers, soccer kickers, swimmers and gymnasts are just a few of those who may need to increase their range of motion in order to be more effective in their chosen activities.

The Effects of Aging on Connective Tissues

Our connective tissues are 60%-70% water when we are young. As we age our connective tissues become more brittle. By age 70 we have lost about 20% of the water content that was in the connective tissues when we were born. In addition, our collagen becomes thicker so we become stiffer and less flexible.

An effective stretching program can reduce the aging of connective tissues. Even those who have not been careful to stay flexible can undo much of the damage of inactivity by beginning to stretch in the ways described in Chapter 13.

Should All Athletes Stretch?

Recent research is making us question our previously unquestioned reliance on stretching for warm up, to reduce delayed onset muscle soreness (DOMS), and to reduce injuries. While we have always thought that stretching was good and more stretching was better, there are now a number of questions. Is stretching as a warm up good for some people and not good for others? Is it good for the treatment of some injuries but not for others?

Certainly when you need a greater range of motion, stretching is essential. The question is, how much range of motion do you need for your sport? If you are a cyclist, you may not need much. If you swim the backstroke you may not need as much shoulder flexibility as a butterfly swimmer, yet both may need some extra flexibility for their sprint turns. A jogger or marathon runner probably doesn't need extra hip flexibility, but a sprinter might. Certainly a gymnast needs great flexibility, as do participants in the martial arts. How much do you really need to perform your exercise or to compete in your competitive event?

Stretching during a warm up increases injuries for at least some people. A couple of studies of 10K runners have found that those who stretched had more injuries than those who did not. The question is, is it the stretching itself or just poor stretching technique that is the culprit?

Relative to injury, one study found that when one joint had at least a 15% greater flexibility than the corresponding joint, the more flexible joint was 2.6 times more likely to be injured.[6] A hypothesis for this might be that the stretching exercises lengthen the connective tissue surrounding the muscle fibers which then requires the fibers to absorb all of the force of the eccentric contractions — the muscle lengthens while it is being contracted, such as

19

returning the barbell to the starting position after it has been lifted. The theory is that too much force was placed on the fibers, and they overstretched and were injured.

Stretching may decrease injuries, at least for some people. In a study of military recruits, the group that had 3 hamstring stretching exercises added to its physical fitness regime both increased their hamstring flexibility and reduced the rate of overuse injuries to the legs from 29.1% in the control group to 16.7% in the group which stretched.[7]

How we measure flexibility affects what we find. At the present time we have no way of knowing just how much we are stretching the muscle fibers and how much we are stretching the various connective tissues involved. When the research relates to injuries, the studies have not reported whether the injuries were to the muscle fibers, the tendons or the ligaments. They also don't report on whether the injury was acute (an injury from a single specific movement) or a chronic overuse injury due to repeating the same movement patterns thousands of times, perhaps on a surface that contributes to the injury, such as running on concrete versus running on grass or in the sand.

Are muscular injuries such as strains or pulls increased or decreased by stretching? Does stretching before the exercise increase the susceptibility of the muscle fibers to injury during the activity when the muscle's job is to shorten?

The muscles are stretched more than the connective tissue. This can set the muscle up for more injury and reduce the muscle stiffness by relaxing the muscles.[8]

To understand a bit better, we must remember that while tendons may be stretched to 4% before injury and muscles can usually be stretched to 20% to 30% before they are injured, each of us, and each muscle and tendon, differ somewhat. We therefore don't know exactly how far any of our own muscle groups can be stretched before some injury either occurs or becomes more probable with our ensuing exercise.

At the Duke University Medical Center an interesting study was performed with leg muscles in the front of the lower leg of rabbits. It was found that when the muscles were stretched by 20%, they didn't seem to have their potential contracting force reduced. Muscles stretched 30%, however, were not able to exert maximum force. Additionally, the fibers near the tendons at the end of the muscle belly showed ruptures of some of the fibers and bleeding. Certainly the 30% stretch injured some fibers. Is this what causes more injuries in 10K runners who stretch? The study also concluded that when the fibers lost their ability to contract to the fullest, they also increased their chance for injury.[9]

Naturally, much of the work on stretching muscles or tendons to the breaking point has to be done with animals or excised muscles from dead animals. Do these studies hold true for human tissue? If a rabbit's front leg muscle fibers can withstand a 20% stretch without ill effect, does that mean that a human leg muscle fiber can only withstand 20%? What about a human neck muscle? What about another rabbit's leg or neck? What about your leg muscle fibers compared to those of your sister, your neighbor, the Olympic sprint champion? Lots of questions! But realistically, studying the muscle fibers of a rabbit's leg or a bird's wing will give us some indication as to how muscles react. And certainly, at this stage of the game, all we are seeing are indications — but indications strong enough that we should take them into account in our training.

The stretch of the muscle can make it less able to contract efficiently. This reduces its "stiffness." A study at the Centinella Hospital Biomechanics Laboratory, a major southern California sports medicine center, may indicate why. The study found that the electrical activity in muscles was generally reduced by stretching, whether the stretching was before or after a warm up. This was particularly true for the calf muscles (soleus and gastrocnenius).[10]

Muscle Stiffness

Muscle stiffness may be mechanical, due to the properties in the muscle fibers, or neural, due to increased electrical activity in the nerves which then stimulate the muscle fibers and make them more tense. While the aforementioned "contractures" are excessive stiffness and will reduce one's performance, a certain amount of stiffness is valuable for most athletic movements because power is increased with the right amount of stiffness.

Mechanical Properties of Muscles

Extensibility or stiffness of muscle fibers is related to how easily or difficult it is to lengthen the muscle fibers when a lengthening force is applied to them.[11] We measure the stiffness of muscle by seeing how much it lengthens when it is affected by a force which should stretch it. Muscles which lengthen rather easily are called compliant, those that don't stretch readily are called stiff. More technically, stiffness is defined as the ratio of change in force to the change in the length of the muscle. This stiffness is dependent, to a large degree, on the tension within the muscle fibers. That tension can come from the activation by the nerves or from factors within the muscle.

The myosin and actin proteins, which move across each other when the muscle fiber contracts, thereby shortening the muscle fiber, are attached by what is termed a "myosin cross bridge." The strength of that attachment by the cross bridge is what sustains a muscular contraction and what causes the stiffness of a muscle. The stronger the tension of the cross bridge, the more the muscle resists stretching, so the more it is considered to be stiff. (More on this in the next chapter.)

Some of those factors can be hereditary. Environmental factors may also be present. For example, when a stretch-shortening (plyometric) stress occurs, such as when you jump down from a chair and immediately jump upwards, there is much greater tension developed in the muscle fibers than if you are merely standing on the chair. The tension required in the muscles to absorb the force of jumping from 18 inches above the floor is significant. (In Chapter 10 we will discuss this "stretch-shortening cycle" and plyometric exercises as a method of developing power for your sport.)

Stretching a muscle (as during eccentric or lengthening action) increases the firing rate of the muscle spindles which increases the stiffness of the muscle. The spindles sense the amount of stretch in muscle fibers and signal the information to the spinal column. The stiffness of the muscle will therefore be influenced also by the level of muscle activation.

Continued activity such as running or other exercises in which the muscle lengthens under pressure then immediately contracts (called the stretch-shortening cycle) obviously causes fatigue in the muscles. Part of that fatigue is due to normal fatiguing factors such as increased waste products from the energy generating system, but fatigue also comes from the reduced muscle stiffness caused by exercise that requires more energy to contract the muscles.[12] So muscle stiffness also slows the fatigue factor, especially in strength-speed activities such as running 100 to 400 meters.

Notes:

1. H.A. DeVries, "The 'Looseness' Factor in Speed and O2 Consumption in an Anaerobic 100-yard Dash," *Res Q Exercise. & Sport* 34 (1963): 305-313.
2. G.W. Gleim, N.S. Stachenfield and J.A. Nicholas, "The Influence of Flexibility on the Economy of Walking and Jogging," *Journal of Orthopedic Research* 8 (1990): 814-823.
3. G. Lentell, et al., "The Use of Thermal Agents to Influence the Effectiveness of a Low-Load Prolonged Stretch," *Journal of Orthopedic and Sports Physiotherapy* 16.5 (1992): 200-207.
4. B.F. Taylor, C.A. Waring and T.A. Brashear, "The Effects of

Therapeutic Application of Heat or Cold Followed by a Static Stretch on Hamstring Muscle Length," *Journal of Orthopedic and Sports Physical Therapy* 21.5 (1995): 283-286.

5. B.F. Taylor, C.A. Waring and T.A. Brashear, 283-286.
6. J.J. Knapic, C. Bauman, B.H. Jones, J.M. Harris and L. Vaughan, "Preseason Strength and Flexibility Imbalances Associated with Athletic Injuries in Female Collegiate Athletes," *American Journal of Sports Medicine* 19 (1991): 76-81.
7. D.E. Hartig and J.M. Henderson, "Increasing Hamstring Flexibility Decreases Lower Extremity Overuse Injuries in Military Basic Trainees," *American Journal of Sports Medicine* 27.2 (1999):173-176.
8. D.C. Taylor, J.D. Dalto, A.V. Seaber, and W.E. Garrett, "Viscoelastic Properties of Muscle-Tendon Units: The Biomechanical Effects of Stretching," *American Journal of Sports Medicine* 18 (1990): 300-309.
9. T.J. Noonan, T.M. Best, A.V. Seaber, and W.E. Garrett, Jr., "Identification of a Threshold for Skeletal Muscle Injury," *American Journal of Sports Medicine* 22.2 (1994): 257-261.
10. K.J. Mohr, M.M. Pink, C. Elsner and R.S. Kvitne, "Electromyographic Investigation of Stretching: The Effect of Warm-Up," *Clinical Journal of Sports Medicine* 8.3 (1998): 215-220.
11. D.C. Taylor, J.D. Dalto, A.V. Seaber, and W.E. Garrett, 300-308.
12. J. Avela and P.V. Komi, "Interaction Between Muscle Stiffness and Stretch Reflex Sensitivity After Long-Term Stretch-Shortening Cycle Exercise," *Muscle Nerve* 21.9 (1998):124-127.

4

Understanding the Muscles and Nerves and Their Relationship to Strength

This chapter is about getting stronger and more powerful. If your sport requires speed, power or strength, this chapter is essential. If you are a dancer, volleyball player or basketball player who wants to jump higher, a gymnast who wants to be stronger, or a soccer player or swimmer who wants to be faster, you should understand how to make your muscles stronger and more powerful. You will want to eliminate the parts of your conditioning program that may actually reduce your strength potentials.

Since the mission of this book is to make your conditioning program as scientific as possible, it is essential that you understand why we propose the things that we do. Of course, you can always skip this chapter and just believe what we say later in the book. But without understanding the basic anatomy and physiology, you can't really understand if or why your conditioning program makes sense.

In this chapter we will try to bring everyone up to speed so that the rest of the book makes sense. If you have a college degree in kinesiology, physiology or physical education, you can probably skip this chapter. But if you are a reader who has little understanding of what is happening in the deepest parts of your muscles, this chapter is essential.

A mistake that is continually made, and one this book is attempting to clarify and correct, is the belief that merely lifting weights is the best way to become a better athlete. While typical strength training exercises will help you or the athletes you are training, traditional strength training may not be the best use of an athlete's time. The best use of an athlete's strength conditioning time is to make the movements sport specific and power oriented, just as they are in a game. Recently there was a photo in a newspaper showing a swimmer lifting weights over her head in a standing press. She was wasting her time. Swimmers don't need that type of strength. However, if she had been a platform diver, such overhead work would have been essential because doing hand stands is an essential part of the diving repertoire.

Many studies have shown that while resistance training has increased an athlete's strength, it does not necessarily positively affect her sport performance. This has been shown in sprinting.[1] It has also been shown in throwing.[2] As we will indicate, there is more we must be concerned with than pure strength. Pure speed of a muscle fiber is largely inherited and is dependent on the percentage of "fast twitch" muscle fibers. Effective training can increase the strength of each of those fast fibers, however, so that each can move more weight quickly. And quite possibly more important is the working of your brain in telling which muscle fibers to contract.

Our Muscles and How They Work

To understand how our bodies move, and to appreciate the marvels within us, we should be aware of what our muscles are and how they allow us to move. We have 434 muscle groups in our bodies that move parts of our

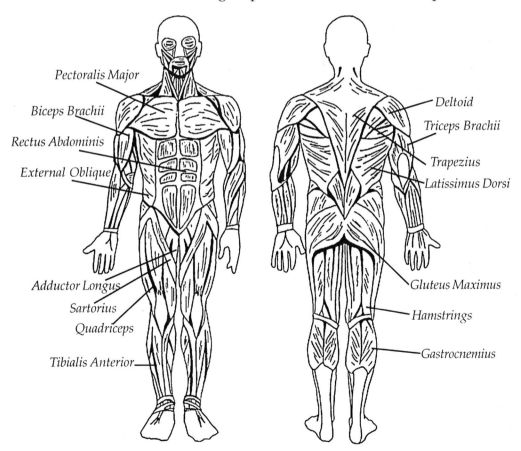

anatomies. Only about 150 are primary movers. Each muscle is made up of thousands of individual muscle fibers having a very small diameter, from 1/300 to 1/2500 of an inch — much smaller than the diameter of a straight pin. These muscle fibers have the ability to shorten, or contract, by sliding one part of fiber (called an actin filament) past another filament (called myosin). Each fiber either contracts totally or not at all (called the "all or none" principle).

There are two major factors which affect our ability to move effectively with strength — the number of muscle fibers contracting at one time and the efficiency of the lever (joint and muscle attachments). Every joint is part of a lever which varies in efficiency. The biceps muscle in the front of the upper arm works on a more efficient lever than does the calf muscle (gastrocnemius), which allows one to rise up on the toes. These levers also vary in efficiency from person to person. Those who have shorter bones generally have better lever actions than those with longer bones. (The effect of levers will be discussed later in this chapter.)

When we see our muscles bulge under our skin we are seeing the outline of the muscle "belly." That "belly" of the muscle is actually made up of millions of muscle cells and billions of working elements within those cells. This chart illustrates what goes into your bulging biceps or your shapely calf (see diagram on the opposite page).

The major theory on muscle contraction holds that there is one band (titin) which anchors the thickest band (myosin) to one end of the sarcomere. The other end of the myosin thread is attached by another thin thread

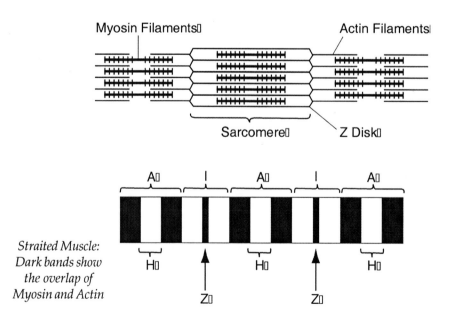

(actin). The actin fiber looks like a double strand of beads which are twisted. The myosin has outcroppings from its body which seem to grip the sides of the actin "beads" to slide the actin along the side of the myosin. Not all of the fibers in a muscle will contract at the same time, but every fiber contracting will do so to its maximum ability. This is known as the "all or none" principle. The greater percentage of fibers which a person can make contract at one time, the greater the force which can be exerted.

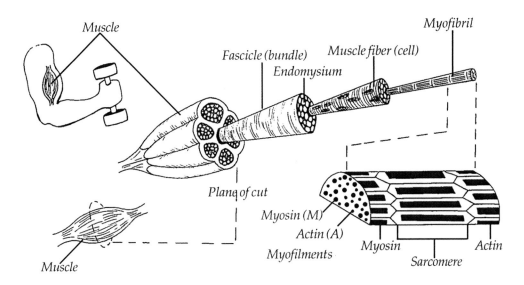

The muscle belly is made up of large numbers of fasciculi (generally containing 100 to 150 individual muscle fibers).

The individual fibers vary in length from 1 to 40 millimeters (mm) about 0.04 to 1.6 inches in length and 10 to 100 micrometers (a micrometer is a millionth of a meter, or 0.00004 of an inch) in diameter.

Each individual fiber is made up of slender threads called myofibrils. Each myofibril is about as long as the muscle fiber but only about 1 to 2 micrometers in diameter.

Each myofibril is made up of a number of sarcomeres. These are the parts of the fiber which actually shorten. (They are about 2 micrometers long.)

The myofibrils are made up of still smaller segments called myofilaments. There are over 1,000 of these in each sarcomere.

These cells and parts of cells are made from amino acids which form the protein which is a major building block of each cell. About 20% of a muscle is made of protein (amino acids), about 75% is water and the remaining 5% is made up of other things such as salts, phosphates, and minerals. The amino acids are formed according to directions sent by the DNA (deoxyribonucleic acid) genes in the chromosomes of the cells of the muscles.

Within the sarcomere are the fibers which produce the contraction. While we don't know exactly how a muscle cell contracts, there are some theories. Since the threads creating the contractions are about 5 to 15 millionths of a meter long (about 1 ten millionths of an inch) and a diameter which is much smaller, it is a wonder that we know anything at all!

In this contraction the sarcomere can shorten by 20%–50%. This contraction begins by the reception of a nerve impulse. That impulse requires that there be sufficient fuel in the cell to make the contraction. That fuel is called ATP (adenosine triphosphate). As one phosphate is broken off from the larger ATP, molecule energy is produced. We don't have an unlimited amount of ATP, so the phosphate has to be replaced. This is done by taking the phosphate from creatine phosphate (CP) which is also in the muscle.

There is generally three to five times more CP in the muscle than ATP, so it makes an efficient molecule to resynthesize the ATP. Some people supplement their diets with creatine phosphates to help in this action (more on this in Chapter 22.) This type of energy production can last only a few seconds before the fuels are exhausted. This is called anaerobic activity and is the type of muscle fueling which is found in heavy weight lifting or in short sprinting.

If the activity is to last more than several seconds, energy from glycogen (sugars) and oxygen must be used to resynthesize the ATP. This is called aerobic (with air) exercise. This begins when you take your first breath during exercise so the oxygen begins to aid in the resynthesis of the ATP in well under a minute.

To clarify what is meant by some key terms, here are a few definitions:
• *Maximum strength* is the amount of weight that one can lift one time. It is determined by the number of muscle fibers which the brain can stimulate at one time and the cross sectional area (diameter) of the muscle fibers which are contracting.
• *Speed* is how fast you can move. It may be limited to the speed of one joint action, or it can be a combination of joint actions, such as in sprinting or swimming fast.
• *Power* is the combination of strength and speed. It is necessary in many sport activities which require a fast action with maximum force, such as putting the shot, swimming fast, leaping high in sport or dance, kicking a goal in soccer, lifting a heavy weight fast, serving a cannonball tennis serve, etc. While power is often defined as merely the amount of work performed during a certain amount of time, in sport we generally think of it as work being performed in a relatively short time, sometimes over a time span of less than a second.
• *Endurance* is how long a muscle, or the entire body, can perform an activity. Running a marathon or swimming a mile or two would be examples.
• *Strength endurance* is how long the body or a muscle can perform an exercise which requires less than maximum strength. Sprinting 200 or 400 meters or swimming 100 meters would be examples of events that require strength endurance. Playing a volleyball match where continued jumping for blocking or spiking is required is another example.

While you may not be able to measure the amount of ATP and creatine in your body, the size of the muscle is a good indication. In a Swedish study evaluating the effectiveness of sprint training, it was found that "... After training, all subjects showed a gain in body weight (average 1.4 kg) and in thigh circumference (average1.5 cm) indicating a larger leg muscle volume and consequently also an increase in total ATP and CP." [3]

What Do Athletes Need?

The types of exercises you do or that you prescribe for your athletes should be selected based on their potentials for developing strength, hypertrophy (size), speed, quicker force production, strength endurance or aerobic endurance. Each is gained differently. Consequently you need to know what you want each muscle group to do before you determine your whole workout schedule. If every athlete does the same workout, some are not utilizing their time to their best advantage. In addition to making the lifting movements sport specific we need to know how the exercises should be performed, depending on whether we want strength, size, speed or power. As Bill Kraemer, one of the world's authorities in this area, has determined, we need to know whether the athletes require "predominantly eccentric, isometric, slow-velocity, or high-velocity strength or power in their athletic event, this will dictate the time commitment to each component and form the basis for designing individual workouts." Additionally, "program variation over a training period is essential to maximize gains and prevent overtraining." [4]

Specificity

Knowledgeable conditioning coaches will always talk about the principle of specificity. The problem is that many don't know how to make the exercise as specific as the action needed in the competition.

Helpful Terminology
Rep — (repetition) one full exercise movement RM —repetition maximum 1 RM —the amount of weight which can be lifted only one time 10 RM — (ten repetition maximum) the amount of weight which can be lifted only 10 times Set — the number of repetitions to be done at one time, commonly 6, 8, or 10 Intensity — the maximum amount of weight handled in a lift, using high weight with low repetitions would be an example of intensity in a workout Volume — the total amount of weight lifted in an entire workout

- In tennis some of the specific movements would be the serving and overhead action, the forehand and backhand actions, running forward and back and running or shuffling to each side in a rally.
- In dance the specific movements and leaps will vary depending on the type of dance (i.e. ballet, modern, jazz) and the choreography of the specific dance.
- In volleyball or basketball the running, shuffling and jumping actions should be made sport specific. For example, if a three-step approach is used to spike the volleyball, the same movement should be used in training.

Specificity of strength and power training, as in other aspects of training for your sport, must be as exact as possible. This means that when using resistance training, the velocity of the lift, the joint angle and the posture of the player should be as close to the game situation as possible. [5]

Once weight training became a part of most athletic conditioning programs, the coaches and athletes copied the body builders and weight lifters in designing their programs. This doesn't make as much sense as it would appear. Remember that power lifters work on the bench press and squat — the same exercises they do in competition. Olympic lifters work on the clean, clean and jerk and snatch — the same movements they do in competition. Body builders just want big muscles. They don't have to perform any specific power movements in their competitions. Then why should we, as coaches or athletes, follow what makes sense for these other activities? The exercises they do don't apply nearly as much to other sports.

To illustrate the specificity of exercise that can be developed, let's take the crawl stroke in swimming. Coaches attempting to get more specific strength have used several approaches. Some have analyzed the crawl stroke action and determined that the latissimus dorsi and the triceps are the primary movers. Then they look at the typical exercises which work those muscles and come up with the lat pull down and the French curl, perhaps using 10 RMs. But these don't imitate the swim stroke in any way, the best exercise is a straight arm pull down on the lat machine.

Others will use the Swim Bench, in which the swimmer lies on the bench and does the stroke action. This is good, but if the swimmer pulls as hard as she must in the water, she will pull herself right off the bench. The Swim Bench does have the advantage of putting the swimmer in the correct posture — prone. If someone holds the swimmer's legs so that she doesn't slide off the bench, and if the resistance is adequate, this can be an effective specific exercise. Swim coaches have traditionally used many repetitions with light weights, but the sprint swimmer is pulling with maximum force on every stroke. This requires both power and strength endurance. Consequently, the best program would be a reverse pyramid starting with the heaviest weight and reducing the resistance at each level where the swimmer is exhausted. The total reps would be 75 to 200 for sprinters. Such a program would be sport specific.

A German company has developed a strength training machine for discus throwers. The athlete stands in the middle of the circular machine, which is angled at the ideal angle for a discus throw. The athlete then moves the weight while in the correct posture and at the correct angle. This is sport specific. A Nordic company has developed a similar machine for the javelin.

If you were coaching shot putters, you would want incline presses at a 40 to 43 degree angle — the most efficient angle for a throw. And rather than a two arm press, it would be more realistic if it were a dumbbell press. The ideal, of course, would be where it could be done standing where the last part of the putting action could be perfectly simulated.

Take the basketball lay up as another example. After stopping the dribble, the player takes one step, then another and leaps as high as possible. Compare this with the squat, where both legs move together and the body is standing. It isn't as specific to the action needed in the game.

While there is no harm in being able to do a bench press or a biceps curl, it is the strengthening of the specific athletic movement, rather than the individual muscles, which is the most important part of the off the field conditioning. A few strength coaches are now working more to develop such specific training.

Specificity applies to every aspect of training. It applies to the coordination of the joints; to whether the training is to be for strength, power or endurance; to the posture (body position) in which the exercise is done; and to the speed of the exercise. Endurance training, such as running, can make the muscle fibers more ready to work through many repetitions. However, strength training of the same muscles will have a quite different effect on the fibers. These two types of training are actually rather incompatible and may interfere with power training necessary for your sport.

Training for strength is somewhat specific to the speed at which the exercise is performed. Fast action better recruits the fast twitch fibers.[6] So if you want power (speed x force or strength) you will want to design your lifting to include the power aspects of the movement, not just slow brute strength.

All of the muscle fibers in a muscle belly don't work in any one exercise. The brain seems to select the motor units (nerve and muscle fibers) which will do the most efficient job. For example, in doing a biceps curl, the lateral fibers were more likely to work. But if the hand is supinated (turned upward) during the exercise, the medial (middle) fibers are more apt to work.[7] So if developing your biceps is important, as it is in lifting (such as in cheerleading, dance, gymnastics, rowing, tackling in rugby, rebounding in basketball, etc.), you will want more than one bicep exercise. You will want a pure flexion and an exercise in which the hand is turned from the pronated to the supinated position during the exercise.

Strength

We know that when young people begin strength training, their initial progress is quite fast. This is because their nervous systems are learning how to do the movements efficiently.[8] This holds true for both doing strength exercises and for doing sport-related exercises. It is the latter in which we are primarily interested — as you will see as the book unfolds.

Most of us have heard the story of the mother who lifted a car off her son when the jack had collapsed. We have probably also had the occasion to perform a feat of strength or speed in the heat of a game or when overcome by fear. Certainly the brain's ability to contract more muscle fibers is critical to developing the strength-power which makes us better athletes. But now let's take a look at the muscles because they are the elements which actually perform the strength and power needed in the games.

When a muscle belly is exerting force, not all of the individual fibers in that muscle belly contract. Generally, it is a relatively small percentage of the total fibers. A major objective of strength training is to teach the brain to contract more individual muscle fibers at one time. "Neuromuscular activation is increased after training allowing for more weight to be lifted with fewer fibers."[9]

One study reported strength increases of 160%–200% in the first 12 weeks of strength training. But the maximum isometric force which could be generated was increased by only 3%–20% over that same 12-week period.[10] This indicates that a large part of the ability to lift weights in the early weeks is an increase in the ability of the nervous system to stimulate either more fibers or the most appropriate fibers to allow for an efficient contraction.

Part of this neural adaptation is moderated by the Golgi tendon organ located in the tendon next to muscle. It measures the tension in the muscle and signals the spinal cord. This signal generally inhibits the muscle's ability to increase its force of contraction past a certain point. However, with training, the inhibiting action of the Golgi organ's messages to the spinal column can be reduced so that more fibers can be allowed to contract at one time. So part of the early increase in muscle strength is due to the inhibition of the Golgi organ's action. This increase in strength development obviously occurs without any increase in muscle size. It is entirely independent of the fiber size.

The complexity of the exercise a person is performing is also related to how much of the early strength increase is related to learning to do the exercise and how much is related to muscle hypertrophy.

The Nervous System's Contribution to Strength

The signal for a muscle to contract comes from the nervous system, usually the brain but sometimes as a reflex action from the spinal cord. A motor unit is the nerve and the muscle fibers it innervates. One nerve can stimulate as few as 3 muscle fibers or as many as 800. Where fine coordination is required, such as in the eyes or fingers, fewer fibers work with one nerve. Where gross motion is desired, such as in the thigh or gluteal muscles, one nerve might stimulate several hundred fibers. When stimulated, all the fibers in the one motor unit contract.

All the fibers in the motor unit are of the same type, slow or fast twitch, categorized on how quickly they contract. (See Chapter 5 on muscle fiber types for a more complete explanation.) The slow twitch motor units have fewer fibers working with one nerve. Ten to 180 fibers would be the normal range for the slower motor units. In contrast, the fast twitch motor units will generally contain 300 to 800 fibers per nerve. Because of these facts, when a small amount of weight is being moved, the brain is more likely to use the smaller slow twitch motor units. When a larger weight is to be moved the brain will likely call upon the fast twitch motor units. This is the reason that heavy weights are often used for power sport activities, because they are more likely to require the fast twitch fibers to work.

Muscle Size

As just mentioned, it is believed that the first adaptation to strength training is involved in the brain and nerves becoming adept at executing the movement. The increase in muscle size seems to come later. (Although some animal studies show immediate changes in muscle size with the first day of strength training.) Muscle size, either hypertrophy (increase in the size of the individual muscle fibers) or hyperplasia (the increase in the total number of muscle fibers), probably comes later. (See Chapter 6 on muscle size.)

In a study of college women doing a biceps curl, leg press and bench press, it was concluded that it took longer for the brain to learn how to coordinate the muscles in the more complex bench and leg press movements than in the biceps curl. This may have delayed hypertrophy in the trunk and legs. The biceps exhibited a greater degree of hypertrophy more quickly along with the quicker neural adaptation. [11]

It has been suggested that during the first two months of resistance training, 40% of the strength improvement is due to the adaptation of the nervous system and that the remaining 60% of improvement is due to the changes in the musculature, such as hypertrophy and fiber type changes. [12]

However, the research hasn't yet told us whether concentric (shortening contractions) or eccentric (lengthening contractions) exercise, or some combination of the two, helps most in developing the brain and nerve input.

In recreational strength trainers, who would emphasize the concentric contractions, there was an increase in the cross sectional area of the muscles and an increase in the number of capillaries bringing blood to the muscles.[13] Both of these would increase the size of the muscle when measuring it from the outside. The increased cross sectional area should increase the potential strength of the athlete, and the increased blood flow should increase the muscular endurance of the athlete.

Lever Action

It is more than the muscles' force that determines how strong a player can be. The way in which the bones act as levers is at least as important. Assume there are two women with the exact number of muscle fibers in their biceps muscles, but one has a forearm 12 inches long, and her biceps muscle attaches an inch away from the elbow joint. This is a ratio of 1 to 12. The second woman has a forearm 9 inches long, but the biceps tendon attaches an inch and a half away from the elbow. This is a ratio of 1 to 6. Even though they have the same number of fibers contracting at the same time, the second woman will be more than twice as strong as the first, possibly four times as strong. For this reason it is easy to see why the tall, thin basketball player will never be as strong as the short, stocky softball player. If you find that a player is not progressing as fast as desired, you might check the lever action of the joints involved in the lifts where she is not progressing well.

The lever action changes during a lift. Every lift has its "sticking point." That sticking point is the point where the maximum muscle force is used. This means that when using free weights, or most machines, the muscle force is not at maximum during most of the exercise. It is essential that athletes work at maximum in that part of the exercise which they will use in a game or in their event — the last few inches of extension of the leg in the jump of a dancer or volleyball player, the last 90 to 120 degrees of the wrist flexion in a tennis serve, the first 90 degrees of elbow flexion of a rower, the first 30 degrees of hip flexion in a soccer kick, etc.

To force a lifter to work at the maximum throughout the lift, spotters can be used to assist the lifter during the hardest part of the lift or to force the lifter to work harder during the easier part of the lift by giving additional resistance to the bar.

Resistance Training Increases Bone Density

Just as the lack of physical activity allows the bones to soften and decompose, stressing the bones through resistance training can increase their size and strength and decrease the chance of fractures. High intensity strain on the bones, even if short term, are best for inducing bone growth. It is not known whether this bone growth is because the normal breakdown of the bones is slowed, whether there is an actual increase in the bone cell formation, whether it is caused by the increased blood flow in the bones, by changes in hormones, or by other factors.[14] So here is another advantage to resistance exercise.

Hormone Changes

Seven trained power lifters and 12 untrained subjects did a single bout of leg presses to exhaustion at 80% of their one repetition maximum. Measurements of several hormones, neurotransmitters (chemicals which conduct a nerve impulse from one nerve to another) and regulatory substances were measured before and after the set. All of these elements were raised by this single set of exercises. Five minutes after the exercise the trained lifters had significantly more of the various substances in their muscles. This is probably because they lifted more weight during the set. [15]

Notes:

1. C. Delecluse et al., "Influence of High-Resistance and High Velocity Training on Sprint Performance," *Medice & Science in Sport & Exercise* 27.8 (1995): 1203-1209.
2. J. Bloomfield et al., "The Influence of Strength Training on Overhead Throwing Velocity of Elite Water Polo Players," *Australian Journal of Science and Medicine in Sport* 22(1990): 63-67.
3. A. Thorstensson, B. Sjodin, and J. Karlsson, "Enzyme Activities and Muscle Strength After 'Sprint Training' in Man," *Acta Physiol Scand* 94.3 (1975): 313-318.
4. W.J. Kraemer, N.D. Duncan, and J.S. Volek, "Resistance Training and Elite Athletes: Adaptations and Program Considerations," *Journal of Orthopedic and Sports Physical Therapy* 28.2 (1998): 110-119.

5. Greg Wilson, speech given at the Norwegian University for Sport, 1998.

6. D. Pearson and R. Newton, "Super Slow Training: Buyer Beware," *Strength and Conditioning Journal* 21.5 (1999): 29.

7. B. Ter Haar Romeny et al., "Changes in Recruitment Order of Motor Units in the Human Biceps Muscle," *Experimental Neurology* 78 (1982): 631-650.

8. D.G. Sale, "Neural Adaptations to Strength Training," *Strength and Power in Sport,* ed. P.V. Komi (Oxford: Blackwell Scientific, 1992): 249-265.

9. L.L. Ploutz et al., "Effect of Resistance Training on Muscle Use During Exercise," *Journal of Applied Physics* 76.4 (1994): 1675-1681.

10. O.M. Rutherford et al, "Strength Training and Power Output: Transference Effects in Human Quadriceps Muscle," *Journal of Sports Sciences* 4 (1986): 101-107.

11. P.D. Chilibeck, A.W. Calder, D.G. Sale, and C.E. Webber, "A Comparison of Strength and Muscle Mass Increases During Resistance Training in Young Women," *European Journal of Applied Physiology* 77.1-2(1998): 170-175; T. Abe, D.V. DeHoyos, M.L. Pollock, L. Garzarella, "Time Course for Strength and Muscle Thickness Changes Following Upper and Lower Body Resistance Training in Men and Women," *European Journal of Applied Physics* 81.3 (2000): 174-180.

12. M.V. Narici et al., "Changes in Force, Cross Sectional Area and Neural Activation During Strength Training and Detraining in the Human Quadriceps," *European Journal of Applied Physiology* 59 (1989): 310-319.

13. G.E. McCall, W.C. Byrnes, A. Dickinson, P.M. Pattany, and S.J. Fleck. "Muscle Fiber Hypertrophy, Hyperplasia, and Capillary Density in College Men After Resistance Training," *Journal of Applied Physiology* 81.5 (1996):2004-2012.

14. P.D. Chilibeck, D.G. Sale, and C.E. Webber, "Exercise and Bone Mineral Density," *Sports Medicine* 19.2 (1995):103-122.

15. W.J. Kraemer, et al., "Acute Hormonal Responses to a Single Bout of Heavy Resistance Exercise in Trained Power Lifters and Untrained Men," *Canadian Journal of Applied Physiology* 24.6 (1999): 524-537.

5

Types of Muscle Fibers

Like most things, there is the simple story, and there is the real story. Physiological investigations in the late '60s and early '70s did a great deal to shape our knowledge of skeletal muscle function and fiber type. The biopsy technique, enzyme histochemistry (analysis of the chemicals in the tissues and cells), and physiological studies all advanced this issue. From this work, we now know that the fiber types differ in their ability to contract fast, in myosin ATPase enzyme characteristics which also control contractile speed, and in the make up and proportions of the different enzymes in the muscle fiber area. From these three differences, three different fiber type classification schemes have emerged. We will start being a bit technical, but as the chapter unfolds the information will become clear. It is impossible to make something as complicated as a muscle very simple. It would be like trying to explain Einstein's Theory of Relativity in a few words.

First they were called slow twitch and fast twitch, based on how fast the cell shortened. This was Phil Gollnick's classification. About the same time researchers Brook and Engle labeled them type I and type II based on the type of metabolism in the cell — the amount of myosin ATPase (energy developing enzyme) in the fiber. Then Dr. J.B. Peter and his group investigated the properties of the two categories of fibers established by Brooke and Engle. They proposed another terminology which recognized both of the earlier ideas. The type I cells were termed Slow Oxidative. The slow fibers had many mitochondria containing enzymes which aided in the use of oxygen for cell energy, and capillaries carrying the oxygen in the blood. They could therefore contract many times before they fatigued. The type II or "fast" fibers had to be further divided into two sub-categories. Type II cells were either fast oxidative glycolytic (FOG) or fast glycolytic (FG). The

FG fibers stored lots of glycogen and had high levels of enzymes necessary for producing energy without oxygen, but contained few mitochondria so they tired quickly. The FOG fibers had the best of both worlds, high speed and glycolytic (energy producing) capacity, plus high levels of oxidative enzymes which allowed for oxygen to be taken up by the cells. These FOG, or intermediate, fibers were labeled type IIa fibers by a fourth research group, Brooke and Kaiser, in 1970. The pure fast fibers (FG) were termed type IIb. This last system seems to have stuck within the physiological research community.

There are actually a much larger number of fiber types, but they are not as prevalent. For example, in one study of abdominal muscles, it was found that type I fibers made up 55%-58% of the subjects analyzed. Type IIa made up 15%-23%, IIb 21%-28% and IIc 0%-1%. The IIc fibers actually are a true intermediate fiber. But since they are found in a very low percentage of fibers, it really isn't worth dealing with them here.

Studies at the University of Salzburg in Austria found, as might be expected, that Type IIa fibers were faster than IIc which were faster than type I. But they also found that there seems to be more than one type of each major type of fiber.[1] In fact, now it appears that there are a number of different fiber types, not merely the three most common (I, IIa, and IIb). So today the known fiber types are listed as: types I, Ic, IIc, IIac, IIa, IIab, IIb and hybrids. The hybrids are fibers that contain more than one type of myosin heavy chain types.[2]

Resistance training can change the myosin heavy chain composition from the type IIb to the type IIa in less than two weeks.[3]

Intense aerobic exercise has similar effects in terms of changing the makeup of the muscle fibers. Eight weeks of high intensity endurance training for four subjects decreased the type IIb fibers in three of them. The decreases ranged from 31%-70%. The fibers were changed to either the slow type I or Ia types. A second part of the study compared 13 professional cyclists who had been training for several years and found a 20 times lower content of type IIb fibers than four sedentary controls who had 80% more of the fast type I fibers. In another part of the study, eight sprinters were compared to non-athletes. There was almost no difference between the two groups in terms of their type I and type IIb fibers.[4] So the highly aerobic work, such as wind sprints, may reduce the types of fibers which are needed most in developing maximal power.

On the other hand, a Canadian study found that strength training reduced the mitochondria while the fibers were getting larger.[5] This might mean that muscular endurance could be reduced while the muscles were

Different Types of Muscle Fibers:			

- Myosin ATPase refers to the major anaerobic fuel within a muscle fiber, ATP (adenosine triphosphate).
- Oxidative capacity refers to the ability to use oxygen as a fuel (aerobic capacity).
- Mitochondria refers to the energy producing sites within a fiber.
- Capillaries are the smallest blood vessels bringing oxygen and blood sugar (glycogen) to the muscle fibers.
- Myoglobin content is the potential for oxygen storage capacity in a fiber.

Types of Fibers			
Characteristic	Slow Oxidative(I)	Fast Oxidative(IIa)	Fast Glycolytic (IIb)
Myosin ATPase activity	LOW	HIGH	HIGH
Speed of Contraction	SLOW	FAST	FAST
Fatigue Resistance	HIGH	Intermediate	LOW
Oxidative Capacity	HIGH	HIGH	LOW
Anaerobic Enzyme	LOW	Intermediate	HIGH
Content of Fibers			
Mitochondria	MANY	MANY	FEW
Capillaries	MANY	MANY	FEW
Myoglobin	HIGH	HIGH	LOW
Color of Fiber	RED	RED	WHITE
Glycogen Content	LOW	Intermediate	HIGH
Fiber Diameter	SMALL	Intermediate	LARGE

(Used with permission from Dr. Steven Seiler, Agder District College, Kristensand, Norway)

becoming larger and stronger. We might assume, however, that if the athlete were trained for muscular endurance while being trained for strength, this might not occur.

A study of female dancers looked at the possible changes in fiber types when they were training and after 32 weeks of detraining. While they were active they averaged 63% of type I fibers, 26% of IIa, 8% of IIb and 3% of IIc. After detraining it was found that the cross sectional area of the type I fibers actually increased significantly and the other types increased in size only a small amount.

Depending on what you read, you may find the same fi- ber type listed differently so here are the similarities.		
SLOW TWITCH	INTERMEDIATE	FAST TWITCH
Type 1	Type IIa	Type IIb
Slow oxidative	Fast Oxidative Glycolytic (FOG)	Fast Glycolytic (FG)
Red	Red	White

The conclusion was that the type I fibers were more likely to be attributed to heredity factors while the others were more likely to be due to training.[6]

For coaches and athletes it is important to understand that the fast (type IIb) fibers can transition to "intermediate" (type IIa) fibers with long term endurance training, which can even include strength training. Biopsies of elite endurance athletes reveal that after years of training, they have almost no fast IIb fibers, but often have a significant percentage of the intermediate IIa fibers. However, the majority of the available research suggests that type IIa fibers do not transition to type I.

So you must decide what types of fibers you want to develop for your sport. If you run 100 meters, you will want a high percentage of fast twitch IIb fibers. If your event is a 100-meter swim, you will want more type IIa fibers. If you run 10Ks, your need is for far more type I fibers. As a basketball or volleyball player, you would want a combination of speed, muscular endurance and pure endurance. This will change the type of conditioning workout which will be best for you.

The fast twitch type II fibers contract about three times faster than the slow twitch fibers. But since the slow twitch fibers have more endurance potential, the body recruits them first. So if you are a tennis player doing heavy triceps extensions (straightening the arm while holding a dumbbell) to increase your serving speed, the slow fibers will be recruited early. Only if more force is needed will the fast twitch fibers come into play. But in a game, if you need a quick extension of the elbow in your serving action, your triceps exercise might not have given you all of the results you wanted. So the triceps extension and the arm movement in your serve in a match have quite opposite speed and strength requirements.

In a test of the knee extensor muscles of females, Swedish researchers using progressively increasing isometric force lasting 5 seconds found that fiber types were a major factor in the strength generated. A greater number of type IIb and IIa fibers was important. [7]

In a study in Spain involving 16 women and 66 men, age 14 to 36, 10 of

40

Fast- and Slow-Twitch Fibers

1. Type I (previously called the red fibers) are slow-twitch fibers that have more blood supply and more enzymes than the other fiber types. These help in utilizing oxygen. They contract more slowly, but they also have more endurance so they can contract without tiring many more times than the other fibers.
2. Type IIa (previously called the intermediate type or the fast-twitch oxidative type) is a relatively fast twitch fiber which can pick up oxygen better than the type IIb, but not as fast as the type I. In one study they were found to have five times the power of the type I fibers.[9]
3. Type IIb (previously called the white or fast-twitch fibers) fibers are the largest, strongest, and act the most quickly. These are the fibers most involved in strength and speed activities. In the study listed above, these were found to have five times the power of the type IIa fibers, and 25 times the power of the type I fibers. Other studies have shown a peak power output of four times that of slow-twitch fibers.[10]

---

them sedentary and 72 athletes, the chemical characteristics of the vastus muscle fibers were studied. Muscle biopsies were processed histochemically using the myofibrillar ATPase (muscle enzyme) method, and were classified according to gender, sport activity and type of exercise. The average diameter of muscle fibers was larger in men than in women and in trained individuals than in sedentary ones. The largest percentage of slow type I fibers was found in long distance runners, the smallest number in those performing karate and triple jump. The largest percentage of intermediate type IIa fibers was found in swimmers and the least in soccer players. The largest percentages of fast twitch type IIb and IIc fibers were found in soccer players. The largest average diameters of type I and type II fibers were found in swimmers and in long distance athletes, respectively.[8]

An interesting study of weight-trained women at the University of Ne-

---

As one might expect, speed and power athletes have more fast-twitch fibers than endurance athletes. The approximate average percentages of fast-twitch fibers for several sports follow:

Percent of Fast-Twitch Fibers

Sport	Male	Female
Distance runners	31%	39%
Cross-country skiers	36%	40.5%
Cyclists	41%	49%
Untrained subjects	54%	49%
Shot putters	62%	49%
Sprinters	63%	72.5%
Jumpers	63%	51.5%

braska may also be applicable. Twenty-four women completed a 20-week, heavy-resistance weight training program for the legs. Workouts were twice a week and consisted of warm-up exercises followed by three sets each of full squats, vertical leg presses, leg extensions, and leg curls. All exercises were performed to failure using 6-8 RM. Weight training caused a significant increase in maximal isotonic strength (1 RM) for each exercise. After training, there was a decrease in body fat percentage and an increase in lean body mass with no overall change in thigh girth. Biopsies were obtained before and after training from the vastus lateralis muscle. Six fiber types (I, Ic, IIc, IIa, IIab, and IIb) were distinguished following a chemical analysis of the cells. The heavy-resistance training resulted in significant hypertrophy of all three major muscle fiber types. Type I increased 15%, IIa increased 45%, and IIab and IIb increased 57%. These data are similar to those in men. The study also showed a conversion of many type IIb fibers to IIa.[11]

Sex Differences in Fiber Number and Type

Dr. Karin Hendriksson-Larsen of Sweden has been a major researcher in the area of the physiological status and concerns of females in sport. In a study concerning the number, distribution and size of various muscle fiber types in the tibialis major muscle (front of the lower leg), she found that the pattern was slightly different from that in which she did the same type of analysis on the male tibialis anterior, women having 30-40% less total muscle tissue, having fewer and smaller fibers than men. For females in whom she found no difference in the number and types of fibers in the left or right leg, the type II fibers varied in size and were larger deeper in the muscle.[12] Karin also has found that, at least for quadriceps muscles, the power of the muscular contraction is primarily dependent on the fiber types in the muscle.[13]

Fiber Type — Fixed or Changeable?

There is some question as to whether the number of each type of fiber is set at birth[14] or whether they can actually change. However, it is clear that depending on the type of stress placed on the muscle (endurance or strength exercises), fibers can develop the characteristics of another type of fiber. It seems easier to change the characteristics from strength to endurance than from endurance to strength, yet both are possible. Endurance training can convert IIb to IIa, while sprint training can change the IIa to IIb.[15]

A number of other studies have shown that the fastest and most powerful fibers, the type IIb fibers, are reduced and converted into IIa, which are slower but have more endurance through strength training.[16] What does this mean for athletes and coaches? Let's say that you are coaching soccer. If you have a goalkeeper who never plays in the field, you may want only quickness and no strength training. But what about the field players? They need much more endurance with their kicking and jumping strength. Is it, therefore, better to strength train knowing that they will lose some quickness but will develop more endurance?

Body builders don't have any more fast twitch fibers than the general population.[17] So contrary to popular opinion, general weight training doesn't seem to give the type IIb fibers necessary for maximum speed.

Racial Differences in Fiber Types

A small study of untrained students at the University of Tennessee (14 blacks and 14 whites) found that the blacks had a greater percentage of type IIb fibers (22.8% vs. 18.3%) and IIa fibers (40% vs. 36.6%) and a smaller percentage of the slow twitch type I fibers (39.5% vs. 44.9%). While these differences are not considered to be statistically significant, they do make us wonder about the general genetic make up of different groups and what different types of training might do to change those percentages.[18]

So keep this chapter in mind as we look at other research that should be considered for the various sports and playing positions. Speed and endurance muscle fibers are only a part of the equation necessary for your development of a maximally effective conditioning program for higher level athletes.

Notes:

1. K. Hilber and S. Galler, "Mechanical Properties and Myosin Heavy Chain Isoform Composition of Skinned Skeletal Muscle Fibers from a Human Biopsy Sample," *Pflugers Arch* 434.5 (1997): 551-558.
2. R.S. Starone et al., "Fiber Type Composition of Four Hindlimb Muscles of Adult Fisher 344 Rats," *Histochemical Cellular Biology* 111.2 (1999): 117-123.
3. A.C. Fry et al., "Correlation Between Percentage Fiber Type Area and Myosin Heavy Chain Content in Human Skeletal Muscle." *European Journal of Applied Physiology* 68 (1994): 246-251.
4. H. Baumann et al., "Exercise Training Induces Transitions of Myosin Isoform Subunits Within Histochemically Typed Human Muscle Fibres," *Pflugers Arch* 409.4-5 (1987): 349-360.
5. P.D. Chilibeck, D.G. Syrotuik, and G.J. Bell, "The Effect of Strength Training on Estimates of Mitochondrial Density and Distribution Throughout Muscle Fibers," *European Journal of Applied Physiology* 80.6 (1999): 604-609.

6. M. Dahlstrom et al, "Muscle Fiber Characteristics in Female Dancers During an Active and an Inactive Period," *International Journal of Sports Medicine* 8.2 (1987): 84-87.

7. B. Gerdle et al., "Dependence of the Mean Power Frequency of the Electromyogram on Muscle Force and Fibre Type," *Acta Physiol Scand* 142.4 (1991): 457-465.

8. J.R. Ricoy et al., "Histochemical Study of the Vastus Lateralis Muscle Fibre Types of Athletes," *Physio Biochem* 54.1 (1998): 41-47.

9. J.J. Widrick et al., "Force-Velocity and Force-Power Properties of Single Muscle Fibers from Elite Master Runners and Sedentary Men," *American Journal of Physiology* 271.2 (1996): 676-683.

10. J.A. Faulkner et al., "Power Output of Fast and Slow Fibers from Human Skeletal Muscles." *Human Muscle Power,* eds. Jones et al (Champaign, Il: Human Kinetics, 1986) 81-94.

11. R.S. Staron et al., "Muscle Hypertrophy and Fast Fiber Type Conversions in Heavy Resistance-Trained Women," *European Journal of Applied Physiology* 60.1 (1990): 71-9.

12. K. Henriksson-Larsen, "Distribution, Number and Size of Different Types of Fibres in Whole Cross-Sections of Female Tibialis Anterior. An Enzyme Histochemical Study," *Acta Physiol Scand* 123.3 (1985): 229-235.

13. B. Gerdle, M.L. Wretling, and K. Henriksson-Larsen, "Do the Fibre-Type Proportion and the Angular Velocity Influence the Mean Power Frequency of the Electromyogram?" *Acta Physiol Scand* 134.3 (1988): 341-346.

14. T. Rowland, *Developmental Exercise Physiology* (Champaign, IL: Human Kinetics, 1996) 168.

15. C.A. Allemeier et al., "Effects of Sprint Cycle Training on Human Skeletal Muscle," *Journal of Applied Physiology* 77.5 (1994): 2385-2390.

16. A.C. Fry et al., "Correlation Between Percentage Fiber Type Area and Myosin Heavy Chain Content in Human Skeletal Muscle," *European Journal of Applied Physiology* 68 (1994): 246-251.

17. D.G. Sale, J.D. MacDougall, and S.Garner, "Interaction Between Concurrent Strength and Endurance Training," *Journal of Applied Physiology* 68.1 (1990): 260-270.

18. W.J. Duey et al., "Skeletal Muscle Fibre Type and Capillary Density in College-Aged Blacks and Whites," *Journal of Human Biology* 24.4 (1997): 323-331.

6

Muscle Size
Hypertrophy and Hyperplasia

*M*uscles adapt to various types of stresses. Lifting very heavy weights (as in Olympic weightlifting), lifting somewhat lighter weights for a long period of time (as in body building), and working a muscle thousands of times without much resistance (as in marathon running) each force the muscles to make different types of adjustments. Studies with animals, particularly with birds, even show that prolonged stretching of a muscle with a weight will increase the number of fibers.

The prolonged endurance exercise of a distance runner will result in an increase in the muscle's ability to use and store oxygen. One of the reasons is the increase in mitochondrial volume or density. This is the energy producing site in the muscle cell. There is also an increase in the number of capillaries — the very small blood vessels that bring blood to the muscle fibers. The blood, of course, carries both oxygen and sugars for energy. The myoglobin, which can store oxygen for future use, is also increased. Additionally, there is an increase in the enzymes which increase the ability of the cell to utilize oxygen.

These changes in the muscles generally don't make the muscles larger. In fact, some elite marathoners have smaller muscle fibers than people who don't exercise. It should be obvious that this type of aerobic endurance work is not what is needed for basketball. Running long distances may prepare an athlete for a soccer game in which she will run several miles, but it is not the type of conditioning useful for softball. We will discuss strength-endurance work later as a more valuable type of conditioning for swimmers and rugby players. So if you have been running several miles for aerobic conditioning, you may not be helping yourself if you are not in a pure endurance-type sport, and you should be able to make better use of your time.

If you are a high jumper, weight thrower or sprint swimmer, you are among the strength-power athletes, and you need more muscle size and more ability to contract a larger number of muscle fibers in one contraction. You would need more contractile protein, the material that makes the muscle fibers shorten quickly. You need each muscle fiber to increase more in size because the larger the cross sectional area of a fiber, the more force it can generate in a contraction. This is called hypertrophy. You should also benefit from developing a greater number of muscle fibers. This is called hyperplasia.

Fifty years ago we thought that weightlifting increased the number of muscle fibers (hyperplasia). Then the research showed that it was the muscle fibers which were increasing in diameter (hypertrophy), so we thought that was the sole answer to why muscles got larger. It was decided that no new fibers were being developed. Then some research with birds and cats showed that they were increasing the number of fibers in their muscles when they were subjected to stresses. While it was easy to cut into an animal's muscle and count the fibers, no humans volunteered to have a whole muscle belly cut and the fibers counted.

The Role of Muscle Cell Damage in Hypertrophy and Hyperplasia

It seems that both hypertrophy and hyperplasia occur because of damage to the individual muscle fibers. This damage can occur because of a shortening (concentric) contraction but is more likely to happen with a lengthening (eccentric) contraction. It can also occur when a muscle is stretched while holding a weight.

For a number of years, some human subjects have allowed muscle biopsies (small, nearly microscopic, needle sized excisions) that allowed us to see some fiber types and measure muscle fiber size. But they didn't allow us to see whether additional fibers were actually being developed. More recently, using muscle biopsies of body builders we have found that while they have much greater than normal muscle bulk, their muscle fibers are often not much larger than normal. This leads us to believe that their type of workout has allowed them to develop more muscle fibers.

In a study at the University of Maryland both young men (ages 20 to 30) and older men (ages 65 to 75) did leg extensions with one leg, 3 days a week (5 sets of 5 to 20 reps at near maximum) for nine weeks. Muscle biopsies were taken from both the non-exercising leg and the exercised leg before and after the program. The biopsies taken before the experiment showed muscle fiber damage in from 0%-3% of the fibers. After exercising the exercised leg showed damage to 6%-7% of the fibers. The damage was generally

46

to only one or two of the contracting elements in the fibers (sarcomeres). Additionally, both groups increased in strength 27% in the trained leg. (So we old coaches can get as much as our players if we work as hard!)[1]

The study was repeated for women. Older women exhibited more muscle damage in the front of the thigh (vastus lateralis) than younger women when doing equivalent training. The University of Maryland study used a group of 20- to 30-year-old women and compared them with a group of women 65 to 75 years old. Prior to the study, the younger women showed 2%-4% of their muscle fibers were damaged. The older women showed 2%-5% damaged. Both groups then did leg extensions with only one leg, 3 days a week for 9 weeks. At the conclusion of the study, both groups increased their strength — 38% in the younger women and 25% in the older women. At the conclusion of the study, muscle damage was again measured. The younger women still had 2%-4% of their fibers damaged, but the older women showed a damage rate of 5%-17%.[2]

We don't know exactly how hypertrophy occurs, but it seems to happen more with the eccentric contraction than the concentric contraction. It seems that when the weight is lowered under stress, there is more damage to the smaller parts of the muscle fiber. This damage seems to be the key. There seem to be multiple causes for this.

Eccentric contractions have been shown to disturb or damage the Z discs that anchor the actin filaments and attach one myofibril to another. The exercise also releases proteins from the muscle into the blood. The damage can continue for some time after the exercise has been finished. It is not known exactly why the damage occurs, but various theories include free oxygen radical damage and both energy and protein metabolism or reduction. Exactly what happens within the muscle fibers is also not known. It may be that the weakened parts of the fibers are eliminated or die and are then replaced by stronger elements.[3] We don't really know exactly how or what is happening — only that *something* is happening.

Hypertrophy – increase the size of the muscle.

When one trains with fairly heavy weights, the muscles generally respond by producing more of the contractile protein (actin and myosin) in the myofilaments within the small elements (myofibrils) of the muscle fibers. Additionally, more myofibrils develop within the individual muscle fiber. This will increase the size of the total muscle belly (hypertrophy).

The force a muscle can develop is related to the cross sectional area of the muscle fibers which are contracting. A force of 22 to 28 newtons per square centimeter of muscle fiber cross section is the normally accepted estimate of force. (A newton is the amount of force necessary to move one kilogram of weight one meter per second.) However, studies have indicated a range of from 16 to 100 newtons per square centimeter of cross sectional area.[4] With magnetic resonance imaging (MRI) we have been able to get a clearer picture of where hypertrophy occurs. It is more pronounced in the widest part of the muscle and occurs much less at the origin and insertion areas. [5]

Hyperplasia — increase the number of muscle fibers

One study compared four highly-trained body builders with four active non-body builders. The biopsies showed similar size of muscle fibers in both groups, but the fact that the body builders had much larger muscles indicated that they had many more muscle fibers. So it was assumed that the difference was due to hyperplasia not hypertrophy. [6]

A study of cats done at the University of Texas, indicated that new muscle fibers are created in this mammal, also. Many people in the past have theorized that the new cells were formed either by splitting the existing cells or by the development of nearby "satellite" cells into new muscle fibers.[7] Weightlifting, at least with cats, can increase both the size of the muscle (hypertrophy) and the number of muscle fibers (hyperplasia). In a study using cats lifting weights with increasing resistance (averaging 57% of their body weight) on one wrist for two years, the cats were found to have increased their muscle weight by 11% and the number of muscle fibers by 9% when the exercised leg was compared with the non-exercised leg.[8] After examining the training variables that predicted muscle hypertrophy, scientists from Dr. Gonyea's laboratory found that the lifting speed had the highest correlation to changes in muscle mass. (The cats that lifted the weight in a slow and deliberate manner made greater muscle mass gains than cats that lifted the weight quickly.)

Developing hyperplasia through long-term, continuous stretching has been done with birds. In the early 1970s research on birds indicated that if a weight that was 10% of the bird's weight was attached to the bird's wing, the muscles in the back that were supporting the wing and being stretched increased their total number of muscle fibers. Studies showed that in a month the number of muscle fibers increased by 16%[9] to 75%.[10]

In a study using weights attached to one wing of 26 different quails, increasing the weight from 10% of body weight at the beginning of the study to 35% of body weight by the 17th day, the stretching of the muscles increased the total muscle mass by 174% after 12 days and 318% after 28 days. The wing without the weight served as the control. The number of muscle fibers in the stretched wings increased by 82% after 28 days.[11] The quail wings were stretched for one day with 10% of the body weight, then rested for two days, then stretched with 15% body weight and rested for two more days. This approach was used up to the 11th day, when 25% of the quail's weight was used for four days, followed by two days of rest. Then from days 17 to 37 it was increased to 35% of the quail's weight

Antonio's research on the quails showed the maximum hypertrophy occurring after 16 days of stretch. By this time the weight being suspended from the wing had been increased to 25% of the bird's body weight. The number of damaged muscle fibers at this point was between 0.7% and 3.7%, with the most damage occurring around the 16th day. This was also the point where the greatest cross sectional area increased in the slow-twitch fibers. The fast-twitch muscle fibers cross sectional areas were greatest at days 12, 16 and 20. The control wings, as might be expected, showed almost no damage.

Some studies have shown fiber damage as high as 25% in the stretched wing. The conclusions of Antonio's study included the theory that the hyperplasia was most likely to occur in the hypertrophied muscle cells after they had reached a maximum cross sectional area. It was surmised that perhaps the cell was not able to metabolize effectively if the cell became too large, so it split into two or more fibers.[12] There is a question as to whether muscle cells are increased because they split after a certain amount of hypertrophy has taken place or whether cells that are near the fibers, satellite myogenic cells, become full muscle fibers.

While the study of animals is very valuable in the search for the causes and the mechanisms for increasing muscle size, number and strength, the way that animals are trained seldom is similar to that of human athletes.[13] We certainly don't hang 50 pounds on the arms of our shot putters for a month or two. It would be rather difficult to take a history test while writing with a dumbbell and a pen in her writing hand!

However, the increased size or number of muscle fibers is only part of the story. Increasing the blood supply to the exercised muscle also increases the measurable size of the entire muscle. In recreational strength trainers there was an increase in the cross sectional area of the muscles and an increase in the number of capillaries bringing blood to the muscles.[14]

We need to consider just how much hypertrophy, if any, would be ideal for each of us. Will that hypertrophy make us stronger, quicker, more powerful? If we want larger muscles there is a right way to work for them, and we will discuss that later in this book.

Notes:

1. S.M. Roth et al., "Ultrastructural Muscle Damage in Young vs. Older Men After High-Volume, Heavy-Resistance Strength Training," *Journal of Applied Physiology* 86.6 (1999): 1833-1840.
2. S.M. Roth et al., "High-Volume, Heavy-Resistance Strength Training and Muscle Damage in Young and Older Women." *Journal of Applied Physiology* 88.3 (2000): 1112-1118.
3. C.B. Ebbeling and P.M. Clarkson, "Exercise-Induced Muscle Damage and Adaptation," *Sports Medicine* 7.4 (1989): 207-34.
4. R. Alexander and A. Vernon, "The Dimension of Knee and Ankle Muscles and the Forces They Exert," *Journal of Human Movement Studies* 1 (1975): 115-123; J.G. Hay and J.G. Reid, *Anatomical and Mechanical Basis of Human Movement* (Englewood Cliffs, NJ: Prentice-Hall, 1982); M.J.N. McDonagh and C.T.M. Davies, "Adaptive Response of Mamallian Skeletal Muscle to Exercise with High Loads," *European Journal of Applied Physiology* 52 (1984): 139-155.
5. W.J. Roman et al., "Adaptations of the Elbow Flexors of Elderly Males After Heavy Resistance Training," *Journal of Applied Physiology* 74 (1993): 750-754.
6. L. Larsson and P.A. Tesch, "Motor Unit Fibre Density in Extremely Hypertrophied Skeletal Muscles in Man," Electrophysiological Signs of Muscle Fibre Hyperplasia," *European Journal of Applied Physiology* 55.2 (1986): 130-136.
7. C.J. Giddings and W.J. Gonyea, "Morphological Observations Supporting Muscle Fiber Hyperplasia Following Weightlifting Exercise in Cats," *Anat Rec* 233.2 (1992): 178-195.
8. W.J. Gonyea, D.G. Sale, F.B. Gonyea, and A. Mikesky, "Exercise Induced Increases in Muscle Fiber Number," *European Journal of Applied Physiology* 55.2 (1986): 137-141.
9. O.M. Sola, D.L. Christiansen and A.W. Martin, "Hypertrophy and Hyperplasia of Adult Chicken Anterior Latissimus Dorsi Muscles Following Stretch With and Without Denervation," *Experimental Neurology* 41 (1973): 76-100.
10. S.E. Alway, W.J. Gonyea and M.E. Davis, "Muscle Fiber Formation and Fiber Hypertrophy During Onset of Stretch-Overload," *American Journal of Physiology* 269 (1990): C92-C102.
11. J. Antonio and W.J. Gonyea, "Progressive Stretch Overload of Skeletal Muscle Results in Hypertrophy Before Hyperplasia," *Journal of Applied Physiology* 75.3 (1993): 1263-1271.

12. J. Antonio and W.J. Gonyea, 1263-1271.
13. B.F. Timson, "Evaluation of Animal Models for the Study of Exercise-Induced Muscle Enlargement," *Journal of Applied Physiology* 69.6 (1990): 1935-45.
14. G.E. McCall et al, "Muscle Fiber Hypertrophy, Hyperplasia, and Capillary Density in College Men After Resistance Training," *Journal of Applied Physiology* 81.5 (1996): 2004-2012.

7

Muscle Contractions and Muscle Action in Exercise

———

Now that we have looked at the fibers and how they develop and work, let's look more specifically at the science behind strength training.

Types of Muscular Contractions

There are three types of muscular contractions: concentric or isotonic (same tone), in which the muscle fiber is shortening; static or isometric, in which the muscle is contracted but does not change its length; and lengthening or eccentric (pronounced ek-sen-trik), in which the muscle is lengthening.

Both concentric and eccentric exercises cause muscle cell damage. The eccentric exercises not only damage more muscle cells, but also damage them more severely. One study in which one arm contracted concentrically and the other arm eccentrically showed that while fewer muscle fibers were activated in the eccentric exercise, the force generated in those fibers involved was very high. Severe damage was shown in 13% of concentric contracting muscles and 17% of eccentric contracting muscles.[1] Both the increase in muscle cell size and the increase in the total number of muscle cells occur faster with eccentric exercise. The damage done to the individual fibers seems to account for this.

In a study done at the University of Southern California, eccentric-only work was found to be significantly more effective than the concentric/eccentric exercise which is commonly done. The study dealt only with shoulder strength.[2] This indicates that rather than the typical way of exercising (lifting the weight nearly as fast as possible, then returning the bar to the starting point at about the same speed) may not be best for strength and size gain. For bench press strength you may be better served starting with a weight heavier than your 1 RM at arms length, then lowering the weight as slowly as possible to the chest. Two spotters would be essential for such maximal eccentric exercises.

Types of Exercises

Exercises can be isotonic (concentric), eccentric, isometric, isokinetic or plyometric. Each has its place in developing the various types of size, strength and power which make people more effective athletes. Isotonic (iso means "same," and tonic means "muscle tone or strength") is the type of exercise done when lifting a weight such as a barbell. In an isotonic exercise, the weight stays the same during the contraction. Most of the exercises you will do will be isotonic.

Most isotonic exercises will have an eccentric component. When the athlete lifts the weight in a biceps curl, the return to the beginning position is eccentric. Because of the muscle-damaging action in the eccentric part of the exercise, many people return the weight slower than it was lifted. If it was lifted in two counts, it can be returned in four to six counts. This should aid in developing muscle size.

Muscle strength, however, comes from more than just muscle size. The ability of the nervous system to stimulate a great number of muscle fibers also seems to be important.[3] However, the research hasn't yet told us whether concentric or eccentric exercise, or some combination of the two, helps this to happen best. We also don't know the best speed to lift for each type of strength or power that we want.

In isometric ("same measure") exercises, the joint does not change positions. Standing in a doorway and pushing out on the jamb would be isometric. Of course, if you break the door, a la Samson, it would become isotonic. Isometrics are a way of maintaining strength when you are on vacation and do not have access to resistance machines. Isometrics can also be used in rehabilitation when there is little ability to move a joint. This type of exercise has the lowest transfer to most sport needs. However, a soccer player

Running utilizes both concentric and eccentric contractions. The power of the push off is concentric, but as the leg moves forward, it is being stretched eccentrically.

53

The neck should be stiffened (isometric contraction) to transfer the shock of the ball from the head to the torso.

who heads the ball could profit from stronger neck muscles gained by isometric contractions, as can a woman in a rugby scrum. Isometric strength would also be useful for the biceps, forearm, hand, lats and lower chest in carrying the ball in rugby.

Isometric strength gain is pretty much limited to the joint angle at the time of the contraction. For example, a study done on previously untrained women showed that when the quadriceps was exercised at 45 degrees there was a 27% increase in strength at that angle after six weeks of training, but at a 75 degree angle the strength increase was only 7%.[4] Because of the joint specificity, if you choose to work isometricly the work should be done at about every 15 degrees through the range of motion.

While isometric work can make the muscles stronger in working against isometric resistance, such training does not increase the speed of muscular contractions. In a Canadian study designed to test for whether the motor unit (nerve and muscle fibers) would fire faster if the muscle's contracting force was increased, it was found that the change in strength did not change the speed of the contraction. This is another indication of the role of the nervous system in strength.[5]

Eccentric (lengthening) exercises seem better for increasing size and strength and are an essential part of plyometric exercises which increase speed and power. They are also a part of the sport-specific movements in running and some jumping.

Maximal eccentric force is about 1.3% of the 1 RM (130 pounds if your RM is 100 pounds). However, eccentric work is generally done with about 120% of the 1 RM load. The lifting of heavy weights is generally done with the assistance of spotters during the concentric phase of the lift, then the weight is lowered slowly, taking 3–4 seconds to complete the eccentric phase in the desired range of motion. If a player is using only one limb, such as a dumbbell curl for the biceps or a one-legged leg press, the opposite limb can be used to assist the movement through the concentric part of the lift.

Eccentric exercises may do more than just strengthen the muscles. A recent study at the University of Southern California found that eccentric exercise increases bone density more than concentric exercise, so stronger bones are another advantage of eccentric exercises.[6] You must be cautioned, however, that the risk of injury is higher in eccentric work, so the athletes using this method must already be well trained.

While supra-maximal eccentric loads are often used by elite power lifters, they may not provide more strength for you. One study found that normal concentric training was as effective in developing quadriceps strength as was supra-maximal eccentric exercise. Isometric, concentric and eccentric exercise were compared. During 12 weeks of training, those exercising isometrically increased their force production by 35%. The cross sectional area of the muscle increased 5%, which did not account for the increase in force production. Those working concentrically increased their isometric force production by 15% and their cross sectional muscle area by about 5%. Those working eccentrically (with a 45% greater load than those working concentrically) increased their force production by 11% and also had about a 5% increase in the cross sectional area of the muscle fibers. The researchers concluded that during the first 12 weeks of training the increase in strength is due more to the amount of force a muscle unit can produce than to the cross sectional area of the muscle. [7]

So now we have yet another theory as to how strength is produced:. The three major theories of how strength is produced are: 1) the increased potential force of the increased cross sectional area (hypertrophy) of the muscle fibers, 2) the number of muscle fibers that can be contracted at one time by the nervous system, and 3) the possibility that an individual muscle fiber can "learn" to generate a greater amount of force as it is trained.

Isokinetic (same energy) exercises require a special type of machine that keeps the speed nearly constant while the force is maximized. This has a high transfer to athletic events that require speed. Machines that rely on fluids, air or braking mechanisms are usually isokenetic. The possible disadvantage is that the lifter must make certain that she is contracting her muscles to the maximum. It is easy to cheat on isometric machines.

Plyometric (increase measure) exercises use a combination of eccentric then concentric contractions. Exercise physiologists call this the "stretch shortening cycle." This type of exercise is most likely to develop more speed and power in the athlete. However, because of the type of muscular contractions involved, more injury to the muscle is likely. Plyometrics should therefore be done only by well-trained athletes, and they should be done only under the supervision of a qualified person who will limit the number of plyometric repetitions.

Don Chu, one of the leading authorities on plyometrics, recommends not using lower body plyos until the athlete can squat 1.5 times her body weight, or upper body plyos unless the bench press is at least equal to one's body weight.[8]

The theory of why plyometrics work is that: 1) a stretched muscle reacts faster than a relaxed muscle (that it has "stored" energy by being stretched), and 2) when a muscle is already contracting in an eccentric contraction, such as when the foot hits the ground while running or when landing after jumping off of a box, it is more able to initiate its concentric contraction. If a person jumps from a 2-foot high box, the number of muscle fibers in the calf muscle required to contract in order to allow the body's weight to be absorbed effectively is higher and quicker than the person could probably elicit in a concentric contraction. If the person lands and quickly jumps, this increased number of fibers can be called upon to continue to contract in the ensuing concentric contraction. The chances are that more muscle fibers will be called on to contract than could normally be elicited if one were merely standing then jumped upward.

To increase the number of fibers contracting, the person can jump from higher and higher boxes — up to 3 or 4 feet high. (Most recommend a maximum of 1 1/2 to 2 feet for the box jump.) This will require that more fibers will eccentrically contract when landing and will then be available for the immediate jump up to another box. This training should teach the nervous and muscular systems to contract more and more fibers on the one contraction. This results in an increase in power — which is what is desired in ballet dancing, jumping and sprinting.

If you want strength for moving something, you probably should move something in your exercise. So concentric types of exercises would seem to be best for developing strength and power, but isometrics can be effective where non-movement strength is useful, such as when the neck is "bulled" during heading a soccer ball. And, as mentioned earlier, more size may be gained by emphasizing the eccentric phase of the exercise. If that increased size can be converted to strength and/or power, eccentric exercises should be valuable. But as shown above, in short term studies the eccentric work alone did not increase the concentric potential for strength and power needed in a power lift, a jump or a sprint.

The research studies which have been done often don't give us the results we had expected. For example, a study of team handball players in Italy found that those who trained for strength, while they gained throwing strength, didn't gain vertical jumping strength. Those who merely played but didn't do extra strength training did improve their vertical jumps.[9]

In a study of female team handball players, those who practiced the game and trained on the bench press, a non-sport specific exercise, improved the velocity of their throws by 17% while those who only practiced improved their throwing velocity by only 9%.[10] In a study of karate participants, those who strength trained and practiced improved their punching velocity over those who either only strength trained or only practiced karate.[11] Based on such research, it is more effective to strength train and practice the sport-specific movements during the same period of time that we are doing more traditional strength exercises. It is also quite clear that the more we make the strength or power movement sport specific, the better the outcome of the resistance training relative to game performance.

Speed of the Exercise

It is impossible to know the best speed at which to perform exercises for each type of strength or power that we want. That speed can vary from no movement as in an isometric exercise, to a very fast movement such as a plyometric exercise. Research indicates that athletes who perform low-velocity, high intensity strength training concurrently with high-velocity training are superior in tests of isokinetic strength at high velocities when compared to athletes who only perform low-velocity, high intensity training. This may be due to training or to genetic factors. [12]

Types of Resistance

The most common types of resistance are free weights: barbells (for two-hand exercises) and dumbbells (for one-hand exercises). These have the advantage of being relatively inexpensive and useful in many types of exercises. They also require that the lifter use other muscles than the primary lifting muscles in order to balance the weight. The amount of force these balancing muscles exert is, however, very small.

The disadvantage of free weights is that they are less safe than other types of resistance systems, such as those done on machines. If the weights are not secured properly, they may slip off. And with the heavier barbell exercises, a spotter is necessary to assist the lifter in case she loses balance (as in a squat) or lacks the strength to replace the weight on a rack (such as in a bench press). The only deaths recorded for strength trainers were teenage boys who were doing bench presses alone at home and suffocated when they couldn't get the weight off of the neck.

Weight machines are safer than the free weights and also allow the resistance to be changed by simply sliding a pin to another weight. This allows for more people to exercise in a shorter period of time. Sliding a pin in a weight stack doesn't take nearly as much time as it does to change a weight on a barbell or dumbbell. The major disadvantage is that in some of the exercises the lifter cannot gain as full a range of movement as can be done with free weights.

The variable resistance machines add a different element by using cams to change the resistance during the exercise. If you were using free weights and doing a biceps curl, it would be easy as you started the exercise but would become increasingly more difficult as you lifted the weight. By using the specially designed cam, however, the muscle can be forced to work harder than normal at the beginning of the exercise as well.

Machines often allow the athlete to work at a posture which is more sport specific. While a bench press with the hands very close together would be better than the traditional wide grip for a shot putter, it would also be best to do the exercise in a vertical position. Only a machine can allow this type of action.

Isokinetic machines allow the user to exert constant, or nearly constant force against the machine. The force is measured on a gauge. This way the lifter can use full power over the entire range of motion. Also, the exercise is isokinetic, the best type for an athlete. Unfortunately, many people want to "pump iron" and thus overlook the benefits of working on an isokinetic machine.

Springs and elastic bands are often used as part of a home gym but are seldom seen in schools or gyms. They have the advantage of being inexpensive. Their disadvantage is that their resistance increases as they are expanded, so you do not get a true level of resistance throughout the exercise.

Manual resistance from a partner or yourself (called dynamic tension by the famous bodybuilder Charles Atlas) is the use of one muscle against another. There are some very real advantages in this type of resistance for neck exercises and for some of the smaller muscles, such as the wrist and fingers, but it is of no value in developing leg strength or bench-pressing strength. Of course, its greatest advantage is that it is cheap and you can't help but take your equipment with you on vacation.

Isometric work can be done using a number of non-movable types of resistance. Pressing a barbell upward against the pins in a squat rack would be one example. Using a spotter's resistance added to the weight of a bar can also allow for isometric work. Isometric work is generally done at the sticking point in a lift to attempt to increase the force development at that specific joint angle.

Body Movements When Lifting

Weight-training exercises are often described in technical anatomical terms. So lying face down is called being in the prone position. Lying face up is called being in the supine position. Bent means bending at the waist while standing. Other positions are kneeling and standing, which certainly need no explanation.

Resistance Weight Machines vs Free Weights	
Machines	
Advantages	*Disadvantages*
Expensive	Many limit action to one joint
Less versatile unless you have	a complete set of machines Easier to use
Bulky, not portable	Calibrated resistance (many change resistance throughout the exercise)
Quicker to set resistance	
Free Weights	
Advantages	*Disadvantages*
Cheaper	More chance of injury if lifts are improper
More variety of exercises	Often need a spotter
Easily maintained	More skill required (balance)
Usually require additional muscles to stabilize	Easily stolen
	Unless assisted by a partner, the maximum force is exerted only for a few degrees in the movement.

Joint actions

As strength training has become more scientific, it has begun using the names for body movements which have traditionally been used in anatomy and kinesiology. In this book we will generally use these more scientific terms.

- Flexion means to decrease the angle of a joint. A biceps curl is an example of elbow flexion.
- Extension means to return the joint to its normal position.
- Hyperextension means to bring the joint to a position past normal extension.
- Abduction means to move a limb away from the body.
- Adduction means to bring the joint back from the abducted position.
- Other terms are used for rotation of a joint, such as the shoulder or neck, or the complicated movements of the ankle and wrist.

59

Planning a Program for Increasing Muscle Size

In the earlier cited study women training on a knee extension and a chest (bench) press 8-12 repetitions to exhaustion, three days a week for 12 weeks increased muscle size 19% for the knee extension but 27% for the chest press. For women the upper body increased in size 10%-31% and the thigh 7%-8%. It was concluded that upper body increases occurred earlier than lower body increases.

A high volume workout in which a large number of sets and repetitions and a great total amount of weight is lifted, works best to develop muscle size. Additionally, heavy eccentric training using 120% of one's 1 RM in a 3–4 second eccentric contraction may increase the micro-traumas in the muscle and thereby promote both hypertrophy and hyperplasia. The exerciser should concentrate on the lengthening (eccentric) part of the exercise. During the exercise period, the rest periods between the sets should be short. Two to 3 days rest between exercise periods should be taken to allow the body to make the repairs to the muscles.

One study indicated that hypertrophy occurs best using 75% of one's 1 RM.[13] In an attempt to compare strength training, power training and high repetition training, three groups were compared: a heavy weight group which worked with a 90%–100% 1 RM, a power group working fast with 45% of the 1 RM and a high repetition group using 70% of its 1 RM.[14] The workouts and results were:

	Load	*Sets and Reps*	*Hypertrophy*
Heavy weight	90%–100%	3 x 3, 2 x 2, 1 x 1	10%
Power group	45%	5 x 8	10%,
High repetition	70%	3 x 12	18%

A Japanese study investigated whether or not doing a fatiguing concentric exercise before doing an eccentric exercise would increase the muscle damage and, therefore, increase the potential for muscle gains in size. The women in this study did 12 eccentric contractions of elbow flexion (biceps curls) with one arm. With the other arm they did 100 isokinetic concentric contractions, then did the 12 eccentric contractions. The results showed that the muscle damage was less in the arm that first did the concentric exercises. This was evidenced by a smaller increase in biceps size as well as enzyme changes in the muscles. In another study done by the same group it was found that a muscle warm up also reduced the muscle damage.[15]

Planning a program to increase muscle size, either through hypertrophy or hyperplasia definitely requires a fairly large number of reps (8 to 15) with 60%–80% of the 1 RM. The last repetition must result in muscle failure

60

(exhaustion). Larger numbers of sets are also profitable. Schmidtbleicher also suggests periodization with 11 to 30 reps at 50 to 75% of 1 RM for two weeks, then the use of 75%–80% loads for two weeks. The first period increases strength endurance and gains some aerobic benefits while the second period increases the production of contractile protein and an increase in the cross sectional area of the fibers along with an increase in strength and creatine phosphate for anaerobic abilities.[16]

A study at Marquette University used middle-aged runners and compared them with a sedentary group of people. After the muscles were biopsied from the subjects, it was found that the sedentary people's individual fibers were both larger and stronger than those of the runners. But after adjusting for the cross sectional areas of the individual fibers, it was found that the strength was directly related to the cross sectional areas of the fibers. While the runners' fibers had more ability to contract a greater number of times because of the fuel supply, this endurance ability did not transfer to the fibers' ability to shorten with force. This study also found that the ability to generate force was five times as great for the type IIa as the type I fibers while the type IIb fibers were twice as strong as the IIa fibers. Studies such as this strongly indicate that if we want to develop peak force and power, we need to work on developing more of the type II fibers, especially those which are in the type IIb and the other related types.

Since there is a strong relationship between muscle size and strength, these types of exercises are suggested:

- The use of heavy eccentric contractions (120%–130% of 1 RM)
- Functional isometrics — finishing a concentric contraction with a strong isometric contraction at the sticking point or near the end of the lift
- Isokinetics — working on machines that allow for full force to be exerted throughout both the concentric and eccentric parts of the exercise
- Optimal spotting — allowing for increased resistance in both the concentric and eccentric phases of the exercise by using a spotter to manually increase the resistance

Gaining Strength

We have long known that the cross sectional area of a muscle fiber is related to the strength with which it can contract. However, not all studies indicate that the increased size, when developed by eccentric contractions, translates directly into the increased concentric strength or power (speed-strength) that is needed in most sports. We also realize that the brain is a

61

major factor in strength development and the use of maximal force. The more muscle fibers that can be contracted at one time, the greater the strength.

Athletes' strength needs are sport-specific. Becoming very strong in the bench press is helpful for team handball defenders who block with their arms extended, but it is not nearly as important for basketball players, unless more passing strength is needed. Pulling in on a rowing machine develops the strength needed for rowing, but such an action is seldom used by a tennis player.

Studies have shown that for most people an exercise increases strength primarily through the movement pattern utilized. If a girl did quarter squats, but in a game she needed strength from a 90-degree flexed knee position, she would need to do squats with the knees flexed to 90 degrees.

Strength is not only gained primarily in the angles exercised, but it is also dependent on the angle of the joint while exercising. If you want serving strength for volleyball or shooting strength for basketball, you would want to have your body at the appropriate angle during the exercise — a standing position.

Still another factor affecting maximum strength gain is the posture used by the lifter while exercising. It should be the same as used in a game. For example, a machine that allowed a swimmer to exercise her lats while standing would not be as effective as if she exercised in the prone position.

In setting up a strength program you must be aware of the exercise methods that will increase the muscle size and the potential strength of each muscle fiber and you must have programs for teaching the brain to be able to stimulate more muscle fibers at the same time. High volume exercises will tend to increase muscle size while high intensity will be more likely to increase the type of strength needed for the weight events in track and field or for those who do power lifting or Olympic weightlifting. It is this high-intensity type of workout that is used by many professional football teams. One set of high intensity work both saves time and increases the athlete's effective strength. A little over a third of the pro football teams now use the high intensity programs and more successful college programs, such as Michigan State, are adopting this approach. It is done with both machines and free weights.

One High Intensity Set

For years in sports we have followed the lead of bodybuilders and used the 3 set approach to strength training. This is in spite of the pioneering work of Richard Berger from the late 1950s and early 1960s that showed that a single set of 10 RM was about as good as three sets.[17] This has been borne out in nearly every study since, but we still cling to the three set standard.

In a recent University of Florida study of male weight trainers ages 33 to 45, with an average of 4.6 years of training, who had been performing one set of each of 9 different exercises, the question was whether they would gain significantly more strength doing three sets of each exercise. In the 13-week study in which some continued their 1 RM exercises while others increased to three sets, no significant difference occurred in lean body mass, 1 RM or muscular endurance.[18]

However, Bill Kraemer, certainly one of the top three experts in the world on strength training, has suggested that as strength gain plateaus develop a few months into the training period, the lifter can go to three sets as a way of periodizing the training.[19] The obvious disadvantage of three sets in the added time.

Spotter-Assisted Training

Since eccentric contractions will cause more fiber damage that will result in greater muscle size and strength, eccentric contractions should be included in an effective resistance program. Eccentric exercises can be done by using more than 100% of the 1 RM with a spotter assisting in the lifting of the weight, or by having a spotter give hand pressure downward on the bar which carries a 1 RM load or a lighter weight. The spotters must be careful to not give too much pressure. Some people may want to joke around, but too much pressure can cause muscle injury more severe than that which will give maximal development.

Spotter assists can also be used in concentric exercise. Since the muscle is only working at maximum during a few degrees of the total range of motion, additional pressure can be applied to the bar through the range where the muscle is not working with maximal force. The spotters' techniques require learning to apply just the right amount of pressure at the correct angles.

Super-Slow Training

There are two commonly used methods for increasing the strength-building stimulus without adding much time to the workout. One method is to increase the length of each repetition by slowing down the speed of the movement. Slower movement produces more muscle force and more muscle tension than faster speeds. For example, in one subject the maximum effort isokinetic leg extension performed when the weight was lifted at 60 degrees per second produced 174 foot-pounds of muscle force, whereas the maximum effort isokinetic leg extension performed at 120 degrees per second produced only 132 foot-pounds of muscle force."[20]

There is little research on this type of training, but there are a number of people who have reported success using it. The hypothesis is that in the slow movements more motor units are recruited to work as the additional time is required for the exercise. This allows for more muscle fibers to be utilized and exhausted.

Super-slow training seems to work for size and strength. One suggestion is to use 50%–70% of the 6 RM but using 6 seconds for the concentric part of the lift and 8 seconds for the eccentric part of the lift. The load should be heavy enough so that only 4–6 reps can be completed at exhaustion. Once muscle failure has occurred in the super slow period the repetitions are immediately done at normal speed.

In an 8-week study of beginning strength trainers using Nautilus machines, Westcott found that those using the standard Nautilus program of a 2 second concentric lift and a 4 second eccentric return to the starting position gained an average of 22 pounds in strength compared with a slow-lifting positive emphasis group using 10 seconds to lift and 4 seconds to return which gained an average of 27 pounds of strength.[21]

In another approach to slow-training, Westcott investigated slow positive training (10 seconds lifting the weight and 4 seconds in an eccentric contraction returning the weight to the starting position) and slow negative training (4 seconds in the concentric contraction and 10 seconds in the eccentric contraction). The slow positive exercises were used for leg extensions, biceps curls, and chin-up exercises. The slow negative exercises were used on leg curls, triceps extensions, and bar-dips. After 6 weeks of training the slow positive weight loads increased by an average of 22 pounds and the slow negative exercises by 26 pounds.

Breakdown Training

In a study on breakdown training, 45 beginner-level participants performed standard Nautilus training for the first month. During the second month of training, half of the group continued their training while the other half did the same training but, when reaching exhaustion, dropped the weight by 10 pounds and did an additional 2 to 4 reps. Those using the breakdown technique increased their average weight load by 25 pounds. The group that continued their traditional training increased theirs by 18 pounds.[22]

Reverse Pyramid Training

For elite athletes in some sports, the author has found that the reverse pyramid works well.[23] He first used it with an Olympic hopeful in the breaststroke in 1960. The boy had been an All-American swimmer from the time he was 10, so was well conditioned. Since this was before weight machines were available, an overhead pulley was set up with two nylon ropes on two pulleys attached to a bar on one end and attachments for barbells to be hooked to the other end. The boy's estimated 1 RM was 60 pounds. He did his straight arm lat pull down with 60 and completed 3 reps. Then 50 pounds was quickly attached to the ropes and that was pulled down for 12 reps, then 40 pounds for 27 reps and finally 30 pounds for 70 reps. A total of 112 reps were done for this first session. This was because swimming a 100- or 200-meter race was a strength-endurance activity. By the sixth day of the routine (the third week), he did 6 reps with 90 pounds, 9 with 80 pounds, 16 with 70 pounds, 42 with 60 pounds, and 150 with 40 pounds. The actual goal for that workout was 200 reps. Immediately after the strength workout he went to the pool, and during his swimming workout, he broke his best 100 breaststroke time by 2 full seconds, then beat the future Olympic champ in a 100-meter freestyle time trial.

The same type of reverse pyramid has been used with power lifters, but the total number of reps was 25. The pure strength-power demands of a power lifter do not require such a great number of reps. This type of extreme strength or strength-endurance exercise should only be used in certain sports and only with elite athletes.

Power Training

When lighter weights are lifted, the brain seems to activate the slower twitch fibers. With heavy weights, or when power is needed, the fast twitch fibers are required to contract in developing the initial force. When we want power in our sport, we will want a good part of our work to be lifting either heavy or fast.

Soreness

Soreness of the muscles generally occurs when untrained athletes work too hard. There are several possible causes. Very small injuries to either muscles or connective tissue are probably the major factor. Eccentric contractions during strength training exercises or such activities as running downhill or plyometrics are often the culprits. The soreness will likely last up to seven days. [24]

Recovery

The positive changes in the muscle fibers occur during the recovery period. While the exercise damages the muscle fibers and forces them to make adjustments, those adjustments are made during the recovery period. That period should be between two and three full days. Highly conditioned strength trainers who are close to their maximal potentials may only need a day to recover.

The amount of rest the muscle needs to adjust and mend depends on the condition of the athlete, the types of contractions (eccentric contractions do more damage and require a longer recovery), the intensity of the workout, and the age of the lifter. The rest period does two things. It allows the body to repair the small damages to the muscle fibers while the lactate and hydrogen ions (byproducts of the exercise) stimulate the pituitary gland to allow for the secretion of more human growth hormone.[25] Human growth hormone is the strongest natural steroid and helps to increase muscle size.

A traditional Monday, Wednesday and Friday whole body workout would not leave enough time for recovery. Consequently, a Monday, Thursday, Sunday, Wednesday, Saturday, Tuesday, Friday, Monday schedule would appear to make more sense for maximum gain based on adequate recovery. Another option would be a split routine working upper body on Monday and Thursday and lower body on Tuesday and Friday. If you have your athletes do split routines, be certain that they are not using the same muscles on consecutive days — such as presses and dips one day then deltoids and triceps on the next day. The same muscles are involved in both days' workouts.

An example of a four day upper/lower body split routine would be:
    Mon./Thurs. – pectorals, deltoids, lats, neck, arms and forearms,
    Wed./Sat. – quads, hamstrings, calves, abdominals and lower back
An example of a three-way split routine would be:
    Mon./Thurs. – pectorals, deltoids, triceps brachia
    Tues./Fri. – lats, lower back, biceps brachia, forearms
    Wed./Sun. – quads, hamstrings, calves, abdominals

Rest Between Sets

You must rest between sets, but not too long. Generally, if you are doing an isolated movement such as a biceps curl or a triceps exercise, 1 to 1 1/2 minutes is sufficient time for a rest. For a multi-joint exercise such as a press or a squat, two to three minutes (maximum) should be enough.

The fewer reps you are doing to exhaustion, the longer the recommended rest period is. A 2 RM set will require a longer rest than a 6 RM set. However, if you are working with lighter weights attempting to develop endurance, your rest periods should be much shorter.

A French study evaluated the rest periods during bench press sets. Ten sets of 6 reps were performed. The rest periods between sets were evaluated when using a 1-minute rest between sets, a 3-minute rest and a 5-minute rest. When the 3- and 5-minute rest periods were used, there was no problem with reduced power or with the amount of blood lactate from the previous set reducing the performance. The reduction of performance in the lifting when the lifter was given only a minute rest between sets was attributed to the drop in creatine phosphate. (Supplementation with creatine will be discussed in a Chapter 22.)[26]

Notes:

1. M.J. Girala et al., "Changes in Human Skeletal Muscle Ultrastructure and Force Production After Acute Resistance Exercise," *Journal of Applied Physiology* 78.2 (1995): 702-708.
2. S.C. Bast et al., "The Effects of Concentric Versus Eccentric Isokinetic Strength Training of the Rotator Cuff in the Plane of the Scapula at Various Speeds," *Bull Hosp Jt Dis* 57.3 (1998): 139-144.
3. J.Y. Seger, B. Arvidsson and A. Thorstensson, "Specific Effects of Eccentric and Concentric Training on Muscle Strength and Morphology in Humans," *European Journal of Applied Physiology* 79.1 (1998): 49-57.
4. J.P. Weir et al., "Effects of Unilateral Isometric Strength Training on Joint Angle Specificity and Cross Training" *European Journal of Applied Physiology* 70 (1995): 337-343.
5. C. Rich and E. Cafarelli, "Submaximal Motor Unit Firing Rates After Eights Weeks of Isometric Resistance Training" *Medical and Scientific Sport and Exercise* 32.1 (2000): 190-196.
6. S.A. Hawkins et al., "Eccentric Muscle Action Increases Site-Specific Osteogenic Response," *Medicine & Science in Sport & Exercise* 31.9 (1999): 1287-1292.
7. D.A. Jones and O.M. Rutherford, "Human Muscle Strength Training: The Effects of Three Different Regimens and the Nature of the Resultant Changes," *Journal of Physiology* (London) 391 (1987):1-11.
8. W.R. Holcomb, D.M. Kleiner and D.A. Chu, "Plyometrics: Considerations for Safe and Effective Training," *Strength and Conditioning Journal* 20.3 (1998): 36-39.
9. E.M. Gorostiaga et al., "Effects of Heavy Resistance Training on Maximal and Explosive Force Production, Endurance and Serum Hormones in Adolescent Handball Players," *European Journal of Applied Physiology* 80.5 (1999): 485-493.

10. H. Hoff and B. Almasbakk, "The effects of Maximum Strength Training on Throwing Velocity and Muscle Strength in Female Team Handball Players," *Journal of Strength and Conditioning Research* 9.4 (1995): 255-258.

11. M. Voigt and K. Klaussen, "Changes in Muscle Strength and Speed of an Unloaded Movement After Various Training Programmes," *European Journal of Applied Physiology* 60 (1990): 370-376.

12. A.J. Blazevich and D. Jenkins, "Physical Performance Differences Between Weight-Trained Sprinters and Weight Trainers," *Journal of Science, Medicine and Sport* 1.1 (1998):12-21.

13. M.H. Stone et al., "A Theoretical Model for Strength Training," *Journal of Sports Medicine* 21 (1981): 342-351.

14. D. Schmidtbleicher and M. Buehrle, "Neuronal Adaptations and Increase of Cross-Sectional Area Studying Different Strength Training Methods," *Biomechanics X-B*, ed. G.B. Johnson (Champaign, Illinois: Human Kinetics, 1987) 615-620.

15. K. Nosaka and P.M. Clarkson, "Influence of Previous Concentric Exercise on Eccentric Exercise-Induced Muscle Damage," Journal of Sports Science 15.5 (1997): 477-483.

16. D. Schmidtbleicher, "Training for Power Events," *Strength and Power Training in Sports*, ed. P.V. Komi (London: Blackwell Scientific Publishers, 1992) 381-395.

17. R. Berger, "Effect of Varied Weight Training Programs on Strength," *Research Quarterly* 33 (1962): 168-181.

18. C.J. Hass, L. Garzarella, D. de Hoyos and M.L. Pollock, "Single Versus Multiple Sets in Long-Term Recreational Weightlifters," *Medicine & Science in Sport & Exercise* 32.1 (2000): 235-242.

19. W. Kraemer, "Everything You Wanted to Know About Strength Training but Were Afraid to Ask," General Session, IDEA Personal Trainer Conference, Anaheim, CA, March 23, 1996.

20. W. Westcott, *Strength Fitness: Fourth Edition* (Dubuque, IA: Brown and Benchmark, 1995.

21. W. Westcott, "Exercise Speed and Strength Development," *American Fitness Quarterly* 13.3 (1994): 20-21.

22. W. Westcott, "High-Intensity Training," *Nautilus* 4.1 (1994): 5-8.

23. R. O'Connor, "Scientific Weight Training: Part 3, Specific Sports Programs," *Scholastic Coach*. Nov. 1964: 43.

24. P. Komi, "Neuromuscular Fatigue: Disturbed Function and Delayed Recovery after Intensive Dynamic Exercise," World

Congress of Sports Medicine, Orlando, FL, May 31, 1998.

25. W. Kraemer, "Physiological Basics for Resistance Training Programs," World Conference on Sports Medicine, Orlando, FL, June 2, 1998.

26. D. Abdessemed et al., "Effect of Recovery Duration on Muscular Power and Blood Lactate During the Bench Press Exercise" *International Journal of Sports Medicine* 20.6 (1999): 368-373.

8

Exercises that Strengthen
One-Joint Action

————

Sometimes you will want to strengthen an individual muscle while other times you will want to work on a combination of actions in a more complicated movement. If you want to strengthen your abdominal muscles, you are concerned with only one-joint action. If you want to be able to jump higher, you will be concerned with a number of muscles — the hip and knee extenders that straighten the legs, the calf muscles that push you off from your toes, and a number of other muscles that aid in your jump. The rotator cuff muscles of the shoulder are muscles that are more easily strengthened by a one-joint exercise.

This chapter will deal with exercises that isolate one-joint action. The next chapter will give you exercises that use several joint actions together — compound exercises. For maximum strength you will want to do both. For example, if you are a volleyball player or a dancer who wants to be able to jump higher, you may want to work each individual muscle you will use in jumping, then combine them in a total jumping action such as a squat or a plyometric exercise. Another reason to use single joint exercises is for rehabilitation. If you have injured a bone, muscle or tendon, you will have to begin to regain the strength lost when your muscle or joint was incapacitated.

In your weight training program you will have exercises that work a single joint action and exercises that work multiple joint actions. Determine what muscles you want to develop and whether you want to isolate them or use them in combination. This chapter will show you the single joint exercises. Look for the muscles you want to exercise then select the exercise you want to do. Often you will have more than one choice. Remember, too, that you want the exercise to be as sport-specific as possible

Selecting The Equipment

Selecting the best equipment is your next task. If you have only free weights, it will be more difficult for you to work effectively on the muscles below the shoulders because you won't be able to use pulleys. Or, if you want to exercise at home but have no weights, you will have to do manual resistance exercises in which you work one of your muscles against another.

Keep in mind that for most people, strength gain is very specific. You will generally gain strength at the exact angle and through the exact number of degrees at which you work. For example, if you were a dancer whose jumps generally began with the knee flexed at about 30 degrees, but you were doing 90 degree squats, you would be using more degrees in your exercise than you used in your performance. Since your joints are more effective during the last degrees of a squat than at the 90 degree angle, you would probably be better served doing your squats at 30 to 45 degrees of flexion but with more weight. For your specific sport you will, therefore, want to exercise the muscle at the exact angle where you will want your maximum strength. You will also want your posture to be as close to what you will be doing in your activity, for example: prone for swimming the crawl or standing for softball, volleyball, tennis or basketball.

If you are using free weights your muscles will work at different levels of intensity from the beginning to the end of the exercise. This can be corrected by exercising on an isokinetic machine or a machine using cams. Isokinetic machines use air, liquid, or a special braking mechanism to control your speed of movement. The problem with isokinetic machines is that you will have to push as hard as possible to get maximum gains, so it is easier to cheat by not working to the maximum.

Now decide whether you are going to work for strength (1–7 reps with 80 to 100% of your 1 RM), bulk (10–30 reps with 75%–80% of your 1 RM), speed (about 45% of the 1 RM done very fast) or muscular endurance in which you might do as many as several hundred reps with a weight.

Isolating the Joint Action

You can seldom isolate just one muscle, but you can isolate a joint action. Flexing the elbow by contracting your biceps is such an action. It is not just your biceps muscles that are working when you lift a barbell in a curl. There are two other muscles which work when the biceps do. You will also exercise the muscles in the front of the forearms and hands which are contracting because they are gripping the bar.

71

THE EXERCISES
Neck Exercises

Figure 8-1

Figure 8-2

Neck exercises are important in activities in which your head may take a blow from an opponent or from a fall. Soccer, the martial arts, rugby and gymnastics are such activities.

Some gyms have head harnesses on which the lifter can hang weights from the head and lift the weights with the neck. There are some machines, usually isokinetic, that have neck strength stations. But the simplest, and most effective, way to gain neck strength is to use your own arm strength.

With your hands behind your head and your head forward, push your head back resisting with your arms as much as possible. This is a good exercise for posture when one carries the head too far forward (see figure 8-1, left).

Place your hands on your forehead and tilt your head back. Bring your head forward as far as it will go while resisting with your hands. This should be a major exercise for soccer players who "head" the ball. For soccer, finish with an isometric contraction pushing as hard as possible against your hands but not allowing the head to move (see figure 8-1, right).

Place your right hand on the right side of your head. Allow your head to tilt all the way to the left, then force it right against the resistance of your right arm and hand. Repeat the exercise to the left side (see figure 8-2, left).

Place your right hand against your right temple and twist your head until you are looking over your right shoulder. Repeat with left hand at left temple until looking over your left shoulder (see figure 8-2, right).

Shoulders

The shoulders are involved in every lifting, pushing, throwing and hitting activity. They are, therefore, very important in athletic competition.

Figure 8-3

With a dumbbell in each hand and your palms pointed inward, raise the dumbbell forward as high as possible (see figure 8-3). The exercise can be done with both arms working at the same time or you can alternate them. Athletes who throw underhand or runners, particularly sprinters, should use this exercise. If you are a softball pitcher, turn your hand forward, just as if you were pitching. Volleyball players who dig the ball will want to do this exercise with both arms and with the wrists in the same position used in the dig.

Figure 8-4a

Figure 8-4b

While standing with dumbbells in your hands and at your side, lift the dumbbells directly to the side and overhead with the backs of your hands upward. (If you turn your hands palms up you will be able to lift more weight because you will be allowing the upper chest muscles to join in the work. You probably don't want this.) Swimmers, surfers and Olympic-style weightlifters can use this exercise (see figures 8-4a and b).

Figure 8-5a

Figure 8-5b

73

Figure 8-6a

Figure 8-6b

Figure 8-6c

Bend 30 to 45° degrees, or up to 90° if you rest your head on a table to reduce the lower back strain. Raise the dumbbells from directly below the shoulders to as far up as they will go. Keep your arms straight or nearly straight. This muscle action would be used by rowers, paddlers, surfers and riders. It is also a good posture exercise for holding the shoulders back (see figures 8-5a and b).

The rotator cuff muscles turn the upper arm in the shoulder socket. These very important muscles come into play in most throwing and hitting actions. They are particularly important in throwing or hitting a softball, serving or spiking a volleyball and hitting a golf ball. Because these muscles are quite small, they are often injured. They should, therefore, be exercised for both maximum strength and for injury prevention.

While lying on your back on a bench or on the floor and holding a dumbbell with your elbow at a 90-degree angle to your side, bring the dumbbell to a vertical position. Continue the action until the weight is touching your abdomen. Return to the starting position. This exercise will work two different actions of the rotator cuff muscles (see figures 8-6a, b and c).

Lie on the floor with your left side to the lower pulley of a machine, your left elbow next to your hip with your elbow flexed to 90 degrees and your left hand on the handle. Pull the handle across your body by rotating your

74

Figure 8-7a   Figure 8-7b

upper arm and keeping the elbow flexed. From the same position take the handle in your right hand and pull the handle across your body. Change to lying with your right side to the machine and repeat the exercises above. The pulleys give you better resistance than the dumbbell exercise illustrated in because the amount of force required to do the exercise is nearly constant throughout the entire range of motion.

While standing bent at the waist with dumbbells in each hand, pull the weights back toward your waist and turn them to the inside. This is particularly good for swimmers. If you are a volleyball player and have a high pulley available, you can stand or sit facing away from the pulley. Then move your shoulder through the action needed for your spike (see figures 8-7a and b).

Upper Chest

The upper chest muscles are used in any pushing or throwing action. The lower chest muscles are used in pulling yourself upward such as in swimming or gymnastics.

Figure 8-8a   Figure 8-8b

Figure 8-9

The front of the deltoids will work with the upper part of the chest muscle. If the exercise is done flat on your back, the pectorals will do more of the work. If you are on an incline with your head high, the deltoids will do more of the work (see figures 8-8a and b).

Free weights lend themselves well to the type of shoulder muscle isolation in lateral raises. Lie down on your back with a dumbbell in each hand. Allow the weights to come at least to the level of your body. Then raise them with slightly bent arms until your arms are vertical. This exercise can help in any throwing type action, including spiking or serving a volleyball. For throwing or spiking it is better if done standing, so if there is a machine available that will allow you to sit or stand while doing this flying motion, use it.

To add flexibility you can do the exercises on a narrow bench and let the dumbbells come down past your body before lifting them. In order to get a maximum stretch, use very light dumbbells.

Lower Chest

Working the lower chest muscles requires that you bring your arm toward your hips while you are working against resistance. This means that for best results you will either have to be on a steep incline with your head down or work with overhead pulleys. Gymnasts and some martial arts participants can use this type of strength.

Using pulleys, start with your arm at about a 45-degree angle from vertical, then pull the resistance across your body in front of your shoulders finishing at your opposite hip. This exercise will emphasize the lower part of your chest, but it also works the upper chest (see figure 8-9).

Another pulley exercise that works your lower chest is the straight-arm pull down. Facing sideways to the pulley with your arm overhead, pull down the handle until your arm is at your side. This is particularly good for backstrokers. However, it is even more effective for them if the handle is moved behind the plane of the body, just as it is when actually swimming (see figures 8-10a and b).

Decline lateral raises, in which your head is lower than your torso while you are on an incline board, require only dumbbells rather than a pulley set up. From the decline position with your arms to the side, bring the arms to the vertical position then return them to the your side (see figures 8-11a and b).

Figure 8-10a   *Figure 8-10b*

Figure 8-11a   *Figure 8-11b*

Upper Back

The upper and middle back muscles are used in posture. They also assist in any pulling action. They would, therefore, be essential in swimming, rowing, paddling, martial arts, gymnastics and cross-country skiing.

For the top of your back, the upper part of your trapezius, do the same exercise that develops the top of the shoulders. (See standing fly.)

You can also do standing shoulder shrugs with a barbell. In this exercise you stand holding the barbell in front of you with your arms straight. Just lift your shoulders up without bending your arms. The trapezius muscle is quite strong, so a lot of weight can be handled in this exercise (see figures 8-12a and b).

For the middle part of the trapezius, the same exercise that works the back of the deltoids (bent flys) will do.

The lower part of your upper back is best developed by pulling down on a pulley. Face the machine. With your arms straight, pull down with little or no bend in the elbows until you have pulled the bar to your hips.

Figure 8-12a

Figure 8-12b

Figure 8-13

This will also work one head of the triceps muscle. Since your arms will start at about a 30-degree angle from vertical, you will get most of your strength gain in the area in which you are working the muscle. If you want to gain strength in the top 30 degrees of the pull, either face away from the machine and start your pull with your arms directly overhead or do pull-overs on the bench. This is an absolutely essential exercise for all swimmers and is helpful for surfers, rowers and gymnasts (see figure 8-13).

There are some machines that allow you to sit while you perform this exercise. Bent-arm pullovers increase the range of motion in which your muscles gain strength because the weight starts at a lower position. You can use either a dumbbell or barbell for this exercise (see figures 8-14a and b).

 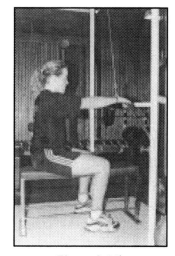

Figure 8-14a   *Figure 8-14b*

The previously mentioned side pull down for the lower chest will also work the lower part of your upper back. (See sideways pull down on low pulley.)

Abdominals

Most people are aware of how important it is to have abdominal strength. It helps to keep our bellies tucked in for better posture. In fact, the abdominals along with the lower back are the two most important areas for strength in our bodies. In athletics the abdominals help to stabilize the hips, so they are essential in every action that involves the hip joints — running, jumping, swimming, gymnastics, skiing. In order to attempt to isolate your abdominals, you should flex your knees as much as possible so that the muscles that flex the hip joint (bringing the thighs forward and upward) will not work as well. You should also keep your hips on the mat when doing an abdominal exercise. Whenever your hips are pulled off the mat or bench, your hip flexors are working. This is particularly harmful for girls and women who generally have more curvature in their lower backs. This curvature places a higher pressure on the outside of the discs in the lumbar region. It can cause many problems as the person grows older.

The reason that hip flexion exercises can increase the curvature of the spine is that there are some muscles deep inside the pelvis, such as the iliopsoas, that attach from the lower vertebrae to the thigh bone. As they get stronger they pull in on the lower spine and increase the curvature. You will often see this extreme lower back curve (technically called "lordosis") in female gymnasts.

Abdominal curl-ups are done by lying on the floor or on a bench with

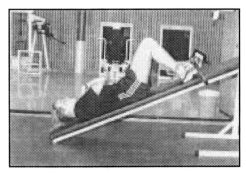

Figure 8-15a   *Figure 8-15b*

your knees flexed and your hands on your chest or shoulders. Curl your shoulders forward until your hips are about to leave the floor. Usually you will be able to touch your elbows to your thighs. A normal range of motion for abdominals is under 40 degrees (see figures 15a and b).

If you do the curl-ups on an inclined board with your head lower than your feet, you will also increase the resistance you are lifting. If you are working for strength, hold weight plates on your forehead or chest in order to increase resistance. Gymnasts, divers and dancers are more likely to want extra strength in the abdominals, but most people are looking for muscular endurance for running. If this is what you want, just do many repetitions. Herschel Walker, the former professional football player, did 3,500 repetitions daily.

Some people aren't sufficiently strong to do this exercise correctly the first time. If this is true for you, do the exercise this way. Grab the backs of your thighs with your hands and pull yourself up to the proper position. When this becomes easy, use only one hand on one thigh to help you curl up. Soon you will be able to do the exercise without using your hands to assist you. The exercise is easier with your hands on your hips, harder with your hands on your chest, and most difficult with your hands on your head.

Another exercise that is often done for the abdominals is the abdominal crunch. In this exercise you will lie flat on your back then bring your knees and shoulders upward at the same time.

Side sit-ups are done for additional strength for the muscles on the side of your abdominal area. For this exercise most people will have to have their feet held down. They can be hooked under a barbell or a sofa or held by a partner. Lift your shoulders from the mat or bench. This exercise will not only work the abdominal oblique muscles but also the muscles on one side of your lower back and the rectus abdominis on the side to which you are bending (see figures 16a and b). The rotary abdominal machine is the best way to exercise the abdominal obliques (see figure 8-17).

Figure 8-16a

Figure 8-16b

Figure 8-17

Checklist for Abdominal Exercises

1. Flex your knees so that your hip flexors cannot contract effectively.
2. If your hips leave the bench or floor, your hip flexors are contracting.
3. Think of yourself as "curling" up rather than "sitting" up.
4. Look at the ceiling throughout the exercise.

Lower Back

Exercises for the lower back are probably the most important for the average person to do because lower back injuries, especially muscle pulls, are so common. Gymnasts also have a large number of lower back muscular problems. These muscles aren't highly visible, so we often overlook them.

The lower back muscles are particularly important in weightlifting, swimming and skiing. And, of course, they are essential in maintaining good posture because they are the muscles that hold our chests up by pulling our rib cages down and back. This raises the front of the rib cage and our chests.

81

Figure 8-18a   *Figure 8-18b*

Back arches can be done on the floor. Just lie face down and raise your shoulders and knees slightly off the floor. Current thinking is that the back should not be hyperextended.

In a gym there may be a Roman chair available, if so, this increases the resistance you can gain in your exercise. In a Roman chair you will put your hips on the small saddle, hook your feet under a bar, bend forward at the waist about 30 degrees, then straighten your back. If you desire strength, hold weight plates or a dumbbell behind your head. If you want muscular endurance, do as many repetitions as you can (see figures 8-18a and b).

The deadlift is a commonly used exercise for the lower back, but we do not recommend it. In the deadlift, the knees are slightly flexed. With the weight on the floor, grip the bar with your palms toward your body. While keeping your back straight and head up, straighten up to the standing position.

The problem with this exercise is that excess stress can be put on inside edges of the discs of the lower spine. This could weaken them. Also, the weight being lifted is at its maximum while the pressure on the disks is at its maximum. In addition, the amount of force your muscles are required to exert diminishes during the exercise. By the time your back has moved through 30 degrees of motion, your muscles are lifting only 50% as much weight as they did when the weight was first being lifted from the floor. As mentioned earlier, we do not recommend this exercise but mention it only because it is commonly done.

The good morning exercise is similar to the deadlift, but the weight is carried on the back of the shoulders. The waist is allowed to bend forward until reaching a 90-degree angle, then straightened back up to the standing position. This commonly done exercise is not recommended for most people because of the great pressure on the inside of the spinal discs in the lower back.

Hip Flexors

The hip flexors bring our thighs forward, so they are essential in any running or jumping activity as well as diving. As previously mentioned, hip flexion exercises might be harmful for some people, especially females. However, many people need strength in the hip flexor muscles. Gymnasts, dancers, and anyone who needs to run fast must have hip flexor strength.

Those susceptible to excessive lower back curvature should take special precautions. They should keep the connective tissue in their lower backs flexible by doing toe touching exercises. They should also keep their abdominals strong to reduce the

Figure 8-19

tendency of the front of the hips to drop forward, increasing the curve of the lower spine.

Hip flexors are exercised when the thigh is brought forward. This can be done several ways. You can do them hanging or standing. You can do them without weights, with a weighted boot or with an ankle attachment to a pulley on a machine.

While hanging from a high bar, bring one leg forward with your knee bent. Touch your knee to your chest.

While hanging from the high bar, bring your leg forward without bending your knee.

Using the lower pulley of a weight machine, hook your ankle into a handle or use an ankle strap to secure your ankle to the pulley. Raise your leg straight forward (see figure 8-19).

While standing, brace yourself with your arms, lift one leg forward as high as it will go. Bring it up slowly. This can be done with or without weighted boots.

Leg lifts are done from the supine position. Lift one or both legs from the floor to the vertical position.

While standing and steadying yourself by holding a table or bar, and with a partner resisting, move the thigh through a full flexion then extension movement.

If no steadying possibilities exist, the exercise can be done outside with the exerciser lying and the partner resisting. This is a particularly good warm-up method for outside running sports such as soccer, rugby, track and field, and softball.

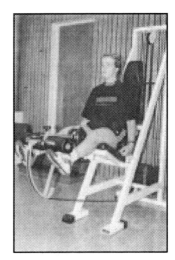

Figure 8-20a   *Figure 8-20b*

Figure 8-21

Knee Extensors (Leg Extension)

Extending the knee means straightening it. The knee extensors are, therefore, used in any running, jumping, or competitive weightlifting activity. Some of the major knee extensor muscles also flex the hips, so the following exercises will also strengthen your hip flexors.

On the leg extension machine, hook your feet under the padded bar. Straighten your legs. This exercise can also be done with a weighted boot (see figures 8-20a and b).

With a partner to provide resistance, sit on a table and let your partner put both hands on your ankle. Straighten your leg while your partner gives you just enough resistance to allow you to make the movement. This manual resistance exercise is probably more effective than the straight concentric exercise and may approach an isokinetic exercise in effectiveness (see figure 8-21).

Figure 8-22

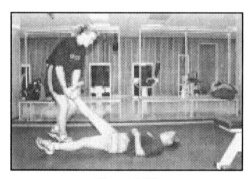

Figure 8-23

Figure 8-24

Hip Extensors

The hip extensor muscles bring the thighs from a forward position back to a straight position. They will also bring the thighs farther back than straight. This is called hyperextension. The hip extensors are the muscles that supply power when you are running or jumping.

On a hip extension machine starting from a hip flexed position, extend your thigh (see figure 8-22).

With a partner, lie on your back and bring your leg up. Let your partner hold your ankle and apply resistance as you lower your leg to the floor (see figure 8-23).

While standing and bracing yourself for balance, bring one leg backward as far as you can (see figure 8-24).

Knee Flexors (Leg Curls)

The knee flexors shorten the angle of the knee. They generally work with the hip extensors, so they are useful in running. If the front of the thighs

85

Figure 8-25a

Figure 8-25b

Figure 8-26

(the quadriceps or knee extensors) are strengthened, the knee flexors must also be strengthened. An imbalance of strength sets up the weaker muscle for injury. On a leg extension machine, lie face down and hook your ankle under the bar. Bend your leg back at the knee joint. This exercise can also be done standing with a weighted boot (see figures 8-25a and b).

With a partner, lie on the floor. Let your partner supply resistance by putting her hands on the back of your ankle as you flex your knee (see figure 8-26).

Ankle Plantar Flexion

Ankle plantar flexion occurs when the sole of your foot moves closer to your calf muscle. This action occurs when you rise up on your toes. This is a key area for strength and power in running and jumping, for diving or dancing, and for pushing off on a turn in swimming.

Holding a barbell on your shoulders, rise up on your toes. This is better done with your toes on a riser board because your calf muscle will be gaining flexibility as you stretch down (see figures 8-27a and b).

On a weight machine and with your legs straight, allow the weight to bring your ankles back stretching your Achilles tendon. Then push the weight out with your calf muscles (see figure 8-28).

While holding a table for balance, rise up on one foot. This will give you

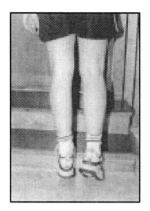

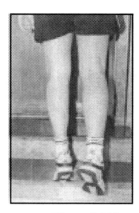

Figure 8-27a   Figure 8-27b

Figure 8-28

Figure 8-29a   Figure 8-29b

Figure 8-30   *Figure 8-31*

the same resistance as holding a barbell that equals your body weight and doing the exercise with two legs. For example, if you weigh 150 pounds and hold a barbell that weighs 150 pounds, each of your calf muscles will be lifting 150 pounds. If you hold no weight but do the exercise with only one leg, the calf muscle will still be lifting 150 pounds (see figures 8-29a, b).

Other Ankle Exercises

You can also do ankle exercises to increase dorsal flexing strength (bringing the top of your foot forward) or turning the foot inward or outward. There are some weight machines that can help you do this, but these exercises are more easily done with a partner or by giving yourself the resistance. These can be helpful in preventing or rehabilitating ankle sprains.

Dorsal flexion (bringing the back of the foot closer to the front of the knee) is done by pushing down on the top of your foot with your hand then allowing the muscles in the front of your lower leg to bring your foot upward against the resistance of your hand (see figure 8-30).

Eversion of the ankle joint occurs when you bring the outside of your foot upward. This action can be done to strengthen your ankle if you have had an ankle sprain. The sprained ankle damaged ligaments that will take years to totally repair and shrink. But by strengthening the muscles in the outside part of your lower leg, you may be able to prevent further ankle sprains. To do this exercise, push down in the area of your little toe and bring your foot upward and outward against the pressure of your hand (see figure 8-31).

Inversion of the ankle occurs when the sole of the foot is brought inward. This is not an action which is particularly useful, but if a person had an injury to those muscles and wanted to strengthen them, she would simply put her hand under the foot applying pressure to the outside edge of the sole, then turn the foot inward against that pressure. There may be times when joggers who have been diagnosed with pronation or eversion may want to strengthen the muscles which will hold the inside of the foot upward. However, orthotics are usually an easier and more effective solution to this common running problem.

Arm (Or Elbow) Flexion

Arm flexion occurs when you bend your elbow forward. The biceps curl is the exercise which strengthens this action. The curl can be done with a barbell, dumbbell or a set of dumbbells. The bi-

Figure 8-32

ceps are used in weightlifting to get the bar to shoulder height, in rowing to pull the oar, in basketball for rebounding, and in many other sports.

The barbell biceps curl is the most common biceps exercise. With the barbell in your hands, palms facing forward, and your arms extended down, curl the barbell upward. The gripping of the bar will give you some isometric strength in the front of your forearms (see figure 8-32).

If you want some additional strength in the back of your forearms you can grip the bar with your palms facing inward at the start. This is called the reverse grip. This additional strength in the back of the forearms may be helpful for tennis players or golfers (see figures 8-33a and b).

Figure 8-33a

Figure 8-33b

89

Figure 8-34

Alternating dumbbell curls are done by curling one dumbbell then the other. This exercise is really just a variation of the barbell curl previously mentioned.

Another biceps exercise is done in the sitting position while bracing your upper arm against your thigh and curling the dumbbell, thus eliminating cheating by swinging the weight (see figure 8-34).

On a weight machine you can use the bench press station to curl or you can use the lower pulleys.

Arm (Or Elbow) Extension

The triceps are used to straighten your arms. They are, therefore, used in pushing something away from the body and in throwing. In ice skating and dance they aid in lifting one's partner, in swimming they assist throughout the whole stroke, in gymnastics they are used in handstands and vaults, in softball they are used to both throw and hit, in basketball they are used to shoot and pass, in tennis they are used in the serve, in soccer for the throw in, and in golf they assist in the downswing. In short, they are used a great deal.

The best exercise for this action is the standing one-arm triceps extension. The exercise being done in this position gives maximum stretch to the triceps muscle. Start with the arm holding the dumbbell extended overhead. Steady that elbow with the other hand by holding just below the el-

Figure 8-35a

Figure 8-35b

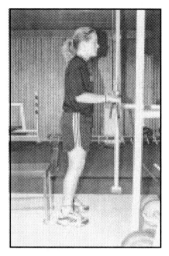

Figure 8-36a

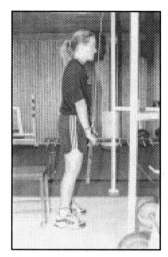

Figure 8-36b

Figure 8-37a

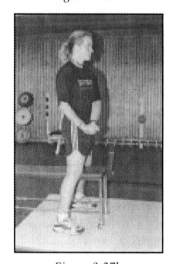

Figure 8-37b

bow on the extended arm. Allow the dumbbell to lower as much as possible for maximum flexibility. Then raise the dumbbell overhead for strength (see figure 8-35a and b).

On a weight machine use the high pulley station. Grip the bar, and with your elbows at your side, bring the bar down by straightening your arms. This exercise does not give as much flexibility, but it will give a more even pattern of resistance throughout the exercise (see figures 8-36a and b).

Some people like to exercise both triceps at the same time. If you prefer this, use either a dumbbell or a barbell, lower it behind your head and extend it overhead. The problem is that it is almost impossible to do this exercise without bringing in other muscles that move the shoulder joint. Also,

Figure 8-38a

Figure 8-38b

Figure 8-39a

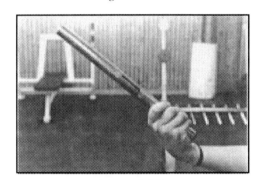

Figure 8-39b

using a heavy barbell can pull you off balance — especially if your arms are perpendicular to the floor in the maximum stretching position (see figures 8-37a and b).

To use your own muscles to give you resistance, flex one arm, put the hand of the other arm against the wrist of the bent arm. Straighten the flexed arm while resisting with the other hand.

Wrist Flexion (Front Of Forearms)

The wrist flexors are used an any throwing or hitting motion. They put the curve on a curve ball and the fast in a fast ball. They supply much of the power in a tennis serve, and they supply some of the power in the golf swing, the tennis forehand, badminton and racquetball forehands and overheads, and in hitting a softball.

Sit down while straddling a bench. With a barbell in your hands, your palms up, and the back of your forearms on the bench, let the weight hyper-extend your wrist then flex your wrist forward. This exercise can also be done with a dumbbell exercising one wrist then the other (see figures 8-38a and b).

Some people will use a weight attached by a rope to a handle. The exer-ciser raises the weight by rolling the handle by alternate wrist movements.

Figure 8-40a

Figure 8-40b

Figure 8-41a

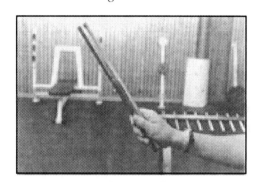

Figure 8-41b

This is not good for maximum strength gain, but it is fine for bulk work or muscular endurance.

A simple way of exercising this muscle at home is with a broom or mop handle. Grab the end of the handle, and with your palm facing up, lift the opposite end of the broom up. This is a particularly good exercise for the tennis serve and for golf (see figures 8-39a and b).

Wrist Extension (Back Of Forearms)

The wrist extensors are important in stabilizing the wrist in any backhand action — tennis, racquetball, badminton, squash or golf. They are also essential in weightlifting competition because they tend to be the weakest link in the cleaning action that brings the bar from the floor to the chest.

While sitting on and straddling a bench, grasp the barbell palms down. Let the barbell flex your wrists downward, then extend your wrists upward. This exercise will strengthen the back of your forearms. You will probably be able to use only about 2/3 of the weight you were able to do in the wrist flexion exercise (see figures 8-40a and b).

At home you can take a broom or mop handle and, with your palm facing down, lift the broom up using only your wrist. This is effective in strengthening the muscles in the back of the forearm for the tennis, racketball,

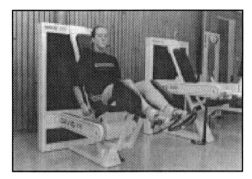

Figure 8-42a

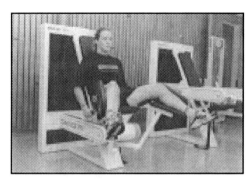

Figure 8-42b

Figure 8-43

badminton or squash backhand stroke. It will also aid in preventing or curing tennis elbow (see figures 8-41a and b).

Hip Abduction

Hip abduction means moving your leg sideways in a lateral plane. It uses the muscles on the outside of the hips. It is used by anyone who wants to move laterally while facing ahead: basketball players playing defense, dancers and gymnasts. Golfers use it in developing the leg power of their swings, and any racket sport player will also use these muscles.

If you have an adduction machine sit in the seat, hook your legs into the stirrups and push both legs outward (see figures 8-42a and b).

Lie on your back with your partner holding the outside of your feet or lower legs. Push your legs apart as far as they will go while your partner resists (see figure 8-43).

While standing sideways to the machine at the

Figure 8-44

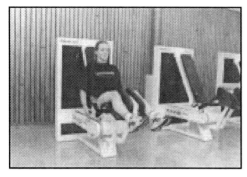

Figure 8-45

Figure 8-46

Figure 8-47a

Figure 8-47b

low pulley station, hook the foot which is farthest from the machine into the handle or ankle strap and pull your leg away from the machine (see figure 8-44).

Hip Adduction

Hip adduction exercises strengthen the muscles on the inside of the thigh.

Sit in the seat of an abduction-adduction machine. Put your feet in the stirrups and squeeze them together (see figure 8-45).

With your feet apart, have your partner put her hands on the inside of your feet or lower legs and give you resistance as you squeeze your legs together (see figure 8-46).

Stand sideways to a machine with a low pulley, with the foot nearest the machine attached to the pulley by an ankle strap. With that leg abducted about 30 degrees, squeeze your leg in toward your body pulling the handle away from the machine (see figures 8-47a and b).

9

The Traditional Multiple
Joint Strength Exercises

*M*any of the traditional strength developing exercises are multiple joint exercises. The bench press, for example, strengthens the upper chest, the front of the deltoids and the triceps. The lat pull-down strengthens the lower chest, latissimus dorsi and biceps. People who are using strength exercises to increase their potential in a sport are often advised to use such multiple joint exercises.

THE EXERCISES
Bench Press

The bench press exercises the triceps, upper chest and the front of the deltoids. If any of these muscles are weak, they can be strengthened by the specific muscle exercises given in the previous chapter. The bench press is done on a bench rather than the floor because your arms should be able to come below your shoulder level to increase your flexibility and the range of motion in which the muscles will gain strength. Your grip should be wide enough to allow you to lower the bar to your chest. Your forearms should be perpendicular to the floor. A wider grip will require more work from your chest muscles. A narrower grip will work the triceps more (see figures 9-1a and b).

Your back should remain on the bench throughout the exercise. If you arch your back, more of the lower chest muscles will come into play so more weight can be lifted. However, this is considered cheating.

Starting with the bar above your nose and at arms length, slowly lower the bar to your chest, over the nipples, then push it upward to the starting position over your nose. The exercise can be done on a machine or with free weights using two spotters — one on each end of the bar. The spotters en-

96

Figure 9-1a

Figure 9-1b

Figure 9-1c

Figure 9-2a

Figure 9-2b

sure that the weight does not get out of control. While the exercise is generally done with a barbell, it can also be done with dumbbells.

Despite the popularity of the bench press, it doesn't have a great deal of application to women's sports unless you are a power lifter, then, of course, it is a required lift. If you are a shot-putter or a gymnast or you play flag football, it might help some. Some martial arts participants might profit from this, especially for punches. A basketball player's chest pass can also be strengthened with this exercise, but because of the posture, it would be more effective if done on a sitting bench press machine (see figure 9-1c).

Incline Bench Press

Adjust the bench to the angle at which you wish to work. The higher the angle, the more work the anterior (front) deltoids do and the less the lower

| *Figure 9-3a* | *Figure 9-3b* | *Figure 9-3c* |

pectorals do. The triceps are also major movers. Perform the press just as the bench press was done. It can also be done with dumbbells. This is an essential exercise for shot-putters — particularly when done one handed with a dumbbell. A basketball player might improve shooting strength by doing this exercise with a dumbbell in the shooting hand. It is not particularly useful for any other sport (see figures 9-2a and b).

Overhead Press

This action strengthens the muscles used by dancers or ice skaters in lifting a partner — the upper deltoids, triceps and the highest part of the upper chest muscles. They are also used in doing hand stands.

The overhead press can be done sitting or standing. The weight is generally held in front of the upper shoulders but can also be done with the weight starting behind the neck. While generally done with a barbell, it can be done with dumbbells. If you were a platform diver or gymnast it would be important for doing hand stands (see figures 9-3a, b and c).

Lat Pull-Downs or Chin-Ups on a High Bar

For this exercise you need a pulley weight machine. While sitting, kneeling or standing, take a wide grip on the bar and pull it down behind your back or to the front of the shoulders. The pull-up can also be done by pulling yourself up to a high bar and bringing your head in front of or behind the bar (see figure 9-4).

Generally, the palms face forward, but your reasons for doing the exercise can determine which grip is more desirable. If you are attempting to increase your strength for climbing a wall (as is required in police training and the military) or you were a rock climber, your hands would be facing

Figure 9-4

Figure 9-5

Figure 9-6a

Figure 9-6b

forward and you would finish with the bar in front of your shoulders. If you were attempting to gain strength for climbing a rope, you would be better served grasping the cable rather than the bar on the machine or grasping the upright standard on a horizontal bar.

Squats (Quarter, Half or Full Leg Extensions)

Squats exercise the hip and knee extensors (gluteals, quadriceps). Be certain that the angle of the knee is not less than 90 degrees (thighs approximately parallel with the floor). At about this point, the ligaments on the side of the knees that attach to the menisci pull the menisci back and create a fulcrum that can put additional stretch on the tendons and ligaments in the front of the knee, thereby giving them an undesirable stretch. This can weaken the structure of the knee. This undesirable action is greatly increased if the muscles of the back of the thigh and those of the calf touch, because an

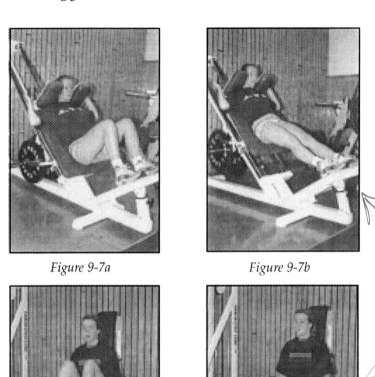

Figure 9-7a   Figure 9-7b

Figure 9-8a 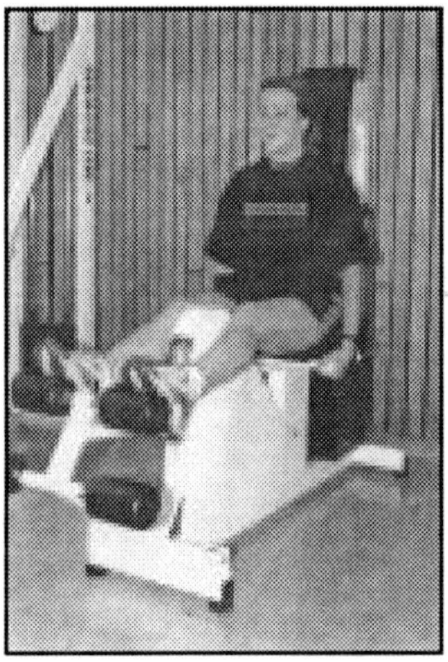   Figure 9-8b

additional fulcrum is created still farther away from the knee joint. For maximum safety the exercise must be done in a squat rack. Set the pins at the point past which you will not lower the weight.

The most common foot positions are with the feet directly under the shoulders and pointed forward or with the feet wider than the shoulders and pointed slightly outward. The feet will remain flat on the floor during the entire lift. Your back will be slightly arched and your head up to reduce the strain on the lower back (see figure 9-5).

Don't let your knees get too far ahead of your toes. This would indicate that you are carrying too much weight forward and could lose your balance. Also, don't bounce up from the deep position because additional pressure can be put on the knee ligaments. During the squatting action, the bar should move up and down in a vertical path.

Figure 9-9 *Figure 9-10*

On a leg press machine, the safety is built in. Not only is there no strain on the lower back, but it is easier to do calf rises at the end of your leg extension series (see figures 9-7a,b and 9-8a,b).

If you don't have a full weight set and a squat rack, you can still do squats. Hold on to a table for balance and do one-leg squats to the 45- to 90-degree level. This will give you the same effect as doing a two-leg squat carrying a weight equal to your body weight.

Anyone who runs or jumps will profit from this multi-joint exercise — basketball and volleyball players, gymnasts, high and long jumpers. Since women tend to have more knee injuries, it is particularly important that they not exercise through more degrees than is necessary in the sport. For example, if rebounding in basketball uses a less than 30-degree knee flexion, there is no need to do much more than the 30 degree flexion in the exercise. And the less flexion used in the quarter or half squat, the more weight that can be handled.

Lunges

This exercise works the same muscles as squats. With a barbell held behind your neck or with dumbbells held at your sides, take a long step forward and bend the forward leg as you settle into the lunge. Your knee should be no farther forward than your toes. Push yourself back up and bring your forward foot back to the starting position. You may need two smaller steps to return to the starting position. This is valuable for runners and jumpers (see figure 9-9).

Upright Rowing

Upright rowing exercises the biceps, deltoids, and upper trapezius. It can be done with a barbell, dumbbells or on a low pulley on a machine. Grip the bar with the palms facing the body and the arms extended downward. Lift the bar to your chin, always keeping the elbows higher than the bar. This would be important if you were a competitive weightlifter (see figure 9-10).

101

Bent Rowing

This exercise works the biceps, lats, rear deltoids and the trapezius. It is very useful for those who like to row a boat. Bend at the waist to an angle of about 60 degrees and keep the knees slightly flexed. Grip the bar with the palms facing your body. Lift the bar to your chest (see figure 9-11). This can also be done on a rowing machine or on a low pulley while sitting on the floor (see figure 9-12).

The more you bend at the waist, the greater the strain and possible damage to the spinal discs. To reduce the strain, the exercise can be done with a dumbbell using the opposite hand on a table to support your shoulders. If there is a rowing machine available it is even better. If you are a paddler or rower this would be an essential exercise.

Figure 9-11

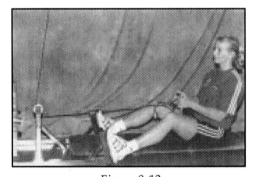

Figure 9-12

Power Clean

This exercise is useful for those wishing to develop full body extension power. It develops the knee and hip extensors, the ankle plantar flexors, the lower back, the deltoids, upper trapezius, and the biceps.

Checklist for Safety
1. If one is available, use a rack for all heavy lifts.
2. If no rack is available, use two spotters, one on each end of the bar. If only one spotter is available he or she should stand where the weights can be best controlled. This is usually behind the lifter.
3. Do not do bench presses alone. Lack of control of the weights is the leading cause of death among strength trainers.

Figure 9-13a   Figure 9-13b   Figure 9-13c

With your feet about shoulder width apart and the barbell close to your feet, flex your legs and flex your back to about 30- to 45-degrees from vertical. Take a wide grip with your palms facing toward you. Start the cleaning action with an explosive jump quickly extending your knees, hips and ankles. Use the velocity generated by your lift to pull the bar to chest level. At the top of the movement, quickly bring your wrists back and thrust your elbows forward while slightly bending your knees and allow the bar to settle on the top of your chest. Return the bar to the floor. It is definitely useful for competitive weightlifters and might be useful for anyone who jumps in their sport (see figures 9-13a,b and c).

Figure 9-14a   Figure 9-14b

Power Snatch

This exercise adds the triceps to the muscles working in the lift, and it adds the coordination needed for lifting a weigh overhead. The lift begins the same as the power clean but with a lighter weight. The body explodes as in the power clean, but the weight is pulled as high as possible. Just as it reaches its highest point, the knees are bent to drop the body under the bar and the arms are locked straight. The knees are then straightened to complete the lift (see figures 9-14 a and b).

The most common mistakes are letting the bar move too far from the body and letting the elbows drop just as one is completing the pull and making the hop under the bar.

10

Plyometrics

*I*n sport we are primarily after speed and power. The Russians seem to have been the first to recognize what we now refer to as "plyometrics," "pliometrics," or the "stretch-shortening cycle." This training method is based on the fact that when a muscle is under eccentric (lengthening) tension then immediately begins a concentric (shortening) tension, more force can be developed. This is because either the stretched muscle fibers are "pre-loaded" and more ready to contract maximally and/or more muscle fibers are involved in the eccentric contraction and so are more ready to contract in the concentric contraction. If this is true, more muscle fibers can be involved in the concentric contraction than would be possible to involve in merely concentrically contracting the muscles.

For example, if you were to merely jump as high as possible from a standing or crouching position, you would be concentrically contracting your muscles. But if you jumped from a box, your leg and thigh muscles would have to absorb the force of the fall. If you quickly jumped upward immediately after landing, the muscle fibers and tendons would be under more tension than they were in the pure concentric jump. This should allow you to jump higher on your rebound from the floor.

How It Works

Plyometric training seems to work on two parts of the neuromuscular system. The muscle spindles, which register the stretch of the muscle fibers, and the smallest parts of the muscle fibers (myofibrils), which do the contracting, are both trained in the stretch-shortening cycle of plyometric work.

It also works on the anaerobic energy system, particularly on the creatine phosphate and the lactic acid systems. The creatine phosphate system allows for the adenosine tri-phosphate (ATP) system to replenish itself when phosphates from the ATP are released to create the energy needed to contract the muscle. That ATP phosphate is replaced by the phosphate in the creatine phosphate, so it is ready to again provide more muscle energy. Since there is about five to six times more creatine phosphate than ATP, the anaerobic energy can be continued five to six times longer. It usually takes between 5 – 15 seconds to deplete these two energy sources. Plyometric work in this 5 – 15 second range taxes the creatine phosphate system.

The lactic acid system comes into play in the anaerobic development of energy. As the ATP and creatine phosphates are depleted and the stored muscle sugar (glycogen) is utilized for energy, there are several breakdown products from this utilization of the glycogen. Lactic acid is one of these. As oxygen is breathed in, it reconverts the lactic acid back to glycogen. This, of course, is the aerobic source of energy for the muscles. This system is more effectively trained when the athlete exercises hard for 30 – 90 seconds or more. While plyometrics can affect this system, it is probably better to train this system with running or swimming or whatever other sport specific needs you have.

Plyometric training was one of the secrets of Valerie Borzov, who won the 100- and 200-meter sprints in the 1972 Olympics. Today most sprinters use plyometrics as part of their training. If strength or power is a requirement for your sport, you should consider this training method. It is probably the best method for developing dynamic force. You must, however, be aware of the injury potential in doing plyometrics. Most running injuries occur when the hamstrings (back of thighs) are transitioning from the stretching action of moving forward to the immediate concentric backward hip extension. This is a perfect example of the stretch shortening cycle in sport.

As with other elements of conditioning (strength, flexibility, endurance), the overload principle is essential. While increasing the number of repetitions will increase muscular endurance it is the progressive increase in the power requirements which develop greater speed or power (speed plus strength).

Training

In plyometric exercise you must consider the quickness of the stretch and the following concentric contraction. According to Paavo Komi, perhaps the leading researcher in this area, it is not the length of the stretch but the quickness of the stretch which is paramount.[1] With this in mind, you must emphasize the quickness of the movement. If you are jumping, you want to minimize your time on the ground. If you are working with a medi-

---

Terminology

bounding — a series of plyometric moves, usually alternate legs to gain horizontal distance.

countermovement jump — a standing jump in which the hips drop and the arms swing down and back in order to achieve maximum height as the arms lift and the hips are extended. There should be no hesitation between the downward stretching movement and the forceful jump.

depth jump (drop jump) — jumping from a height (a bench or box).

frequency — how often an exercise is performed.

intensity — full maximal muscular contraction(s).

hopping — repeated contacts on just one leg.

in-place jumps — a series of vertical jumps.

jump squats — from the squat position several repeat plyometric jumps are performed with 30-60% of one's RM.

long jump — jumping in a horizontal direction.

medicine ball — a weighted ball, usually filled with cloth or rubber.

multiple response — a series of jumps or movements.

prancing — a series of high knee running movements.

reactive strength — the strength one has in reacting to a stretch, such as the height one can achieve after hitting the floor in a depth jump.

single response drill — a single movement, such as a jump.

squat jump — jumping from the squat position without the immediately preceding countermovement.

vertical jump — jumping upward.

volume — the total amount of work done in an exercise (or plyometric) session.

---

cine ball for arm or chest power, you want the catch and throw to be as quick as possible.

The overload principle can be followed by both making quicker movements and by making more powerful movements. In a jump you might jump quicker or jump higher. Jumping from increasingly higher boxes or using progressively heavier medicine balls would be methods of increasing your power — assuming that the contact time (feet on the ground or ball in the hands) is not slower.

Upper body work generally uses medicine balls weighing 3 to 10 pounds. These are probably not heavy enough to sufficiently overload the arms in the exercise. But they may aid to some degree in gaining power.

Safety Precautions

There are some cautions to using plyometrics. In jumping plyometrics the legs must absorb three to six times the body weight, and injuries can occur. Very young athletes should not do them until they are sufficiently strong. They should also not do them until they are pretty well grown. A common knee problem with active adolescents is Osgood-Schlatter's disease, which is caused primarily by youngsters running or jumping before the leg bone (tibia) is fully hardened. Bones harden from the middle outward. The growth of the child continues to occur until the bones are fully hardened. Excessive force exerted by the quadriceps muscle (front of thigh) can pull out on the attachment of the tendon which is just below the knee. The softer bone can not only be pulled outward, creating a bump, but the condition can be quite painful. It is most common in boys between the ages of 12 and 14, but it can happen to girls also. Tall, thin girls are most likely to be affected if they run and jump a great deal before the bones are fully hardened. The jumping plyometrics can increase the tendency for this condition to occur.

Plyometric jumping, hopping or bounding exercises should be done on a surface which has some resiliency. Grass, rubber flooring, gymnastic mats or carpeting are surfaces which can reduce the trauma to the joint surfaces of the bones.

It has long been suggested that a person should not start plyometric jumping until she is able to squat 1 1/2 to 2 times her body weight. Such a requirement is probably too high. However, stronger athletes will generally be able to progress faster in their depth jumps than their weaker counterparts.

Another factor which contra-indicates plyometrics is muscle or tendon injury to the muscles which will be plyometrically stretched. The tendency for microscopic injury from the stretch-shortening cycle in an area which already has micro- or macro- injuries is obvious.

A great deal of concern has been voiced about the effect of the various phases of the menstrual cycle on strength or endurance. A French study comparing anaerobic tests of normally menstruating women with others who were on the contraceptive pill found no significant differences in their performances. The only possibility for variation was among those experiencing premenstrual tension. It was thought that perhaps those symptoms might have some effect on the stretch-shortening cycle.[2]

Rest is essential when an athlete is doing high quality maximal work. When doing maximal intensity work, such as a depth jump, 2 to 3 minutes of rest is recommended. For repeat, low intensity work about 30 seconds of rest is sufficient. And, as with strength work, 72 hours of rest between plyometric sessions is suggested. Remember that it is the eccentric work which causes the most muscle fiber damage and that most muscle pulls and tendon injuries occur in the transition of the stretching muscle to a concentrically contracting muscle. The plyometric action is the transition from a

During school-low intensity

108

powerful eccentric contraction to a powerful concentric action, so the injury potential is high.

In a study at the University of Jyvaskyla, Finland (where most current research on plyometric activity is performed), 10 men were tested on a 20 inch (50 cm) drop jump then exercised at a lower-than-maximal level on a special machine that required the same stretch-shortening action. They were tested 2 hours, 2 days and 4 days after the exercise. There was an initial decline in performance, then an increase, then a further decrease at 2 days, then a recovery at 4 days. There was also a reduction in the enzyme that helps to mobilize the creatine phosphate which took a similar time to return to normal. Muscle stiffness was also affected by the work to exhaustion. It was suggested that there is initial muscle fiber damage, then a recovery, then a secondary level of muscle damage. This may indicate that plyometrics should only be done with a 4 day interval between the exercise bouts.[3]

Specificity

The major message of this book is to work for the specific athletic movement desired in most exercises. For this reason a basketball player or a volleyball spiker or blocker would want to emphasize vertical jumps — pri-

Figure 10-1a

Figure 10-1b

Figure 10-1c

Shoulder

Shin Splints

Toe walking
Outside
heel
Outside

Around Floor
twice.

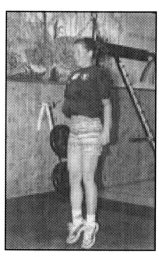

| *Figure 10-2a* | *Figure 10-2b* | *Figure 10-2c* |

marily from a box 8 inches to 2 feet high. However, a basketball player going in for a layup would be doing a one-footed long jump, so this would require another type of plyometric exercise. Swimmers and divers would need two-legged push-off work, but the diver would also want one leg work for the hurdle step. Swimmers would want both the long jump action for the start and vertical jumping for their turns. Sprinters, gymnasts and skaters would also want to work on both one- and two-leg power. Any people involved in running would want alternate leg work. Soccer goalkeepers would also want lateral long jumping power. Slalom skiers would want side-to-side one- or two-legged striding or jumping.

Komi and Bosco investigated the results from depth jumping from various heights and concluded that, on average, a 29-inch drop in a depth jump is best for developing speed, but that dynamic strength is best developed when jumping from a height of 43 inches. Higher than 43 inches takes so long to cushion the shock of landing that the muscles can't concentrically contract fast enough to make maximal gains.[4] Of course individual differences, particularly in height and musculature, can increase or reduce the maximal drop distance.

More recent studies have questioned whether the earlier recommendations of drops from 30-45 inches were really necessary. Later studies suggested maximum heights of 16-24 inches and still later studies suggest 8-16 inches. It is definitely recommended that the heels not touch the ground before rebounding in drop jumps.

An Austrailian study lasting six weeks in which the subjects performed 70-90 drop jumps per week, some working only for height from the drop and others working for a combination of minimal time on the floor and height, found that the group jumping for height but with the minimal time on the ground increased their strength by 20% but did not increase their vertical jump height from pre-test to post-test. The increase in strength did not transfer to the standing vertical jump.[5]

To increase one's ability to do a standing, two-legged vertical jump, low heights should be used in the drop jump. To increase the height of a running jump (one foot take off), a higher drop seems to be more effective.[6]

Upper Body Work

There has been little research on the effectiveness of plyometrics for the upper body. In a study utilizing both stretch-shortening exercises and bench throws (throwing a barbell upward in a bench press action), it was concluded that not much could be gained from the plyometric upper body action because the range of movement was so great that the prestretch did not have the same effect on the arms as it did the legs in plyometric work.[7]

If this is true, a plyometric stretch for a shot-putter, a discus thrower or a softball pitcher might not be as effective as we had hoped. However, if a short arm action is required, such as in a throw in for soccer, plyometric work might help in developing the strength-speed required for a longer throw.

To develop the double overarm throw, as is necessary in soccer, a medicine ball can be suspended from a rope. This is done to make certain that the ball will continually return to the player's hands at the exact spot each time. It can be done with one or two players playing "catch."

The same could be done with a softball underhand throw or a volleyball spike or serve. Field events in track, such as the shot-put, discus or javelin probably won't be as likely to benefit as significantly, because as pointed out a few paragraphs ago, a long eccentric "catching" period would reduce the value of plyometric work for the arms.

Notes:
1. P. Komi, "Measurement of the Force-Velocity Relationships in Human Muscle Under Concentric and Eccentric Contractions," *Medicine and Sport: Biomechanics III* 8 (1973): 224-229.
2. M. Giacomoni et al., "Influence of the Menstrual Cycle Phase and Menstrual Symptoms on Maximal Anaerobic Performance," *Medicine & Science in Sport & Exercise* 32.2 (2000): 486-492.

3. T. Horita et al., "Effect of Exhausting Stretch-Shortening Cycle Exercise on the Time Course of Mechanical Behaviour in the Drop Jump: Possible Role of Muscle Damage," *European Journal of Applied Physiology* 79.2 (1999): 160-167.
4. C. Bosco and P. Komi, "Mechanical Composition and Fiber Composition of Human Leg Extensor Muscles" *European Journal of Applied Physiology* 41 (1978): 275-284.
5. W.B. Young, G.J. Wilson and C. Byrne, "A Comparison of Drop Jump Training Methods: Effects on Leg Extensor Strength Qualities and Jumping Performance," *International Journal of Sports Medicine* 20.5 (1999): 295-303.
6. W.B. Young, G.J. Wilson and C. Byrne, "Relationship Between Strength Qualities and Performance in Standing and Run-up Vertical Jumps." *Journal of Sports Medicine Physical Fitness* 39.4 (1999): 285-293.
7. Robert U. Newton et al., "Influence of Load and Stretch Shortening Cycle on the Kinematics, Kinetics and Muscle Activation that Occurs During Explosive Upper-Body Movements," *European Journal of Applied Phys and Occupational Phys* 75.4 (1997): 333-342.

11

Aerobic and Anaerobic Conditioning

In this chapter we will look at both anaerobic and aerobic conditioning. We will look not only at the sport-specific types of conditioning needed but also at the general advantages of aerobic fitness that are essential throughout our lives. While the major reason for this book is to help competitive athletes and coaches understand what science is indicating today, we understand that this book will also be read by women who are interested in a deeper understanding of how to condition most effectively for their health.

Sport-Specific Conditioning

As with strength and power training, your conditioning needs to be specific. Softball base running requires full-speed for 20-40 yards then allows a rest. Volleyball requires short bursts of speed, often laterally, and often ending with a jump. Tennis has similar conditioning requirements, but the sprint generally doesn't end in a jump. Soccer requires a good deal of jogging with some short bursts of speed for 10-40 yards. Swimming and running require different types of conditioning depending on whether one is in an anaerobic sprint or in a purely aerobic distance event.

Further specificity comes into play depending on the exact movements of the athlete. For example, a tennis player playing the baseline might run back and forth or might shuffle and slide more. A volleyball blocker would want more plyometric two-foot jumps. A softball infielder would generally start a movement with a sideward pushoff. A swimmer would want both the two-foot dive and pushoff power along with the shoulder power or strength endurance required for the swim.

The Effects of Aerobic Conditioning

Aerobic conditioning is what gives us stamina. It also gives us the health benefits of reduced heart disease, increased immunity and protection against some cancers. The major benefit of exercise has correctly been focused on the heart and circulatory system, but it should be noted that the bones and ligaments, digestive and excretory systems, and the lymphatic and respiratory systems all benefit.

The well-conditioned person not only is able to ward off infectious diseases and cancers better than the poorly-conditioned person, but the chances of developing heart disease, strokes, diabetes, and other types of degenerative and chronic diseases are also lessened.

A study in Minnesota of 40,000 women, aged 55-69, showed that as little as one day a week of exercise significantly reduced their death rates. But the more physical activity they got, and the more vigorous it was, the lower their death rates.[1] Good physical condition can aid women in reducing most of the diseases of aging. Exercise also aids in relieving the menstrual discomforts that are often experienced. The high body heat and the increased blood circulation that occur during exercise aid in relieving the congestion of blood in the uterus, a major cause of discomfort.

A Harvard University study found that female runners produced a less potent form of estrogen than did their non-exercising counterparts. This was held to be a factor in the 50% reduction of expected cases of breast and cervical cancers and a 65% reduction in a type of diabetes that is more common among women than men.

Do Women Have Better Endurance?

There is now a question as to whether women can have greater endurance than men because of their larger fat stores. The marathon is a 26 mile (42.2km) race. Women continue to reduce the margin between themselves and the faster men. However, in the supermarathon events, women's times often equal men's times when they run 35 to 43 miles (56 to 70 km). Many women then become faster than the men. This is probably due to lighter body weight, more fat stores, and a better ability to convert fat into sugars for energy, according to studies at the University of Cape Town.[2] Other studies do not bear this hypothesis out, but the arguments do stimulate our curiosity.

Exercise and Age

Age is a factor in choosing the types and amounts of exercise that one should do. A woman who has been exercising regularly will be physiologically "younger" than a woman who has not been exercising. That is, the condition of the woman's body, its biological age, will be less than that expected for a person of that chronological age.

If someone has not exercised much, the body may appear older than it is. The bones can be softer, the blood pressure higher, the amount of artery hardening greater, the blood supply less, the digestive processes slower, and many other such factors that we associate with age can be present. But if that same person begins an effective exercise program, those results of aging can be slowed, stopped, or even reversed.

Osteoporosis (porous bones) an affliction of many older women and some thin men, can be prevented or reversed by weight-bearing exercise. Walking, running, weight lifting, or calisthenics can all slow or prevent its development. Swimming, while an effective endurance exercise, does not prevent the disease because the water, not the body, supports the weight.

People can continue to exercise throughout their lives. Evidence indicates that such exercise should help to prolong life because it keeps the body younger. A few years ago, a San Francisco man made headlines. He was over 100-years-old, but he ran seven miles each day — on his way to work as a waiter. When he finally retired from that job, he took a job working in a gym.

You may have heard of the Abkasian peasants in the USSR who live to be very old. Their longevity is attributed to their exercise. Not long ago, one of the men from this area was accepted into medical school. After his graduation, he took his mother to live with him in the city, thinking that she deserved a rest in her old age. Although she had been healthy when she arrived, her health failed rapidly in the city. When she returned to the farm and working in the fields, her health returned to normal.

Exercise can make you feel better and live longer, no matter when you begin your program. If you begin when you are young and continue the program, you may add years to your life — and life to your years. But you are never too old to begin. After all, exercise may be the next best thing to the fountain of youth.

Cardiopulmonary Endurance

Endurance is the ability of the body to continue to work or exercise over a long period of time. Stamina is developed by exercises that make the heart beat fast over a relatively long period of time — a minimum of 20-30 minutes. This is the most important aspect of physical fitness.

The more common physiological terms for endurance are either cardio-vascular (heart-blood) or cardio-pulmonary (heart-lung function) endurance. Those who have developed such fitness have trained their bodies to use oxygen efficiently. Since oxygen is just as important in developing energy as is blood sugar but cannot be stored like sugar, the ability to use oxygen effectively must be developed.

The heart is really a double pump. One pump (the right side of the heart) receives "used" blood that has just come from the tissues after delivering

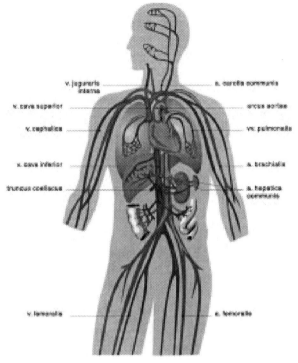

Blood Vessels

The effects of endurance exercise on the circulatory system are:

- The red blood cells become more numerous. These are the cells that carry oxygen from the lungs to the muscles and other tissues of the body. The increase in these blood cells enables each beat of the heart to carry more oxygen to the tissues. This begins to occur almost immediately after beginning an effective aerobic exercise program.
- The number of blood vessels being used in the muscles is increased. This gives the muscles more capacity for using the oxygen that is brought to them in the blood. This takes longer to develop.
- Some of the muscle fibers will develop a greater ability to contract over longer periods of time because of an increased ability to store and use oxygen.
- The heart enlarges, enabling it to pump more blood in less time to the muscles and tissues that need it. The enlarged heart beats slower than a normal heart when resting. It has a longer rest period between each beat. This normally takes many months or years to develop.

Circulation System

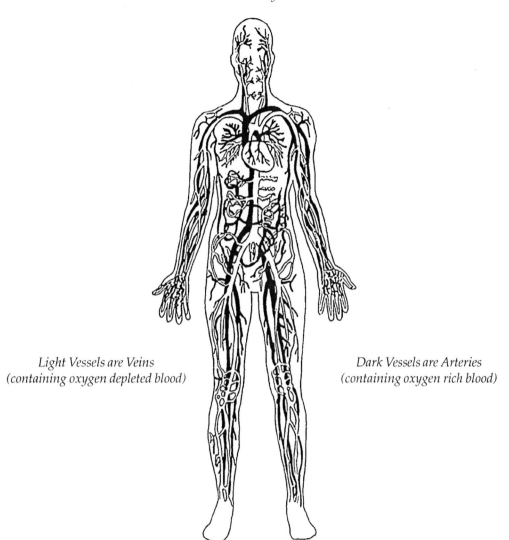

Light Vessels are Veins
(containing oxygen depleted blood)

Dark Vessels are Arteries
(containing oxygen rich blood)

nutrients and oxygen to them. The blood is received into the right atrium, the top chamber of the right side of the heart. It is then pumped into the right ventricle where the next heart beat pumps this dark, bluish-red blood to the lungs where the blood gets rid of a waste gas (carbon dioxide) and picks up a fresh supply of oxygen that turns it a bright red again. The second pump (the left side of the heart) receives this "reconditioned" blood from the lungs in the left atrium. The next beat pushes the newly oxygenated blood into the heavily muscled left ventricle. The next beat pumps the blood out through the great trunk-artery (aorta) to be distributed by smaller arteries to all parts of the body.

The heart is a very strong pump. Each day it pumps about 13 tons of blood. Each minute it pumps the total volume of the body's blood through the circulatory system. During heavy exercise, it may pump the entire volume of the blood of the body nine times each minute. That's a lot of work for a 12-ounce organ.

The heart can enlarge normally, because it has been forced to work hard to pump the blood of a person who exercises for long periods of time. Swimmers, basketball players, and long distance runners usually have such enlarged hearts. This normal enlargement is generally considered to be good.

Abnormal heart enlargement is found in many people for various reasons. These people's hearts have been forced to beat rapidly for reasons other than exercise. The heart of an obese person will have to beat many more times each day just to pump blood through the excess fat of that person. Some people have abnormally enlarged hearts because their heart valves do not function efficiently. Many have abnormally enlarged hearts because their arteries are clogged and narrowed so the heart must push the blood at a much higher pressure to get the blood to the organs and muscles.

A normally enlarged heart will beat slower than normal as it enlarges. An abnormally enlarged heart will generally continue to beat relatively fast since it has enlarged because of extreme stresses. Its enlargement would allow more blood to be pumped with each beat, but because of the great demands of the body (such as in obesity) or because of the heart's inefficiency (such as in damaged valves), enlargement is not enough. The heart must, therefore, continue to beat at a relatively fast rate.

Women athletes have been found to have a relatively smaller amount of muscle in the left ventricle than men. This reduces the amount of blood that can be delivered to the organs with each heart beat. This has been estimated to be 68% responsible for the lower VO2 max in women. This smaller ventricular size combined with the greater amount of body fat in women has been found to account for about 99% of the difference in VO2 max between women and men.

The pulse rate is the number of heart beats per minute. The average heart beats 70 to 80 times per minute when the person is at rest. But the lower the pulse rate, the better conditioned the person is. Some athletes have pulse rates in the 30s. A pulse rate of 50 would be very good for the average person. A former Swedish tennis great had a pulse rate of 28. This was achieved because of the way he practiced, continually running while hitting for several hours every day.

There are several methods of finding your pulse rate. First you must find an artery that is near to the skin. The most common places are just inside the muscle at the side of the neck; at the base of the neck just inside the collar bone, on the inside of the wrist about two inches below the base of the thumb, or directly over the heart. Place your fingers, not the thumb, of one hand on one of these spots. If your fingers are at the correct place, you will feel a throbbing. Each throb is a pulsation of blood from the heart. Count the number of beats for one minute. Or, count the number of beats for 15 seconds and multiply by four. This will give you your resting pulse rate in beats per minute. If you are exercising and don't want to take the full 15 seconds, you might count your pulse for six seconds then multiply by 10 to get your pulse rate for 60 seconds.

A heart that beats 70 beats per minute has one-half of a second to fill with blood. This resting phase is called the diastolic period. If the pulse rate is increased to 120 beats per minute, the resting phase is reduced to one-fourth of a second. In spite of the shorter resting phase, the heart still remains functional to about 160 beats per minute. At that point the resting phase may be so short that the right atrium of the heart cannot fill completely with blood, and each beat may pump less blood.

Even though the resting phase of the heart is diminished, there are other things that happen to keep the heart efficient. The blood pressure increases. This pushes more blood into the heart. The veins may be being massaged by the muscles as the muscles contract. That aids in the more rapid return of blood to the heart. The blood becomes more acidic due to the lactic acid formed in the muscles as a result of the use of sugars for energy. This acidic quality makes the hemoglobin in the red blood cells more able to pick up the oxygen in the lungs. These factors enable the heart to pump four to ten times as much blood during heavy exercise as during rest.

The well-conditioned person's heart gets more resting periods than does the heart of the person in average condition. If a person's heart were to beat 20 times less per minute (i.e., 60 rather than 80 beats per minute), it would save nearly 10,000 beats during a night's sleep and nearly 30,000 beats in a 24-hour day. It would get 18 days per year more rest than the heart with the higher pulse rate.

Red blood cells carry the oxygen from the lungs to the body tissues, by means of an iron compound called hemoglobin. These red blood cells are 1/3500 of an inch in diameter. They are formed in the bone marrow and live about three months. When red cells are destroyed, the body reclaims most of the iron and uses it to form new red cells. If one's diet is deficient in iron, it will probably result in anemia.

Various studies have shown that female runners and cross country skiers have 2.5 to 15% less hemoglobin than the men in those sports. On the other hand, women seem to have a higher concentration of a compound (2,3 diphosphoglycerate) that increases the release of oxygen to the tissues. This seems to compensate for the lower hemoglobin values.

The more blood and red cells present in each unit of blood, the greater the oxygen-carrying capacity of the blood. If a person lives high above sea level, the body's need for oxygen increases. This is because the air at high altitudes is less dense, so there is less oxygen per cubic foot of air. The body then manufactures more red blood cells so that a greater proportion of the oxygen in the air is absorbed. The Aymara Indians of the Andes Mountains have an average red cell blood count of 8 million per cubic centimeter of blood. The average person at sea level has a red cell count of about 4.5 million. Strenuous exercise and high altitude living both have the same effect on the red cell count. As the body's need for oxygen increases, the red blood cells increase to accommodate that need — if the diet contains sufficient iron.

Trained endurance athletes seem to have a more effective type of red blood cell. The average person's blood cells are rather stiff and have some trouble in moving through the capillaries where they release their oxygen and pick up carbon dioxide. According to one study of trained cyclists compared to non-exercisers, the cyclists had red cells that are able to "deform" and move more easily through the capillaries so that they could exchange the gasses more quickly.[3] The red cells can therefore make more trips between the lungs and the muscles.

Exercise increases the total amount of blood in the body. The average person can increase the total amount of blood by 10-20% during 10 weeks of effective endurance training. This can increase the blood volume by up to two quarts. Well-trained athletes may have over 40% more blood circulating in their bodies than average people. This means that the heart doesn't have to pump as often to get the needed oxygen to the muscles and other tissues because each spoonful of blood carries more red cells and, consequently, more oxygen. While women generally have about 30% less blood volume than men, when we look at the body weight of the athletes, the values actually are very close.[4]

The condition of the muscles is another factor in one's endurance. Only the muscles that are specifically involved in the activity gain endurance. The legs of a long distance runner or cyclist and the chest and upper back muscles of a swimmer will have developed changes when they become well-conditioned. The number of small blood vessels (capillaries) being used by the muscle will increase so that more blood will be able to circulate through the muscle. This allows more oxygen and blood sugars to be available for energy.

A Swedish study of fatiguing the shoulder muscles found that the women in the study who were performing 150 isokinetic shoulder flexions tended to fatigue progressively for the first 40 repetitions, then a plateau was reached. It was concluded that this was the level of fatigue for the type 2 muscle fibers.[5] Of course with endurance training for those muscles we would expect more type IIa fibers to be developed along with more blood vessels and endurance to be increased – probably at the expense of the fast twitch IIb fibers.

As mentioned earlier, long distance training will change the muscle fiber types from the fast twitch (type IIb) to a slower twitch type such as type IIa or I. This will permit more glycogen to be available for fuel for the muscle fiber. Additionally, the number of capillaries available to carry red blood cells to the muscles is proportional to the number of type 1 slow twitch fibers.[6] Consequently, the presence of more type I fibers indicates a double advantage for endurance athletes.

Endurance activities can be continued throughout life, or they can be begun as we get older. A number of people participate in masters-level competition. This competition usually begins in the 30 to 40 year age range and can go to 100. There are competitions in running, swimming, orienteering, rowing, cycling, volleyball and nearly every other sport one can imagine.

Masters level participants have been shown to be more interested in their health than the general population, as shown by their increased use of seat belts when driving and a greater propensity to see a doctor if something seemed wrong. And more important, their outlooks were happier and their lives seemed more fulfilling.

If you are a masters level athlete you can follow the same training rules as the younger athletes, but generally your strength potential will not be as great as it was when you were younger. If you were not highly conditioned as a younger person, you can easily be better conditioned than you were.

How Much Exercise Do I Need?

Let's start with general aerobic fitness. In the past we have looked upon fitness as a maximum level of cardiovascular endurance. It required increasing your heart rate significantly for 30 minutes a day with walking, swimming or other such endurance activities. This was based on the earlier aerobic theories of Dr. Ken Cooper that were further developed at Stanford University then adopted by the American Academy of Sports Medicine. This standard required that we start with a maximum heart rate of 220 beats per minute then adjust it for age by subtracting our age to get the maximum heart rate for our age. We were then advised to exercise at a rate of 65%-85%

of that adjusted heart rate for 20 to 30 minutes at least three or four times a week. Some have now widened that range from 60%-90% of one's maximum heart rate. The higher number is for the better conditioned athletes. Certainly every athlete should have at least such a minimal level of fitness. If you participate in a non-aerobic sport, you should still have this minimal level of fitness.

Exercising for Better Aerobic Fitness

Effective aerobic exercise, according to The American College of Sports Medicine (ACSM) report of 1990, requires that aerobic exercise be done 3-5 times per week for 20-60 minutes each session at an intensity of 60%-90% of maximum heart rate or 50%-85% of maximal oxygen consumption.

As mentioned earlier, you should determine your target heart rate zone (where your heart rate should be while exercising to increase cardiorespiratory fitness). To do this you must first determine your maximal heart rate. This is done by subtracting your age from 220. Then, you can determine the limits of your intensity by multiplying your maximal heart rate by between .6 and .9. (The higher number is for better conditioned people.) For instance, if you are 20 years old, then your maximal heart rate is 220 - 20 = 200. To determine your minimal target heart rate, multiply 200 x .6 = 120 beats per minute. For the top of your target heart rate zone, multiply 200 x .9 = 180 beats per minute. Beginners should begin at the low end of the target heart rate range, and slowly increase their exercising heart rate as their body adapts to the increased physical demands of exercise.

As you improve in your conditioning, your resting heart rate will drop. While the average male pulse rate is 72 and the average women's pulse is 78, it doesn't take long to drop those levels with effective endurance training. It is quite easy to get into the 60s and even the 50s for resting pulse rates. But it does require more than walking a few minutes a day and doing some gardening.

Physiologists use another measure to determine cardiorespiratory fitness. Most elite level endurance athletes have been tested for their maximum volume of oxygen levels (VO2 max). The VO2 max is the major physiological measurement used by exercise physiologists. It determines the amount of oxygen that a body can use to develop energy while exercising. The maximum amount of oxygen used is the number of milliliters of oxygen per kilogram of body weight per minute.

Males generally have about a 20% higher average VO2 max than females. Age also influences it. A 20-year-old woman will probably average 40 to 50; a 40-year-old will probably drop to 35, and a 70-year-old to 30. The top

In a study at the Marshall University Human Performance Laboratory 81 men and 81 women were tested relative to the actual VO2 max rate they achieved at each level of target heart rates. Their results showed a higher VO2 max level for each target heart rate than the ASCM had assumed. [10] The ratings were:

ACSM Max heart rate	ACSM VO2 Max (assumed)	Marshall Univ. study Max heart rate (actual)
55	40	63
70	60	76
85	80	89
90	85	92

conditioned athlete in the world, a Norwegian cross country skier, has a 95 VO2 max, and a top Italian cyclist had a level of 94. While you will probably never get to that 95 level of conditioning, you can certainly improve your own level through exercise.

A study from the Czech Republic analyzed the VO2 max for several types of sports for men and women. The average VO2 max was higher for the longer duration performances. But it was also higher when the athlete did a specific test for VO2 max. For example, a rower showed higher VO2 max when on a rowing ergometer than on a treadmill or bicycle ergometer. Canoeists did better on a paddling ergometer than on a treadmill or bicycle ergometer. This shows the importance of specificity in testing. People who row or swim may have very high VO2 maximums, but their true level will be shown when doing a sport-specific test.

A study of highly trained female triathletes found differences in VO2 max depending on whether the athletes were running or cycling. While the exercise intensity was the same, the VO2 max for treadmill running was 74% but for cycling on a cycle ergometer it was only 62.7%. So even the same athletes doing different activities, both of which are specific to their training, do not measure the same. It was also found that these triathletes did not have as high a VO2 max as single sport athletes, such as runners or cyclists. This was probably due to the fact that they did not exercise as intensely at either event as did runners or cyclists who did long single sport training. [7]

An interesting study done at Auburn University in Alabama compared the energy costs of running forward, backward and sideways for athletes. For similar distances and speeds running forward increased the pulse to 113 beats per minute. Running backward increased the pulse rate to 132 and

---

Karvonen's Formula

1. First take 220 minus your age ___. This is your maximum heart rate (MHR). Next you will need to determine your resting pulse rate. Take this while lying in bed in the morning before you get up. Use your index and middle fingers and locate your pulse either on the side of your neck (carotid artery) or on the wrist just above the thumb. Count the number of pulse beats in a minute or take your pulse for 15 seconds and multiply by 4 to determine the total for a minute.

2. Resting pulse rate (Rest HR) ___

3. Subtract the resting pulse rate from the maximum pulse rate.
   Answer for first question minus the answer for the second.
   MHR ___ - Rest HR ___ = ___ heart rate reserve (HRR)
   Now you will determine your maximum and minimum pulse rates for an effective work out. For the average person your high end will be your heart rate reserve multiplied by 80% (.80) then add to that number your resting pulse rate.

4. ___(HRR) x .80 = ___ + ___ (Rest HR) = ___ Maximum desirable heart rate during exercise.
   Next find the minimal acceptable level for your work out by taking the heart rate reserve (HRR), multiplying it by 60% (.60) then adding in your resting pulse rate.
   ___ (HRR) x .60 = ___ + ___ (Rest HR)= ___ Minimal desirable heart rate during exercise.
   These two percentages (60% and 80%) are not set in stone. If you had medical problems or were in very poor condition you might use a number between 40% and 55% to set your minimal pulse rate. If you were very fit or a competitive athlete you might use 85 or 90% to set your high end exercise pulse rate.
   An example of how an average 20 year old would determine the target training pulse range. Assume that her resting pulse rate was 70.
   Minimum target heart rate (220-20=200-70= 130) x .60=78 then add the resting pulse rate of 70=148
   Maximum target heart rate (220-20=200-70=130) x .80=104
   Then add the resting pulse rate of 70= 174
   So this 20-year-old should exercise at a heart rate of between 148 and 174.
   For a 40 year old with a resting pulse of 65 the target heart rates would be:
   Minimum target heart rate (220-40=180-65=115) x .60= 69
   Then add the resting pulse of 65 = 134
   Maximum target heart rate (220-40=180-65=115) x .80= 92 then add in the resting pulse rate of 65 = 157
   So this 40 year old should exercise with her heart rate between 134 and 157.

going sideways to 140. The amount of oxygen used per kilogram of body weight was 12.42 going forward, 15.95 for going backward and 22.10 for moving sideward. [8] Again we see the need for specificity in training.

These illustrations should underscore the essential concern of athletes to condition themselves specifically for their event. While cross-training may prevent boredom and perhaps reduce the chance of one experiencing the overtraining syndrome (See Chapter 12), doing non-specific training does

---

Rockport Fitness Walking Test

1. Measure out one mile on either an indoor or outdoor surface.
2. Walk as fast as possible throughout the mile.
3. Record the time it takes you to walk the mile.
4. Record your heart rate immediately upon completion of the mile walk. This can be easily and quickly done by taking your heart rate for
   a. 6 seconds and multiplying that number by 10
   b. 10 seconds and multiplying that number by 6
   c. 15 seconds and multiplying that number by 4
5. Determine what your mile time is in minutes and hundredths of a minute. For instance, if your walk time was 10 minutes, 15 seconds = 10.25. This is the number you will plug into the following formulas.
6. Use the following gender-specific formulas to determine maximal oxygen consumption rates (VO2 max).

Male	Female
_____ = 0.0947 x body weight	_____ = 0.0585 x body weight
_____ = 0.3709 x age	_____ = 0.3885 x your age
_____ = 3.9744 x mile time	_____ = 2.7961 x mile time
_____ = 0.1847 x mile heart rate	_____ = 0.1109 x mile heart rate

7. Add these four numbers together. Put that number here _____. For women, take 116.579 and subtract the number you found in step 7 to determine your VO2 max.
116.579 - _____ = _____ VO2 max
(Men would take 154.899 and subtract the number found in step 7 to determine their VO2 max. 154.899 - _____ = _____ VO2 max)

---

not increase the sport-specific requirements in either endurance, strength or power, or in sport-specific skills.

A study at the Human Performance Laboratory of the Milwaukee Heart Institute bears this out. Ten men and 20 women, all well-trained runners, were divided into 3 groups. One continued the running training, one ran 10% more per week than normal and one did the normal running workout then added an extra 10% of swimming workout. The results were that adding 10% to the workout, whether by more running or by swimming, increased the running speed and conditioning, but adding more running was much more effective in increasing running conditioning. [9]

Working at a Percent of Maximum Heart Rate

The ACSM (American College of Sports Medicine) recommendation of using 220 heart beats per minute then subtracting your age to get your maximum heart rate for exercise is actually based on the VO2 max concept. To achieve a 40% VO2 max, it was assumed that one needed to exercise at 55% of one's maximum heart rate. For a 60 VO2 max, one needed to exercise at 70% of one's maximum heart rate, and for an 80% VO2 max, the target heart rate should be 85% of one's maximum heart rate. Recent work seems to indicate that the actual VO2 max achieved at each of these target heart rates may be higher than originally assumed.

Many fitness professionals are now using a heart target rate formula developed by the Finnish physiologist Karvonen. It adds another component to find the maximum heart rate, that is, the heart reserve. This takes into consideration one's resting heat rate in addition to one's maximal heart rate. (See box.)

To determine your maximal oxygen consumption rate (VO2 max), you can do the Rockport Fitness Walking Test [11], as this has been validated by ACSM as an appropriate fitness test.

Now that you know your maximal oxygen consumption, you can test to see whether your cardiorespiratory fitness program is working by occasionally repeating the above test. As your fitness level increases, your VO2 max will increase because cardiorespiratory fitness relies on the effective delivery and use of oxygen to make energy. You can also measure your progress by noting the changes in your resting pulse rate. As you get into better condition, your resting pulse rate should drop.

Beginning Aerobic Fitness for New Athletes

If you are in poor or average condition and desire to increase your fitness level, be sure that you begin with a low-intensity activity such as walking or use a low intensity level on a stationary bike or a stair climber. Whichever approach you take, start slowly. If you begin any exercise program too quickly, you will probably have some muscle soreness for the first few days. This soreness discourages some people, but it will disappear and will probably never return as you get into condition and keep fit.

Keep improving by increasing the amount of time spent exercising and/ or the intensity at which you exercise. Eventually you will reach your fitness objectives. When you reach these objectives, you can continue to work at that level for maintenance.

As you progress in your athletic aerobic conditioning, you can continue to increase the overload for better conditioning. Of course, the sport you have chosen will determine how much you will exercise aerobically and how important that aerobic conditioning is. Obviously in cycling, distance running and the triathlon, aerobic conditioning is the most important element of your conditioning. It is certainly important in basketball — but if you worked only on aerobic conditioning and forgot to practice your jump shot and free throw shooting, you wouldn't be much help to your team. But luckily, most basketball coaches work their aerobic conditioning into most of their drills.

Coaches are well advised to condition during their drills. Aerobic over-load can be included in many sport drills. For example:

- In volleyball the blockers can be worked aerobically by having two setters and two to four hitters working against them. One setter sets to one side of the court, the block forms and jumps, then another setter sets to a hitter on the other side of the court and the blockers must move down the net and prepare for another block. This series of setting a hitter right then a hitter left is continued for 30 to 40 seconds or more. This will develop the sort of strength-speed endurance necessary for a game.
- In soccer three or four attackers can attack the goal and shoot, then move to the outside of the field and sprint back to the starting point while another group does the attacking. Two or three groups of attackers can be used.
- In basketball a series of fast break or zone press drills can be used in succession.
- In tennis the common "lob, overhead, attack the net" drill works well.

Drills such as these incorporate the game skills, fun and aerobic conditioning that are essential for an effective sport drill.

When to Exercise

Just about any time is a good time to exercise. However, if you exercise just before you go to bed, you will increase your metabolism, that may make it more difficult to sleep. If you exercise just after eating, you will force your body to divide the available blood between the stomach, that needs it for digestion, and the skeletal muscles, that need it for exercise. But if you exercise just before a mealtime you may find that you don't desire as much food. If you use your exercise sessions to give you energy, you may choose to exercise in the morning. If you use your exercise sessions to relieve the stress and tension of your day, the evening would be a more appropriate time.

In a study measuring anaerobic capacity in the morning and evening it was found that the anaerobic capacity was 26% better in the afternoon than in the morning. [12]

In a study on aerobic power, 12 men and 12 women were tested maximally on an ergometric cycle. The time to exhaustion was 9% longer in the afternoon than in the morning. The VO2 max was 7% higher in the afternoon. [13]

A further refinement of that study showed that for high intensity exercise, female athletes who trained in the morning were better able to perform at high levels in the morning. Those who trained in the afternoon were better able to obtain their highest intensity exercise in the afternoon. The drop in effectiveness for those who trained in the morning then were tested in the afternoon were identical to the drop in performance of the afternoon trained people when tested in the morning. [14] This again points to the importance of specificity in training. This might indicate that if you were training on the West Coast for a competition on the East Coast (which is 3 hours later) perhaps the training time should be moved up 3 hours to correspond with the actual time on the East Coast.

Warm-Up and Cool-Down for Aerobic Exercise

Endurance exercise requires a proper warm-up and a vigorous activity period. It may be desirable to also have a cool-down session. When the athlete has been working at a very high pulse rate level, slowing to the point where the pulse drops to about 100-105 may be wise.

Even well-conditioned people often show abnormal electrocardiograms when they exercise without a proper warm-up. However, they will show normal electrocardiograms when they are warmed-up prior to exercising. A warm-up is designed to increase blood flow to the muscles you are going to work. So, a brisk walk or a slow jog would be an appropriate warm-up to a jog, and a few minutes on a rowing machine or a slow swim would get the blood flowing to your upper body before a swimming workout. You can also perform the activity you plan to engage in for your workout at a very light intensity for a proper warm-up. A good indication that you are properly warmed up is when you begin to sweat. Five minutes is usually sufficient to get your body ready for your workout.

Aerobic Workouts for Endurance Athletes

In a study of female track athletes running on a treadmill at their maximum velocities, it was found that on average they reached their VO2 max (about 52 milliliters of oxygen per kilogram of body weight per minute) in about 4 minutes (234 seconds) and sustained it for nearly a minute (56 seconds).

So while the VO2 max can be achieved at a high velocity run, it is often not sustained long. The study concluded that working at less than 60% of the maximum time (ie. the time for your race) is not effective conditioning. [15] Consequently, we might assume that in training in over or under distance, the time of the exercise should not be over 33% less than the time of the race. So if the athlete were working for an 800 meter run in 1:54 the under-distance should be no less than about 500 meters. The over-distance runs might be 1200 or so meters. Remember the principle of specificity.

Anaerobic Considerations

Anaerobic exercise is that which happens before the body begins to use the oxygen that has been breathed in. In order to tell you how this increase in anaerobic capacity occurs, we must get a little bit technical. There are a number of chemical actions that supply energy to the individual muscle fiber. The primary energy source is called ATP (adenosine triphosphate). This ATP is used for energy in all cells. As the name implies, there are three phosphates in the molecule. Energy is released when one of these phosphates is broken off from the ATP. This energy supplies the power for the muscle fiber to contract. There is enough ATP in the muscle to last for almost a second. If it is not resynthesized, there will be no more fuel for the muscle.

The ATP is resynthesized by taking the phosphate in creatine phosphate that is also present in the cell. But just as the ATP storage in the cell will last for only about a second, the creatine phosphate available will last for only about five seconds. The use of these substances for energy is called anaerobic (without oxygen).

In order to continue to supply the muscles with an energy source, the cells use the food (carbohydrates, proteins, and fats) and the oxygen that is in the blood and is continuously being breathed in. The muscle fibers are now being fueled aerobically—with oxygen.

Anaerobic work is very short term, such as lifting a weight in an Olympic lift, the beginning of a running or swimming sprint, a jump or vault, a golf swing, a tennis serve, or an exercise in strength training. For these short-term activities, supplementation with creatine monohydrate has been found useful to increase the length of time that muscles can work anaerobically. They also aid in developing more force in the muscles so that more weight can be lifted or a sprint start might be faster. The supplementation with creatine can also help in aerobic sports where there are occasional bursts of energy, such as in soccer, volleyball or tennis. (How creatine can be supplemented is covered in Chapter 22.)

While some sport activities are purely anaerobic, most sports utilize anaerobic energy sources during parts of their activity. Soccer players may use anaerobic energy when sprinting, a goal keeper would use anaerobic energy when moving quickly to stop a ball, softball players will use it in hitting and in beating out a single, double or triple. Of course, marathoners will use nearly no anaerobic sources for their energy.

There has been some disagreement on how long a rest is needed for people doing an anaerobic sprint. One minute of rest per 10 yards of sprinting has been suggested. In a French study that investigated rests between sprints of 30 seconds, 1 minute, 3 minutes, 5 minutes, 10 minutes and a full

Benefits of Aerobic Exercise
1. An increase in the number of blood vessels. When this occurs in the heart, it increases one's chances of avoiding or surviving a heart attack.
2. Control of body fat. One-half hour of proper exercise daily will keep off (or take off) 26 pounds of fat per year.
3. There is an increase in the basal metabolism for several hours after exercising, that may take off additional pounds.
4. An increase in HDLs (the good blood cholesterols).
5. A strengthening of the diaphragm, the major muscle used in breathing.
6. In improved immunity system to fight off degenerative and infectious diseases.
7. Stronger bones and connective tissue.
8. A reduction in minor aches, pains, stiffness, and soreness.
9. There is an increase in productivity.
10. A reduction in chronic fatigue.
11. An increased ability to relax and to sleep well.
12. An increase in endorphins in the brain (if the exercise is sufficiently long), making one feel exhilarated.
13. Improved digestion and bowel function.
14. Increased mental capabilities (i.e. increased alertness) due to an increase in oxygen to the brain.
15. Increased muscle tone.
16. Increased self-esteem. Increased creativity and imagination.
17. Decreased muscle tension and stress.
18. Decreased PMS symptoms and menstrual cramps.
19. Decreased labor pain and faster recovery time from giving birth.
20. Lower resting heart rate from a larger stroke volume.
21. Lower resting blood pressure.
22. Increased life expectancy and better quality of life.

day of rest found that the power between the sprints remained unchanged.[16]

To illustrate the percentage of anaerobic to aerobic sources of energy in middle distance running events. In tests for a 400 meter run (about 50 to 55 seconds), an 800 meter run (about 1:50 to 2 minutes) and a 1500 meter run (about 4 to 4 1/2 minutes) it was found that for the 400 meter run about 60% of the energy source was anaerobic, for the 800 meters it was about 35% and for the 1500 meters it was 20% or less. [17]

Percent of Entergy from Anaerobic Sources

Event	Women	Men
400 meter	62%	63%
800	33%	39%
1500	17%	20%

Effects of Menstruation

A study using six normally menstruating athletes, six normally menstruating non-athletes and six amenorrheic (not menstruating) athletes studied the ventilation (VO2 max, carbon dioxide production) and the time it took the women to fatigue on a bicycle exerciser during the luteal phase of the menstrual cycle. The luteal phase is between ovulation and the first day of menstrual flow. It averages 14 days but has a normal range of 10 to 17 days. The non-athletes' performances were decreased during the luteal phase. The athletes' performances were not. [18]

While it is often believed that the luteal phase of the cycle is the more effective for competition, a Japanese survey of college athletes indicated that they believed that the earlier follicular phase was more productive. After the survey the researchers took top level basketball players and subjected them to increased levels of exertion on cycle ergometers and measured a number of physiological responses. The study found that the heart rate was higher during the luteal phase both when the athletes rested and exercised. On the other hand, the volume of oxygen consumed and the speed of breathing (respiratory rate) as well as the lactic acid production were all higher during the follicular phase. Still in comparing one phase to the other, the results did not leave a firm conclusion as to which phase of the cycle was more productive for sport performance. [19]

A French study analyzed the anaerobic force production of 17 women in three tests. Some women were on oral contraceptives. Tests were done during menstruation (days 1-4), during the midfollicular phase (days 7-9) and the mid-luteal phase (days 19-21). There were no significant differences of force production during the different phases of the cycle, and there were no significant differences between those on oral contraceptives and those who were not. The major negative factor was premenstrual or menstrual pain. This seemed to reduce the neuromuscular capabilities of the stretch-shortening cycle. [20]

While early studies of the effects of menstruation generally asked the athletes to recall when they were most and least effective during their menstrual cycles, modern studies usually use body temperature and cervical mucous methods of determining more accurately when ovulation occurred. The earlier studies found that the athletes believed they performed best after menstruation and into the mid-cycle period and performed worst during the premenstrual phase. Studies of adolescent swimmers found that they performed best during the menstrual and post menstrual period, but studies with older swimmers showed no differences. A study of cross country skiers showed their performances to be better just after ovulation and just after menstruation. The point is, that there seems to be a great deal of difference between the athletes. [21]

In a study of eight normally menstruating runners working at 55 and 80% of their VO2 max, working at 55% didn't seem to make a difference in their aerobic capacity. But at 80% of their VO2 max, their running economy was significantly less during their mid-luteal phase (about days 20 to 24 after menstrual flow) compared to the early follicular phase (about days 1 to 4 after flow). It was felt that the differences were due to lessened ability to ventilate effectively and to changed mood states. [22]

The Effects of Oral Contraceptives on Performance

Let's begin with the fact that more studies are needed, but based on those studies available:

- One study found an increase in performance in 8% of the women on the pill.
- Other studies have found no effect or a reduced aerobic capacity.
- Elite athletes can regulate their cycles so that their performances will not be decreased during menstruation. Menstruation can usually be delayed for a week or more by taking additional pills when the pill usage should be stopped to allow for menstruation. They can also use fewer pills each month and shorten the cycle so that the competition will occur just after menstruation. [23]

An article from the Sports Medicine Center of the University of Ottawa suggests that for athletes with menstrual dysfunction, oral contraceptives may help. Oral contraceptives may also even make their hormonal variations more predictable. It has been recommended that the triphasic and the newer progestin contraceptives may be preferable. [24]

Pregnancy and Exercise

Physical training and activity during pregnancy is very common today, and many women even continue training after the 25th week of gestation. Irrespective of its level of intensity, training has not proved to be associated with risk. Moderate training seems to be beneficial by increasing the effect of insulin among those possibly at risk of diabetes during pregnancy. Pregnant women who exercise not only tend to be characterized by better health and self-esteem and a lower incidence of depression during pregnancy, but also find delivery less strenuous. The offspring of women who train during pregnancy show fewer signs of stress during delivery and are usually characterized by better physical condition. [25]

Olympic gold medal winners who were mothers found themselves to be stronger after childbirth.

Notes:
1. L.H. Kushi, *Journal of the American Medical Association* 277 (1997): 1287-1292.
2. J. Bam et al., "Could Women Outrun Men in Ultramarathon Races?" *Medicine & Sport in Science & Exercise.* 29.2 (1997): 244-247.
3. J.A. Smith et al., "Greater Erythrocyte Deformability in World-Class Endurance Athletes," *American Journal of Physiology* 276.6 Part 2 (1999): H2188-2193.
4. K.D. Mittleman and C.M. Zacher, "Factors Influencing Endurance Performance, Strength, Flexibility and Coordination," *Women in Sport*, ed. B. Drinkwater (Oxford: Blackwell Science, 2000) 25.
5. B. Gerdle, J. Elert and K. Henriksson-Larsen, "Muscular Fatigue During Repeated Isokinetic Shoulder Forward Flexions in Young Females," *European Journal of Applied Physiology* 58.6 (1989): 666-673.
6. W.J. Duey et al., "Skeletal Muscle Fibre Type and Capillary Density in College-Aged Blacks and Whites," *Journal of Human Biology* 24.4 (1997): 323-231.
7. D.A. Schneider and J. Pollack, "Ventilatory Threshold and Maximal Oxygen Uptake During Cycling and Running in Female Triathletes," *International Journal of Sports Medicine* 12.4 (1991): 379-383.
8. H.N. Williford et al, "Cardiovascular and Metabolic Costs of Forward, Backward, and Lateral Motion." *Medical Science in Sports and Exercise* 30.9 (1998):1419-1423.
9. C. Foster et al., "Effects of Specific Versus Cross-Training on Running Performance," European Journal of Applied Physiology 70.4 (1995): 367-372.
10. Swain DP, Abernathy KS, Smith CS, Lee SJ, Bunn SA"Target heart rates for the development of cardiorespiratory fitness." Med Sci Sports Exerc Jan, 1994, 26(1):112-116
11. Kline, Porcari, Hintermeister, Freedson, Ward, McCarron, Ross and Rippe, 1987.
12. P.D. Marth, R.R. Woods and D.W. Hill, "Influence of Time of Day on Anaerobic Capacity," *Percept Mot Skills* 86.2 (1998): 592-4b.
13. D.W. Hill, "Effect of Time of Day on Aerobic Power in Exhaus-

tive High Intensity Exercise," *Journal of Sports Medicine and Physical Fitness* 36.3 (1996): 155-160.

14. D.W. Hill et al, "Temporal Specificity in Adaptations to High-Intensity Exercise Training," *Medicine & Sport in Science & Exercise* 30.3 (1998): 450-455.

15. D.W. Hill and A.L. Rowell, "Responses to Exercise at the Velocity Associated with VO2 Max," Medicine and Science in Sports Exercise 29.1 (1997): 113-116.

16. S. Blonc et al, "Effect of Recovery Duration on the Force-Velocity Relationship," *International Journal of Sports Medicine* 19.4 (1998): 272-276.

17. D.W. Hill, "Energy System Contributions in Middle-Distance Running Events," Journal of Sports Science 17.6 (1999): 477-483.

18. R.B. Schoene et al., "Respiratory Drives and Exercise in Menstrual Cycles of Athletic and Nonathletic Women," Journal of Applied Physiology 50.6 (1981): 1300-1305.

19. N. Mesaki et al, "Effect of Menstrual Cycle on Cardiorespiratory System During Incremental Exercise," *Nippon Sanka Fujinka Gakkai Zasshi* 38.1 (1986):1-9.

20. M. Giacomoni et al, "Influence of the Menstrual Cycle Phase and Menstrual Symptoms on Maximal Anaerobic Performance," *Medicine & Sport in Science & Exercise.* 32.2 (2000): 486-492.

21. C.M. Lebrun, "The Effects of the Menstrual Cycle and Oral Contraceptives on Sports Performance," *Women in Sport*, ed. B. Drinkwater (Oxford: Blackwell Science, 2000) 43-44.

22. T.J. Williams and G.S. Krahenbuhl, "Menstrual Cycle Phase and Running Economy," *Medicine & Sport in Science & Exercise.* 29 (1997) 1609-1618.

23. C.M. Lebrun, "The Effects of the Menstrual Cycle and Oral Contraceptives on Sports Performance," *Women in Sport*, ed. B. Drinkwater (Oxford: Blackwell Science, 2000) 54-56.

24. R.J. Frankovich and C.M. Lebrun, "Menstrual Cycle, Contraception and Performance," *Clinical Sports Medicine* 19.2 (2000): 251-271.

25. K. Henriksson-Larsen, "Training and Sports Competition During Pregnancy and After Childbirth, Physical Training is Beneficial for Mother and Child," *Lakartidningen* 96.17 (1999): 2097-2100.

12

High Performance Problems

John Dryden long ago told us, "The wise, for cure, on exercise depend." However, some people exercise excessively and can develop some health problems as a result of their heavy work schedules. There is no question that effective endurance exercise is a great benefit to the health of the woman exercising. It reduces high blood pressure, reduces heart attack risk, and reduces the risk of some cancers. It also builds up immunity to fight off other diseases. There are times, however, when a person gets far more exercise than her body or mind can handle. Then problems can result. While usually temporary and reversible, negative outcomes of physical or mental stress from exercise must be taken into account. The negative effects discussed in this chapter are most likely to happen to elite athletes or to recreational exercisers who work out far more than normal.

Overtraining

Some athletes, particularly in the endurance sports, suffer from what is called "overtraining syndrome" or "chronic fatigue syndrome." It has also been called staleness or burn out. The symptoms may include any of the following: a loss of motivation, increased injuries or illnesses, loss of appetite, loss of body weight, irritability or other mood changes, depression, insomnia, nightmares, a loss of sex drive, and generally below-average performances. Women can also develop menstrual problems. (See the Female Athlete Triad on page 138.) Any one symptom can be an indication of the effects of overtraining.

It is more likely to occur in men running over 64 kilometers (40 miles) a week or women running over 48 kilometers (30 miles) a week.[1] However, others have found it to be as high as 150 to 175 kilometers (about 100 miles per week). [2] Often athletes think that increasing the workout will bring in-

The effects of overtraining or overfatigue can be:
• mechanical (stressing of bones, ligaments, muscles and tendons);
• metabolic (depletion of carbohydrates, inadequate amounts of adenosine triphosphate [ATP] which is essential in the release of energy in the muscles, an excess of stress-related hormones [particularly cortisol])
• systemic (involving the whole body or the mind-body relationship) such as mental staleness, general tiredness, etc.

creased results. This isn't always true. In one study, doubling the swimming workout reduced the performances of the swimmers. In speed skating it has been found that practicing more than 15 hours a week is counterproductive. If you are a competitive athlete, gauge yourself so that your workouts maximize your performance and don't lead to overtraining and a reduction in your competitive abilities.

Overtraining is often common at the beginning of a sport season, particularly if the woman has engaged in interval training — short, intense bouts of exercise for 1-5 minutes each. Monotonous long distance training can also be a factor. Varied workouts are more likely to keep one's psychological spirits up.

Ten percent of the elite college swimmers in the United States have suffered some of these symptoms. This might well be expected since it is not uncommon for elite swimmers to swim 4-6 miles twice a day during the season. Coaches realize this and generally will "taper" the workouts as the championship meets approach. During the tapered programs there is more sprinting and far less total distance.

The amount of time necessary to recover varies with the problem. Bones and tendons take longer to recover than muscles. Replenishing carbohydrates may take only a day or two but mental staleness may take some time. Effective recovery depends on several factors. Your age, your own physiological make up, the altitude at which you are exercising, the temperature, and your level of fitness are among the factors which will affect your speed of recovery.

A Finnish study at the Research Institute for Olympic Sports compared two groups of elite distance runners, one continuing their normal workouts and the other continuing their normal workout but increasing the high intensity parts of the workouts by 30%. They were measured on submaximal and maximal treadmill tests for their VO2 max and heart rates. They were also measured on their moods as well as on certain hormones that are related to stress-cortisol, catecholamines and noradrenaline. Five of the 9 females who were exposed to the extra work showed signs of overtraining.

Their VO2 max decreased from an average of 53 to an average of 50.2. Their optimal treadmill work (amount of oxygen demand) reduced from an average of 56 to an average of 52.2. Their maximal heart rate decreased from an average of 190 to an average of 186. They also showed mood disturbances. Blood levels of adrenaline and noradrenaline also decreased. While there are a number of individual differences among these athletes, it was concluded that hormone levels during exercise be monitored for elite athletes to determine or predict their approaching a state of overtraining. [3]

In a study at the University of Wisconsin, a group of active college women was compared with a group of elite college female swimmers. All answered a mood questionnaire and had their cortisol levels taken from their saliva. The swimmers increased their swimming workouts from 2000 yards a day in September to 12,000 yards a day in January (the overtraining period). Then as the championship season approached, they reduced (tapered) their workouts to 4,500 yards a day. The swimmers experienced significant alterations in tension, depression, anger, vigor, fatigue and total mood levels with the increase and decrease of their workout volume, compared to the controls. Salivary cortisol was significantly greater in the swimmers compared to the controls during baseline and overtraining, but was not different between the groups following the taper. Salivary cortisol was significantly correlated with a depressed mood during overtraining, but not at the beginning (September) baseline or the taper period (February). Those swimmers who had overtrained had greater depression and negative mood changes and a higher level of cortisol. [4]

One researcher in the United States monitored the moods of swimmers. If their moods were up they were given more work, if their moods were low, their work load was reduced. This seemed to indicate that the mood of an athlete was somewhat predictive of the onset of the overtraining syndrome.

Individual tolerance to excess workouts has been verified at the Institute for Theory in Training and Movement, German Sport University, Cologne. Working with elite athletes in several sports using several tests, it was recommended that for elite athletes, their tolerance for exercise should be evaluated every few days. Their measures were primarily physiological using the levels of creatine kinase as a measure for effective metabolism. [5]

If you believe that you may be suffering from the overtraining syndrome because of excess tiredness or poor performance, you should see your doctor. It is possible that your symptoms are caused by something other than overtraining. Psychological problems related to home, school or work and physiological problems related to drugs, alcohol or excessive sexual activity can also cause fatigue related symptoms. You may not be able to blame your tiredness and irritability on your exercise program!

Branched chain amino acids (BCAA) increase the amount of glutamine available to the immune system. For this reason, BCAA may need to be supplemented in the diets of endurance athletes. If laboratory tests show low iron stores, the doctor may prescribe iron supplementation. As you know, low iron is a common problem with most women. There is no evidence at this time that extra vitamin or mineral supplements will help you avoid the overtraining syndrome. This was verified by a study at the University of Tennessee.

The major symptoms of overtraining include decreased exercise performance, altered mood states, and depleted muscle glycogen stores. These closely resemble the effects of a low level of the brain neurotransmitter serotonin, the level of which is dependent on the blood level of the amino acid tryptophan to the branched-chain amino acids (BCAA). To test the level of BCAA, 10 highly-trained distance runners had their training volume increased by 40% for two weeks. This amounted to a state of overtraining. This was followed by a reduction of 41% below their normal training volume. The runners experienced a significant increase in their negative mood states with higher training volume, but it reduced when training was reduced. However, resting heart rate, blood pressure, resting metabolic rate, serum cortisol were not changed. Neither was the level of tryptophan or the level of BCAAs. [6]

The major preventive approach is to individualize one's training so that overtiredness does not occur. Planned rests must be part of the training program. Adequate diet and sufficient fluid intake are also essentials. For many, where it is at least partly related to psychological factors, counseling, relaxation techniques, massage, and other stress reduction approaches may be useful.

The Female Athlete Triad

Female endurance athletes and dancers are often afflicted by a combination of three major problems: eating disorders (anorexia and/or bulimia), amenorrhea (no menstruation) or oligomenorrhea (little menstruation), and osteoporosis (a loss of bone minerals, particularly calcium, resulting in weakened bones).

Eating Disorders

Dancers and gymnasts are most likely to have problems because of a pressure to keep their weights excessively low. Endurance athletes, such as swimmers and marathon runners, may develop the same problems because they are not replacing the calories they lost during their training. So while studies have shown that as many as 15% of female college swimmers may have eating problems, over 60% of gymnasts exhibit such problems in some studies.

The eating patterns among physically active women can range from normal, through inadequate, to the severely neurotic problems of advanced anorexia or bulimia. A low nutritional intake will almost certainly affect the menstrual patterns. Once this happens, bone loss is almost certain to occur.

Dr. Barbara Drinkwater, former president of the American College of Sports Medicine, has been outspoken in her concern for preventing this problem of the female athletic triad. [7] The combination of hard training and the desire to keep weight reduced often results in inadequate nutrition. This is sometimes achieved by bulimic methods, such as vomiting. The results are that one's weight is too low, there is a loss of calcium from the bones, and there is a lack of healthy menstruation.

Anorexia nervosa is starvation by choice. This is a disease primarily seen in young women. It afflicts nearly 1 in 100 women[8] although 5%-10% of its victims are male. In this disease, the person goes on a diet and refuses to stop, no matter how thin he or she gets. About one out of ten people who have this affliction end up starving themselves to death. The disease has a psychological basis, but its physical effects are very real. Medical care, usually hospitalization, is generally required.

It appears that there may be a hereditary predisposition to it. (Identical twins exhibit the disease four to five times more often than non-identical twins.) But our culture, with its high value on thinness, may help it along. Parents who value outward appearance and social achievement, rather than self-esteem and self-actualization, are often associated with the anorexic person. [9] Another factor commonly associated with the problem is an absent or distant father. Coaches are often the problem, especially with gymnasts, but divers and distance runners may also be advised to lose weight.

After the anorexic begins the severe dieting routine, symptoms of starvation may set in leading to a number of physical problems. Abnormal thyroid, adrenal, and growth hormone functions are not uncommon. The heart muscle becomes weakened. Amenorrhea occurs due to the low percentage of body fat. Blood pressure may drop. Anemia is common due to the lack of protein and iron ingested. The peristalsis of the intestines may slow and the lining of the intestines may atrophy. The pancreas often becomes unable to se-

Symptoms of Anorexia Nervosa
• Weight 15% below what is expected
• Intense fear of becoming overweight
• "Feeling fat" even when very thin
• Amenorrhea

Symptoms of Bulimia Nervosa
• Secret binge eating (at least twice a week for 3 or more months) • A lack of control over eating • Purging (vomiting, laxatives, etc.) • Overconcern with body shape

crete many of its enzymes. Body temperature may drop. The skin may become dry and there can be an increase of body hair in the body's attempt to keep itself warm. And the worst effect of the disease is death.

Because dieting is such a common occurrence in our society, anorexia is often difficult to diagnose until one has entered the advanced stages of the disease. However, other symptoms, such as moodiness, being withdrawn, obsessing about food but not being seen eating it, and constant food preparation may be observed by those close to the anorexic. Once diagnosed, there are a number of medical and psychological therapies that can be effective.

Bulimia or bulimia nervosa is more common than anorexia. It is typified by the person restricting calorie intake during the day and bingeing on high-fat, high-calorie foods at least twice a week. Following the binge, the person will then purge in her attempt to rid the body of the excess calories just consumed. Purging techniques include vomiting, laxatives, fasting, and excessive exercise. Some experts do not consider the behavior bulimic until it has persisted for about three months with two or more binges per week during that time. Estimates based on various surveys of college students and others indicate that between 5%-20% of women may be bulimic. It is also more common among men than is anorexia.

Bulimia, like anorexia, stems from a psychological problem. However there may also be a link to physical abnormalities in some cases. The neurotransmitters serotonin and norepinephrine seem to be involved as does the hormone cholecystokinin which is secreted by the hypothalamus and makes a person feel that enough food has been eaten.

Physical symptoms that may be seen depend on the type of purging technique used. The bulimic who induces vomiting can have scars on the back of the knuckles, mouth sores, gingivitis, tooth decay, a swollen esophagus, and chronic bad breath. The bulimic who uses laxatives can cause irreparable damage to the intestines due to constant diarrhea. All bulimics run the risk of throwing off their electrolytes (minerals involved in muscle contractions) due to the constant dehydration suffered. It is this imbalance of electrolytes that can cause the bulimic to have abnormal heart rhythms and can induce a heart attack.

A meta-analysis of 34 studies comparing the relationship between eating disorders and athletic participation showed dancers the most likely to be affected. And, compared with other studies, gymnasts were not particu-

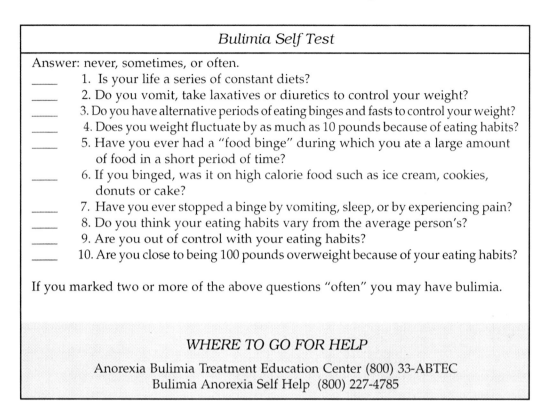

larly affected. Yet athletes appeared to be more at risk than non-athletes. While elite athletes were more likely to be at risk, non-elite athletes, particularly those in high school, had a reduced level of eating disorders. It was concluded that, depending on the level of competition, athletics can be a positive or a negative influence on eating disorders. [10] For elite gymnasts most studies show that they are likely to be affected by eating disorders, this is different from the findings of this meta-analysis.

The National Collegiate Athletic Association (NCAA) assisted in a large study on the prevalence of eating disorders among its athletes. 1,445 student athletes from 11 Division 1 schools were surveyed using a 133-item questionnaire. The results indicated that 1.1% of the females met DSM-IV (Diagnostic and Statistical Manual of the American Psychiatric Association, Fourth Edition) criteria for bulimia nervosa versus 0% for males. None of the student athletes met DSM-IV criteria for anorexia nervosa but 9.2% of the females were identified as having clinically significant problems with bulimia versus .01% of the males. Of the females, 2.85% were identified as having a clinically significant problem with anorexia nervosa versus 0% for males. 10.85% of the females reported binge eating on a weekly or greater basis versus 13.02% of the males. 5.52% of the females reported purging behavior (vomiting, laxatives, diuretics) on a weekly or greater basis versus 2.04% for the males. These results show fewer eating disorders among elite college athletes than earlier studies had indicated. [11]

Amenorrhea and Oligomenorrhea

Menstrual problems in athletes occur primarily because of insufficient caloric intake — either because of an eating disorder or because of not replacing the calories used during the exercise period, even though the meals consumed might be adequate for a non-exercising woman.

It is essential to keep menstruation normal to avoid bone loss. Normally it returns to normal within two to three months of reducing one's training regimen and obtaining adequate nutrition.

Amenorrhea is often related to a reduction of estrogen, the major female hormone. Estrogen levels of most amenorrheic women is similar to women who have entered menopause. Another factor in reducing menstruation is the reduction of the lutieinizing hormone (LH) which is necessary to complete the menstrual cycle. It can be reduced by either an excess of exercise or by a diet too low in calories for the work being done. [12]

Heavily exercising girls and women must eat more if they wish to reduce the possibility of the female athlete triad becoming a problem.

Osteoporosis

Osteoporosis is almost certain to occur when amenorrhea occurs. Some young female athletes have been found to have bone densities similar to 70- and 80-year-old women. Some of the bone loss may be irreversible. The loss of the bone material puts the athlete at increased risk of broken bones. Stress fractures are more easily developed as are fractures of the pelvis, hip and spine.

In a preliminary study done by the British Olympic Medical Center, a group of 34 female long-distance runners whose athletic activity was considered to be the cause of abnormal menstruation or a lack of menstruation (amenorrhea) were tested for bone density. They were divided into three treatment groups: one receiving calcium supplements, one receiving calcium supplements (1000mg/day) and hormone replacement therapy, and one group receiving nothing. In some of the athletes, menstruation returned to normal. Of those who regained normal menstruation there was an increase in hip and lower back

Degrees of Amenorrhea
• Primary amenorrhea means not having had a menstrual period by the time she is 16 years old.
• Secondary amenorrhea means the stopping of menstrual periods once a girl or woman has begun menstruating. No periods for 3-6 consecutive months.
• Oligomenorrhea means a very long time between menstrual flows with a total cycle of 35-90 days.

bone mineral density of about 4% during the first year. Of those who did not regain their menses, there was a loss of bone density of about 6%. The investigators are suggesting a much larger study to look at the problems and treatments for amenorrhea and osteoporosis. [13]

A Swedish study compared normally menstruating and non-menstruating long-distance runners and another group of eumenorrheic (normally menstruating) soccer players. Generally, each group ate similarly, but no group took in an adequate amount of food for energy. Still, body weight, body mass index and percent of body fat were all lower for the amenorrheic group. Body weight was the major predictor of osteoporosis. [14]

Assuming that your diet is adequate, bone density can be increased by weight training. When the bones are subjected to stress, they become stronger. This is particularly important to women who swim because swimming does not stress the bones since the water supports the body. While runners get some help from their weight bearing activities, swimmers do not. It is, therefore, even more important to use resistance exercises in the gym or at home. (See Chapters 8 and 9 on weight training.) However, female athletes often show lower than expected bone density even though they exercise. This seems to relate to the lack of estrogen and its relation to amenorrhea.

In one study it was found that female runners who ran more miles per week had more fractures. The unanswered question, however, was whether these resulted from bone loss or from overtraining and overstressing the bones through the constant pounding on the ground.

Another study found that female rowers who did not menstruate had only 9% less bone density than did the other rowers who were menstruating regularly. While 9% sounds like a lot, it was less than expected. It is possible that the stress on the bones from rowing had a strengthening effect which somewhat counteracted the negative effects of the lack of menstruation.

Reduced Immunity

The immune system can be affected by overtraining. Colds and other minor infections can be more common. This may be because of a reduction of glutamine — one of the non-essential amino acids. Glutamine is an essential fuel for the cells of the immune system. While it is normally released by the body's muscles, its release is reduced by endurance exercise.

Another factor which may be related to the reduction of the immune factors is that cortisol is released. This is a hormone released when the body is stressed. This reduces several types of white blood cells which are disease fighters. After three hours of running, the cortisol level is doubled or tripled, and it stays elevated for about 12 hours. (However, 45 minutes of running

To reduce your chances of becoming ill:
• Make certain that you get enough sleep. • Get enough food, particularly carbohydrates and vitamin C. • Have annual flu shots. • Make certain that you are not losing weight. • Do not inoculate yourself with harmful bacteria or viruses.

does not cause a reduction of the white cells.)

The cancer-killing cells in the body are reduced by as much as 50% as we age. This is a major reason for the increase in cancers later in life. Endurance sports such as marathon running reduce these. However, and more importantly, the positive effect of the running increases these cells for long distance runners when they are resting or running less than 10 miles a day.

In a study done at a recent Los Angeles Marathon, it was found that among those who ran the race, 14% soon developed upper respiratory infections. Among those who signed up for the race but did not race, only 2% developed such problems. We can assume that both were somewhat similarly trained but that the actual running of the marathon reduced the immune factors. [15] The increase in infections seems to occur to people running more than 60 miles a week. This would be approximately equivalent to swimming 15 miles a week or cycling 150 miles a week.

Self-inoculation is a common method of developing a cold or other infection. We all carry some pathogens (germs). Infected people carry more than normal. Often these are found in the mucus membrane areas such as the nose and mouth. If a person with an infection touches his or her nose or mouth then touches something with that germ carrying hand, many germs are left there ready for the next person to come along and get them on her hands then touch her nose or mouth and develop an infection. The most common cites for this to happen are on door handles and sink faucets.

We are indebted to Dr. Barbara Drinkwater of the Pacific Medical Center in Seattle, Washington, and the former president of the American College of Sports Medicine, for her input on this section. She is the leading authority in the world on the Female Triad.

Notes:

1. Russell Pate, symposium on elite athletes, Pre-Olympic Scientific Congress at Dallas Texas, July 11, 1996.

2. H. Kuipers, "How Much is too Much? Performance Aspects of Overtraining," Pre-Olympic Scientific Congress, Dallas, Texas, July 13, 1996.

3. A.L. Uusitalo et al., "Hormonal Responses to Endurance Training and Overtraining in Female Athletes," *Clinical Journal of Sports Medicine* 8.3 (1998): 178-186.

4. P.J. O'Connor et al., "Mood State and Salivary Cortisol Levels Following Overtraining in Female Swimmers," *Psychoneuroendocrinology* 14.4 (1989): 303-310.

5. U. Hartmann and J. Mester, "Training and Overtraining Markers in Selected Sport Events," *Medicine & Sport in Science & Exercise*. 32.1 (2000): 209-215.

6. H. Tanaka et al., "Changes in Plasma Tryptophan/Branched Chain Amino Acid Ratio in Responses to Training Volume Variation," Internation Journal of Sports Medicine 18.4 (1997): 270-275.

7. Aurelia Nattiv, Barbara Drinkwater et al., "The Female Athletic Triad," *Clinics in Sports Medicine: The Athletic Woman* 13.2 (1994): 405-418.

8. M.A. Balaa and D.A. Drossman, *Anorexia Nervosa and Bulimia: The Eating Disorders, Disease of the Month*, (Chicago: Year Book Medical Publishers, 1985) 1-52.

9. Eleanor Whitney and Eva Hamilton, *Understanding Nutrition*, (St. Paul, MN: West Publishing, 1987) 281.

10. L. Smolak, S.K. Murnen and A.E. Ruble, "Female Athletes and Eating Problems: A Meta-Analysis," *International Journal of Eating Disorders* 27.4 (2000): 371-380.

11. C. Johnson, P.S. Powers and R. Dick, "Athletes and Eating Disorders: The National Collegiate Athletic Association Study," *International Journal of Eating Disorders* 26.2 (1999):179-188.

12. A. Loucks, symposium on elite athletes, Pre-Olympic Scientific Congress, Dallas, TX. July 11, 1996.

13. J.H. Gibson et al., "Treatment of Reduced Bone Mineral Density in Athletic Amenorrhea: a Pilot Study," *Osteoporosis International* 10.4 (1999): 284-289.

14. U. Pettersson et al, "Low Bone Mass Density at Multiple Skeletal Sites, Including the Appendicular Skeleton in Amenorrheic Runners," *Calcif Tissue Int* 64.2 (1999): 117-125b.

15. David Neiman, symposium on elite athletes, Pre-Olympic Scientific Congress, Dallas Texas, July 11, 1996.

13

Flexibilty, Stretching, Warm Up and Posture

———

Flexibility is generally defined as the range of motion of a joint. It is related to the length of various connective tissues in the joints, such as the ligaments and tendons. Every athlete needs a certain amount of flexibility. But excessive flexibility may set us up for injuries. The amount of flexibility you need depends on your activity; ballet dancers, gymnasts and hurdlers need more flexibility than distance runners or swimmers.

Flexibility results when a person stretches connective tissue: ligaments (which hold bone to bone), tendons (which hold muscle to bone), fascia, and small pieces of connective tissue that hold the muscle fibers together.

Connective tissue shrinks somewhat if it is not stretched occasionally. We often feel a tightness in our back or a lesser ability to touch our toes as we age. But shrunken or tightened connective tissue can be stretched relatively easily, and normal flexibility can usually be regained within a few weeks time if the proper stretching exercises are done daily. Of course, it is best to stay flexible all of our lives.

Acute and chronic changes in flexibility are likely to occur with stretching exercises, but it is how flexibility is measured that gives us different results. Flexibility can be measured three ways:

1) Static range of motion — a simple measurement of how many degrees a person can move a joint before it becomes uncomfortable. This is the typical measure we use.

2) Dynamic-passive — a relaxed muscle being stretched by a partner or therapist.

3) Dynamic-active — a muscle being stretched actively by the subject.

The latter two types of stretches are useful in determining whether a muscle is stiff or compliant (see Chapter 3). Once stretched the change in flexibility or the loss of muscle stiffness can be temporary or longer term. However, it is difficult to distinguish between changes in stretch tolerance (the amount of stretching ability due to the connective tissues and muscles) as opposed to changes in muscle stiffness.

While stretching has been shown to assist in healing some injuries, in aiding posture, and in some warm up exercises, the research on stretching is not as complete as we would like. In fact, there are few scientific papers on it. For that reason in the following paragraphs you will see that one study may show one thing while another contradicts it. But by understanding that all of the facts are not yet in, you may be able to appreciate that there is a great deal more to learn about this type of exercise. In fact, although most of us have stretched for years and stretched our teams both before and after practice, there is no scientifically based prescription for flexibility training and no conclusive statements can be made about the relationship of flexibility to athletic injury. The literature reports opposing findings from different samples, frequently does not distinguish between strain, sprain and overuse injury, and rarely tells us how intense the exercise was that the athlete performed.[1]

Do You Need Additional Flexibility?

If your posture is poor or you cannot execute the movement required for your sport because of being too tight, you probably need additional flexibility. If you are active in sports or dance there is a chance that you can be more flexible in order to make your movements easier as well as to avoid injury by moving a joint past its normal range of motion, thus damaging ligaments or tendons. If you cannot make the required movement for your sport because your joints are too tight stretching for flexibility should help.

We have talked about muscle stiffness as generally being positive for athletes. However, if the muscles are too stiff they will resist the normal eccentric action involved in most athletic events and the muscle fibers can be damaged when they are forced to contract while stretching. Landing from a jump or a running stride are examples. If you have tight calf muscles, quadriceps or hamstrings, even when they are not contracting you may have problems in both the efficiency of your movements and the potential for injury. An abnormal stiffness in the muscles is called passive muscle stiffness because the muscles are extra tight even when not contracting. The muscles may be extended and relaxed after a number of stretching sessions. One stretching session won't do it.[2]

Typically, specific flexibility needs and patterns are associated with specific sports and even positions within sports. The relationship of flexibility to athletic performance is likely to be sport-dependent — more flexibility

147

needed for one sport and more muscle stiffness and reduced flexibility for another. Decreased flexibility has been associated with increased efficiency in straight ahead running and walking. Increased muscle stiffness may be associated with increased isometric and concentric force generation. And where the stretch-shortening (plyometric) action is part of the sport (such as in sprinting, repeated volleyball or basketball rebounding jumps, gymnastic tumbling or slalom skiing), increased muscle stiffness is desirable and excessive ligament and tendon flexibility is undesirable.

A Japanese study found that when comparing performances in a vertical jump in which the person crouched, waited, then jumped with a counter-movement jump, the stiffness of a quadriceps tendon was not important when the subjects did the normal squat jump. But when they did the more plyometric countermovement jump, tendon stiffness was very important. The stiffness of tendon structures has a favorable effect on stretch-shortening cycle exercise, possibly due to adequate storage and recoil of elastic energy.[3] This may mean that when your sport uses countermovement, flexibility may not be desirable. This would be particularly true for spikers and blockers in volleyball and rebounders in basketball. It might also be important for sprinters and for gymnasts in vaulting and tumbling.

When Is the Best Time to Stretch?

It is always more effective to stretch after you have done some full-body warm-ups such as jogging or jumping jacks. Stretching before an activity is done to get your muscles and connective tissue ready to be active. Recent research, however, indicates that stretching prior to activity may increase the risk of muscular injury and may reduce effective strength and power. Most of the work has been done with distance runners but some has been done on weight lifters and swimmers.

If you are attempting to increase your general flexibility, it is better to stretch after you have warmed up or after your workout because the connective tissue is more likely to be accommodating to the stretch and you can move the joints through a greater range of motion. This allows them to be stretched farther, then while the stretch is still in progress the muscles may be cooled. This seems to allow the full stretch to be accommodated or "set," and is more effective in holding the gain in flexibility.

The stretching should be done immediately after the muscles have reached their higher temperatures because they cool rather quickly. If the muscles are warmed 5 degrees Celsius (about 8 degrees Fahrenheit) stretching is maximally effective for only three minutes.[4] But not all research shows that a warm up stretching is essential.[5]

How Can You Stretch Most Effectively?

Stretching exercises can be done very slowly then holding the stretch (static stretch) or while moving (ballistic or dynamic). Moving stretches should never be done with jerky movements. Also, there is a danger of damaging the connective tissues or the muscle fibers, so ballistic exercises should not be done for muscles that have been injured. If you are doing ballistic exercises you would slowly bounce at the end of the stretch. Use a seated toe touch for an example. After doing a static stretch you would bring your hands back several inches from your toes then do a series of bouncing toe touches attempting to go farther downward with each bounce. But don't bounce too hard.

For a sport-specific ballistic stretch, you would merely move through the action you need in your sport. A tennis player may swing through a forehand or backhand action slowly then faster as part of a warm up. A golfer would swing slowly and with a shorter backswing then increase the arc and the speed of the swing. A runner may run with the knees lifted very high in an exaggerated movement. A softball player may swing the bat slowly then faster.

Properly done, the proprioceptive neuromuscular facilitation (PNF) exercises are often found to be the most effective. (Proprioceptive neuromuscular facilitation literally means "helping your muscles and nerves." "Proprioceptive" means being able to sense yourself. "Neuromuscular" means the nerves and the muscles. And "facilitation" means making it easier.) In this type of exercise you move the body part to be stretched as far as possible then you contract the muscles opposite the stretched side of the joint which helps you to stretch farther. For example, if you were doing a sitting toe touch, you would contract your abdominal muscles and quadriceps to allow you to stretch farther. If you were attempting to stretch the upper chest muscles, you would pull back hard with your upper back muscles.

The theory behind PNF is that by contracting the muscle opposite the one that is being stretched, you will reduce the stretch reflex in that stretched muscle. As you know, a stretched muscle is more ready to react and shorten thereby fighting the stretch. (Remember the doctor hitting you below the knee cap and having your stretched quadriceps muscle fight back and kick out your lower leg? This indicates that a stretched muscle is more ready to contract than is a relaxed muscle.) The muscle that you are contracting is called the agonist. The opposite muscle, in this case the muscle you are stretching, is called the antagonist.

A partner may be used to help you. The partner would push to help you stretch farther as you are stretching and contracting the opposite muscles.

This helps the person stretching achieve a greater amount of stretch, but the partner must not stretch the joint too far or tissue damage may result. Consequently, this technique should be done by experts or supervised by experts. Not all studies have found that PNF is better. There is nothing wrong with pure "static" stretching, [6] so if you are not being supervised just stick to the simple static stretches to get maximal results without the possibility of injury.

If you are attempting to increase your range of motion, the stretch should be held in a position where there is some pain. If you are merely warming up for an activity, it seems to be enough to stretch almost to the point of pain, but then contract the muscle which you had stretched. If you are getting ready for an activity that would use your upper chest muscles (throwing, serving a volleyball or tennis ball, doing a bench press, or any activity that involves pushing away from your body) you could stretch by pulling your elbows back as far as possible at your shoulder level. Then you could bring your hands forward and push them against each other.

Holding a stretch for 30 seconds seems to give the maximum benefits for the exercise. Some studies indicate that if this is followed by a ballistic motion, the stretch would be more effective. If you did a sitting toe touch for 30 seconds, then did a little faster stretch moving your hands from about midway up your shin bone to below your toes, your total flexibility might be increased.

Which Stretching Exercise Should You Use?

While hundreds of stretches have been developed, the intelligent method of stretching for sport specific flexibility is to do the exact movement needed in the sport. As examples, after warming up the muscles and joints to be stretched:

- Golf — Take the address position then pull the club back. When you reach the point of resistance have a partner assist in the stretch by applying pressure to your hands. Hold for 30 seconds. Then move to the exact follow through position that you want and have your partner push on your hands to increase your range of motion.
- Butterfly Swimming — Bend forward then move slowly through the full butterfly motion, emphasizing the recovery. A partner can assist in stretching and moving the arms through the high over water recovery.
- Pike Position in Diving, Gymnastics or Long Jumping — From a sitting position stretch forward then, with your arms grasping the backs of the knees, pull the shoulders toward the thighs.

- Ankle Plantar Flexion (for divers, gymnasts, ballet dancers, soccer goalkeepers for punting) — While sitting with the legs straight out in front, use the calf muscle to point the toes downward. Apply pressure (yourself or a partner) to the top of the foot by pushing it toward the floor.

Whatever range of motion you need for your sport can be similarly imitated. Just remember that a range of motion increase in a joint where you don't need the extra flexibility can set you up for an injury. More flexible joints are more likely to be injured. Flexibility just for the sake of flexibility is not a good idea.

Additionally, the flexibility you need for your sport should be developed outside the sport season. The same cautions about stretching as a part of the warm up apply here. Stretching will stretch the muscle fibers as well as the connective tissue. The stretched fibers are more likely to be injured. If you stretch for flexibility months before your sport season begins, your muscles will have time to heal and the stretched ligaments and fascia that were limiting your flexibility will stay stretched for the sport season.

Safety Concerns

There are a few safety concerns in stretching. It is best to keep the connective tissue in the abdominal area tight. Therefore, back hyperextensions are not recommended. Many are also concerned that the ligaments in the back of the neck can be too easily stretched. That is the reason that abdominal curl ups are now done with the neck straight and the eyes looking at the ceiling instead of with the head forward. A third major area of concern is overstretching the knee. In exercises such as the deep-knee bend or the hurler's exercise there is an excessive stretching of the connective tissues in the front of the knee, a crushing of the cartilage (meniscus) in the back of the knee joint and some stretching of the tissues on the sides, particularly the inside, of the joint. Because women have many more knee ligament injuries than men, women should be particularly careful about stretching exercises which could stretch the knee ligaments. With these points in mind here are some exercises which are questionable or contraindicated.

1. Back bend or back hyperextension
2. Deep knee bend
3. Hurdler's exercise (with toes out or in) excessive flexion of the knee
4. Standing toe touch
5. Trunk twists with a barbell
6. Shoulder stand or plow

The back bend (standing and bending backward) not only stretches the abdominal connective tissue, which is not desired, but it crushes the rear of the spinal discs as the vertebral column bends back. It also reduces the stability of the vertebral column by stretching the ligaments in the front of the spine. It is an exercise done by many dancers and gymnasts, but is not needed by the general population.

The deep knee bend stretches the ligaments in the front of the knee and crushes the cartilage in the rear of the knee. If the knee bend is less than 90 degrees there is no problem but past that point there may be damage. Further damage can result when the calf muscle contacts the rear of the thigh. At this point a lever action is created that intensifies the stretching and crushing. Only Olympic-style weight lifters need this type of stretch.

Figure 13-1

The hurdler's stretch is done by extending one leg forward and putting the other leg to the side. The sideward leg can lie next to the extended leg or be abducted to the side to approach the actual body position of a hurdler. The exercise is often used to stretch the quadriceps, especially if the person lays the torso backward. The greatest danger is when the leg to the side is next to the body. It causes the same kinds of problems as does the deep knee bend. Hurdlers do this exercise with the thigh that is at the side at a 90-degree angle to the outstretched leg. This would be one way of stretching the ligaments that restrict their hip abduction. Dancers or gymnasts might also do it. However, there are usually better abduction flexibility exercises (see figure 13-1).

The standing toe touch (see figure 13-2) generally does not stretch the back and hamstrings as much as does a sitting toe touch because the hamstring muscles in the back of the thigh fight the stretch because of the stretch reflex. Also, if it is done using a bounce, tissue can be overstretched. The tissues are better stretched from a sitting position in which the abdominals and quadriceps pull the body forward and the muscles of the back and hamstrings are relaxed because of the reciprocal enervation. (The stretched muscles relax because the nervous system does not want them to fight the contraction of the other muscles.)

The trunk twist with a barbell (see figure 13-3)or a twist done too rapidly can tear connective tissues or muscles because of the inertia caused by the excess force. Trunk twists should be done slowly and never with a bar-

Figure 13-2

Figure 13-3

bell. The barbell does nothing but compress spinal disks. It doesn't aid in stretching.

The shoulder stand or plow or any exercise that flexes the neck forward is not recommended. In a shoulder stand, the neck is bent 90 degrees in order to make a base of support with the shoulders. In the plow, the legs are allowed to come to the floor on the same side of the body as the head (flexion of hip).

Posture

While in some physical activities such as ballet or gymnastics, posture is extremely important, most of us would like to have an attractive and functional posture.

One of the chief causes of poor posture is tight connective tissue in the front of the body. When the tissue in the front of the shoulders is allowed to shrink, it pulls the shoulders forward resulting in round shoulders. When the tissue that connects the front of the lower hips to the front of the thigh is allowed to shorten, it pulls the hips forward and a pot belly develops. We do so much sitting that our hips are in a flexed position so the connective tissue in the front of the hip is allowed to shorten because of not being used.

Two flexibility exercises that help to prevent poor posture or assist in regaining good posture are the chest stretcher and the lower hip stretcher.

The exercise that best stretches the front of the shoulders is done by pulling the shoulders and arms back as far as they can go in a slow stretch. This not only stretches the front of the shoulder area but also strengthens the upper back which will aid in helping to pull the shoulders back (see figure 13-4).

The exercise that best stretches the front of the lower hip area is done by

Figure 13-4

taking a normal stride forward, tightening the abdominal muscles (so that they will not be stretched) then pushing the hips forward until the stretch is felt in the front of the lower hips.

Good posture requires not only the flexibility to allow the shoulders and hips to be able to assume the proper alignment, but also the strength to hold that alignment. The major muscle groups that hold one in a good posture are: the gluteal muscles of the buttocks, which pull down on the back of the hips, in turn raising the front of the hips; the abdominal muscles, which pull up on the front of the hips; the lower back muscles, which pull down on the rib cage, raising the chest; and the upper back muscles which hold the shoulders back.

The best exercise to strengthen the abdominal muscles is the curl-up. The trunk is curled forward as far as possible without letting the top of hips rise from the floor. Keeping the hips on the floor and the knees bent makes it nearly impossible to use the muscles in the lower hip area. These are the muscles that tend to pull the hips forward, giving one a pot belly and a sway back. Put your hands on your chest, look up at the ceiling, and curl forward. This exercise should be done 50 times or more each day. If you can't do the exercise, grab the back of your thighs with your hands and pull yourself up. In this way your biceps will aid you in doing the curl up.

The exercise that strengthens all of the back muscles is the back extension. Lie on the floor face down. Raise the shoulders and legs upward about 4 inches, then relax. This should also be done 10 to 50 times. This may be the most important exercise you can do. Since the lower back muscles are the most often injured, it behooves us to keep them as strong as possible to minimize the chance of injury. This exercise will strengthen the muscles that hold your shoulders back, your lower back and your gluteals. If you have access to a gym, using a Roman chair or other back machine will be more effective because you can move the muscles through a greater range of movement before your back begins to hyperextend.

Think tall for better posture. Stand tall, walk tall, sit tall. When you stretch upward to be as tall as possible, all of the right things happen. The abdominal and lower back muscles tighten. The chest is raised while the abdomen is flattened. However, if your shoulders are rounded or your head is held forward, "standing tall" will not change these. When you stand tall, the shoulders are rotated backward so that gravity and the large chest muscles

Types of Stretches
—Static stretch occurs when you hold the position.
—Ballistic stretch is a stretch done moving.
—Active stretch occurs when you supply the power for the stretching.
—Passive stretch occurs when you are relaxed and another person or a device aids you in stretching.

do not exert as much forward pull on them. This makes it easier to hold them back.

General Flexibility Exercises

Three areas of the body are important for general flexibility: the upper chest stretch (shown above), a lower back and hamstring stretch, and a calf (gastrocnemius) stretch. However, there are many stretches that can be used if different parts of the body need additional flexibility.

The best exercise for trunk flexibility is done standing with the legs spread 14 to 18 inches apart. Reach up with the left arm and twist your body as far as it will go to the right. Push with the shoulder to accentuate the twisting action. The stretch is very good for the lower back and may be felt in the knees or ankles, if done correctly. Then do the twist with your right arm raised and twisting to the left.

The best exercise for stretching the lower back and the back of the thighs is done in a sitting position. Reach down as far as possible. This exercise is more effective when sitting than when standing because the back of the thighs are relaxed when sitting (see figure 13-5). When standing, they are under tension so they resist the stretch. Another low back stretch is done by rolling into a ball (see 13-6).

Stretching the calf muscle is done standing. With your right foot on the floor, take a long step forward with your left leg. Bring your hips forward until you feel a stretch in the back of your lower leg and heel. If you take a

Figure 13-5

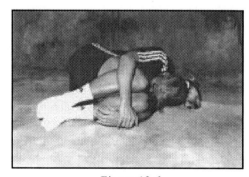

Figure 13-6

Figure 13-7

short stride, your rear foot should be flat on the ground. If you take a long stride, which will also stretch the tissue in the front of the hip, the heel may leave the ground (see figure 13-7).

If you wish to stretch your upper back and triceps, you can pull one arm across the body. While not necessarily required for general flexibility, these stretches may be helpful for swimming, volleyball and other sports.

Stretching as Part of Your Warm Up

Scientific evidence indicates that the traditional stretching exercises used for warm up for many years may actually be harmful. An effective warm up procedure is covered in Chapter 16.

Stretching to Prevent Injury or to Aid in Recovery

Some sports injuries are the result of a sudden trauma. Others occur because the tissues are overused over a long period of time. To reduce the chances for sudden injury, one would need to stretch then contract the muscle. A few years ago 11 members of the Dallas Cowboys football team sustained serious hamstring pulls. The next year an exercise was begun in which a player on his back would lift one leg as far as possible. His partner would then attempt to gently push it a bit farther. (This would be the PNF type of stretch explained earlier.) Then the partner would resist the leg as it was returned to the ground. This then allowed the muscle to contract while being resisted. This was done several times with each leg each day. That year only one Cowboy suffered a hamstring pull. It is difficult to determine whether it was the PNF stretch or the muscular contraction or both which contributed to the injury reductions.

Overuse injuries are quite common in sports where there is a long term continuous strain on part of the body. For example, tennis players can have elbow problems, and runners have foot, thigh and leg problems. Stretching to increase one's range of motion may reduce some of these problems.

One problem that often affects runners is an excess of muscle tension in the hamstrings and calf muscles. This excess tension is called contractures. Often the problem can be corrected with effective stretching of the affected part.

Lower back pain afflicts nearly 7 million people. It is often a result of poor posture, but can also be caused by muscle strain, mental stress, poor sleeping habits and other causes. Often it can be relieved or cured by the proper lower back stretches recommended earlier in the chapter.

Hammer toes is a condition in which the toes curl under. If surgery isn't required, the toes can be stretched upward with the hands.

Plantar fascitis is an inflammation of the tendons which extend forward from the heel bone under the foot. Stretching the toes and the Achilles tendon are highly recommended for relieving the pain and preventing a reoccurrence. A cure often takes six months to a year and is speeded by a proper orthotic shoe insert.

Shin splints may be relieved by pushing downward on the top of the foot to stretch the tissues in the front of the lower leg.

Notes:
1. G.W. Gleim and M.P. McHugh, "Flexibility and Its Effects on Sports Injury and Performance," *Sports Medicine [New Zealand]* 24.5 (1997): 289-299.
2. J.P. Halbertsma, A.I. van Bolhuis and L.N. Goeken, "Sport Stretching: Effect on Passive Muscle Stiffness of Short Hamstrings," *Arch Phys Med Rehab* 77.4 (1996): 688-692.
3. K. Kubo, Y. Kawakami and T. Fukunaga, "Influence of Elastic Properties of Tendon Structures on Jump Performance in Humans," *Journal of Applied Physiology* 87.6 (1999): 2090-2096.
4. D.W. Draper and M.D. Ricard, "Rate of Temperature Decay in Human Muscle Following 3 Mhz Ultrasound: The Stretching Window Revealed," *Journal of Athletic Training* 30.4 (1995) 304-307.
5. W.L. Cornelius et al., "The Effect of Warm Up on Acute Hip Joint Flexibility Using a Modified PNF Stretching Technique," *Journal of Athletic Training* 27.2 (1992): 112-114.
6. W.L.Cornelius et al., "The Effects of Cold Application and Modified PNF Stretching on Hip Joint Flexibility in College Males," *Research Quarterly for Exercise and Sport* 63.3 (1992): 311-314.

14

Developing Speed

*M*any people want to be able to run faster, whether to improve sports performance, to have a better kick when finishing a distance race, or to compete in a sprinting event. While your genes play a major role in your ability to run fast, there are ways to train that can significantly improve your running speed. Not everyone has the speed to be a sprinter, but everyone can run a little faster with the proper form and training. If running faster is one of your goals, read on!

Sprinting

Sprinting is a matter of mechanical efficiency and transmitting nerve impulses from the brain to the muscles involved. One important factor in a good running style is the optimal combination of stride frequency and stride length. Both increase as we run faster, with stride length increasing more than frequency.

To be able to enhance good sprint performance, you have to develop a combination of physical, physiological and psychological skills. Your speed depends on a combination of the following skills and attitudes:

- reaction time (the speed with which the brain can transmit impulses to the muscles)
- acceleration ability
- maximum running velocity
- running technique and coordination skill
- curve running technique
- maximal power
- elastic strength/explosive power
- anaerobic capacity
- aerobic capacity
- flexibility/mobility
- mental strength
- will power
- goal setting

Several variables can contribute to stride length and frequency of strides, including leg length, muscle strength, quickness of reflexes, distance of the run, and how tired the runner is. The more skilled the runner is, the more precise the relationship between optimal stride length and frequency. Because the skills needed and their coordination are rather complex, this chapter will be a bit technical.

The main objective for a good sprinter is to develop the greatest possible velocity in a race. That running velocity is a product of stride frequency and the stride length. The aim of a good sprinter is to optimize the relationship between those parameters. In a 100-meter sprint, sprinters on a national level use between 45 and 55 strides and the average stride frequency is 4.5-5.5 strides per second. In the 200 and 400 meter events, the stride length is a little shorter and the frequency is slower.

Your Body's Energy

You get your energy from the oxygen you breathe and the food you eat, but there are also some body chemicals involved in your energy production. At the beginning of an activity, your energy comes from anaerobic sources — sources in which oxygen is not a factor. But within seconds oxygen becomes a factor, and your energy is primarily aerobic. While in sprinting 100 yards, 80% of your energy will come from anaerobic sources. The longer the workout or race, the more comes from the oxygen you breathe. (This was more fully discussed in Chapter 11.)

The energy needed to run the 100 meters is 8%-20% aerobic and 80%-92% anaerobic. In the 200 meters the ratio is 20%-30% aerobic and 70%-80% anaerobic, and in the 400 meters it is about 25%-40% aerobic and 60%-75% anaerobic. Research results vary somewhat, so the calculations of energy from aerobic and anaerobic sources are not exact.

Running Technique

Running is a fundamental skill and differs from other skills in that the movement pattern is designed to be continuous, without interruption. We move one foot in front of the other, with the arms on each side moving synchronously with the opposite leg.

The goal of motor learning is to develop the ability to perform without thinking about it. Frequent practice of a complex skill (in this case the short sprints) helps make the movements automatic.

Good running performance depends primarily on an economic running technique. Many runners find their own way to move according to specific developed skills and the inner feelings for the running movement. Some people, however, do not have the natural ability to coordinate neuromuscular activity. In that case the sprinting movement becomes very uneconomical. These people have to learn the sprinting technique from the scratch.

From a mechanical point of view, it is possible to characterize the ideal running technique. But ordinary men and women are not robots so there has to be some individual variations according to the differences in body types, physical abilities and neuromuscular functioning.

Biomechanical Principles of Sprinting

In running, muscular activity produces force. In the short sprints, this force can start, accelerate and decelerate in running straight forward, as in the 100 meters. An additional skill is required when running a curve, as in the 200 and 400 meter distances. In each stride the sprinter will have a slight loss of velocity in the airborne or flight phase. This loss of velocity has to be compensated for by the force production of the supporting leg at the push-off.

In order to optimize the movement pattern in sprinting, the linear and the angular motion need to be integrated. This means that the specific sprinting movements in the various planes need to be complementary and coordinated.

The body has three axes of rotation: frontal, sagittal and transverse. The frontal plane rotation represents inversion and eversion (the downward or upward movement of the long arch in the bottom of the foot). The sagittal plane rotation is found in plantar and dorsal flexion (the toe of the foot moving away from the knee or toward the knee). The transverse plane rotation represents abduction and adduction (the moving outward or inward of the hip joint).

If we take a close look at the different movements in a sprint running stride we will see that the legs are extending backward from the time the foot lands until it pushes off the ground at the end of the stride. (Technically the landing of the foot is called the "front support" phase of the stride, which then becomes the "back support" phase as the hips extend.) After the push off the leg enters the "swing phase" of the stride. Here the hip flexes (moves the thigh forward) and the knee flexes (bringing the foot closer to the hips). While the swing phase is happening, the other leg is in its extension or power phase, pushing backward. As the legs are going forward and back, adjustments are being made by the hips and back. The hips move up and down thereby forcing the thighs to be abducted and adducted (moving slightly out and in as they extend backward) and the spine is rotating and flexing to each side as each stride is taken.

In the sprinting stride, the action against the ground in the landing will create a reaction from the surface that generates a force equal to the impact force, that gives the sprinter a forward and upward direction opposite to that impact.

In order to accelerate the body, you must push hard against the ground to develop an optimal reaction force-power or speed. The magnitude of the normal force depends on the force with which a sprinter presses against the ground and to what extent she activates hip, knee and ankle extensors as the leg straightens and pushes backward. If a person weighs 154 pounds, the reaction force exerted on the body by the ground while sprinting, will be approximately 700 Newtons (the force needed to push one kilogram forward at one meter per second). When landing in a sprinting stride, the force on the ground can be as much as 3-4 times the runner's weight.

When the sprinter swings the arms, the normal force is also changed. Arm movements serve to alternately increase and decrease the body's force on the ground. The actions of the arms also create forces that act on the rest of the body, such as in creating a rotation of the spine.

We can divide the reaction force into horizontal and vertical components. The horizontal component generates the force which moves the body forward while the vertical force moves the center of gravity (in the middle of the hips) up and down. If you are starting from the blocks, as in a track meet, the ability to gain velocity quickly is critical to your success in the race. In order to obtain an optimal reaction force, you have to push hard against the ground. This is called the resultant force. That resultant force is distributed into both horizontal and vertical forces. The horizontal force to get you moving forward is critical. If you get too much vertical force you will stand up too quickly. Our ability to run fast in the short sprints depends in part on the force we can generate backward with our hip and ankle extensors and in part on the lever arrangement in the involved bones, muscles and joints.

In the body the bones form the lever arms and the joints are the axes around which the bones move. When the muscles used in the sprinting action generate tension and exert force, one end of the bone will move more than the other. In principle, the longer the length of the lever, the greater the potential linear velocity (speed) at its end. In sprinting, however, this principle is utilized in the opposite way. In the swing phase, the knee of the recovery leg and arms are bent in order to shorten these limb levers and bring them forward with less energy. If a sprinter has good leverage, he or she has a mechanical advantage for more economical running.

Technical Analysis of the Specific Sprint Stride

Let us define a running cycle as consisting of two strides — each leg striding once. The duration of a cycle is from the instant the right foot strikes the ground to the end of the take-off of the left foot. A stride is the movement of one leg from the landing and support phases until the push off is completed. During running, the support phase accounts for about 40 percent of the total cycle time and the airborne recovery phase takes about 60 percent of the time.

The Sequence of a Sprint Running Stride

I. Support Phase

1. Contact — The support phase begins by landing on the ball of the foot, with the foot slightly in front of the midline of the torso until the foot is directly under the torso, or center of gravity of the body. In the landing it is important to work on the following details:
   - While sprinting the body has to be in an upright position, when the foot lands. The hip is high with a small bend in the knee and ankle joint.
   - The placement of the foot on the ground should be high on the toes, near to the vertical line of the body's center of gravity.
   - The foreleg (shin bone) movement should be an active movement down and backward against the ground like a grabbing movement.
   - The knee on the opposite, recovering leg should be in a position near the landing knee.
   - The swings of the arms and legs should be relaxed.
2. Midsupport — This is the moment when the center of gravity of the body is directly over the foot.
3. Later Support and Take-off — The duration of this movement is from the midsupport until the full extension of the hip and ankle at take off. In the take-off it is important to work on the following details:
   - Contract the hip and leg extensors to get a strong push backward against the ground with the leg.
   - The hip muscles should start the extension followed by the knee and ankle joints.
   - Fully extend from the hip.
   - Full extension in the knee and ankle joints is not necessary; the knee will stay slightly flexed.
   - Keep the body in an upright position with the hip in a high and forward rotated position.
   - The arm opposite to the landing leg needs to have an active but relaxed swing in order to keep the body balanced and to add force to the leg drive. (One of the body's reflexes is called the

cross extensor reflex. The arm on one side of the body moves with the leg on the other side. The arm can assist the leg with speed and power movements through this reflex action.)

- Drive the opposite arm backward in a controlled way with the elbow leading the action.
- Look forward and relax the neck and cheek muscles when you are pushing your arms.

II. Airborne Recovery Phase

1. Follow-through – This is the phase from the time the rear foot leaves the ground until the bent knee passes the vertical line of the body's center of gravity in the middle of the hips.
2. Forward Swing — The forward swing starts from the time the thigh is vertical to the ground and continues with a natural knee lift and forward movement of the thigh.
3. Foot Descent — The foot descent is the period beginning when the foot starts to move downward and backward toward the ground for the footstrike. In the airborne recovery phase it is important to concentrate on the following details:

   - The airborne phase is the relaxation period of the running stride — the important thing is to focus on loose, swinging movements with both arms and legs.
   - At the same time the body should be kept in an upright position with a slight forward lean.
   - Try to prevent a backward lean because the force of the push-off will move the body more upward than forward.
   - Be prepared for the leg action and foot strike in the coming support phase.

Conditioning for Sprinting

As has been noted, people who must sprint during their event (basketball, softball, soccer, tennis, field hockey, etc.) need strength and power in their push off, the speed to bring the recovering leg forward quickly, a strong abdominal muscle group to stabilize the hips, and strength and speed in other areas of the body, such as the shoulders and arms.

The leg and ankle power is developed by doing half squats, hip and leg extensions, and calf rises. (See Chapters 8 and 9 for the best exercises for these.) Sprinting short sprints (10-20 yards) from a standing or running start helps your overall speed. Running uphill fast will also increase your power. If no other exercises are done, just running uphill will increase your power by about 3% in 10 weeks. Repeats of 25- to 200-yard uphill runs are recommended. Plyometric work, such as bounding, will also develop your leg power.

Strengthening and speeding up the hip flexors can be done with the hip flexor and knee extensor exercises shown in the strength chapter. Sprinting downhill, a technique pioneered by Russian coaches, will help you to make the recovery quicker.

Strong abdominals are extremely important in sprinting. All abdominal exercises illustrated in Chapter 8 should be done, including curl-ups, side sit-ups, and twisting.

Plyometrics for Speed

An Australian study compared two types of drop jumps and the effects on the standing vertical jump and the running vertical jump. One group was a control group which did not train. A second group did 72-90 drop jumps (jumping from a box then springing as high as possible) per week emphasizing jumping high. The third group emphasized both getting off the ground quickly and jumping high. (The time on the ground was measured by a device in the floor.) Getting off the ground quickly is considered

Checklist — Sprinting
Posture
• run tall
• high hip position
• feel strong in upper body
• eyes should look straight ahead
• no downward rolling of the shoulders
Arms
• arms swing far behind, with the elbow as high as the shoulder
• on the forward swing, the hands will be shoulder high or higher
• hands held in a loose fist
• elbows brush the shirt as they swing by or they can be just wide of the shirt
Legs
• work for increased stride length through a strong push off, not by reaching forward.
• swing the thigh fully forward
• lift the knee high
• run high on toes
• have an active foot stike, aggressively "claw" the ground
• to make your strides quicker, imagine that you are running on hot bricks
• to keep your stride light, imagine running on eggs

Direct Performance Indicators for Sprinters

- High stride frequency and average stride length (45-55 strides per 100 meters at 4.5-5.5 strides per second)
- Short duration of the whole stride cycle (0.20 to 0.30 of a second)
- Short support time (ground contact of 0.8-0.12 sec)
- Large upper leg angle at take-off indicates a full powerful stride
- High upper leg velocity during the support phase of the other leg
- Active touch-down with a fast reverse velocity of foot (leg quickly moves from a forward to a backward action)
- Small "foot-to-body" touch-down distance
- Touch-down with the heel high
- Stiff supporting leg during the ground contact
- Knee joint slightly flexed at take-off, in contrast to hip and ankle joints that fully extend
- Small deviation of pelvis from the vertical
- Small body lean forward
- Short distance between knees at touch-down
- Center of gravity in hips during support phase
- No rotation of shoulder and hip axis
- No delay of return movement of arms
- No rotation of shoulders axis

---

a major objective in stretch shortening cycle work and in sprinting. The group that worked for quickness off the ground gained 20% in reaction strength over the other two groups. Scientifically this is very significant, however, no group increased their vertical jumping abilities significantly.[1] This again shows that specificity is essential in training. Despite the fact that coaches have long considered vertical jump ability to be essential to many sports, it does not seem to be a valid measure. While it definitely applies to volleyball and basketball, it doesn't apply to base running in softball or to sprint speed in soccer.

While isokinetic strength work (see Chapter 7) and plyometrics (see Chapter 10) are the most common types of exercises for speed increase, these approaches don't always work. For example, softball players were tested on speed of throw and on various isokinetic tests. One group worked isokinetically while another worked on plyometrics. The isokinetic group improved on all isokinetic tests. The plyometric group, which was tested on isokinetics but not given additional training in them, showed no change on their isokinetic strength. But neither group improved in speed of their softball throw.[2] This might indicate that traditional speed developing programs may not always work, but more research is needed.

Speed and Muscle Fiber Type

Sprint speed seems to be nearly totally dependant on the number of fast twitch fibers. In a study of 25 sprinters, with 100 meter times between 10.4 and 11.8, the percentage of fast twitch fibers was positively related to speed and negatively associated with endurance. The faster sprinters (average 10.7) had an average of 66% of fast twitch fibers, the slower spinters (average best time of 11.5) had 50.4% of their muscle fibers of the fast twitch type.[3] Additionally, those with more fast twitch fibers were significantly stronger and more powerful than those with more slow twitch fibers.

As noted earlier, endurance training can convert the fast type IIb muscle fibers to the slower IIa while pure sprint training can change the type IIa fibers to IIb.[4] But merely strength training may not make these same changes. One study followed nine elite weight lifters for two years. Despite their heavy resistance training, their percentage of fast twitch fibers did not change, in fact there was a non-significant small decrease from 57.1%-55.4%.[5]

Notes:

1. W.B. Young, G.J. Wilson and C. Byrne, "A Comparison of Drop Jump Training Methods: Effects on Leg Extensor Strength Qualities and Jumping Performance," *International Journal of Sports Medicine* 20.5 (1999): 295-303.
2. B.C. Heiderscheit, K.P. McLean and G.J. Davies, "The Effects of Isokinetic vs. Plyometric Training in the Shoulder Internal Rotators," *Journal of Orthopedics and Sports in Physical Therapy* 23 (1995): 125-133.
3. A. Mero et al., "Relationship Between the Maximal Running Velocity, Muscle Fiber Characteristics, Force Production and Force Relaxation in Sprinters," *Scandinavian Journal of Sports Science* 3 (1981): 16-22.
4. C.A. Allemeier et al, "Effects of Sprint Cycle Training on Human Skeletal Muscle," *Journal of Applied Physiology* 77.5 (1994): 2385-2390.
5. K. Hakkinen et al., "Neuromuscular and Hormonal Adaptations in Athletes to Strength Training in Two Years," *Journal of Applied Physiology* 65 (1988): 2406-2412.

15

Sport-Specific Strength and Power Exercises

As noted in the previous chapters, not many of the traditional multi-joint weight training exercises apply to multiple sports. Each athlete may profit some from general strength or flexibility exercises, but the time spent on nonsport-specific exercises may be largely wasted.

Here are some sport-specific ideas that you might want to use for your specific sport conditioning. A book could be written for each sport. Just remember the basic principles in developing your own exercises:

1. How much flexibility is needed for your sport?
2. What are the requirements for your sport: speed, power, pure aerobic endurance, speed endurance, continuous activity, start-stop activity, strength, etc.
3. What body position will you be in during your activity: standing, running, prone, supine, crouched, etc.

Develop your sport-specific exercises based on these requirements where possible. Here are a few ideas for a number of sports. They are suggested merely to give you an idea for making your sport-specific movement more effective when off the field or out of the pool.

Archery

The arm that holds the bow needs isometric strength in the total shoulder area as well as in the hand and wrist. A partner can help by applying pressure to your outstretched arm (see figure 15-1). First apply pressure from above so that your isometric force is upward, then from below so your isometric force is downward, then from inside so that your isometric force is inward, then from the outside so that your isometric force is outward. The same gains can be made by using weights or pulleys (see figure 15-2a and

167

Figure 15-1

b). To increase strength in your biceps and shoulder extensors, you can use a heavier bowstring pull or a high pulley in a gym (see figures 15-2a and b). This will help you draw the bowstring. In every exercise be certain that your hands are in the same position they would be if you were shooting.

Badminton

Wrist flexing power is necessary for the smash and the clear. Wrist curls will accomplish this. The back of the wrist, being weaker than the front, needs additional work. See wrist extension and hyperextension.

Quickness and speed can be attained by practicing a 2 or 3 step sprint to the right, left, front or back from the ready position.

Basketball

Basketball players most often utilize a two-legged jump for rebounds or jump shots and a one-legged jump on a driving shot. When practicing your jumps make them explosive as you would do in a game. Perhaps use a shuffle under the basket then practice jumping and reaching to the rim for the rebound. For the driving shot, take the two steps allowed before the lay-up then leap as high as possible. You can measure your progress by practicing near a wall and touching it. Some chalk on your finger will make it easier to see.

Figure 15-2a

Figure 15-2b

For jumping power, have a partner stand behind you and put her hands on your shoulders to give resistance when you jump. Once you have left the ground, she must take her hands off your shoulders so that your landing will be soft.

The clean action will increase the strength of the jumping muscles. Plyometric box jumping is perhaps the best exercise for explosive jumping power. Remember, however, that the recommendation is a total of only 30 plyometric repetitions twice a week. Both the one- and two-leg extensions are important so both one- and two-leg vertical jumps are recommended.

Your sideways shuffling on defense can be practiced for quickness by working side to side in the key and noting how many times you can go from one line to the other and back in 5 seconds.

To increase your two-handed passing strength, work on a sitting chest press machine. As you press the bar, keep your arms at the same distance apart and the same position as they would be in passing. Since your hands are open when passing, they should be open when pressing. Set the bar on your hand rather than your fingers for maximum pressing potential. Sometimes work with your 1 RM, but generally work for power by using only 40%-50% of your 1 RM working at top speed.

For rebounding you will want pulldowns from an overhead position. While most gyms will use a bar on the lat pulldown station, it is best to attach a medicine ball to the cable so that the exercise is really sport-specific. You can always grip the cable, however, so that your hands are in the same palms-facing-inward position as they would be in a rebound. Your hands should be basketball width apart.

For one-handed shooting strength, the best exercise is to have a partner stand behind you holding a rope. Place your hand in a shooting position, with the rope looped around your fingers (as close to the finger tips as possible). As your partner provides gentle resistance on the rope, perform the shooting action while standing on the floor. Don't perform a jump-shot action because the rope would pull you out of the shooting angle. If you have a hook shot, however, the same principle would apply.

Cycling

The best type of sport-specific cycling exercise is done on an exercise bike. Start with the tension very high, and reduce it as the cyclist tires. This is the reverse pyramid approach done with the primary idea of muscular and aerobic cardiovascular endurance.

For long events endurance is the key factor. Working the reverse pyramid but finishing with a much longer higher tension workout would be

169

effective. For short sprints, high-level reverse pyramid work is essential. The work is primarily anaerobic.

Dance

The amount of flexibility required depends on the type of dance (ballet, modern, jazz, etc). That flexibility should be gained early in the career of the dancer.

When leaping is important, one- and two-leg plyometrics jumps are necessary to develop maximum power. See basketball for more actions that also apply to dance.

Field Events
Long jump

While we would assume that one-leg plyometrics would be valuable for any runner or jumper, a study at the University of Iowa using eleven elite female long jumpers, indicated that it didn't help in gaining more height in the long jump. What was important was the degree of flexion at the knee and the length of the calf muscles along with the speed of the eccentric and concentric contractions. All of this might suggest that if plyometrics are to be used, they should utilize both maximum stretch and speed of the calf muscles and a degree of knee flexion that will give the maximum jump height.[1]

High jump

While back hyperextension is not a recommended exercise for the general public, it is essential for the high jumper. Hip flexibility for the lifting leg is also essential, as is the speed with which it can be lifted. To improve the flexibility of the lifted leg, put it forward and attempt to do the splits. For leg power and speed, do hip flexions and extensions on a low pulley. For hip strength attach an ankle harness to a rope. With the harness on the kicking leg ankle, have a partner resist the kicking leg — but not too hard. You are looking for speed with some resistance (10%-50% of 1 RM).

General Fitness

For general fitness you do not need sport-specific skills. You will, however, want to concentrate on your lower back and your abdominal muscles for strength. You will also want to do either aerobic fitness walking, running, biking or swimming for 20-30 minutes at least three times a week (60%-90% of your maximum heart rate — see Chapter 11). This will reduce your heart attack risk and increase your immune factors, which should prevent or reduce your infection rate and protect somewhat against many cancers. For weight loss you would want to do an hour or more at 45%-60% of your maximum heart rate. The longer exercise period allows for the mobilization of body fat as fuel. The shorter workout uses more blood and muscle glycogen (sugars) for fuel.

Golf

The back side of the leading wrist (the left wrist for right-handers) and arm can be strengthened by both concentric and isometric wrist exercises. For the isometric exercise, stand in your golf stance next to a door jamb. Place the back of your left hand against the door frame with your hand where it will be when you address the ball. Contract your arm and wrist muscles just as they would contract in your down swing. Repeat the exercise several times, each time moving your feet 6, 12 and 18 inches to the left of your starting position; then 6, 12, and 18 inches to the right of your starting position. When practicing with your partner, take your addressing position and let your partner apply pressure to the back of your left hand. Move your arms through a 45-degree backswing then forward 90 degrees so that you have had pressure applied through that essential 90-degree arc around the ball.

You can also stand in your address position and put the palm of your right hand on the back of your left hand and contract isometricly through the 90-degree arc near the ball. Isometrics are more effective if the contractions are done every 10 degrees through the total swing action.

Gymnastics

The requirements of gymnastics necessitate strength and power in every muscle group. Every strength exercise, particularly the multi-joint exercises, can provide the strength necessary for the various events. Do 1RM maximal strength and 40-50% of 1RM power work. If one is to press into a handstand, the most effective exercise would be the handstand press with manual resistance from a teammate rather than the standing (military) press — although it, too, would help. Plyometrics are important in vaulting and tumbling routines. Flexibility work should be done early in the career.

Ice Skating

For flexibility the type of range of movement depends on the movements in the skating routine. Sitting toe touchers, front-rear and sideways splits are all useful. Plyometric jumps from both one and two legs are useful to gain elevation in the jumps.

171

Figure 15-3a

Figure 15-3b

Rowing

For rowing, flexibility is not a factor, with the possible exception of wrist hyperextension. If the rower cannot hyperextend the wrist to 90 degrees, the oar will not be parallel with the water on the recovery and there will be a greater chance of "catching a crab."

Strength endurance is the major factor. The lower back, biceps, and lats are critical. Leg extensions are also useful. Each of these muscle groups can be strengthened individually, but with the prevalence of rowing machines in gyms, it is quite simple to work a sport-specific movement in the exact posture necessary in a race. A reverse-pyramid type of workout is absolutely the most effective. After a warm-up of 20-50 reps, start with a 1RM and exercise to exhaustion. Have a partner decrease the weight quickly and continue until the total number of repetitions done is greater than will be used in the race. About 10% more should be sufficient (see figures 15-5a and b).

Running Distance

The best way to train for distance running is simply to run long distances. However, if your event requires running hills, such as cross country running, you can profit by the same types of power exercises used by sprinters. These exercises will also help in your sprint at the end of a race. Obviously, if you run the 400, your training will be quite different than if you run the marathon. Training needs to be specific. Runners in the 400-meter will want to do a great deal of speed endurance work (repeat 200s, repeat 300s, repeat 400s, repeat 500s), while the marathoner will be primarily interested in long-distance work. It is a good idea to use heart rate monitors that can be set for maximum and minimum rates for the desired race intensity. This will help to keep the athlete in an effective training zone.

Do as much of your work on soft surfaces (grass or sand) as possible. Work on roads, outdoor or indoor tracks, or other hard surfaces increases the chance of chronic injuries such as lower leg stress fractures, shin splints, bone bruises and plantar fasciitis.

Downhill Skiing

In downhill skiing, the emphasis is on the quadriceps. Using 40-50% of your 1 RM, do a series of half squats at 5 degrees lower than you would flex your knees in a race until exhaustion. For plyometrics, side to side hops are effective, especially when they are done hopping from platforms angled at about 30 degree tilts. Cut oil drums are sometimes used for this type of plyometric drill.

Cross Country Skiing

Both single-leg hip extensions and single-leg quadricep work are needed here. Because cross country skiing is a pure endurance activity, it is its own best training.

Soccer

A soccer player will generally run 5-7 miles in a game played over a total of approximately 2 hours. About 12% of that time is involved in sprinting, with the average sprint being only about 30 yards. Accelerating from a standing start to a maximal sprint occurs 40-60 times a game, and direction is changed about every 5 seconds.2 This would translate into a workout in which repeat 30-yard sprints are run as wind sprints or as parts of drills.

Figure 15-4a

Figure 15-4b

For kicking and passing, the hip flexor and hip adductor muscles must be strengthened. This is done with work on low pulleys or by attaching a rope to the foot of one player who practices the various kicking movements while a teammate holding the other end of the rope provides resistance.

Throw-in strength can be increased using a high pulley, with the player grasping a handle or cable (not the bar). The hands must be in the same position they would be in when making the pass. This can also be done using a rope attached to a ball with a teammate holding the other end of the rope.

Goalkeepers can increase their throwing strength by throwing small medicine balls. Care must be taken to condition the rotator cuff muscles with strength training exercises before a heavy ball is introduced into the training process. For punting, use a low pulley with an ankle attachment. From a hyperextended position, move the leg through the flexed hip position at least 90 degrees forward. Quadriceps extensions will also help.

Sprinting

Since sprinting is an important component of many sport skills, let us look first at some exercises that can improve speed. Speed can be increased by both lengthening the stride and by increasing the stride frequency. Increasing stride length is generally easier to do, but both are important.

Hip extensor strength seems to be the key ingredient in sprinting speed, but ankle plantar flexion and hip flexion are also important. Along with the single-leg hip extension and hip flexion exercises and the ankle plantar flexion exercises, one-leg vertical jumps, pure speed work (such as 10 to 40 yard sprints), and plyometric work (such as one- and two-leg bounding) are particularly useful. Stretch-shortening cycle work (see Chapter 10) is essential to increasing both the speed and the power of the hip flexion and extension and the ankle plantar extension. Bounding (very long strides with powerful leg and ankle push off), sprinting uphill to increase the work of the hip extensors and ankle planter flexors, and running downhill to speed the stride frequency are important sport-specific exercises.

For jumping power, have a partner stand behind you putting her hands on your shoulders to give resistance when you jump. Once you have left the ground, she must take her hands off your shoulders so that your landing will be soft.

Additional resistance can also be added by wearing a harness with a small parachute attached to your back (commercially available or homemade) or a harness held by a partner behind you that forces you to push harder than normal in your hip and ankle extension.

Since pure sprinting on a track team is primarily anaerobic work, the sprint workouts should emphasize anaerobic conditioning. They should also emphasize pure speed in 10- to 100-meter sprints.

Swimming

The best exercise for a freestyler or butterflyer is a reverse pyramid on the overhead pulley. After a warm-up of several reps at about 70% of the 1 RM, grip the bar with both hands near the center. Starting with your 1 RM, make the full pull, then try a second rep. Work with a partner who will change the weight and note the weight and the number of reps for each weight. The partner quickly inserts the pin at the next weight down, and the exerciser does as many reps as possible — always to exhaustion. Drop to the next lowest weight and repeat to exhaustion, continue this process until 200 total reps have been completed. This will approximate swimming a 400-meter race with maximal contractions for each stroke.

Because most competitive swimmers have exceptional muscular and cardiovascular endurance, it is likely that there will be a weight that can easily be lifted 30 or more times. So when you have done 25-30 reps, move the pin back up to the next higher weight. After exhaustion drop the pin again as was done earlier in the exercise.

Backstrokers should use a single-handed high pulley. A machine with high pulleys placed several feet apart would work best. The swimmer stands or sits between the two high pulleys and pulls the handle in the same direction as when swimming the backstroke.

Manual resistance can be used if no weight machine is available. The exerciser should bend forward for freestyle or butterfly or lie on the back for backstroke, and grip a handle attached to a rope held by one or two teammates. The exerciser will pull through using the exact arm action used in the stroke. The partners giving the resistance allow the exerciser to move, but only under maximum force production. Once a week the exercise should be done with maximum force with a 200 repetition limit, then after a 3 day rest it should be done with reduced resistance for speed and power (30-40% of the maximum).

For dive and pushoff strength, do the snatch or clean movements with the Olympic barbell. You can also push off the wall holding a kickboard parallel to the wall. Vertical jumps are also effective. From the blocks, using a shoulder harness attached to a line held by a teammate, push off and make the full racing dive. The teammate should allow you to get to the pushoff point before applying pressure, then let the rope go as the toes are finishing their push.

175

An Australian study found no benefit in increasing the speed of the flip turn by the use of plyometrics.[3]

Tennis

Serious tennis players should get into condition by merely playing. However, the start-stop nature of the game makes it more difficult to get into maximum cardiovascular condition. While jogging a few miles may help the general caridovascular fitness, a quicker series of side-to-side sprints should be used, such as running the 24-foot singles court width or sliding side-to-side, like a defensive basketball player. This gives a greater opportunity for speed endurance rather than the pure endurance one gains from simply jogging.

Pure speed is necessary to move forward, backward and side-to-side to get the difficult balls. For pure speed, 10-yard sprints with a 1-minute rest between is best. You might also do 5-yard sprints with a 40-second rest between them. Your sprints should be varied, doing some from the ready position to the left and some to the right, and also doing some forward and some backward.

The wrist is a primary concern for a tennis player. Whether it is the snap of the front of the wrist in the serving action or the strain on the back of the wrist in the backhand action, the wrist is a major area for strength and power for a tennis player.

Volleyball

For your serving or spiking action, use a high pulley on a weight machine. Using a single handle, not a bar, face away from the pulley and use

Figure 15-5a   *Figure 15-5b*

Figure 15-6a

Figure 15-6b

your hips, shoulders, arm and wrist in an action that mimics your serve or spike. The high pulley can increase the sport-specific strength while also strengthening the rotator cuff muscles which are often injured in volleyball. See Chapter 8 for specific rotator cuff exercises (see figures 15-5a and b). This exercise can also be done with a partner standing behind you holding one end of a rope (see figures 15-6a and b). The end you hold should have a loop or handle so that your hand can be open and facing in the direction of your serve or spike. (A tetherball or an old, rag-stuffed volleyball with the rope running through it would be ideal.)

For your jump for a block or spike, take the steps that you would ordinarily take to get to that position, perhaps shuffling sideways for the block or using a 3- or 4-step approach for the spike, then use your 2-footed jump. You can do this at the net or against a wall. Mark the spot on the wall where your highest jump was recorded. Check yourself weekly on your progress (see figures 15-7a and b).

Figure 15-7a

Figure 15-7b

For jumping power you can have a partner stand behind you with her hands on your shoulders to give resistance when you jump. Once you have left the ground, she must take her hands off your shoulders so that your landing will be soft.

The clean action (see Chapter 9 on multi-joint exercises) will increase the strength of the jumping muscles. Plyometric box jumping is perhaps the best exercise for explosive jumping power. Remember that the recommendation is a total of only 30 plyometric repetitions twice a week.

To protect and strengthen your fingers for setting and blocking situations, simply squeeze a tennis ball.

Notes:

1. J.G. Hay, E.M. Thorson and B.C. Kippenhan, "Changes in Muscle-Tendon Length During the Take-Off of a Running Long Jump," *Journal of Sports Science* 17.2 (1999): 159-172.
2. M. O'Toole, "Physiological Aspects of Training," *Women in Sport* ed. B. Drinkwater (Oxford: Blackwell Science, 2000): 77.
3. J.M. Cossor, B.A. Blanksby and B.C. Elliott BC, "The Influence of Plyometric Training on the Freestyle Tumble Turn," *Medicine & Sport in Science & Exercise.* w2.2 (1999): 106-116.

16

Warming Up Effectively

*M*ost coaches have been taught to warm-up their athletes by doing a number of stretches and some movement exercises such as running. It was believed that stretching made the muscles more ready to contract, reduced delayed onset muscle soreness (DOMS), and reduced the chance for muscle injuries. The research, while inconclusive due to the relatively few studies so far done, indicates these reasons are invalid for most people who exercise.

A number of studies indicate that:

- The muscles do not function as well after stretching because the stiffness required for maximal force is reduced by the stretching.
- Delayed onset muscle soreness does not seem to be reduced by stretching or massage.
- Muscle and connective tissue injuries are generally higher among those who stretch.

An analysis of all or most of the known studies in the area shows that stretching alone generally does not prevent injuries. In some cases it increases injuries.

In further summarizing literature of basic physiology and anatomy it was found that:

- Stretching doesn't increase the compliance (effective action) of a muscle during eccentric contractions. These lengthening contractions are the sort of contractions most often associated with muscle and tendon injury.
- Stretching can produce damage of muscles and tendons at the cellular level.
- Stretching seems to mask muscular pain in humans. This seems to be

why stretching an injured muscle or tendon may make it feel better even though additional damage may be occurring.

- Stretching before an exercise will have no positive effect on a muscle that will not be required to elongate during the activity, such as jogging or walking. Yet studies of joggers and slow running indicate that stretching can cause injuries. [1]
- Stretching as a part of the warm up reduces power by 4%- 8%.

Most muscle injuries occur in the normal range of motion, not in a lengthened state, so stretching will not reduce the causative factors.

Should Stretching Be Part of Your Warm-up?

One thing we know is that we are all individuals with our own potentials or problems relative to our muscles and connective tissues. Some people like to do stretching exercises as part of their warm-up, some do not. You may need to experiment with stretching versus non-stretching in your warm-up. If you stretch, you may want to experiment with the types of stretches you do and whether or not you should stretch to the maximum degree possible.

Now that stretching is actually being investigated as a warm up activity, we have found a number of studies show that it decreases one's power. The various studies show that stretching during warm up decreases your power by 4%-8%. There is a question as to why. Some, like Dr. Arnold Nelson at Louisiana State University, believes that it is because the tendons are stretched so they become more slack. The contracting muscle must, therefore, take up the slack of the stretched tendon before it can tighten the tendon sufficiently to move the joint. Others believe that the problem lies in the sarcomere, the small muscle cell that holds the contractile elements. It is thought that the contractile elements, actin and myosin, are pulled farther apart by the stretching, so the muscle contraction must make up for that separation before the contraction can begin to be effective. [2]

As has been indicated earlier, research on stretching has not answered all, or even most, of our questions about when and how to stretch. Is stretching a poor warm-up for a distance runner, but a necessary factor for a high jumper or dancer? We don't know. However, the reduction in power indicates that it would not be good for any athlete who must jump or run fast. Distance runners are currently studied more often than other athletes in terms of the desirability of stretching. So far the results indicate that for long distance running, stretching is not effective as an injury preventive.

A 1983 survey of 500 runners found that those who warmed-up had more injuries than those who did not (87.7% vs. 66%). The frequency of injuries increased with the length of the warm-up. It is assumed that stretch-ing was part of the warm-up, but it was not specifically asked. [3] A few years later a survey of 10K runners in the national championships found that those who stretched had more injuries. But it is not known whether those who stretched did so because they already had an injury and assumed that the stretching would protect them from further injury. [4]

In a year-long study of recreational distance runners, it was found that those who stretched sometimes had more injuries than those who always stretched or those who never stretched. But those who never stretched had fewer new injuries than those who stretched. [5] While the above studies cast a doubt as to the effectiveness of stretching for distance runners, certainly more research needs to be done.

Some people stretch because they believe that it will reduce the soreness which can follow exercise. A Swedish study investigated whether stretch-ing would decrease (DOMS) in women doing eccentric exercise, the type of exercise most likely to increase muscle soreness. No advantages for stretch-ing were found. The amount of soreness and tenderness was not reduced. [6]

In some activities you can stretch too long or too far in your warm-up. If you are entering a sprint race on the track or in the pool, you would want your muscle fibers to be tighter and stiffer. Too much stretch can slow you down. This is also true of high jumpers, long jumpers and weight lifters. But if you are getting ready for a tennis match, a long run, or a leisurely afternoon of skiing, light stretching might not be a problem. [7]

More research is now being conducted into the effectiveness of warm-up stretching for various types of activities. With this newer research in mind, we can say that stretching before a strength training workout should not be a problem. However, if you were in a weight lifting competition, pre-competition stretching might reduce your strength. On the other hand, if you stretch after your workout, when the connective tissues are warmer, you should be able to increase your flexibility effectively.

Warming-up the Muscles to Make Them More Efficient

There isn't any disagreement at this time about using sport-specific move-ments in the warm-up. Running, jumping, swimming, leg extensions and arm exercises all are effective in getting the blood supply opened to the muscles that will be used in the game or practice.

There is basic scientific evidence to suggest that an active warm-up may be protective against muscle strain injury. Warming the muscles should be done by slowly doing your sport-specific movements. If you are in a swim meet, swim slowly then faster for your warm-up. In a track meet, run slowly then faster. For volleyball blockers and hitters, move to the jumping point and jump half as far as you will need in the game or practice. Then increase the velocity and height of your jump, so that when you finish your warm-up, you are working to the maximum. Softball batters and golfers should swing slowly using about only 3/4 of the full arc, then increase the arc and the speed until it is at full swing speed. Whatever your event, move slowly then faster in your warm-up, then eventually at full speed.

If the purpose of stretching is to get the muscle ready to contract more quickly, this doesn't happen. While in the past it was believed that a stretched muscle is more ready to contract, as is shown in the knee-jerk reflex, this does not seem to be true. An electromyographic study of the bicep femoris, soleus and gastocnemius indicates that stretching reduces the firing patterns in these muscles. [8]

In a study covering 55 high school football games, some teams warmed-up and stretched for 3 minutes before the third quarter and the control group did not warm-up. The two groups experienced about the same number of injuries, but the teams that warmed-up had fewer strains and sprains in the third quarter. [9] The problem with this study is that we don't know whether the stretching or the muscular warm-up was responsible for any reduction in strain injuries. The study should have been done with four groups: one with no warm-up, one with stretching only, one with a running warm-up only, and one with a stretching and running protocol.

A study at the University of Pennsylvania indicates that, at least with sprinters, even a slight physical warm-up can increase the ability of the muscles to pick up oxygen through increased mitochonrdial activity. Even a somewhat relaxed movement pattern can help the muscles to bridge the gap from anaerobic to aerobic energy production. [10]

Warm-up and the Positive Effective on the Heart

A New York University study using nuclear imaging of heart function after strenuous exercise, both with and without a warm-up, found no difference in the work of the heart. These findings are contradictory to other such studies. [11]

Warm-Up and Increased Endurance

A French study used untrained young men exercising to exhaustion on a bicycle exerciser at 75% of maximum heart rate. One trial was without a warm-up and one was with a 15 minute warm-up at 50% maximum heart rate. The warm-up was found to allow better adjustment of the heat regulating mechanisms of the body and the blood flow. It also increased the water loss during physical work. For most subjects, these adjustments allowed for improved endurance during the exercise. [12]

Warming-Up the Breathing Muscles

Just as other muscles need conditioning and can profit by a warm-up, so can the breathing muscles: diaphragm, intercostals, abdominals, sternocleidomastoid and others. When the diaphragm contracts, it lowers the bottom of the thorax and enlarges the available space in the thorax which reduces the pressure and creates a vacuum. The outside air then moves in. The external intercostals, the muscles between the ribs and near the skin, also expand the rib cage which also increases the space inside the thorax. When these muscles relax, the area inside the thorax is reduced, and the air is forced out.

During exercise additional breathing muscles can come into play. The sternocleidomastoid can lift the top of the front of the rib cage enlarging it even more. The trapezius can do the same with the back ribs. Also during exercise additional muscles help to force the air out. The abdominal muscles can help to push the diaphragm even higher, and the internal intercostal muscles pull the ribs closer together. Both of these reduce the thorax volume even more, so the internal pressure is increased and the air is exhaled even more forcefully.

A study at Birmingham University in England looked at warming-up the breathing muscles. An untrained group and a group of elite rowers did breathing tests and warm-up exercises. The recommendation after the test was that specific breathing warm-ups be done along with the full body warm-ups. [13]

Recommended Warm-up

Based on the results of the research, it would seem that most people should not stretch. In fact, probably no one should stretch because the stretching reduces muscle stiffness and the muscle's ability to contract to the maximum. It also sets them up for a greater chance of injury during the eccentric contractions that occur in most running and jumping exercises. The exception would be for those with overly tight muscles whose efficiency will be increased by reducing the excessive tightness.

The research tells us that about 15 minutes of exercise at about 60-70% of the athlete's VO2 max should be an effective warm-up.

Taking an average of the ACSM and the Marshall University numbers discussed in Chapter 11, we can suggest that a 60-70% VO2 max warm-up would be about 73-80% of the maximum heart rate level of 220 (minus) the athletes age multiplied by .70 to .80. For a 20-year-old, this would be a 140-

Warm-up Basics
• No stretching for most people. • Warm-up the muscle actively-from slow to faster movements. • If maximum force is to be used (jumping, sprinting, putting the shot, forwards in a rugby scrum, a maximum squat or bench press, etc.), make certain that the muscles get some maximum contractions either by doing the activity, mimicking it in the weight room, or having a partner give resistance for the movement needed.

160 level of heart rate for 15 minutes. We might infer that this would be an effective warm-up for sprinters, but might take too much energy from distance runners, soccer or basketball players, or swimmers. No exact levels have yet been researched for each sport or for each position of each sport.

Certainly the warm-up will have to include some maximal efforts, such as jumping in basketball, kicking in soccer, spiking in volleyball, sprinting for sprinters. Skill sports will also need some mental reminding of the skills that will be used: serving in volleyball or tennis, overhead smash in tennis, free throw shooting in basketball, turning in swimming, etc.

Recommended Cool-down

After the practice or game, stretching may not hurt, but any excessive stretching may set up the muscle fibers for injury during the next practice. There is no evidence that post-exercise stretching will increase flexibility or reduce delayed onset muscle soreness. Stretching for an increased range of motion should be done very early in the sport season, or better yet, immediately after the previous sport season. (See Chapter 13 on flexibility.)

Some post-exercise jogging may assist in reducing the blood pooling in the muscles, but if bruises, strains or sprains were incurred in the practice or game, the extra work might increase the blood flow to the injury. This would increase the swelling when the injury should have been treated with ice or cold to reduce any potential swelling.

There have been few studies on the effects of cool-down. A study in Japan of cardiac patients age 50-70 years old found that after a maximal cardiac exercise, those who used a cool-down period rather than just resting had a more efficient return to normal in terms of breathing. The resting group hyperventilated and had a more uneven return to the resting state. [14]

In a Dutch study using over 300 runners in a 16-week study, half of the runners were given information on preventing running injuries, including how to warm-up, stretch and cool-down. A diary was kept by each runner noting what was done and how many injuries occurred. Those who received the information had 5.5 injuries per 1000 hours of running. Those who did not get the information had 4.9 injuries per 1000 hours of running. [15] The conclusion of the study was that the information was the first step in preventing injuries, but perhaps the study's assumption that warm-up, stretching and cool-down will prevent injuries was wrong, or at least wrong for most runners.

Notes:

1. Shrier, "Stretching Before Exercise Does Not Reduce the Risk of Local Muscle Injury: A Critical Review of the Clinical and Basic Science Literature," Clinical Journal of Sport Medicine, 9.4 (1999): 221-227.
2. Duane Knudson et al., Conference of AAHPERD, Cincinatti, Ohio, April 28 and 29, 2001.
3. J. A. Kerner and J.C. D'Amico, "A Statistical Analysis of a Group of Runners." *Journal of the American Podiatry Association* 73.3 (1983): 160-164.
4. S.J. Jacobs and B.L. Berson, "Injuries to Runners: A Study of Entrants to a 10,000 Meter Race," *American Journal of Sports Medicine* 14.2 (1986): 151-155.
5. S.D. Walter et al., "The Ontario Cohort Study of Running-Related Injuries," *Archives of Internal Medicine* 149.11 (1989): 2561-2564.
6. P.H. Johansson et al, "The Effects of Preexercise Stretching on Muscular Soreness, Tenderness and Force Loss Following Heavy Eccentric Exercise," *Scandinavian Journal of Medicine and Science in Sports* 9.4 (1999): 219-225.
7. G. Wilson, "Applied Resistance Training: A Scientific Approach," unpublished manuscript, Southern Cross University, NSW, Australia, 1998, 25.
8. K.J. Mohr et al., "Electromyographic Investigation of Stretching: The Effect of Warm-Up," *Clinical Journal of Sports Medicine* 8.3 (1998): 215-220.
9. B. Bixler and R.L. Jones, "High-School Football Injuries: Effects of a Post-Halftime Warm-Up and Stretching Routine," *Family Practice Resource Journal* 12.2 (1992): 131-139.
10. S. Nioka et al., "Muscle Deoxygenation in Aerobic and Anaerobic Exercise," *Adv Exp Med Biol* 454 (1998): 63-70.

11. R.M. Chesler et al., "Cardiovascular Response to Sudden Strenuous Exercise: An Exercise Echocardiographic Study," *Medicine & Sport in Science & Exercise.* 29.10 (1997): 1299-1303.

12. S.H. Mandengue et al., "Effects of Preliminary Muscular Exercise on Body Temperature, Water Loss and Physical Performance," *Sante* 6.6 (1996): 393-396.

13. S. Volianitis et al., "The Influence of Prior Activity upon Inspiratory Muscle Strength in Rowers and Non-Rowers," *International Journal of Sports Medicine* 20.8 (1999): 542-547.

14. Y. Koyama et al., "Effects of Cool-Down During Exercise Recovery on Cardiopulmonary Systems in Patients with Coronary Artery Disease," *Jpn Circ Journal* 64.3 (2000): 191-196.

15. W. van Mechelen et al., "Prevention of Running Injuries by Warm-Up, Cool-Down, and Stretching Exercises," *American Journal of Sports Medicine* 21.5 (1993): 711-719.

17

Common Injuries

*M*ore and more women are playing in fast-paced, aggressive sports these days. From basketball to snow skiing to soccer, women are competing and mixing it up with the same ferocity as men. However, an unfortunate side effect comes with all of this dynamic, physical play by women — a disproportionate rate of sports injuries for women athletes.

Since sport activities are designed to stress the body to some degree, injuries often develop. You should be aware of the types of injuries or problems that may occur and how you can prevent or cure the problem. This chapter will give you an idea of some of the illnesses or injuries that may occur during or due to exercise. (For more in-depth coverage of sports injuries and treatment, I recommend *Prevention and Treatment of Athletic Injuries*, by Bob O'Conner and R. Budgett in conjunction with the British Olympic medical team.)

Gender Differences in Anatomy and Kinesiology

The role of monthly hormonal differences relative to strength training, the looseness of ligaments, and susceptibility to injury is still being researched. Decreased fine motor skills have been reported.[1] Perhaps these menstrual problems can contribute to the increased risk of injury we find in this particular group of women. Most such research has focused on athletic injuries to the lower extremity, and in particular, the anterior cruciate ligament. Based on a paucity of current research, no firm conclusions can be drawn regarding the influence of hormonal fluctuations on upper extremity injuries in female athletes.

Common Injuries to Female Athletes
The following injuries have been reported to be more common in females: • Serious shoulder injuries in volleyball • Shoulder pain due to impingement in swimmers • Stress injuries to the distal radial physis in gymnasts • Wrist and elbow injuries in golfers • Thoracic outlet syndrome • Stress fractures due to osteoporosis

Head Injuries

Head injuries are possible in many sports. It is easy to diagnose a head injury when the person is unconscious, but head injuries without unconsciousness are more common. The inability to remember something (such as one's name or the type of competition) or a lack of alertness can signal a concussion. More than 90% of all concussions are of this mild type. However, since even mild concussions can progress to more serious problems, they should also be treated. A skull fracture is another type of head injury. The broken skull bones can penetrate the brain and cause additional injury.

Helmets such as used in American football, ice hockey, motorcycle and auto racing, bicycle riding and in some ski competitions can greatly reduce the incidence of skull fractures and concussions. Helmets may reduce the risk of skull fracture but do not greatly reduce the risk of concussions because they lack the "air management systems" of modern foams and air-filled sacks that dissipate any blow around the skull. The most effective of the helmets are those used in American football where both air and foam padding have been utilized under a strong plastic shell.

In bruising injuries, bleeding below the surface of the skin occurs. With a brain injury, the resulting hematoma can be fatal. Hematomas are most common in the temporal area and are the leading cause of death for sports injuries. Consequently, all head injuries must be assumed to be serious by the athletes, their coaches, and the medical personnel involved. Obviously, head and neck injuries must be treated at an appropriate medical facility. X-rays and scans will be needed to confirm or rule out the severity of the injury.

Headaches can be caused by a number of internal or external factors from psychological to physiological. The stress of anticipating an event or the relaxation after it can both cause psychologically induced headaches. "Weightlifter's headache," on the other hand, is physiologically based. The internal pressures in the torso and skull from holding the breath and lifting maximally can cause a headache that may last for weeks. When this type of headache persists, the person should have x-rays to determine if the spinal discs have been compressed and the nerves injured.

The ears can be a particular problem for some exercisers. "Swimmer's ear" (otitis externa) is an inflammation of the ear on the outside part of the ear drum. The continued wetness of the outer part of the ear can encourage the growth of bacteria which can set up an infection. Mild cases can be treated with over-the-counter ear drops. More severe cases can be treated with prescription drugs. There are also ear drops that can be used immediately after swimming which will dry out the ear and prevent infections.

Dental injuries are a very common type of facial injury. Dental injuries may be as simple as a chipping of the tooth enamel, which may be artificially replaced, or as severe as a tooth being knocked out. When this is the case, immediate care from a dentist or physician is called for. A tooth that has been replanted within 30 minutes has a 95% chance of success while a tooth that was not replanted for 2 hours has only a 5% chance of success. For this reason, if a tooth is knocked out, reinsert it in the proper place immediately and keep constant pressure on the tooth until medical help is found. Do not put it in ice.

Neck Injuries

Neck injuries include the very serious spinal fractures and spinal dislocations but also include muscle strains and sprains of the ligaments. While the muscles to the rear of the spinal column are stronger than those in the front, a neck bending forward will be stopped when the chin hits the chest, so serious forward moving injuries are not too common. When the neck is extended backward, it could go as far back as the head hitting the upper back, so backward extension of the neck is a far more serious problem.

When the neck is extended backward, it is possible to rupture the back part of the disc which separates the vertebral bones. A ruptured disc can be quite serious. A whiplash injury in an auto or sport accident can stretch the ligaments in the front of the vertebrae while also rupturing a disc or two.

Another type of injury is caused by compression of the vertebrae and discs from a fall or a blow in which the force comes to the top of the head — especially when the head is bent forward 20-30 degrees. This type of blow, such as one caused by a fall from a horse or a cycle, can shatter a vertebra and possibly a disc, even sending fragments into the spinal cord. This compression fracture is the most common reason for spinal cord injury and its resulting paralysis. It is not only found in cycling and riding, but also in diving, gymnastic falls (including tumbling and trampoline falls) and hockey head injuries.

A blow to the head is better absorbed if the neck muscles are strong and tensed. The tensed neck transfers some of the force to the lower body so that it is not only the brain that is absorbing the blow but the trunk as well. For this reason strong neck muscles can aid in the reduction of brain injuries and paralysis.

When the injury is to the side of the head, there can be a compression of the vertebrae on the opposite side of the neck. Pain, such as burning, numbness or tingling may be experienced along the arm and possibly to the hand. This "burner" may last several seconds. If it persists, it requires medical attention.

Shoulder

The shoulder is the most complex of the joints commonly used in sports. The fact that it can move the arm in every direction and can rotate it gives it this complexity. Sports in which overuse injuries in the upper extremity are seen frequently include gymnastics, swimming, volleyball, tennis, racquetball and golf. Traumatic injuries to the upper extremity are frequently seen in sports such as alpine skiing, snowboarding, and rollerblading. In general, similar injury rates are seen in men's and women's sports with comparable rules. [2] But certain sport-specific injuries have been reported to occur with higher frequency in females. There is a higher incidence of serious shoulder injuries in female volleyball players despite a similar overall incidence of injury in males and females [3] Shoulder pain secondary to impingement has been reported to be more common in female than in male swimmers [4]

Shoulder pain in female athletes may occur for several different reasons. Relatively poor upper body strength, shorter upper extremities, improper technique, generalized laxity and overuse may be contributing factors. What is called the "impingement syndrome" is associated with rotator cuff tendon problems. This is typically seen in the more mature overhead athlete, such as volleyball or basketball players and swimmers. Degeneration of the tissues, tearing of the rotator cuff and bone spurs are common causes. [5]

Although sport participation in general exposes the female athlete to risk of arm and shoulder injury, participation in sports involving the use of these upper extremities may also serve to prevent neck and shoulder symptoms in young females. A study of 718 high school students found a significantly higher incidence of neck and shoulder symptoms in girls when compared to boys of the same age. Girls involved in sports requiring dynamic use of the upper extremities complained of significantly fewer neck and shoulder symptoms than those participating in activities or hobbies involving static postures of the upper limbs. [6]

190

In younger athletes instability and weakness may be the major problem.[7] Repetitive overhead activities with the arm in abduction and external rotation, such as in a volleyball serve or an overhead softball throw stress the front of the shoulder joint and the rotator cuff.[8]

Athletes may complain of pain while throwing, pitching a softball, serving or spiking a volleyball, performing swimming strokes such as freestyle or butterfly, or weight training using the bench or military press. A lack of endurance in these activities is also a common complaint. There is often no history of traumatic injury. In primary impingement syndrome, night pain is common, as are complaints of inability to sleep on the side of the affected shoulder. Treatment includes rest, physical therapy (stretching and strengthening) NSAIDS (non-steroidal anti-inflammatory agents), and in some cases, corticosteroid injections or surgery. Both prevention and rehabilitation exercises are important. (See Chapter 8.)

Suprascapular nerve entrapment is a recognized cause of shoulder pain in the overhead athlete and is frequently observed in volleyball players.[9] The athlete may complain of pain at the rear of the shoulder. This is often due to the atrophy of the infraspinatus muscle. It has been estimated that 20 percent of high level volleyball players show clinically evident atrophy of the infraspinatus muscle. Treatment includes rest, NSAIDS and strength exercises for the rear of the shoulder.

Fracture of the collar bone (clavicle) can occur with direct trauma, as happens with some falling injuries where a straight arm is used to break the fall, or it can be the result of accumulated stresses, as found in weight lifting and shooting sports. Since the break is usually in the middle of the bone, pushing gently on one end or the other may elicit pain at the fractured area. This test may be used to give an idea as to the type and severity of the injury, but X-rays are always a good idea.

Stress fractures of bones in the shoulder girdle sometimes occur. The diagnosis should be considered in any female athlete involved in an upper-limb dominant activity who presents with insidious onset of pain and bony tenderness. The post-menopausal athlete and the young amenorrheic female athlete may be at particular risk for stress fractures due to lower bone density. [10]

Rib stress fractures may be seen in female rowers and sometimes in golfers and are thought to be due to repetitive stresses applied to the rear and side of the rib cage by the serratus anterior, rhomboids, trapezius, and external oblique muscles.[11] In rowers these fractures are most often associated with long distance training and heavy load per stroke. The athlete will complain of pain in the rear and side of the chest cage. Trunk rotation during the golf swing can also cause the pain as can coughing or deep breathing.

Stress fractures of the humerus (upper arm bone) have been found in adolescent male baseball pitchers and tennis players. They are thought to be due to a high level of repetitive stress placed on immature bone, possibly aggravated by a period of rapid growth. As more young female athletes participate in such activities, the incidence of such fractures may increase. It is a common misconception that, compared with overhead pitching, the underhand motion performed in windmill softball pitching creates less stress on the arm, resulting in fewer injuries. However, it has been shown that high forces are experienced at the shoulder and elbow during the delivery phase of the windmill softball pitch with peak compressive forces equal to 70%-98% of the pitcher's body weight. [12] Thus, the upper am and shoulder in soft ball pitchers may be at risk for repetitive stress injury.

Shoulder separations or dislocations can occur in any direction. A shoulder separation is actually an injury to the ligaments at the acromioclavicular joint. Shoulder separations are generally treated with a sling and a period of rest until the pain is improved. Shoulder dislocations typically occur with a fall onto the outstretched arm or a blow to the upper front of the arm when it is in an abducted and externally rotated position. A fall broken by a straight arm might displace the humerus upward or backward. A force to the upper front of the arm might displace the bone backward and a blow from the top might displace it downward. Once a dislocation has occurred, it is highly likely to happen again because the ligaments that held the humerus in the scapula have been severely stretched. For that reason surgery is often the only satisfactory solution.

Rotator cuff injury is the result of muscle tears from stretching or contracting. These muscles that twist the humerus are relatively easily injured. A hard throwing action, the stopping of a rotation such as might occur when a golfer hits the ground with the club head, or a violent pulling backward of the upper arm which might occur in a fall, are all possible causes of a rotator cuff injury. Pain from the injury is typically localized in the front and side of the shoulder and may radiate to the upper arm.

When throwing a ball hard, the rotation of the humerus can be more than 7,000 degrees per second. That is equivalent to 20 complete 360 degree rotations in a second. Obviously, this puts great strain on these small muscles. All overhead sports athletes can have rotator cuff problems. Tennis, volleyball, badminton, and softball players are most likely to have such injuries. The incidence increases after one has reached 35 years of age.

Chronic overuse of the shoulder, such as occurs with "swimmer's shoulder" results from the continued use of the shoulder muscles — particularly the rotator cuff and the biceps. Half of young competitive swimmers, 65%

of older swimmers and 70% of elite swimmers have had some problems with the shoulder. It may be a severe inflammation of the tendons (tendinitis) or a more chronic variety of the problem (tendinosis).

The Elbow and Forearm

Elbow injuries can occur with a single trauma, a series of stresses that weaken the elbow, or a lesser single trauma to an elbow already weakened by previously absorbed stresses. The chronically stressed elbow can have muscular, tendon or bursa damage and is seen in tennis elbow and other tendinosis such as "little league elbow."

Tennis elbow (lateral humeral epicondylitis) can affect anyone who has continued strain on the front or the back of the forearm. It is the most commonly seen problem of the elbow in athletes. [13] It occurs equally in male and female athletes, but in a study of more than 500 tennis players, it was found that women over the age of 40 had an increased risk of developing lateral epicondylitis, particularly when participating in more than two hours of tennis per week. [14] Other sports requiring repetitive forearm motion such as volleyball, golf and other racquet sports have been implicated in the development of this problem.

"Little League elbow" is the name for damage done to the muscles and tendons on the inside top of the arm bone (ulna) just below the elbow. In children this bone is not yet hardened, so it is easily injured. The snapping down of the elbow, as would be found in pitching a curve ball, is the major cause. It has been reported to occur with increased frequency in males, but it is also seen in females. The probability of developing this problem is increased with activities involving wrist flexion and pronation such as tennis, golf or bowling. It is often caused by hitting the ball late with the head of the racquet behind the elbow during contact.

Prevention can be aided if the muscles around the elbow are strengthened so that they absorb more of the shock of the force. For example, to prevent a tennis elbow, one should do reverse wrist curls or, more simply, grasp the end of broom and, with the palm facing down, lift the broom repeatedly to strengthen the muscles on the back side of the forearm. This strengthens the arm for backhand drives. Some tennis elbow problems occur on the inside of the forearm. To prevent this, lift the same broom with the palm of the hand facing upward. This will also help to develop strength for the serve.

The use of proper technique and equipment should be emphasized. In tennis or other racquet sports proper grip and racquet size are important. They should be appropriate for a player's palm size. Decreasing string tension may also help in dispersion of forces placed on the forearm extensors.

The use of lighter racquets, low vibration materials and playing on softer surfaces may also prevent recurrence.

The Wrist and Hand

The wrist is a very delicate and easily injured joint. With the two forearm bones meeting the wrist and eight bones in the wrist leading to five bones at the top of the hand, you have a large number of ligaments and joints that can be injured by wrist movements or falls.

Wrist injuries are most likely to occur in gymnastics, contact sports, fast pitch softball, throwing and catching sports or racquet sports such as tennis. They can also be injured in falls where the hand is outstretched to break the fall. Hand injuries are more likely to occur in ball-handling sports such as volleyball, softball, basketball, team handball, and for the throwing and catching players on a rugby team. Hand and wrist injuries are more common in children and youth than in the adult populations, and they are the most common types of injuries sustained during athletic competition. [15]

Wrist sprains may accompany a fracture, they are more commonly experienced without one. Use the standard treatment of ice and heat along with compression. Taping around the wrist or using a wrist brace should reduce the chances of an immediate reoccurrence. If the sprain resulted from a backward bending of the hand, you can use several strips of tape on the inside of the arm and hand. The hand should be bent forward before the tape is applied. (The degree of forward bend is determined by the amount of backward extension you feel should be maximal.) Anchor those strips of tape with tape around the hand and around the lower forearm. If the sprain was forward, use the same principles but use the several strips of tape on the back of the hand and wrist.

Overuse injuries to the wrist (tenosynovitis) are most likely to occur in golfers, racquet sports players and fly fishers. The left thumb of the right-handed golfer is particularly vulnerable because the wrist is bent far backward in the backswing. [16] A women's smaller hand may predispose her to developing this syndrome — particularly with the use of ill-fitting gloves and too large of a grip. Thumb injuries are common, especially when the thumb is bent back when grasping an opponent or falling while holding a racquet or pole.

"Handlebar palsy" often occurs to cyclists. It is an irritation of the nerve on the outside of the hand at the base of the little finger. Gripping the handlebar for long periods of time is the cause. The symptoms include tingling, numbness and weakness.

Carpal tunnel syndrome has been reported in athletes requiring wrist flexion with a tight grip, including cyclists and weight lifters. It is seen more frequently in women.[17] Common complaints include pain at night and while driving as well as pain following participating in the offending sport. Treatment consists of rest, splinting and anti-inflammatory medication.

The Chest and Thorax

Rib injuries, including fractures and bruises, are the most common type of chest injury. The painful ribs should have X-rays to determine the extent of any injury. If a fracture is not displaced, merely resting for six weeks can generally heal the bone.

Exercisers over 40 often have pain in the middle of the chest which appears to be rib pain. Generally, this is merely the aging, less-flexible cartilage that holds the ribs to the breast bone (sternum). It is not serious. It is the price we pay for still being alive!

Thoracic outlet syndrome is a relatively uncommon cause of referred pain to the shoulder in athletes. However, it is seen three times more commonly in women than in men. It is sometimes seen in athletes with long, thin necks, especially dancers. It has also been described in aquatic athletes.[18] It is thought to be caused by compression of the nerves and vessels in the shoulder area. Relatively weak shoulder girdle muscles or excessively large breasts may predispose an athlete to this problem. Swimmers in particular are known for their poor posture and forward position of the shoulders which may lead to downward pressure of the collar bone on the first rib. The swimmer may complain of inability to keep the fingers together and control movement of the hand during the pull-through phase of the swimming stroke. Likewise, the water polo player may have difficulty grasping and throwing the ball.

Lumbar Spine

Spine-related problems make up about 10% of all athletic and exercising complaints, and back pain is at least a minor problem for three quarters of all top athletes.

Injury due to immediate trauma, such as a blow to the back, a fall, or a muscle strain while lifting are obvious. The problems or causes of overuse injuries are not quite so easily pinpointed. The repetitive small injuries that result in overuse problems can be caused by continued bending forward or backward, continued quick or strenuous muscle contractions, or by the continued use of vertebral joints that have degenerated or are arthritic. Weight lifting, dancing and jogging can cause such overuse problems. If pain has persisted for a month to six weeks it can be considered chronic. Medical diagnosis is called for.

A major lower back problem in sports occurs when the back is hyperextended, as is common in gymnastics, figure skating, volleyball, and dance. Some experts believe that stress fractures can develop from such repeated hyperextensions. When such stress fractures occur, they should be treated with rest from the offending extension or hyper-extension activity. Occasionally, bracing is necessary.

Chronic low back pain can be caused by a number of factors. Tight buttock and hamstring muscles, tight connective tissue in the lower back, poor abdominal strength, poor posture and muscle strains are the most common. Lifting incorrectly can bring on and continue low back pain. In a study of low back pain in female gymnasts by the Department of Orthopedics at the University of Illinois, it was found that the type of flexibility required, which is not found in other sports, was very detrimental to the lower back. The large number of repetitions of the routines sets the athlete up for a number of overuse injuries, with the most common being lower back pain. In the seven-week study of elite rhythmic gymnasts it was found that 86% complained of low back pain during that seven week period but only one lost practice time, and that was because of an injury. The most common diagnoses were muscle strains and stress reactions from the bony tissues. [19]

Degenerating discs are a major low back problem. Discs are thick, jelly-filled shock absorbers between each vertebra. Problems occur when the disc slips a bit out of place or the jelly-like material inside moves out of its casing. Pain results when the disc puts pressure on the nerves in the area. The most likely symptom is low back pain, which may also be felt in the buttocks and down the legs. This is because the nerves of the buttocks and legs originate between the vertebrae in the low back area. It has been found in exercisers as young as 10 years. Studies have shown that nearly half of adult athletes and 11% of athletes under 18 have some sort of disc related problems. The contributing factors include: a family history of degenerative discs, strenuous lifting (particularly in a lift such as the dead lift where the torso is at a 90-degree angle and the maximum effort in the lift is done at this point), and some collision sports such as soccer, hockey and rugby. The exaggerated hyperextended posture of female gymnasts can also place strain on the back side of the discs.

Forward flexing can cause similar problems. The continual forward flexing can damage the forward part of the discs. Activities such as rowing, competitive diving, dance and strength training can contribute to these problems.

Sharp low back pain may be a result of an acute fracture or a stress fracture. The broken part of the vertebra can move and put pressure on the local nerves. Gymnastics, springboard diving, butterfly swimming, weight lifting, tennis and classical or jazz dance can contribute to the development of stress fractures.

Since there can be several causes of lower back pain, the treatment must fit the problem. If the problem is a tightened fascia in the low back or tight hamstrings, stretching is wise. If the vertebrae are somewhat misaligned, manipulation may ease the pain. But if the problem is a herniated disc, manipulation would be unwise — as it would be for a stress fracture. If the problem increases when the lower back is flexed forward, such as when sitting, a back support can be used when sitting or driving. Rest is often an effective cure, but a combination of rest and participation in a pain-free exercise is often the most effective. Many lower back problems will be resolved after six weeks of rest.

Abdominal Injuries

Abdominal injuries make up about 10% of all sports related injuries. They can be caused by either blunt or penetrating forces. In sport the great majority of injuries are caused by blunt forces such as hitting, being kicked, or falling on an object such as a ball. Falls such as from a horse, a cycle or while rock climbing, or auto racing can also cause injuries to the abdominal viscera.

Muscle strains to the abdominal wall can occur when the abdominal muscles contract forcefully in jumping or in a twisting movement. Muscular spasms or cramping may occur. The area injured is easily pointed out. The sharp pain is usually localized.

A stitch in the side often occurs early in an exercise activity. The cause or causes are not known, but it may be related to a cramp in the diaphragm due to poor conditioning or poor circulation. In some cases it is assumed to be due to eating shortly before the exercise. It may also be related to week abdominal muscles. While the pain may be intense, it rapidly subsides with rest. To ease the pain, bend your torso away from the side with the pain and extend the arm, the one on the side of the pain, over your head. This should stretch the cramped muscle.

The Hip and Pelvis

Hip fractures require a great force to break the normally strong hip bones. In athletes who have osteoporosis, hip fractures may occur with less force or with a seemingly minor injury. The most likely sports for hip fractures are horseback riding, downhill skiing and cycling – sports where falls are most likely to occur. They will normally be surgically treated.

197

Injuries to the tendons of the hips and their insertions into the hip bones are common in adolescent athletes. A violent contraction of the muscles at the same time that it is being stretched (an eccentric contraction as part of the "stretch-shortening cycle") can injure either the tendon or the bone. Sports in which the legs are forced to move quickly, such as sprinting or slalom skiing, are the most likely culprits. Surgery may or may not be required, but 4-6 weeks of rest is generally mandatory.

Injuries to the pubic region (the lower front of the torso) can come with a direct blow but can also develop with a continued overload to the area. Endurance athletes such as cross country skiers, long distance runners, soccer and ice hockey players are often afflicted by such problems. The pain may be due to an inflamed tendon or a stress or avulsive fracture.

Stress injuries in the lower part of the inside of the pelvic bones are often caused by repeated trauma to the bones. Stress fractures of the hip may occur in long distance runners and race walkers and are more common in females than males.

Osteitis pubis is an inflammatory reaction that occurs at the front of the pelvis where the two pubic bones meet. It is sometimes seen in weight lifters and typically responds to rest from heavy lifting and occasionally a corticosteroid injection. It is thought to be primarily due to overuse The kicking by a soccer player and the continued pulling on the bone by the tendons that attach to the thighs as is found in long distance runners and race walkers can create overuse problems.

Thigh Injuries

Muscle pulls are common in the hamstrings. The damage may include, or even be limited to, the tendon. The pull is generally high in the muscle — near the buttocks and is commonly pulled while running fast or jumping. It is usually caused by the quick change from a lengthening action to a shortening action (the stretch-shortening cycle). This is most likely to occur when a person is running fast and has to quickly change the direction of the thigh from being pulled forward by the quadriceps to being pulled backward by the hamstrings. The faster the person is running, the more quickly this action must occur. The small muscle fibers may not be able to take the transition and may become strained. Muscle pulls in the quadriceps are likely to be lower in the muscle and may occur near or in the patellar tendon.

Eccentric contractions which damage the sarcomeres are mechanical. It is hypothesized that the strain disrupts some membranes that permit the hydrolysis of the protein. (In hydrolysis the protein is split and incorporated with a water molecule which also splits.) The muscle protein is thereby damaged and cannot function. Further, the inflammation that occurs further damages the muscle protein. Neither "getting into shape" nor stretching has an effect on preventing this type of injury. But since the actual cause of the injury is merely now a hypothesis, we can't say for certain exactly what happens nor how we can prevent the damage. [20]

Studies at Duke University revealed that certain muscles are more susceptible to strain injury (muscles that cross multiple joints or have complex architecture). These muscles have a low strain threshold for both passive and active injury. Strain injury is not the result of muscle contraction alone, rather, strains are the result of excessive stretch or stretch while the muscle is being activated. When the muscle tears, the damage is localized very near the muscle-tendon junction. The commonly injured muscles have been described and include the hamstring, the rectus femoris, gastrocnemius and adductor longus muscles. Injuries inconsistent with involvement of a single muscle-tendon junction proved to be at tendinous origins rather than within the muscle belly. [21]

Bruises of the thigh muscles are common, especially in contact sports. The quadriceps are particularly vulnerable. Bruises are most likely in contact sports. These bruises (charlie horses) can be on the surface or deep. The deeper bruises are accompanied by a rupture of the blood vessels in the area of the bruise. This causes a hematoma that can be very serious. Its most serious consequence can be the formation of bone bits in the muscle. this is called myositis ossificans.

The Knee

The knee is obviously an essential body part for most sports. Its importance is underlined by injuries by either direct blows that stretch ligaments or by chronic actions that can bruise or otherwise injure the internal surfaces of the joint. Direct blows to the knee are most likely to stretch ligaments and may injure the menisci, the semi-circular cartilage-like cushions that ease the sliding of the thigh bone (femur) on the leg bone (tibia).

Cartilage (meniscus) injuries are most likely to occur when the leg is planted firmly on the ground, and the knee is flexed. When an athlete wears cleated shoes, as in soccer, it is more likely that a blow to the knee can cause a serious injury. A twisting movement may then shear the cartilage and cause a tear in the meniscus. The torn meniscus may cause locking of the knee joint in certain situations, and locking is generally a sign of a cartilage injury.

The cruciate ligaments are inside the knee joint and protect the knee against excessive forward-backward movement. A blow from the front or the back can stretch the ligament that protects the knee from moving in that direction. So a blow to the front of the thigh can stretch or tear the cruciate ligament (anterior cruciate) which is supposed to protect forward-backward movement. Anterior cruciate ligament injuries typically occur either with a hyperextension mechanism, such as landing from a jump, or a twisting mechanism that occurs with the foot planted. This may occur with a quick pivoting movement in a sport such as soccer, skiing or basketball. Less commonly a direct blow to the front or side of the knee can cause a tearing or stretching of the anterior cruciate ligament. This may be accompanied by a tear of one of the collateral ligaments (medial or lateral), which stabilize the knee in a side to side fashion. This type of injury is becoming more common in skiing.

Females are up to five times more susceptible to this injury than males. The reason for this is not completely understood, although it may have to do with differences in the lower extremity alignment. The angle of the femur is greater in men, so the female knee joint is continually under more pressure. Also, there are differences in muscle and ligament strength and size, and hormonal differences between men and women. Combine this with the generally smaller and weaker knee ligaments, and you have the potential for the problem.

An NCAA study of basketball players in the U.S. showed that women are four times more likely to suffer anterior cruciate ligament (ACL) injuries than men. In fact, research shows that in all sports and recreational activities, women suffer ACL tears 6-8 times more often than men. Sports medicine physicians and orthopedists postulate that there are two main reasons why women are more susceptible to ACL tears than men. The first is that when women jump, they put more force on the ligament. The second theory on the higher rate of ACL tears in women is that the ACL is smaller and weaker in women and is thus vulnerable to the sudden stops, rigorous jumping and twists and turns typical in basketball and other court sports like volleyball.

A study by the University of Michigan found that women tend to rely more on their quadriceps (muscle in the front of the thigh) while men use their hamstrings (muscles on the back of the thigh) in stopping forward movement. Quadriceps and hamstring muscles oppose one another and stabilize the knee when one lands from a jump or makes a running cut or twisting motion. The Michigan study concluded that women athletes should place greater emphasis on conditioning and strengthening their hamstrings to take some of the pressure off of the ACL. Others recommend athletes try to land on two feet and round off turns instead of cutting sharply at high speed.

Studies have also found links between menstrual cycles and knee injuries. For example, during childbirth the ligament tissue of the pelvis undergoes a dramatic change in strength. More research is being done into the relation of hormonal fluctuations, the strength of ligaments and knee injuries.

Braces have been developed to reduce the chance of knee injuries. Generally they are heavy metal hinges that attach to the external side of the leg with velcro straps. It would appear that they would protect against injury, but research has not validated that they are effective. Soft neoprene sleeves may be helpful to decrease swelling after a knee injury and provide light support.

Knee pain can affect every aspect of the knee. The posterior cruciate ligament is more commonly injured by a direct blow to the front of the tibia. Pain in the front of the knee (housemaid's knee) can be caused by a number of injuries including damage to the patellar tendon or an inflamed bursa (lubricating sac). It can be caused by continued trauma to the area or by a weakness of the hamstrings when compared with the quadriceps which puts additional pressure on the front of the knee.

Damage to the back surface of the knee cap (patella) is medically termed chondromalachia patella or patelliofemoral pain syndrome, but it is commonly called "cyclist's knee" or "runner's knee." There are many causes including the misalignment of the knee cap caused by a lack of flexibility, muscular weakness in the quadriceps, or a bone deformity or a roughening of the smooth cartilage lining of the patella which doesn't allow it to ride smoothly in its desired track.

Patellar tendonitis is common among runners and jumpers ("jumper's knee") of all ages. The continued flexion and extension of the knee joint during running can cause small damages to the tendon. In more severe cases, the tendon can tear in the area of the patella or closer to the tendon's attachment below the knee.

Lower Leg Injuries

Shin splints (medial tibial stress syndrome) generally are painful in the middle part of the front of the tibia. A sharp pain is more likely to be a stress fracture, but a duller, more diverse, pain is likely to be shin splints. These are generally caused by poor leg or foot alignment, by incorrect shoes for the activity, poor running mechanics, overtraining or by running on hard surfaces. The activity has either caused small muscle tears, stretched the connective tissue between the muscle fibers or overly stretched and damaged the tissues holding the muscle to the shin bone. If you can determine the cause of the injury, you can better direct your healing efforts.

Other than shin splints, most lower leg problems occur in the back of the leg. Tendinitis, stress fractures and stress-caused muscle strains are not uncommon because the calf muscles are used in every running, jumping and dancing activity as well as in some kicking activities such as soccer and martial arts.

The frequency of stress fractures in the lower leg has found that of all stress fractures 34% are of the tibia, 24% of the fibula, 18% of the ankle bones, 14% of the femur, 6% of the pelvis and 4% of other bones. Female athletes in sports involving landing (jumpers, dancers, gymnasts) or cutting (basketball, soccer, team handball) are more likely to develop stress fractures of the fibula. Female long-distance runners are more likely to develop stress fractures of the tibia. The female athlete triad (see Chapter 12) is considered to be a primary factor in female fractures.

Long-legged runners are more likely to have problems with stress fractures than are their shorter-legged comrades. And those who run on an uneven surface, such as on crowned road, are more likely to have problems in the downhill leg. The same is true of running on a banked track. For this reason it is best to balance the leg stress by running as far one way as the other, running on the same side of the street or running the same number of laps in each direction on the embanked track. Running on a soft surface, such as grass or sand, significantly reduces the forces that the tibia and the surrounding muscles and tendons must absorb and may reduce injuries.

Achilles tendinitis or rupture are quite common. The muscles in the back of the calf (gastrocnemius and soleus) are extremely strong and are used in nearly every movement in which we walk, run, jump, dance or ski. These muscles control the tension on the Achilles' tendon. With every step or jump, we put tension on the heel cord and problems can result. They may include a single trauma that rips the tendon or a series of minor injuries that develop a chronic tendinitis. The same kinds of forces that can injure the tendon can injure the muscles fibers and strain or tear them. In high speed stretching of the Achilles' muscle-tendon, it was found that the injuries first occurred in the muscle fibers, then in the tendon units. [22]

A Swedish study has concluded that chronic inflammation of the Achilles tendon does not have clearly defined causes or treatments. There doesn't seem to be much inflammation, but there are changes in the collagen fiber structure of the tendon. These seem to be caused primarily by overuse. While rest and non-steroidal anti-inflammatory drugs (such as aspirin) are often used, they don't always cure the problem. In fact, about 25% of people with this problem will require surgery. [23]

"Tennis leg" is an injury to the tendons of the top of the calf muscle (gastrocnemius) caused by pushing off on the serve, rising on the toes to hit an overhead smash, or pushing off hard to move forward.

Cramps in the calf are quite common in runners, especially during hot weather when excessive amounts of fluids have been lost. Swimmers may also experience such cramps when they extend the toes down forcefully or when the water is cold and reduces circulation. In a cramp a large number of the muscle fibers contract and will not relax. Any muscle with insufficient blood can cramp. For this reason make certain that you have enough muscle nutrients in your diet — water, salt, calcium and potassium.

The Foot And Ankle

As with the wrist, there are a large number of bones that make up the ankle and foot. There is, therefore, a great chance for injury.

Fractures, both stress and direct-force caused, are common in the bones of the feet. Being stepped on or receiving a blow to the foot may cause a bone to break. If there is any doubt in your mind, see a doctor and get X-rays. Otherwise, treat it as a sprained ankle with rest, ice, compression, and a brace. Stress fractures are commonly caused by continued stresses on the foot bones. Long distance walking or running are common causes for stress fractures in the foot. The symptoms of stress fractures are pain, particularly increasing pain with increased exercise.

A sprained ankle is the most common type of athletic injury. It occurs when the outside of the ankle is severely overstretched. The ligaments stretch and may pull off a bone chip where they attach to a bone. Because ligaments take some time to shrink back to their normal length, ankle sprains often recur. In fact 75% of those who sprain an ankle will re-sprain it within a year.

While any of the ligaments in the foot or ankle can be sprained, the most common type is in the lower, outside area of the ankle. The outside part of the foot has moved downward and the athlete's weight stretches the ligaments. This commonly happens when players have jumped then landed on another player's foot. Basketball and volleyball are likely sports for this to happen. In soccer or rugby, a tackle or block from one side may sprain the far side ankle as the force hits higher on the calf while the cleats of the shoe hold the foot firm on the turf. Uneven playing surfaces can also cause sprained ankles. Sometimes a "crack" is heard as the ligament tears. Other times there is only the twisted ankle and the immediate pain. Swelling begins almost immediately. The standard treatment of ice (and later, heat), compression and elevation should be started immediately. Mild sprains will often be sufficiently healed within a week so that activities can be resumed. More severe sprains may take 6 weeks.

Ankle braces can be used on athletes who have sustained a sprain, but they should also be used in any cutting sports in order to prevent the first sprain. While often ankle taping has been used in sports such as basketball, the current ankle braces are always more effective preventers of injury after the first 5-20 minutes of play when the tape has stretched. The major types of ankle braces are the lace up type with hook and eye straps that add additional support to the ankle and the plastic hinged brace. The plastic types are more expensive but do not bind the ankle as tightly, so they allow the type of up and down movement that is essential to running and jumping. High top shoes also offer some protection against ankle sprains, but they reduce the ankle's mobility. The best means of prevention of ankle sprains is a conditioning program that includes strengthening of the muscles on the outside of the ankle (the peroneal muscles) along with proprioceptive training (balance training).

Prevention of running injuries can often be accomplished by the use of orthotics. These are shoe inserts that properly support the bones of the feet and often allow for an effective stretching of the ligaments and tendons which can prevent problems such as shin splints, plantar fascitis and contractures.[24]

A stone bruise is a bruise to the bottom of the heel. It is particularly prevalent with those who go barefoot or wear thin-heeled shoes and step on stones. It also occurs with runners and jumpers who continually land on the base of the heel rather than on the toes. Heel spurs can develop because of the irritation. The pain may be quite sharp and may feel like a stone is in the heel of the shoe.

Plantar fasciitis is a common complaint, especially with older athletes. It is an inflammation of the connective tissue under the foot. It is said to affect nearly 20% of runners. The soreness is under the foot and in the heel or just forward of the heel. The pain is particularly noticeable when getting out of bed in the morning. It may also be evident when arising after being seated for some time. The condition is generally a stress injury where the tendons under the foot are repeatedly stressed, such as in running or in doing heel raises with significant weight on the back.

Another related cause is often that the foot is pronated (the inside part of the foot is closer to the ground). When this is true, a proper orthotic device may both heel the foot and prevent a recurrence. The orthotic may take up to six months to cure the problem. Exercises that strengthen the under part of the foot should also be done. Put a towel on the floor and, with your toes over the edge of the towel, bring it toward you by curling the toes under and pulling the towel.

Blisters are caused by an irritation of the skin in which the skin is rubbed and the outer layer of skin separates from the inner layer. It is most common on the back of the heel, on the toes, or under the ball of the foot. Stiff-heeled shoes, shoes not properly laced, shoes that are to big or too small, and new sport shoes are often the cause of a blister. At the beginning of a sport season blisters are far more likely. Football, basketball and running are the most likely sports in which early season blisters will occur. It is always a good idea to wear two pair of thin socks when breaking in new shoes. The extra sock absorbs some of the rubbing that the skin would otherwise have to endure.

Turf toe is a sprain of the ligaments at the base of any toe. While artificial turf and other hard playing surfaces are generally blamed for the condition, any hyperextension of the toes, such as when starting to sprint, can cause it. It can also be caused by a fall or a trauma to the toe or toe area. In soccer the injury may be caused by a single trauma. In dancers and runners the injury may be caused by a more chronic and continual bending of the toes. Padding, appropriate taping and orthotics may be used to aid in the healing, and orthotics or "toe cups" may be used to prevent the injury.

Altitude Sickness

Altitude sickness results from the reduced amount of oxygen in the atmosphere high above sea level. It is most common in altitudes above 7000 feet (2100 meters) but can occur at only 4000 feet. About 30% will experience it when they go to 10,000 feet (3000 meters) and 75% will be similarly affected at altitudes over 15,000 feet (4500 meters).

The symptoms for moderate altitude sickness include headaches (especially in the front of the head), insomnia, nausea and breathing problems. More severe symptoms can include anorexia, vomiting, tiredness and breathing problems even at rest. The most common treatments include drinking more fluids (water, not alcohol), analgesics such as aspirin, higher carbohydrate intake, rest, and, if not to the final altitude, a slower ascent to the final altitude.

Sleeping at an altitude of over 8000 feet can bring on the symptoms. If you are to go to a higher altitude, it is best to keep your increases in altitude to less than 1500 feet per night for sleeping purposes. One of the negative factors in sleeping at altitude is "periodic breathing" in which the breathing pattern is not rhythmical. This disturbs the quality of sleep — especially the deepest sleep. It is during this deepest sleep period that the most restful sleep occurs. It generally takes 2-4 days to adjust to altitudes in the 8000 foot range. If you were to increase your altitude by only 1000 feet per day, you would probably not experience any negative effects. But if you were to go skiing above 8000 feet, you might experience difficulties.

———

Notes:

1. B.W. Posthuma et al., "Detecting Changes in Functional Ability in Women with Premenstrual Syndrome" *American Journal of Obstetrics and Gynecology* 156.2(1987): 275-278.
2. E.A. Arendt, "Orthopedic Issues for Active and Athletic Women," *Clinics in Sports Medicine* 13.2 (1994): 485.
3. H. Aagaard and U. Jorgensen, "Injuries in Elite Volleyball," *Scand J Med, Science Sports* 6.4 (1996): 228-232.
4. C.C. Teitz, "The Upper Extremities," *The Female Athlete*, American Academy of Orthopedic Surgeons Monograph Series, AAOS, 1997.
5. E.L. Flatow et al, "Excursion of the Rotator Cuff Under the Acromion," *American Journal Sports Medicine* 22 (1994): 779-788.
6. S. Neimi et al., "Neck and Shoulder Symptoms and Leisure Time Activities in High School Students," *Journal of Orthopedic Sports Physical Therapy* 24.1 (1996): 25-29.
7. F.W. Jobe, R.S. Kvitne and C.E. Giangarra, "Shoulder Pain in the Overhead or Throwing Athlete: The Relationship of Anterior Instability and Rotator Cuff Impingement," *Orthopedic Review* 18 (1989): 963-975.
8. J. Walch et al., "Impingement of the Deep Surface of the Superspintaus Tendon on the Posterior Superior Glenoid Rim. An Arthroscopic Study," *Journal of Shoulder and Elbow Surgery* 1 (1992): 238-245.
9. A. Ferretti, A. Carli and M. Fontana, " Injury of the Suprascapular Nerve at the Spinoglenoid Notch. The Natural History of Infraspinatus Atrophy in Volleyball Players," *American Journal of Sports Medicine* 26.6 (1998): 759-763.
10. D.L. Holden and D.W. Jackson, "Stress Fractures of the Rib in Female Rowers," *American Journal of Sports Medicine* 13 (1985): 342-348.
11. K.A. Karlson, "Rib Stress Fractures in Lead Rowers: A Case Series and Proposed Mechanism," *American Journal of Sports Medicine* 26.4 (1998): 516-519.

12. S.W. Barrentine et al., "Biomechanics of Windmill Softball Pitching with Implications About Injury Mechanics at the Shoulder and Elbow," *Journal of Orthopedic Sports and Physical Therapy* 28.6 (1998): 405-415.
13. A.C. Rettig and D.V. Pattel, "Epidemiology of Elbow, Forearm, and Wrist Injuries in the Athlete," *Clinics and Sports Medicine, The Athletic Elbow and Wrist* 14.2 (1995): 289.
14. H.W. Gruchow, "An Epidemiologic Study of Tennis Elbow, Incidence, Recurrence and Effectiveness of Prevention Strategies," *American Journal of Sports Medicine* 7 (1979): 234-238.
15. F.C. McCue, P. Ploska and R.M. Alley, "Athletic Injuries to the Hand and Wrist," *Current Rev Sports Medicine*, eds. R.J. Johnson and J. Lombardo (Philadelphia, Current Medicine, 1994) 42-51.
16. P.M. Murray and W.P. Cooney, "Golf-Induced Injuries of the Wrist," *Clinics in Sports Medicine* 15.1 (1996): 85-109.
17. C. Steyers and T. Schelkun, "Practical Management of Carpal Tunnel Syndrome," *The Physician and Sports Medicine* 23.1 (1995): 83-87.
18. A. Richardson, "Thoracic Outlet Syndrome in Aquatic Athletes," Clinics in Sports Medicine 18.2 (1999): 361-378.
19. M.R. Hutchinson, "Low Back Pain in Elite Rhythmic Gymnasts," *Medical Science in Sports Exercise* 31.11 (1999): 1686-1688.
20. R.L. Lieber and J. Friden, "Mechanisms of Muscle Injury after Eccentric Contraction," *Journal Sci Med Sport* 2.3 (1999): 253-265.
21. W.E. Garrett, Jr., "Muscle Strain Injuries," *American Journal of Sports Medicine* 24.6 Suppl (1996): S2-8.
22. R. Lin, G. Chang and L. Chang, "Biomechanical Properties of Muscle-Tendon Unit under High-Speed Passive Stretch," *Clinical Biomechanics (Bristol, Avon)* 14.6 (1999): 412-417.
23. H. Alfredson and R. Lorentzon, "Chronic Achilles Tendinosis: Recommendations for Treatment and Prevention," *Sports Medicine* 29.2 (2000):135-146.
24. R.D. D'Ambrosia, "Orthotic Devices in Running Injuries," *Clinic Sports Medicine* 4.4 (1985): 611-618.

18

Treating Sport Injuries

There are a number of preferred methods of treating injuries. Some require special equipment available only at the offices of doctors, physical therapists or athletic trainers. Some emphasize cold treatments, some balance them. This chapter will present the method proposed by the British Olympic medical team as shown in the latest book on athletic injuries.[1] Any injury that seems serious or for which the severity is not known should be immediately seen by a competent medical person.

Standard Treatment for Your Injuries

The purpose of standard treatment is to stop the swelling and stop the scar tissue from developing. The first step of standard treatment is to apply some type of pressure, such as with an elastic bandage.

The application of cold compresses or ice is called for in most injuries in order to stop or slow any bleeding. Sometimes the area affected can be immersed in cold water. Sometimes ice will be applied. The ice can surround the joint in the case of treatment for a sprain or it might be applied by rubbing a pulled muscle with an ice cup — a cup of water frozen in a freezer. As the ice melts the paper of the cup can be torn away to expose more ice.

R.I.C.E., the acronym for *rest, ice, compression,* and *elevation* can remind you of the generally preferred initial treatment. The R.I.C.E. treatment is designed to reduce swelling. Pain may also be reduced by using non-steroidal anti-inflammatory drugs (NSAIDs). Aspirin and related drugs are NSAID-type drugs. [2] While the use of NSAIDs has long been recommended for post-injury pain recent studies presented at the American College of Sports Medicine convention report that at least two anti-inflammatory drugs — ibuprofen and flurbiprofen — provide no detectable therapeutic benefit

---

The standard treatment for any injury except a fracture is:

- First three days: icing for 20 minutes every 2 hours (If it is a joint injury begin manipulating the joint during the cold treatment.)
- Second three days: 1 minute hot, 3 minutes cold;
- Third three days: 2 minutes hot, 2 minutes cold;
- Fourth three days: 3 minutes hot, 1 minute cold; Stretch and strengthen the affected area continually.
- Thereafter: 10 minutes hot; When no swelling increase the heat to 20 minutes per session.

(Check with a sports medicine specialist to determine whether or not heat is advised in treating your injury.)

---

as anti-inflammatory agents or as analgesics following muscle injury. [3]

Healing the injury generally requires additional treatment. After bleeding has stopped, heat may be applied to stimulate blood flow and aid the healing process. Both strength and flexibility exercises can aid in the recovery and in keeping you from losing necessary strength or flexibility during the healing process. Proper stretching can also reduce the formation of some scar tissue which might otherwise tighten a muscle. But if the injury is to the muscle fiber, stretching might increase the injury. Let the doctor decide.

Following are more complete treatment suggestions that are common among those who professionally treat athletic injuries. While it is emphasized that the R.I.C.E. treatment is primary, and in many cases is the only treatment needed, often the injury is healed more quickly if heat or electrical stimulation is added to the treatment later in the rehabilitation process.[4] The heat can increase the blood flow to the area which can bring needed nutrients to the damaged area such as calcium to a broken bone. However, when in doubt use only the cold since heat can increase swelling.

Phase One

In the first three days, the goal is to stop and/or reduce swelling. Use ice on the injured area for 20 minutes every two hours. It is better to completely enclose the whole injured area. A sprained ankle could be put into a bucket filled with ice water. A knee would need a larger enclosure. A bath tub would do. The water should be between 55-60 degrees Fahrenheit (13-15 degrees Celsius). The very cold water will reduce the blood circulation and thereby reduce swelling and scarring. The amount of time that each body part may need in cold water or ice may vary. For example, it has been found that if a knee is iced for 5 minutes it is effective, but 25 minutes was four times more effective in decreasing the blood flow to the knee.

209

If, after a 24-hour time period, the swelling has gone down or remained the same, the next step in the treatment would be to begin heat, which promotes healing. If the swelling is stopped in the first 24-72 hour period, continuing to apply cold to the area is acceptable, but it delays the opportunity to begin healing by the proper use of heat.

The body usually gets rid of much of the swelling before it begins to heal the injury area. If there is a lot of swelling, the body will take a longer period of time to begin the healing process. The goal is to stop the swelling as much as possible before adding the heat to help heal the injury.

Phase Two

The second three days are used to both reduce swelling and to promote healing. If the swelling has definitely stopped, some heat can be applied — always followed by cold.

The standard treatment in the second 72 hour period would then be: 1 minute warm, 3 minutes cold, alternating 5 times, ending with 5 minutes of ice to shut down any blood vessels that may have opened due to the heat and begun bleeding again. It is best to submerge the injured area in warm water, but hot packs can also be used. While the injured area is in the warm water, the blood vessels are opening, bringing all the nutrients and enzymes into the area and beginning the healing process. Heat should be about 105-110 degrees Fahrenheit (41-44 degrees Celsius). It should not be applied for too long a period of time.

What to do for plantar fasciitis:
• Stretch the Achilles' tendon by standing a few feet from a wall and allowing your hips to drop toward the wall. Bend the ankle forward and feel the pull at the back of the heel.
• Use a soft rubber heel cup may ease the pain by cushioning the heel bone (and the probably heel spurs) when the heel hits the floor. The heel cup also reduces the tension of the Achilles tendon and the stretch of the ligaments under the foot. You can also use a felt or sponge rubber donut with the hole surrounding the spot where it is sore.
• The use of an appropriate orthotic show insert may aid in recovery.
• Softer more flexible well cushioned shoes, rather than stiff shoes, are also generally recommended.
• NSAIDs, such as aspirin, may reduce the inflammation and the pain.
• Don't walk or run on your toes, walk or run on hard surfaces, or walk in bare feet.
• Exercises which strengthen the under part of the foot should also be done. Put a towel on the floor and with your toes over the edge of the towel, bring it towards you by curling the toes under and pulling the towel.

Phase Three

The third three-day period emphasizes increased healing by more use of heat. During this period of treatment you will subtract 1 minute from the cold water and add that minute to the warm water, so there will be 2 minutes in the warm water, 2 minutes in the cold. Alternate this treatment 5 times, ending with 5 minutes of cold to shut down the blood vessels that are still not completely healed.

This should be done 2-5 times a day, if possible. If your daily schedule is quite full, you may need to make a few adjustments in order to maximize your healing process. An example would be to get up a half hour earlier in the morning. Treat your injury once before going to the office or to school. If you have a break during the morning give it another treatment. You may need to use hot packs (which can be heated in a small pan of water) and cold packs (ice cubes or a pack which can be put in the freezer) at this time. At lunch time you have another opportunity for a treatment. Repeat after school or work and before you begin your exercise program. (If you exercise, do not repeat the program immediately after the practice. Rather, use "ice" or cold water to reduce any swelling caused by the practice.)

Your last treatment of warm and cold will be just before bedtime. This schedule would give you five treatments even during a busy day. But remember, the more times the warm and cold treatment is done, the more the healing process is accelerated.

Phase Four

The fourth-three day period is done using 3 minutes warm, 1 minute cold, alternating 5 times and ending with 5 minutes of cold five times a day. At the end of the fourth 72-hour time period, which is 12 days, the treatment

What to do to treat a blister:
• Use a donut-shaped pad around the blister to eliminate any more pressure.   • Use a skin lubricant, such as Vaseline, over the blister to protect from any additional stress.   • Keep the area clean because the blister may pop on its own and you do not want to invite infection.
To prevent blisters:
• File down any calluses so that blisters do not develop under them.   • Always wear socks when you are wearing shoes.   • Use two pair of socks, especially early in the sport season.   • Buy shoes with a proper fit and break in new shoes gradually.

What to do for "pump bumps":

- Use an ice cup in a circular motion to reduce the inflammation.
- Wear shoes with softer heel sections and which do not put pressure on the Achilles' tendon.
- Use a donut pad over the inflamed area.
- Do not do exercises which use the calf muscle (heel raises, jumping, running)

---

is 10 minutes of hot treatment four to five times a day. Do not try to accelerate the treatment by using more than 10 minutes because more problems, such as unwanted swelling, are more likely.

If you notice any swelling, go back to the previous 72-hour time period recommendations — cut down on the heat and add more cold to control the swelling. If necessary, go all the way back to 1 minute of hot and 3 minutes of cold, the second 72 hour time period, and work back up again. After 24 days you should be nearly back to normal.

Additional therapy during this time will include exercises. These should be begun as soon as possible after the injury. The earlier you begin with the exercises, the less scar tissue will be formed. While the injured area, particularly a joint, is being iced, move it through a full range of movement.

Let's assume that your ankle has been sprained. Check the range of motion to see how far you can move your ankle in every direction. Take the ball of the foot and press the foot upward. Then move it downward. Then move the foot inward so that the sole of the foot is facing toward the other foot (inversion). Then roll the foot outward so that the sole is facing away from the other foot (eversion).

During the first 72 hours do these movements 10 times during the icing phase of your treatment. In the second 72 hour period, while doing 3 minutes of ice, do a great deal of movement of the joint. Because the ice is shutting down the blood vessels, the swelling can be controlled.

This standard treatment will help pulled muscles, twisted knees, twisted or sprained ankles, elbow problems, shoulder injuries and low back pain due to injury. It will not affect broken bones. No matter how much heat is applied, it will not heal any sooner than 4-6 weeks.

Moving more quickly through the phases is possible if you are well-conditioned — the circulatory system is usually more efficient, so the enzymes and nutrients are brought to the injury quickly and continuously. Often heat may be started almost immediately, possibly within a 24 hour period. On the other hand, a person in poor physical condition may have to go through the phases as three day periods.

Protecting The Injury

Injuries, whether blisters or large muscle bruises, can be protected. Protecting an injured area is important if you plan to continue in your sport while the injury heals. When an injury is to soft tissue, such as the skin or to the muscles, a doughnut type of pad is used to keep the pressure off of the injury and distribute it to the surrounding tissue. Depending on the size of the injury an appropriately thick pad is used.

For a small blister, a few thicknesses of gauze pads will do. To protect a larger area, a thick felt or heavy sponge rubber doughnut will work. Athletic training suppliers, pharmacies and many sporting goods stores usually have round or oval-shaped pads specifically made for such protection. This will then be covered with a thicker pad that protects the injury and directs any pressure to the underlying doughnut. Protected in this way, the injury will not be further irritated.

Athletic training taping can often be used to protect an injured joint or muscle. It may be used to limit the action of a joint, such as when taping an ankle or wrist, or it can be used to completely immobilize a joint, such as a finger or thumb. Certified athletic trainers are employed by most universities. Physical therapists are also generally adept at taping and are readily available in private practice.

Finding the Best Professional Treatment

A good sports medicine doctor is generally your best bet for effective treatment. Not all doctors understand the most effective methods to get you back on the field or into the pool quickly. For back injuries an effective chiropractor will often work wonders. It is generally best, however, if he or she works with a sports medicine specialist. Sometimes podiatrists can help with foot problems. For pain, acupuncture often works. A number of medical

What to do for shin splints:
• R.I.C.E.
• Strengthen the muscle by moving your foot upward against the pressure of your hand.
• Wear orthotics or arch supports (orthotics) and/or better cushioned shoes. (Commercial shoe inserts should also help.)
• Don't expect shin splints to heal themselves. They will get worse if you don't correct the problem.
• If the problem is caused by running, run on soft sand or soft grass rather than a hard track or a roadway.

What to do for cramps:
• Break the cramp by bending the ankle forward. It is best to have a second person break the cramp for you. Lie on your back, extend the leg up, let the other person forcefully push down on the ball of your foot to break the cramp. • Sometimes the cramp will reoccur shortly. Just repeat the procedure and massage the muscle to increase the circulation.

doctors have taken special training in acupuncture. Magnet therapy also often works, especially to speed the healing of fractures.

Psychological Factors In Injury And Recovery

An Australian study measured the anxiety of college athletes and their visual changes and reaction times during stress. The subjects were also evaluated according to their social support, their life events, and their stresses from them. The finding was that the major predictor of future injury was their negative stress from their lives outside of sport. [5]

Notes:
1. B. O'Connor et al., *Prevention and Treatment of Athletic Injuries* (United Kingdom: Crowood Press, 1998).
2. ACSM, Athens, Ohio, June 7, 1999.
3. R. Pfeiffer and B. Mangus, "Concepts of Athletic Training."
4. *ACSM's Handbook for the Team Physician*, ed. B. Kibler (Baltimore: Williams & Wilkins, 1996).
5. M.B. Andersen and J.M. Williams, "Athletic Injury, Psychosocial Factors and Perceptual Changes During Stress," *Journal of Sports Science* 17.9 (1999): 735-741.

19

Nutrition

─────

Our ability to become better conditioned is limited if we do not get sufficient amounts of the essential nutrients. This chapter on general nutrition will also point out some of the relationships between food and exercise. This should give you a more complete picture of this area of conditioning.

Nutrition

A basic understanding of the science of nutrition is essential to healthy living. An informed person will be aware of the nutrients necessary for minimal and optimal functioning, then put that knowledge into practice by developing a proper diet. Unfortunately, very few people consume even the minimum amounts of each of the necessary nutrients — protein, fat, carbohydrates, vitamins, minerals and water (the essential non-nutrient). The first three nutrients listed (protein, fat, and carbohydrates) bring with them the energy required to keep us alive in addition to other specific contributions to our bodies.

The calorie used in counting food energy is really a kilocalorie, one thousand times larger than the calorie used as a measurement of heat in chemistry class. In one food calorie (kilocalorie), there is enough energy to heat 1 kilogram of water 1 degree Celsius (2.2 pounds 1.8 degrees Fahrenheit), or to lift 3,000 pounds of weight one foot high. So those little calories you see listed on the cookie packages pack a lot of energy.

Most people need about 10 calories per pound just to stay alive. If you plan to do something other than just lie in bed all day, you may need about 17 calories per pound of body weight per day in order to keep yourself going. Most athletes, particularly the endurance athletes, need much more.

215

Activity	Calories per kilogram per minute	Calories per pound per minute
Badminton	6.4	2.9
Basketball	9.8	4.5
Canoeing	7.3	3.3
Cycling	12.0	5.5
Field hockey	9.5	4.3
Football/soccer	9.4	4.3
Golf	6.0	2.7
Gymnastics	4.7	2.1
Judo	13.8	6.3
Resting	1.2	0.5
Running (6 min. mile)	17.9	8.1
Running (8 min. mile)	14.8	6.7
Squash	15.1	6.9
Swimming (non-competition)		
Crawl	11.1	5.0
Backstroke	12.0	5.5
Tennis	7.7	3.5
Volleyball	3.6	1.6
Walking (easy)	5.7	2.6

You can roughly figure your caloric needs using these figures. These figures are for recreational athletes, not top level athletes.

Protein

Protein is made up of 22 amino acids. These are made up of carbon, hydrogen, oxygen, and nitrogen. While both fats and carbohydrates contain the first three elements, nitrogen is found only in protein. Protein is essential for building nearly every part of the body — the brain, heart, organs, skin, muscles, and even the blood.

There are four calories in one gram of protein. Adults require .75 grams of protein per kilogram of body weight per day. This translates into one-third a gram of protein per pound. So, an easy estimate for your protein requirements in grams per day would be to divide your body weight by 3. For instance, if you weigh 150 pounds, you need about 50 grams of protein per day.

Physically active adults have been thought to require more protein than is recommended by the United States Recommended Daily Allowance

(USRDA), which is set at .8 grams per kilogram of body weight per day. In fact, most active people need not eat additional protein if they keep 12-15% of their total calories as protein. Since active women need to consume more calories per day than their inactive counterparts due to their increased energy expenditure, active women who keep their protein intake around 15% of their total calories will eat more protein per day and thereby fulfill their body's protein requirement. Excess protein consumption (above the body's requirement) will be broken down and the calories will either be burned off or stored as fat.

However, when involved in a strenuous strength training regimen, it may be necessary to increase your protein intake percentage depending on the amount of total calories you consume per day. Strength trained athletes have been shown to adapt to diets considered low in protein (.86 grams per kilogram per day) by decreasing their overall body protein synthesis. This is not a good idea since the purpose of strength training is to build muscle, and you don't want to do anything to hamper this process. Therefore, those who participate in heavy resistance training may choose to follow a diet higher in protein (1.4 grams per kilogram per day) to elicit maximum benefits from their workout.

In order to make any body organ, including muscle, you must first have all of the necessary amino acids. Some of them your body can manufacture, while others you must get from your food. Those amino acids that you must get from your food are called the essential amino acids, while the others that you can make are known as the non-essential amino acids. During childhood, 9 of the 22 amino acids are essential, but in adulthood we acquire the ability to synthesize one additional amino acid, leaving us with 8 essential amino acids.

Amino acids cannot be stored in the body. Therefore, people need to consume their minimum amounts of protein every day. If adequate protein is not consumed, the body immediately begins to break down tissue (usually beginning with muscle tissue) to release the essential amino acids. If even one essential amino acid is lacking, the other essential ones are not able to work to their full capacities. For example, if methionine (the most commonly-lacking amino acid) is present at 60 percent of the minimum requirement, the other seven essential amino acids are limited to near 60 percent of their potential. When they are not used, amino acids are deaminated and excreted as urea in the urine.

Animal products (i.e., fish, poultry, and beef) and animal by-products (i.e., milk, eggs, cheese) are rich in readily usable protein. This means that when you eat animal products or by-products, the protein you consume can be converted into protein in your body because these sources have all of the essential amino acids in them. These foods are called complete protein sources.

Incomplete protein sources are any other food sources that provide protein but not high levels of all of the essential amino acids. Some examples of incomplete proteins include beans, peas, and nuts. These food sources must be combined with other food sources that have the missing essential amino acids so that you can make protein in your body. Some examples of complementary foods are rice and beans, or peanut butter on whole wheat bread.

Another reason to be aware of specific food combinations is to enhance the absorption of the protein consumed. The person who is aware of the varying qualities of proteins can combine them to take advantage of the strengths of each. For example, if flour is eaten at breakfast (i. e., as a piece of toast or coffee cake) and washed down with coffee, and then a glass of milk is consumed at lunch, each of the protein sources would be absorbed by the body at a lower potential. But if the bread was consumed with the milk at either meal, the higher protein values of both would be absorbed by the body immediately.

Protein supplements are used by some people, particularly weight trainers and athletes. These supplements may not be a good value because they usually fall far short of an effective balance of the essential amino acids. While six of the essential amino acids are usually present in good quantities in these supplements, methionine and tryptophan are usually found in lesser amounts — and they are the most commonly lacking of the aminos. Since 6

The essential amino acids and some foods in which they are contained:

- Iso-leucine: fish, beef, organ meats, eggs, shellfish, whole wheat, soya, milk.
- Leucine: beef, fish, organ meats, eggs, soya, shellfish, whole wheat, milk, liver.
- Lysine: fish, beef, organ meats, shellfish, eggs, soya, milk, liver .
- Methionine: fish, beef, shellfish, egg whites, milk, liver, whole wheat, cheese.
- Phenylalanine: beef, fish, egg whites, whole wheat, shellfish, organ meats, soya, milk.
- Threonine: fish, beef, organ meats, eggs, shellfish, soya, liver .
- Tryptophan: soy milk, fish, beef, soy flour, organ meats, shell fish, egg whites.
- Valine: beef, fish, organ meats, eggs, soya, milk, whole wheat, liver.

The amount of nutrients recommended for each person per day are Daily Values. These values were established in 1995 and are required for 10 nutrients with an additional 22 optionally listed food components. From 1973 such recommendations were called RDA (Recommended Daily Allowances) and prior to that MDR (Minimum Daily Requirements).
₅

grams per pound of methionine (13 mg per kg) and 1.6 grams of tryptophan (3.5 grams per kg) per day are the recommended daily allowances, you might check to determine how much of these are actually contained in a supplement. This is especially important if your diet is lacking in either one or both of these amino acids and you are relying primarily on the supplement to account for most or all of your protein needs. A better and cheaper source of protein for one needing a supplement would be powdered milk. If your diet is deficient in protein, you might also consider using egg whites (or egg substitutes), milk or chicken. It may prove less expensive and more nutritious.

Fats

Fat is made of carbon, hydrogen and oxygen. There are nine calories in a gram of fat. In the body, fat is used to develop the myelin sheath that surrounds the nerves. It also aids in the absorption of vitamins A, D, E, and K, which are the fat-soluble vitamins. It serves as a protective layer around our vital organs, and it is a good insulator against the cold. It is also a highly concentrated energy source. And, of course, its most redeeming quality is that it adds flavor and juiciness to food!

Just as protein is broken down into different kinds of nitrogen compounds called amino acids, there are also different kinds of fats. There are three major kinds of fats (fatty acids): saturated fats, monounsaturated fats, and polyunsaturated fats. A more newly recognized fat is called a trans-fatty acid which occurs when an unsaturated fat is converted to a harder saturated-like fat in foods. This occurs when oils, such as corn and safflower, are hardened to make margarines.

Saturated fats are "saturated" with hydrogen atoms. They are generally solid at room temperature and are most likely found in animal fats, egg yolks, and whole milk products. Since these are the fats that are primarily responsible for raising the blood cholesterol level and hardening the arteries, they should be minimized.

Monounsaturated fats (oleic fatty acids) have room for two hydrogen ions to double bond to one carbon. They are liquid at room temperature and are found in great amounts in olive, peanut, and canola (rapeseed) oils. Dietary monounsaturated fats have been shown to have the greatest effect on the reduction of cholesterols, particularly the most harmful LDLs, thereby contributing a positive effect on atherosclerosis. They have also been found to reduce breast cancer risk. [1] The best sourcs of these are canola (rapeseed) oil and olive oil. Many nuts also contain high amounts of monounsaturates.

Polyunsaturated fats (linoleic fatty acids) have at least two carbon double bonds available, which translates into space for at least four hydrogen ions. Polyunsaturated fats are also liquid at room temperature and are found in the highest proportions in vegetable sources. Safflower, corn, and linseed oils are good sources of this type of fat. Polyunsaturated fatty acids of the omega-3 type, found primarily in fatty fish (especially salmon, trout and herring), may also contribute to the prevention of atherosclerosis.

Desirable essential fatty acids

Everyone has heard of the benefits of fish oils in reducing heart disease. These essential fatty acids (EFA) were given the name of "vitamin F" in the 1920's. While desirable, they are no longer viewed as vitamins. These oils are part of the polyunsaturated fats (PUFA) group. Most people obtain enough of these fatty acids in their diets-particularly if they consume vegetable oils, meats, fish or poultry. The most important of these essential fatty acids are: linoleic, linolinic, and arachidonic acids. Some vegetable oils contain linolenic acid but they do not contain eicosapentaenoic acid (EPA) or docosahexaenoix acid (DHA) which fish provide. Fish are able to convert linolenic acid into EPA and DHA. The human body does not have this ability. These fatty acids are precursors to develop the hormone-like substances called prostaglandins.

The 100 prostaglandins have a number of functions. Some constrict or dilate the blood vessels (altering blood pressure), some affect the passages of messages along the nerves, some affect the excretion of water from the kidneys. One, called thromboxane, made from the fatty acid arachidonic acid, increases blood clotting. The EPA and DHA may also be implicated in the reduction of cholesterol and triglycerides which reduce heart attack risk.

When your skin is cut you want your blood to clot quickly. However clots in your blood are the major causes of heart attacks and cerebral vascular accidents (CVA or stroke). Clots are continually being made in the blood and are generally dissolved. However if one sticks in an artery where it is formed it is called a thrombus. If it is formed in the blood and floats to another area it is called an embolism. Most heart attacks are caused by a thrombus sticking in an artery which "crowns" the heart (coronary) and nourishes the heart muscle. This is called a coronary thrombosis. Embolisms are often the cause of strokes as they float to an artery of the brain and cut off its blood supply thereby deadening that area of the brain.

Years of observation and study have shown that people who eat lots of fish have fewer blood clotting problems, so fewer heart attacks and strokes. This is because the fatty acids in the fish fat change the production of thromboxane and thereby reduce the clotting ability of the blood.

Omega 3 Fatty Acids

There are actually six different omega 3 fatty acids. The most important of which are (alpha) linolenic acid, DHA and EPA. Heavily exercising people generally have lower than normal levels of omega 3 fatty acids. So it seems important for athletes to get plenty of this substance.

There are fish oil pills which can be consumed but they don't seem to be as effective as eating fish. Also, we don't know what the proper dosage of pills might be and whether there are any adverse side effects from their use. So here is one area where the "natural" food seems better than the pill. You should consume fish about three times a week or more. We also don't know if the benefits from eating fish come only from the oil or is there some hidden benefit from the non-oily parts of the fish. Still, fish oil supplements, from fish muscle, have been tried in a number of studies and have proven somewhat effective in reducing pain. The ideal dose seems to be 2-3 grams of omega 3 oil daily. It must be mentioned, however, that increasing the amount of omega 3 fatty acids requires a greater intake of vitamin E because vitamin E is reduced when omega 3's are increased.

Since the omega 3 fatty acids are more easily destroyed by oxidation, the antioxidant vitamins (E, C, and beta carotene) are essential to protect them from disintegrating. The increase of omega 3 oils and anti-oxidants can reduce the less desirable omega 6 oils mentioned below. They can therefore reduce pain.

Omega 6 Fatty Acids

There are six omega 6 fatty acids. The most important of which are linoleic acid, arachidonic acid and linolinic acid . Heavily exercising people seem to have more of this fat than normal in their blood. This type of fatty acid seems to produce more of the inflammatory prostanoid types of byproducts. In our Western diets we seem to have much more of this than we need. Present day ratios range from 10-50 times more of the omega 6 than omega 3. The ideal range is under 5 to 1 and our Stone Age ancestors were closer to a 1 to 1 ratio. [2]

The higher rate of inflammatory products produced by too high a level of omega 6 fatty acids may be implicated in arthritis and other inflammatory diseases—such as those pains felt when exercising. We therefore don't need any more of this fatty acid. While we need some of it, we're getting too much.

Trans-Fat

Trans-fat is another type of fat. It is generally commercially made. As people demanded fewer saturated fats in their diets, manufacturers began adding hydrogen atoms to polyunsaturated fats to harden them. If you read the nutrition labels on foods you will often see "partially hydrogenated",

How to read a food label
• Read the ingredients. Generally the ingredients are listed according to the proportions used in the product. If you are concerned with the amount and types of fats in the product look for: whole eggs or egg yolks, cream or whole milk, butter or other animal fats, margarine or hydrogenated vegetable fats (sometimes listed as partially hardened fats), palm kernel oil or coconut oil. These are primarily saturated fats.
• Look at the nutritional analysis.
1. How many calories (Kcal) are there per serving.
2. What is the percentage of total fat. (Multiply the number of grams of fat by 9 then divide that number into the total calories.) If that number is less than 10% you have no problems. Less than 30% is the maximum recommended.
3. Some labels break down the fats into: saturated, mono-unsaturated, and poly-unsaturated. If this is done make certain that the saturated fats are less than a third of total fats (lower is better).
4. Hydrogenated vegetable fats contain trans-fats which act similarly to saturated fats but will be listed on the label as unsaturated fats so you must refer back to the ingredients list to check for hydrogenated vegetable fats or partially hardened fats. There may be more saturated fat than appears on the label.
5. Look at the fiber included. Any fiber is good, more than 4 grams is excellent.
6. If vitamins are listed, check the percentage of the recommended level. If the less common vitamins, such as B-6, B-12 and E are included that is good.
7. Check the minerals if you are salt sensitive. Sodium raises your blood pressure. (See mineral chart in Chapter 20.) More potassium than sodium is a good sign.

"hydrogenated" or "partially hardened" then the name of a polyunsaturated fat such as soy oil, corn oil, or safflower oil. In this type of fat the added hydrogen atoms are on opposite sides of the molecule. This is called the "trans" configuration. Most natural fats have the hydrogens on the same side of the molecule (called the "cis" configuration).

The trans-fats seem to act similarly to saturated fats in raising harmful cholesterols. Estimates of the percentage of these fats in the diet varies from 2%-15%. It depends on how much margarine, crackers and cookies one eats. Research on the exact amount of harm which these fats might cause is now being done. [3]

We eat too much fat. The minimum requirement for fat in the diet is considered to be somewhere between 10%-20% of the total calories consumed. The absolute maximum should be 30%, which is the amount now recommended for the American diet. While we, as a society, are still above this 30% value, we have been declining since the 1970s, so let's try to keep that trend going. Most of us consume between 35%-50% percent of our total calories in fats. Also, our typical diet is very high in saturated fats, and these are the fats that we want to avoid. Many cancers, particularly breast cancer, are related to our high fat intake.

Our high fat intake, most of which is saturated, tends to raise blood cholesterol levels in many people. For those who are interested in decreasing the chances of developing hardened arteries by lowering their blood cholesterol level, it is recommended that you follow a diet low in fat (with the saturated fat intake at 10 percent or less of the total diet) and consume less than 300 milligrams of cholesterol daily. Put another way, keep the total calories from fat under a third of your total intake and eat twice as much polyunsaturated and monounsaturated fats as saturated fat.

In the past, companies were allowed to merely identify the oil in a product on their labels as vegetable oil under the Food and Drug Administration requirements made in 1976, they are now required to note whether it is corn oil, cottonseed oil, soybean oil, etc., because some of the oils, even though they are not of animal origin, are very high in saturated fat. Palm kernel oil and coconut oil are particularly high in saturated fats.

When buying foods, especially cookies and crackers, always check the type of fat used. Avoid those with palm kernel oil and coconut oil. Also be aware of the hydrogenated oils used. While a hydrogenated safflower or canola oil may still have an acceptable fat ratio, a hydrogenated peanut or cottonseed oil may not contain the desired levels of unsaturated fats. Partially hydrogenated vegetable oils (trans fatty acids) may contribute to the development of heart disease.

Cholesterol in the diet is not as important as saturated fats in the diet in terms of controlling one's blood cholesterol level. For this reason, saturated fats should be reduced. This means that the major sources of saturated fats (red meats, butter, egg yolks, chicken skin, and other animal fats) should be greatly decreased. As an informed consumer you may want to keep track of both your total fat intake and your intake of saturated fat to become better aware of your potential risk for heart disease. For example, one raw or poached egg contains 5 grams of fat, all of which is in the yolk. 1.6 grams is saturated fat. It also contains 213 milligrams of cholesterol. An equal weight of fried hamburger contains 11.3 grams of fat, of which 4.5 grams are saturated, and 89 mg of cholesterol.

Olive oil contains several effective antioxidants whose levels depend upon where the olives were grown, how they were ripened and how the oil was extracted. Both the monounsaturated fat content of the olive oil, which is more resistant to oxidation than are other fats, and the phenolic antioxidents which reduce the oxidation of the other fats, reduce the levels of the harmful low density phospholipids (LDLs). The LDLs, as you remember, are the "bad" cholesterols. [4]

Carbohydrates

Carbohydrates are made from carbon, hydrogen, and oxygen, just as are fats, but "carbs" are generally a simpler type of molecule. There are four calories in a gram of carbohydrate. If not utilized immediately for energy as sugar (glucose), they are either stored in the body as glycogen (the stored form of glucose) or synthesized into fat and stored. Some carbohydrates cannot be broken down by the body's digestive processes. These are called fibers and will be discussed later. Of the digestible carbohydrates, there are two categories: simple and complex. Simple carbohydrates are the most readily usable energy source in the body and include such things as sugar, honey, and fruit. Complex carbohydrates are the starches. Complex carbs also break down into sugar for energy, but their breakdown is slower than with simple carbs. Also, complex carbohydrates bring with them various vitamins, minerals and fibers.

People in the United States often eat too many simple carbohydrates. These are the so-called "empty calories." They are empty because they have no vitamins, minerals, or fibers. While a person who uses a great deal of energy can consume these empty calories without potential weight gain, most of us find these empty calories settling on our hips. The average person consumes 125 pounds of sugar per year, which is equivalent to one teaspoon every 40 minutes, night and day. Since each teaspoon of sugar contains 17 calories, this amounts to 231,000 calories or 66 pounds of potential body fat if this energy is not used as fuel for daily living.

High-carbohydrate diets that are especially high in sugar may be hazardous to your health. They can increase the amount of triglycerides produced in the liver. These triglycerides are blood fats and are possible developers of hardened arteries. Also, a diet high in simple carbohydrates can lead to obesity, which may then result in the development of late-onset diabetes. But if your exercise regime uses a great many calories each day the triglycerides will be reduced. This will then reduce the "bad" low density lipoproteins or cholesterols (LDLs) and thereby increase the ratio of the good HDLs (heavy density lipoproteins).

Fiber

Fiber is that part of the foods we take in that is not digestible. Fiber helps to move the food through the intestines by increasing their peristaltic action. Vegetable fibers are made up chiefly of cellulose, an indigestible carbohydrate that is the main ingredient in the cell walls of plants. Plant-eating animals, such as cows, can digest cellulose. Meat-eating animals, such as humans, do not have the proper enzymes in their digestive tracts to metabolize cellulose.

The most common protein foods were ranked according to protein quality by the Food and Agricultural Organization of the United Nations in 1957 and revised in 1973.[6] The higher the rating, the better the essential amino acid ratio — that is, more of the essential amino acids are present. According to the ranking, whole eggs have the highest quality of protein with a ranking of 94%. Cow's milk is second with a biological rating of 84%; fish rate 83%; beef = 74%; soybeans and brown rice = 73%; white potatoes = 67%; whole grain wheat = 65%; beans = 58%; and peanuts = 54%.

Most Common Protein Foods

The higher the rating, the better the essential amino-acid ratio – that is, more of the essential amino acids are present. According to the ranking:

	Biological Value	Amino-acid Score
Whole eggs	94%	100%
Cow's milk	84%	98%
Fish	83%	100%
Beef	74%	100%
Soya beans	73%	63%
Brown rice	73%	59%
White potatoes	67%	48%
Whole-grain wheat	65%	45%
Beans	58%	46%
Peanuts	54%	55%

Bran (which includes the husks of wheat, oats, rice, rye, and corn) is another type of fiber. It is indigestible because of the silica in the outer husks. Some of the fibers, such as wheat bran, are insoluble. Their major function is to add bulk to the feces and to speed the digested foods through the intestines. This reduces one's risk of constipation, intestinal cancer, appendicitis, and diverticulosis.

Some types of fibers are soluble; that is, they can pick up certain substances such as dietary cholesterol. Pectin, commonly found in raw fruits (especially apple skins), oat and rice brans, and some gums from the seeds and stems of tropical plants (such as guar and xanthin) are examples of soluble fibers. These pick up cholesterols as they move through the intestines.

Foods high in fiber are also valuable in weight-reducing diets because they speed the passage of foods through the digestive tract, thereby cutting the amount of possible absorption time. They also cut the amount of hunger

In 1972, the Food and Agricultural Organization refined their findings by rating the quantity of each amino acid in a food. Here is an example of the rankings based on the percentages of three of the essential amino acids:

	Lysin	Methionine (and cystine)	Tryptophan
Hen's egg	167	138	107
Cow's milk	169	79	100
Soybeans	167	67	100
White wheat flour	86	55	105
Mixture of 1/3 milk and 2/3 flour	93	93	95
Mixture of 1/3 soybean and 2/3 flour	93	93	93

From the above chart, you can see that even the highly rated milk or soybeans are relatively low in methionine and cystine. But if we combined them with wheat flour, we can bring their protein quality into the 93 to 95 range. And the flour, which rated 86% in tryptophan, was raised to 93%.

experienced by a dieter because they fill the stomach. A larger salad with a diet dressing might give the person very few calories but still enough cellulose to fill the stomach, cut the hunger, and move other foods through the intestinal passage. If the diet dressing contains either guar or xanthin gum it will take away cholesterol from the digestive tract.

Food processing often removes the natural fiber from the food. This is one of the primary reasons that we, in America, have relatively low amounts of fiber in our diet. For instance, white bread has only a trace of fiber — about 9 grams in a loaf — while old-fashioned whole wheat bread has 70 grams. Also, when you peel a carrot or an apple, you remove much of the fiber.

Dietitians urge that people include more fiber in their diets. People should be particularly conscious of the benefits of whole-grain cereals, bran and fibrous vegetables. Root vegetables (carrots, beets and turnips) and leafy vegetables are very good sources of fiber. The average American diet has between 10-20 grams of fiber in it per day. We also have about twice the rate of colon cancer in this country versus other countries whose citizens eat more fiber. This is why it is the National Cancer Institute that has recommended that we consume between 25-35 grams of fiber per day.

Water

Water is called the essential non-nutrient because it brings with it no nutritional value and yet, without it, we would die. Water makes up approximately 60% of the adult body, while an infant's body is nearly 80% water. Water is used to cool the body through perspiration, to carry nutrients to and waste products from the cells, to help cushion our vital organs, and is a principle ingredient in all body fluids.

The body has about 18 square feet of skin that contains about 2 million sweat glands. On a comfortable day, a person will perspire about a half pint of water. Somebody exercising on a severely hot day may lose as much as 7 quarts of water. This needs to be replaced or severe dehydration can result. It is therefore generally recommended that each person drink eight, 8 oz. glasses of water, or its equivalent in other fluids, daily. This amount is dependent on the climate in which you live, the altitude at which you live, the type of foods that you eat, and the amount of activity in which you participate on a day to day basis.

Notes:

1. M.W. Pariza, "Animal Studies: Summary, Gaps, and Future Research," *American Journal of Clinical Nutrition* 66.6 Suppl (1997): 1548S-1556S.
2. H. Skjervold, "Lifestyle Diseases — Human Diet," *Meieriosten* 19: 527-529.
3. S. Shapiro, "Do Trans Fatty Acids Increase the Risk of Coronary Artery Disease? A Critique of the Epidemiologic Evidence," *American Journal of Clinical Nutrition* Oct. (1997): 1011S-1017S.
4. R. Masella et al., "Antioxidant Activity of 3, 4-DHPEA-EA and Protocatechuic Acid: A Comparative Assessment with other Olive Oil Biophenols," *Redox Rep* 4.3 (1999): 113-21.
5. J.A. Pennington and V.S. Hubbard, "Derivation of Daily Values use for Nutrition Labeling," *Journal of American Dietetic Association* 97.12 (1997): 1407-1412.
6. FAO/WHO: Energy and Protein Requirements, FAO Nutrition Report No. 52; WHE Tech. Report No. 522, Rome and Geneva, 1973; FAO/WHO: Amino Acid Content of Foods and Biological Data on Proteins, No. 24, Rome, 1970.

20

Vitamins, Minerals and Phytochemicals

Vitamins

Vitamins are organic compounds which are essential in small amounts for the growth and development of animals and humans. They act as enzymes (catalysts) which facilitate many of the body processes. Although there is some controversy as to the importance of consuming excess vitamins, it is acknowledged that we need a minimum amount of vitamins for proper functioning. Now that the destructive impact of free oxygen radicals (see below) has been established, it is generally recommended that certain vitamins be included in the daily intake of these nutrients at higher than the levels earlier recommended.

Some vitamins are soluble only in water; others need fat to be absorbed by the body. The *water-soluble vitamins*, B complex and C, are more fragile than the fat-soluble vitamins. This is because they are more easily destroyed by the heat of cooking and if boiled, they lose a little of their potency into the water. Since they are not stored by the body, they should be included in the daily diet.

The fat-soluble vitamins, A, D, E, and K, need oils in the intestines to be absorbed by the body. They are more stable than the water-soluble vitamins and are not destroyed by normal cooking methods. Because they are stored in the body, there is the possibility of ingesting too much of them — especially vitamins A and D.

Nutritional researchers disagree as to whether vitamin supplements are necessary. But they are generally in agreement that natural vitamins are no better than synthetically prepared vitamins. Thus, synthetically-made ascorbic acid is vitamin C.

Free oxygen radicals are single atoms of oxygen that can combine with many molecules and tissues. They are harmful substances produced by many natural body processes. Physical exercise, for all of its benefits, is one producer of free oxygen radicals. So is smoking and air pollution. In fact just the normal processes of living, even sleeping, produce some free oxygen radicals. It seems that between 3%-15% of all oxygen goes through a stage where it is a free oxygen radical.[1]

Free oxygen radicals are also found in the environment. Air and water pollution, any type of smoke, and even dried milk and eggs are some of the environmental sources of these toxins. In animal and human experiments relating to the effect of the anti-oxidant properties of vitamins C and E against air pollution and smoke, it was found that vitamin C is more effective in protecting against nitrogen dioxide, while vitamin E is more effective against ozone's oxidative effects. It should be noted, though, that for maximal protection against the harmful effects of air pollutants, the recommended dietary allowances for both of these vitamins should be increased.

The free oxygen radicals are implicated in many diseases, particularly mouth, throat, skin, stomach, prostate, colon, esophagus and lung cancers. They are also suspected of being one of the substances that can start the lesions that develop into hardened arteries and heart disease. The have also been suspected of causing cataracts (a hardening and damaging of the lens of the eye) and infertility. They are also linked to about 50 other diseases including ulcers, asthma, and high blood pressure.

Vitamin A is necessary for eye sight as well as skin. During World War II, Denmark began exporting large amounts of butter while supplementing Danish diets with margarine. Many children developed vision problems. It was eventually discovered that the lack of vitamin A in the margarine was responsible for the eye problems. The minimum vitamin A requirements, which the Danes had been consuming when they were eating butter, were reduced when they substituted margarine. Vitamin A was then added to the margarine and no further problems developed.

It is possible to get too much vitamin A. When this happens the liver can enlarge. There can be a loss of appetite or weight, loss of hair, severe bone and joint pain, and cracking lips. It probably requires 20 times the minimum daily requirement over a long period of time before this would occur. Here we are talking about vitamin A which comes from animal sources such as liver, milk and butter, not the plant sources of beta carotene which the body can synthesize into vitamin A.

Beta carotene is the plant source from which our bodies make vitamin A. Beta carotene does not seem to have the toxicity that the vitamin A from animal sources has. Beta carotene is a powerful anti-oxidant. Along with other anti-oxidants, including vitamins C and E, and the minerals selenium, zinc, and chromium, beta carotene "donates" electrons to free oxygen radicals making them less destructive. Once the beta carotene is converted to vitamin A it is no longer an anti-oxidant.

If you haven't taken in sufficient vitamin A through milk, eggs, liver, cheese, butter or fish oil, 6 units of beta carotene can be converted into one unit of vitamin A. What is left acts as a strong antioxidant. It can lower the risk of cataracts — a clouding in the lens of the eye which blurs vision which often occurs with age. It also reduces the risk of many cancers, particularly lung, bladder, rectal, and the serious skin cancer called melanoma. There is no recommended minimum daily requirement for this substance but the vitamin A which it can make has a minimum recommended daily amount of 4,000 international units (I.U.) for women and 5,000 for men.

The B-complex vitamins include at least 15 substances; only six have been termed essential. The B vitamins seem to work together, particularly in the nervous, circulatory, and digestive systems. Since they work together, an overdose of some could result in a deficiency in others.

Vitamin B1 (thiamin) is used to help to convert sugars (glucose) into an energy source which can be more readily used in the muscles. For this reason, people who are doing aerobic training must make certain that they have sufficient vitamin B. Without the vitamin a disease called "beri beri" develops. This disease results in the victim not having any energy.

Vitamin B2 (riboflavin) has as its primary function to help to convert fatty acids and proteins into sugars which can be used for energy. Riboflavin and vitamin B6 (pyridoxine) deficiencies may prove to hamper one's fitness performance. However, if one is not deficient, there appears to be no additional fitness benefit from further supplementation of these vitamins. With an increase in exercise training, riboflavin stores in the body have been shown to be reduced so it may be important to increase your intake of riboflavin when embarking on or increasing your existing exercise program.

Vitamin B3 (niacin) is necessary for the breakdown of glucose into energy. It is therefore essential for endurance athletes. It has also been found to inhibit the growth rate of some cancer cells in rats. Pellagra, a niacin deficiency disease, can lead to the development of symptoms of mental illness, such as hallucinations.

Vitamin B6 has several roles but its major function is in the development of proteins from amino acids. So if you are concerned with building muscle tissue it may be an important vitamin.

Vitamin B12 is necessary for the development of red blood cells and for maintaining the fatty sheath which protects the nerves. Vegans, those who consume no animal products or by-products, have diets that are usually deficient in vitamin B12. This is a concern because a vitamin B12 deficiency, in extreme cases, can cause a loss of brain function. Also, a group of vegans in England suffered irreversible destruction of nerve fibers in the spinal cord after 10 to 15 years because of their chronic vitamin B12 deficiency.

Folacin (folic acid) is a component of many tissues. If there is not enough of the vitamin present, the work of the cells is impaired. It is now known that it is an essential nutrient for pregnant mothers because a deficiency can cause severe birth defects in their children.

Excessive B vitamins can affect the efficiency of drugs being taken, so it is important to consider where your diet is in terms of your B vitamins when taking prescription drugs. For example, riboflavin can interfere with the effects of tetracycline, an antibiotic. Pyridoxine can interfere with levadopa, which is often prescribed for Parkinson's disease. And folic acid can lessen the effects of an anti-epileptic drug.

Vitamin C is essential in the production of collagen, the protein substance which is the mainstay of the body's connective tissues including tendons, ligaments and other body tissues, such as bones, teeth, and skin. It also is important for healing wounds. In addition it helps the body to use iron and it assists in the creation of the thyroid hormone thyroxin. It is also a powerful anti-oxidant. It is probably the most controversial of all the vitamins.

We know that people do need some vitamin C because without 10 milligrams a day, a person would get scurvy. In years past, before the effects of vitamin C were known, whole armies were decimated by scurvy. It is estimated that over 10,000 seamen died in the early days of sea exploration because they didn't have enough of this vitamin. However, once fresh citrus fruits were added to their diets, scurvy ceased to be a problem.

Vitamin C is made from glucose, a simple sugar found in ordinary table sugar. In order to turn the glucose into vitamin C, a special liver enzyme is required. Humans do not have that enzyme in their systems so they must take in vitamin C from an outside source, such as oranges. Most other animals do have the ability to convert sugar into this necessary vitamin.

Most of the research relating to vitamin C has dealt with whether or not it can cure or prevent the common cold. Since there are at least 113 distinct viruses known to be able to cause a cold, it is unlikely that any one vitamin could work to limit all the viruses. However, it does seem to have some positive effects in protecting against colds. This may be due to the effects of collagen building or its role in building the immune system. The many studies done relating vitamin C and colds have been inconclusive. If vitamin C helps to prevent colds it is most likely to be the strengthening of the immune system before the viruses were encountered.

One group of people may require more vitamin C than the rest of us. That is the smokers. This may not seem surprising in light of the earlier discussion of the protective effects of vitamin C as an anti-oxidant. It has been shown that smokers have lower blood levels of vitamin C than do non-smokers and smokers with a vitamin C deficiency have a greater chance of developing certain oral mucosal lesions than do others in the population

Vitamin D is seldom found to be deficient in the average diet. It can not only be part of the diet but it is also made by the action of sunlight on a cholesterol near the skin. Just two to three 15 minute periods in the sun per week should produce sufficient vitamin D.

Vitamin E, like vitamin C, has many advocates who claim unproven benefits from its use. For example, vitamin E may be able to help cells live longer. This does not mean that vitamin E will slow the aging process, but it may indicate that the vitamin can be a shield against certain environmental stresses, such as smog, radiation, and other pollutants. This is because of its anti-oxidant properties. When cells treated with vitamin E were exposed to such environmental stresses, only 30 percent of the cells stopped reproducing compared to 90 percent of the untreated cells.

Another one of the major effects claimed for vitamin E is that it helps the hearts of humans and has been beneficial in the treatment of animal heart problems. This was first reported at the 1972 American Heart Association meeting. Some research now indicates that effective vitamin E supplementation may reduce heart attacks by as much as 40%. The lower rate of heart disease among those with high vitamin E levels was documented by the World Health Organization which found that a low level of vitamin E was the most important predictor of heart disease. 62% of those dying had such low levels. Heart pain (angina) and cancers also seem to be reduced by adequate intake of vitamin E. One factor which may be responsible is that vitamin E somehow blocks some of the clotting action of vitamin K so it reduces the blood's tendency to clot.

A recent study indicates another aspect of this desirable type of supplementation. Mortality from coronary heart disease in 50-54 year old men was found to be four times higher in Lithuania than in Sweden. Most risk factors were similar between the men in the two countries. The major difference seemed to be in the antioxidant intakes, particularly vitamin E. The Lithuanians were much lower. This corresponds with a study in England which showed that vitamin E supplements of from 400 to 800 IU daily reduced the death rate from heart attacks by 47%. [2]

Vitamin E is a strong antioxidant which also acts as an anticoagulant — that is it reduces the blood's ability to clot so it reduces the risk of a coronary thrombus, a primary cause of heart attack, and brain embolisms, a primary cause of strokes. As the other antioxidants, it reduces the risk of some cancers, of cataracts in the lenses of the eyes, and it increases immunity to other diseases. In those who exercise Vitamin E also seems to reduce injuries to the small muscle fibers and may be important in preventing such conditions as shin splints.

Reports in the British Medical Journal indicate that 2000 units of vitamin E delayed both the onset of Alzheimer's and the time of death. [3] In the Cambridge Heart Antioxidant Study 400 to 800 units of vitamin E daily considerably reduced the death rate from heart disease. Vitamin E is measured in either international units (solid form foods) or milligrams (if in oils). They are roughly equivalent measures. The minimum daily requirement is only 10 I.U.'s (international units)

Vitamin K is necessary for two of the fourteen steps necessary for the blood to clot. It is found in many foods and in most people it is produced in the intestines by bacteria.

Minerals

Minerals are usually structural components of the body, but they sometimes participate in certain body processes. The body uses many minerals — phosphorus, calcium, and magnesium for strong teeth and bones; zinc for growth; chromium for carbohydrate metabolism; and copper and iron for hemoglobin production in the blood.

Iron is used primarily in developing hemoglobin, which carries the oxygen in the red blood cells. Women need more iron than men until they go through menopause (18 milligrams a day), at which time their iron requirements drop to that of men (10 milligrams a day). The average amount of iron lost a day by a menstruating woman is about 0.4 to 0.5 milligrams per day for sedentary women. That amount is more than doubled for active women. When this is added to the 0.8 mg that is used or lost in normal daily living, about 1.3 to 2 mg per day should be enough. The problem is that, as with other vitamins and minerals, the amount which can be absorbed from the diet (its bioavailability) is much less than that which is consumed. The great majority of women would have enough iron if they took in 2.8 mg of iron daily. But to actually absorb 2.8 mg most women would need to take in about 56 mg per day.[4] While meat and foods rich in vitamin C aid in the absorption of iron, other foods, such as spinach, and drugs, such as antacids, can inhibit the uptake.

Iron deficiency, common in women athletes, may impair athletic performance and should be corrected with supplementation. If an athlete is exercising hard enough for the body to produce more hemoglobin and more red blood cells but there isn't enough iron to make the hemoglobin, the blood cells can't be manufactured and the endurance of the athlete will be limited in this essential component of endurance.

Some athletes are anemic, either not having enough red blood cells or not having enough hemoglobin (the oxygen carrying element in the red blood cells). The most common finding in athletes is a dilutional pseudoanemia that is caused by a plasma volume expansion, rather than an actual blood loss. It is not a pathological state and normalizes after stopping training for 3 to 5 days. Blood cell loss can occur in a number of ways including menstruation, pregnancy, lactation, the continued injury to a body part (such as the foot strike in running), through small losses in the sweat, and through losses through injury or illness, such as to the gastrointestinal tract or the genito-urinary tract.[5] A number of studies have concluded that female runners lose iron into their intestinal tracts. The various studies show between 8%-85% of female runners lose iron this way. Also, 2% of marathoners and triathletes show visible blood in their feces after races.[6] But the main cause is insufficient iron in the diet.

Magnesium is the eighth most abundant element on the earth's surface. It seems to help activate enzymes essential to energy transfer. It is crucial for effective contraction of the muscles. Exercise depletes this element so supplementation may be called for. When it is not present in sufficient amounts, twitching, tremors, and undue anxiety may develop.

Calcium is primarily responsible for the building of strong bones and teeth. For this reason, it seems obvious that a diet that is chronically low in calcium would have a negative effect on one's bone strength. The result of this is brittle and porous bones as one gets older, a condition known as osteoporosis. This is diagnosed when the bone density shows a loss of 40% of the necessary calcium. It happens quite often in older people, especially women who have gone through menopause or have had their ovaries removed, as estrogen seems to serve a protective function against bone loss.

The inclusion of adequate calcium (which may be higher than the current Recommended Daily Allowance) in teenage and young adult years can aid in the development of peak bone mass, which can help prevent osteoporosis later on in life. Another contributing factor to osteoporosis is the imbalance of phosphorus to calcium in the typical diet. Calcium and phosphorous work together. They should be consumed on a 1 to 1 ratio. However, the average diet is much higher in phosphorus than calcium, leading to a leeching of calcium from the bones to make up for this imbalance.

234

Calcium is also necessary for strong teeth, nerve transmissions, blood clotting, and muscle contractions. Without enough calcium, muscle cramps often result. Skipping milk, with its necessary calcium, may be the cause of menstrual cramping for some girls. The uterus is a muscle and muscles need both sodium and calcium for proper contractile functioning. In the U.S., 1300 mg per day are recommended for girls 9 to 18. For women 19 to 51 is drops to 1000 mg.

Lack of calcium is also a major factor in the female athlete traid. (See Chapter 12.) The loss of bone calcium (osteoporosis) may be reduced or reversed by taking calcium supplements. Calcitonin, a nasal spray, has been found to be effective in replacing lost calcium in the bones. This is particularly true for the lumbar spine area. [7]

Fluoride deficiency may be a primary nutritional deficiency in the Western world. It is a major preventer of cavities and dental caries. Fluoride helps build stronger bones and teeth.

Potassium is a chief mineral in cell growth. A deficiency can cause impaired nerve and muscle functions ranging from paralysis to minor weakness, loss of appetite, nausea, depression, apathy, drowsiness, confusion, heart failure, and even death. It is often low in female diets. It helps to regulate the acid base balance of the blood and to regulate blood pressure. Studies have shown an increase in blood pressure when sodium intake is high. Such studies have also shown blood pressure is decreased when the potassium intake is increased. A 1 to 1 ratio of sodium to potassium is considered good. Most people are much higher than desirable in sodium intake and lower than desirable in potassium intake.

Sodium, along with potassium, helps to maintain the body's water balance. But too much, in some people, can raise the blood pressure because too much water is retained. Since it is the major mineral ingredient in sweat it occasionally needs to be increased in very hot weather or when the athlete perspires too much.

Trace minerals are those that are found in very small amounts. Nearly every element found in the body is "essential," but the trace minerals are required in such small amounts and are generally abundantly found in the diet, so there is little reason for dietary deficiency. Usually foods high in calcium and iron are high in the other necessary trace minerals. A few of the trace minerals are:

Copper helps in the production of red blood cells. It also helps: in the metabolism of glucose (sugar), with the release of energy, in the formation of fats in the nerve walls, and in the formation of connective tissues. Deficiency of copper is very rare.

Manganese is used in fat and carbohydrate metabolism, pancreas development, prevention of bone defects, muscle contraction, and many other functions. It has not yet been observed as a human deficiency.

Zinc is an ingredient in insulin and is used in carbohydrate metabolism. It is necessary for the normal growth of general organs, the prevention of anemia, and the growth of all tissues. It also helps in wound healing. Zinc in excess of the recommended daily amount interferes with copper absorption and decreases the level of HDL cholesterol (the "good" cholesterol) in the blood.

Chromium helps to regulate blood sugar and to metabolize fats and carbohydrates. It is also an antioxidant.

Selenium is a mineral which is part of an essential enzyme (glutathione peroxidase) which protects a naturally occurring antioxidant (glutathione). It works with vitamins C, E and beta carotene. It may, as Vitamin E, reduce micro-injuries to the small muscle fibers. It may also reduce the risk of digestive cancers, especially of the stomach and esophagus. In fact it seems to be protective against all cancers. It is found in greater abundance in North American soils than in European soils. It therefore is found more often in both plants and animals raised in America. [8]

Side effects of an excess of selenium can include hair loss, digestive problems (vomiting, diarrhea, nausea), irritability, nerve cell problems, and fatigue. Supplementation of selenium is optional as long as you are getting 50 to 100 mg. a day. Natural sources include: 3 ½ ounces of tuna (115 mg. of selenium); a half ounce of tortilla chips (120 mg of selenium); 3 ½ ounces of lasagna noodles (96 mg.) or spagetti (65 mg). It is quite easy to get this mineral in a normal diet. Fruits and vegetables are quite low in selenium, but meats, grains and beans are generally high.

Phytochemicals

Phyto (Greek for "plant") chemicals include thousands of chemical compounds that are found in plants. Some of these are vitamins but many have no known effect on humans. However, more and more are being found to be highly beneficial. In the past, the phytonutrients found in fruits and vegetables were classified as vitamins: Flavonoids were known as vitamin P, cabbage factors (glucosinolates and indoles) were called vitamin U, and ubiquinone was vitamin Q. Tocopherol somehow stayed on the list as vitamin E. The "vitamin" designation was dropped for the other nutrients because specific deficiency symptoms could not be established and "vita" means "life" so if the compound could not be found to be absolutely essential for life it was dropped as a "vitamin" but is now classified as a phytochemical.

Various phytochemicals have been found to reduce the chance of cancers developing, reduce the chance of heart attack, reduce blood pressure, reduce the problems of menopause, and increase immunity factors. Few of these have been reduced to pill form, such as vitamin pills, so they must be consumed in fruits and vegetables daily. It is suggested that each of us consume at least five servings of raw fruits or vegetables daily. Since many of the phytochemicals are heat sensitive, cooking can destroy some or all of the active ingredients.

We are a long way from developing highly effective phytochemical supplements because there are so many elements, and they may be destroyed in the processing. Garlic pills, for example, are available. However, with deoderized pills some of the active ingredients have been removed — they were in the chemicals that gave the garlic its aroma.

Several types of phytochemicals are being studied:

Plant sterols are somewhat similar to the animal sterol cholesterol but are unsaturated. These plant sterols compete for the same sites and thereby lower the blood cholesterol levels, often by 10%. Soy is a good source for such sterols. Most green and yellow vegetables, and particularly their seeds, contain essential sterols.

Phenols have the ability to block specific enzymes that cause inflammation. They also modify the prostaglandin pathways and thereby protect platelets from clumping thereby reducing the risk of blood clots. Blue, blue-red and violet colorations seen in berries, grapes and purple eggplant are due to their phenolic content.

Flavonoids is the name for a large group of compounds. They are found primarily in tea, citrus fruits, onions, soy and red wine. Some can be irritating but others seem to reduce heart attack risk. For example, the phenolic substances in red wine inhibit oxidation of human LDL (the harmful low density cholesterols). The biologic activities of flavonoids include action against allergies, inflammation, free radicals, liver toxins, blood clotting, ulcers, viruses and cancer tumors.

Phytoestrogens among the flavinoids and other phytochemicals can occupy the body's estrogen receptors and act like estrogen. Soy, found commonly in Oriental diets, is believed to be responsible for reducing many of the symptoms of menopause. When soy is added to the diets of post-menopausal women, their symptoms often are reduced or disappear. [9]

Terpenes such as those found in green foods, soy products and grains, comprise one of the largest classes of phytonutrients. The most intensely studied terpenes are carotenoids — as evidenced by the many recent studies on beta carotene. Only a few of the carotenoids have the antioxident

237

properties of beta carotene. These substances are found in bright yellow, orange and red plant pigments found in vegetables such as tomatoes, parsley, oranges, pink grapefruit and spinach. Limonoids are a subclass of terpenes which are found in citrus fruit peels. They appear to protect lung tissue and aid in detoxifying harmful chemicals in the liver.

Coenzyme Q 10 (ubiquinone) is another phytochemical and is an antioxident. It has been linked to DNA related problems in both the nerves and the muscles. [10] It also works with both vitamin C and vitamin E in a number of actions in which all three are utilized together. [11]

As often happens, the research of the local scientists can influence the acceptance of the substance. While Q 10 has been studied in the United States, it is not recommend as a daily antioxidant. On the other hand, the work of Jan Karlsson and others in Sweden makes Q 10 a favorite among the Nordic peoples. The Swedish National Food Administration recommends 2 to 20 mg per day. Jan Karlsson recommends 50 to 100 mg per day with elite athletes taking in 100 to 300 mg per day. [12]

Supplementing Your Nutritional Needs Through Vitamin or Mineral Pills

Buying vitamin pills should be determined by what you need. Some people need more of a vitamin than do others. If you are on a weight reducing diet, it is a good idea to take a multivitamin and mineral supplement as it is difficult to get all the vitamins and minerals you need while on a diet.

America's most famous fitness guru, Dr. Ken Cooper, the doctor who started the aerobics revolution, now says that we should supplement our diets with certain vitamins and minerals — particularly the antioxidants. He disagrees with those who advise us to get all of our vitamins and minerals from our diet. Cooper says that it can't really be done. In fact, we need more of some nutrients than we could possibly take in through a normal diet. 13 He recommends: 25,000 units of betacarotene, 1000 mg of vitamin C, 400 mg. of vitamin E (specifically d-alpha tocopherol — the natural form of vitamin E), 400 mcg. of folacin and co-enzyme Q10. His message is, "You can age fast or age slow. It's up to you." Endurance athletes benefit from higher doses of antioxidants, and Cooper suggests that anyone exercising more than five hours weekly should double the recommended dosage to combat excess free radical by-products.

Based on 200 clinical studies, the Alliance for Aging Research (AAR) recommends that people at high risk for cancer, especially asbestos workers and smokers, should not take any beta carotene supplements. For others interested in health promotion and disease prevention, they recommend

---

Foods with anti-cancer acting phytochemicals.

- Highly effective: garlic, carrots, celery, soybeans, cilantro, cabbage, parsley, ginger, parsnips, licorice
- Moderately effective: onions, flax, citrus fruits, broccoli, cauliflower, brussels sprouts, tomatoes, peppers, brown rice, tumeric, whole wheat
- Somewhat effective: oats, oregano, barley, basil, cantalope, berries, mint [15]

---

the following ranges of supplements (in an aging population): 250 to 1000 mg of vitamin C daily, 100 to 400 IUs of vitamin E daily, 17,000 to 50,000 IUs (10 to 30 mg) of beta carotene daily. [14]

Dr. Dean Ornish's Preventive Medicine Research Institute (PMRI) conducts pioneering research on lifestyle (diet, exercise, stress management, and group support) and heart disease. PMRI's research director, Larry Scherwitz, PhD, says that if a three-day nutritional analysis reveals program participants are not obtaining adequate antioxidant levels in the diet, they recommend a range of supplementation: 1 to 3 grams vitamin C, 100 to 400 IUs of dry vitamin E, 10,000 to 25,000 IUs of beta carotene.

If you would like to get your vitamins through food sources, you can get your 1000 mg of vitamin C by eating 13 to 17 oranges or 44 tomatoes a day. Fifteen oranges will add 1100 calories to your diet while the 40 tomatoes will add 950 calories to your daily intake. To get the 400 mg of vitamin E each day, as the recommended alpha-tocopherol, you can eat 50 tablespoons of margarine (50,000 calories), 400 cups of spaghetti (79,000 calories), 260 tablespoons of peanut butter (24,000 calories), 8,000 potatoes (700,000 calories), 300 cups of instant oat cereal (43,500 calories), 6 ½ pounds of potato chips (16,000 calories), or 32 pounds of canned tuna in oil (31,000 calories). Since 3500 calories will put on one pound of body weight for the average person you will gain between 5 and 10 pounds a day if you want to get 400 units of vitamin E through "natural" sources. And the "chemical" in the pill is the same chemical found in the oats or the tuna.

Notes:

1. J. Karlsson, "Advances in Nutrition for High Intensity Training," Presentation at the World Congress on Sports Medicine, Orlando, FL, June 3, 1998.
2. Kristenson et al., *British Medical Journal* March 314 (1997): 7081.
3. M. Pahor and W.B. Applegate, "Recent Advances: Geriatric

Medicine," *British Medical Journal* October 315 (1997): 1071-1074.

4. A.C. Grandjean, J.S. Ruud and K.J. Reimers, "Nutrition," *Women in Sport,* ed. B. Drinkwater (Oxford: Blackwell Scientific, 2000) 124.

5. D.J. Shaskey and G.A. Green, "Sports Haematology," *Sports Medicine* 29.1 (2000): 27-38.

6. S.S. Harris, "Exercise Related Anemia," *Women in Sport,* ed. B. Drinkwater (Oxford: Blackwell Scientific, 2000) 315.

7. B. Drinkwater, "Osteoporosis," Presentation at the World Congress of Sports Medicine, Orlando, FL, June 2, 1998.

8. M.P. Rayman, "Selenium: A Time to Act," *British Medical Journal* February 314.387 (1997).

9. D.T. Zava and G. Duwe, "Estrogenic and Antiproliferative Properties of Genistein and Other Flavenoids in Human Breast Cancer Cells," *Nutrition and Cancer* 27.1 (1997): 31-40.

10. J. Karlsson, *Antioxidents and Exercise* (Champaign, IL: Human Kinetics, 1997) 63.

11. J. Karlsson, "Advances in Nutrition for High-Training," Presentation at the World Congress of Sports Medicine, Orlando, FL, June 3, 1998.

12. J. Karlsson, *Antioxidents and Exercise* (Champaign, IL: Human Kinetics, 1997): 105.

13. Ken Cooper, *Antioxidant Revolution* (Atlanta, GA: Thomas Nelson Publishers, 1994).

14. "To Take Antioxidant Pills or Not? The Debate Heats Up," *Tufts Nutrition Letter* May 12.3 (1994): 3.

15. K. Clark, "Phytochemicals Protect Against Cancer," *ACSM Health and Fitness Journal* May/June (1998): 35.

21

Sensible Eating and Weight Management

Sensible eating requires understanding the basic principles of nutrition discussed in the previous chapters. The nutrients must appear in the diet in proper quantities, and the calories must be the amount necessary in order to maintain one's sports activities and desired weight. There are other factors that the athlete must understand. Caloric needs change according to climate and the amount of activity in which the person participates. It is obvious that hot weather necessitates a greater intake of fluids due to the loss of water through perspiration. There is also a lesser need for calories because the body does not need to burn as many calories to maintain its 98.6° Fahrenheit temperature.

A person using a great many calories, such as an endurance athlete, needs more carbohydrates. It is a myth that athletes need a great deal more protein than non-athletes. While the caloric needs may nearly double for the athlete who is expending a great deal of energy, the protein needs are increased only slightly, usually less than 30%. Another myth concerning athletes is that they require more vitamins and minerals than do others. Additional supplements given to athletes already consuming the required amounts of nutrients have not been shown to improve performance. But antioxidant supplementation may reduce the potential damage of the free oxygen radicals that are increased by the exercise.

Endurance athletes and those involved in dance and gymnastics may be under greater pressure to keep their weight down. This is, of course, a mindset that can lead to the development of the female athlete triad and its serious health implications. (See Chapter 12.) It may be the desire to be thin — which leads to a decrease in the nutritional quality consumed due to the decrease in caloric intake — and not the exercise training that affects the dietary practices of athletes, particularly females.[1]

Important Considerations In Selecting Your Diet

The Federal Department of Agriculture has devised a suggested diet guide. It is often called the food pyramid. There are six food groups in the pyramid:

- Grain products (breads, cereals, pastas), 6-11 servings per day.
- Vegetables, 3-5 servings per day.
- Fruits, 2-4 servings per day.
- High protein meats and meat substitutes (meat, poultry, fish, beans, nuts, eggs), 2-3 servings per day.
- Milk products, 2 servings for adults, 3 for children.
- Extra calories, if needed, from fats and/or sweets.

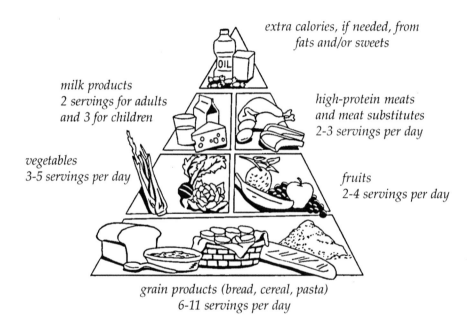

extra calories, if needed, from fats and/or sweets

milk products
2 servings for adults
and 3 for children

high-protein meats
and meat substitutes
2-3 servings per day

vegetables
3-5 servings per day

fruits
2-4 servings per day

grain products (bread, cereal, pasta)
6-11 servings per day

Grain products give the carbohydrates needed for quick energy. A serving size would be one slice of bread, an ounce of dry cereal, or a half cup of cooked cereal, pasta, or rice.

The grains are rich in B vitamins, some minerals, and fiber. Whole grains are the best sources of fibers. Refining grains or polishing rice reduces the fiber, the mineral content, and the B vitamins. This occurs in white and wheat bread (but not whole wheat), pastas, pastries and white rice. The flour is often refortified with three of the B complex vitamins, but seldom with the

	Calories per pound per hour	Calories expended by a 150 lb. person during 20 minutes of exercise
Sleeping uses	0. 36	18
Sitting at rest use	0. 55	27. 5
Sitting at work	0. 60	30
Housework	1.0	50
Walking	1. 2	60
Jogging	1. 75	87. 5

other essential nutrients.

If you are concerned with reducing your cholesterol level (thereby reducing your chances of heart disease), reducing your chances of developing gall stones, or having a softer stool in your bowel movement, eat more of the soluble fibers such as oat bran cereals, whole grain bread with oats, carrots, potatoes, apples, rice bran and citrus juices that contain the pulp of the fruit. If your concern is reducing your risk of intestinal cancers, appendicitis and diverticulosis, eat more insoluble fibers (whole wheat breads and cereals, corn cereals, prunes, beans, peas, nuts, most vegetables and polished rice).

Vegetables are rich in fibers, beta carotene, and some vitamins and minerals. If you are trying to lose weight, many vegetables are high in water and in fibers but low in calories. Among these are all greens (lettuce, cabbage, celery) as well as cauliflower. Actually, most vegetables are quite low in calories. A serving size would be a half cup of raw or cooked vegetables or a cup of raw leafy vegetables.

Fruits are generally high in vitamin C and fiber. They are also relatively low in calories. A serving size would be 1/4 cup of dried fruit, 1/2 cup of cooked fruit, 3/4 cup of fruit juice, a whole piece of fruit, or a wedge of a melon.

Protein sources such as meats, eggs, nuts and beans are high in minerals and vitamins B6 and B12. A serving would be 2 1/2 ounces of cooked meat, poultry or fish, 2 egg whites, 4 tablespoons of peanut butter, 1 1/4 cup of cooked beans. A McDonald's Quarter Pounder would give you two servings. The hidden eggs in cakes and cookies would also count. The best meat products to eat are fish (because of the omega 3 oils that reduce blood clotting), egg whites and poultry without the skin.

Red meat not only has a relatively low quality of protein (after egg white, milk, fish, poultry and organ meats) but it is linked to both cancers and

Approximate number of calories used in one hour.
Soccer – 450
Cross country skiing at 5 miles per hour – 600
Running at 7 miles per hour – 670
Running at 9 miles per hour – 900
Bicycling at 5.5 miles per hour – 250

heart disease. It also carries a great amount of fat, even if the fat on the outside is trimmed off. There is also a great deal of cholesterol in the meat and fat of all land animals.

Of the "flesh" proteins, fish is the best. It is a higher quality of protein than meat or poultry, and it contains the helpful omega 3 oils. Fish are able to convert the polyunsaturated linolenic fatty acid from plants that they eat into omega 3 oils. These work to prevent heart disease by reducing cholesterol and by making the blood less likely to clot in the arteries. They do this by interfering with the production of the prostaglandin thromboxane which increases blood clotting.

Milk and milk products (cheeses, yogurt, ice cream) are high in calcium and protein as well as some minerals (potassium and zinc) and riboflavin. A serving would be one cup of milk or yogurt, 1 1/2 ounces of cheese, 2 cups of cottage cheese, 1 1/2 cups of ice cream, or 1 cup of pudding or custard. Adults need 2 servings daily, children need 3.

Fats and sweets are at the top of the food pyramid. They are there only if a person needs extra calories. Fats over the recommended maximum of 30% of one's diet can be quite harmful — particularly in causing cancers and hardened arteries. Most researchers suggest a maximum of 10%-20% of the diet in fats, most in the form of monounsaturated and polyunsaturated fatty acids.

Sweets may assist in the development of tooth decay but are not otherwise harmful if calories are not a problem for you. An athlete consuming 5,000 calories in a day can probably eat candy bars and ice cream; the person attempting to control one's weight should avoid them.

Keep in mind:
- Avoid milk fat by drinking nonfat milk and milk products, eating ice milk (3% fat) or frozen desserts made without milk fat, and eating no or low fat cheeses. Half of the calories in whole milk come from the 3 1/2% of fat in the milk. Low fat (2%) milk has reduced the fat calories by 40%. When low fat milk is advertised as 98% fat free, it is not that much better than whole milk which is 96 1/2% fat free. Most of milk is water. The

fats in milk are highly saturated — the worst kind of fat. Yet the protein quality of milk is very high.

- Egg yolk should be avoided because it contains a great deal of cholesterol. It is second only to caviar in cholesterol content. Egg yolks are the worst thing for most people to eat because of the high cholesterol and saturated fat content. Egg white, however, has the highest rating for protein quality.

- Reduce salt, because it is related to high blood pressure, and sugars, because they give calories without other nutrients such as vitamins or fibers. Only endurance athletes can safely eat more salt and sugar.

- Reduce fats to between 10%-20% of your calories if you are concerned about heart problems. U.S. guidelines suggest no more than 30%. Use fat free salad dressing or vinegar or lemon juice only. Rather than butter or margarine, buy whole grain bread and eat it without grease. If you must use grease use olive oil, or perhaps olive oil and garlic as they serve in many Italian restaurants. Or, if calories are not a concern and you like sweets, use a jelly or jam.

- Never fry foods in oil, use a non-stick pan. If you must have an oil use canola, olive or safflower oil. Stay away from all fried foods, including potato chips. Fried foods not only add calories and saturated fats but they increase your chances for intestinal cancers — as do all fats.

Beverages

Beverages make up a large part of our diets. We often don't think too much about the kinds of liquids we drink. The most nutritious drinks have been rated by the Center for Science in the Public Interest. They were rated according to the amount of fat and sugar (higher content = lower rating) and their amount of protein, vitamins, and minerals (higher content = higher rating). The results were that skim or nonfat milk was rated a +47, whole milk +38 (the lower rating was because of its fat content), orange juice +33, Hi-C +4, coffee 0, coffee with cream -1, coffee with sugar -12, Kool-Aid -55, and soft drinks -92.

Milk is the best beverage for most people. Adults should drink two cups daily. Our need for milk can be satisfied by other dairy products. For example, two cups of milk are equivalent to three cups of cottage cheese or five large scoops of ice cream. Of course, this choice may taste the best, but there are obvious drawbacks to eating five scoops of ice cream everyday! In addition to its nutrient value as a developer of bones and organs, milk has been found to help people sleep. They go to sleep quicker, then sleep longer and sounder. This is because of the high content of the amino acid tryptophan which makes serotonin, the neurotransmitter associated with relaxation and calming activity.

Coffee contains several ingredients that may be harmful to the body. There are stimulants such as caffeine and the xanthines. There are oils that seem to stimulate the secretion of excess acid in the stomach. And there are diuretics that eliminate water and some nutrients, such as calcium, from the body. Even two cups a day increases the risk of bone fractures. [2] A factor which may add to the risk of bone fractures is that people who drink more coffee usually drink little or no milk.

Brewed coffee contains 100-150 mg of caffeine per cup, instant coffee about 90 mg/cup, tea between 45-75 mg/cup, and cola drinks from 40-60 mg/cup. Decaffeinated coffee is virtually free of caffeine, as it contains only 2-4 milligrams per cup. The therapeutic dose of caffeine given to people who have overdosed on barbiturates is 43 milligrams. Yet a cup of coffee contains up to 150 milligrams of caffeine!

Caffeine is a central nervous system stimulant. It elevates one's blood pressure and constricts the blood vessels. Both of these may assist in the development of high blood pressure. It has also been reported that excess caffeine in coffee, tea, and cola drinks can produce the same symptoms found in someone suffering from psychological anxiety. These symptoms include the following: nervousness, irritability, occasional muscle twitching, sensory disturbances, diarrhea, insomnia, irregular heart beat, a drop in blood pressure, and occasionally failures of the blood circulation system.

Coffee has been a subject of controversy as a beverage for the last several years. The amount of coffee people drink in the United States has been decreasing somewhat since its 1962 peak when people averaged over three cups a day. It is now down to just over two cups a day per person. There are conflicting studies about whether or not coffee is a causative agent in heart disease based on its ability to increase one's blood pressure.

Coffee is an irritant. The oils in coffee irritate the lining of the stomach and the upper intestines. People who drink two or more cups of coffee per day increase their chances of getting ulcers by 72% over non-coffee drinkers. Decaffeinated coffee is no more soothing to the ulcer patient than the regular blend, because both types increase the acid secretions in the stomach. Since an ulcer patient's acid secretion is not as high when caffeine alone is ingested (when compared to the acid levels after the ingestion of decaffeinated coffee), some other ingredient in coffee is thought to be re-

Caloric content of various alcoholic drinks		
Beverages	**Amount**	**Calories**
Ale, 1 bottle	12 oz	148
Beer, 1 bottle	12 oz.	173
Cider, fermented, 1 glass	8 oz.	73
Daiquiri, 1 glass	6 oz.	124
Eggnog, 1 punch cup		338
Gin, dry, 1 jigger	1.5 oz.	107
Manhattan, 1 cocktail		167
Martini, 1 cocktail		143
Whiskey, Scotch, 1 jigger	1.5 oz.	107
Wine, red, 1 wine glass		73
Wine, port, 1 wine glass		60

sponsible for these increasing stomach acid levels.

Some people who are addicted to caffeine find that they suffer from headaches when they do not have their caffeine. If you are one of these people, slowly decrease your caffeine intake over time to allow your body the time it needs to readjust to lower caffeine levels.

Tea is not as irritating as coffee, but it does contain some caffeine and tannic acid, which can irritate the stomach. If you drink large amounts of tea, you should take it either with milk to neutralize the acid or add ice to dilute it. Green tea, the type served commonly in the Orient, contains polyphenols which appear to be anti-oxidants that may reduce cancer incidence. The black tea, served commonly in Europe and America, has less of these protective substances.[3] Not much is known about the effects of herbal teas.

There are seven calories in a gram of alcohol. These calories contain no nutritional elements, but they do contribute to your total caloric intake. Since alcoholic drinks are surprisingly high in calories, they greatly contribute to the overweight problems of many individuals. People who drink alcoholic beverages and eat a balanced diet will probably consume too many calories. If they drink but cut down on eating, they may not develop a weight problem, but they will probably develop nutritional deficiencies that can result in severe illness. Alcohol is also a central nervous system depressant, which causes a decrease in one's metabolism.

In addition to the normal dangers of alcohol in creating alcoholism and destroying brain cells, there are other considerations in drinking. Beer or ale, because of their carbonation, have the effect of neutralizing stomach acid. This might increase the acids secreted by the stomach, which could cause ulcers. Gin contains juniper berries and other substances that are stomach and intestinal irritants.

Studies have indicated that moderate alcohol consumption (less than three drinks a day) may increase the HDL type of blood cholesterol. There seems to be also a protective factor from a substance called reservatrol which is found in the seeds and skins of grapes. For that reason red wine would have even more protective qualities than other alcoholic drinks. Of course reservatrol can also be found in grape juice and in grapes, so there is no need to drink the wine to get the benefits. Before taking up drinking in order to reduce heart attack risk, one should consider that alcohol consumption is related to increased blood pressure and the added calories consumed may increase one's weight. Both of these are negatives in terms of heart disease.

Since Americans drink more beer than milk, 34 gallons of beer a year per person compared to 26 gallons per year per person for milk, health conscious people might consider drinking the best beverage, non-fat milk, rather than the more harmful alcohol. Also, since coffee and alcohol dehydrate the body, athletes who perspire a great deal should be careful of them. You definitely want to keep your fluid intake high.

Food Additives

Sugar is a negative for most people. In fact, it is probably the most harmful additive to the foods that we in the United States eat. We average about 125 pounds of sugar per person per year. This gives us a lot of excess calories that, if we don't use for energy, we will store as fat. As discussed previously, if we exceed our desired weight and become obese, this will lead to increased health risks

Salt can be a dangerous additive to foods because people react differently to salt. Yet most people do not consider adding salt to their food a health risk. But when you look at populations as a whole, it seems obvious that the higher the salt intake, the greater the frequency of high blood pressure.

Since many manufacturers add salt to enhance the taste, sodium is often high. While the desired intake is between 1-2 grams (1,000 and 2,000 milligrams), the average intake in America is five grams.[4] The potential negative effect of a high sodium intake can be combated by ingesting a high level of potassium. However, the desired recommended daily allowance for potassium, 2.5 grams, is not met by the average American, who consumes only

0.8-1.5 grams daily. [5] Most of our foods follow this same pattern — too high in sodium and too low in potassium. Athletes who perspire a great deal may not need to be concerned too much about their salt intake.

Preservatives added to foods give a longer storage life and prevent disease causing germs from multiplying. Most are harmless. Some give protection against intestinal cancers. And some, such as the nitrates in hot dogs, are cancer producing. However the disease of botulism, which they are preventing, is far more of a danger for disease than is the infinitesimal amount in the wiener.

Vitamins and minerals have been added to food for years. In 1973, the Food and Drug Administration suggested that more iron be added to enrich flour after they found that iron is often low in our diets. Vitamins A and D are added to skim milk to make it non-fat milk — milk that has all of the nutrients of whole milk but without the fat. Vitamins A and D are fat soluble and stay in the fat when the fat was removed to make the skim milk.

Vitamins oftentimes need to be added because they have been taken out through processing. For example, white bread is often enriched with vitamins B1, B2 and B3. But this does not replace all of the B-complex vitamins that were removed when the food was processed. Pantothenic acid and folic acid, both B vitamins, are not present in the enriched foods but would be present in the natural foods such as whole grain bread. So, you should be aware that white bread is not the nutritional equivalent of whole grain bread. To be specific, it is lower in vitamin E, some of the B vitamins, and some of the trace minerals such as zinc and chromium than whole grain bread. However, whole grain bread contains phytic acid, which prevents the body from using iron, calcium and other minerals. So, there are positives and negatives to additives, processing, and other procedures used in modern food manufacturing.

Vegetarianism

Vegetarianism is adhered to by people for two major reasons. Some have a reverence for life that precludes their eating of other animals. This is a belief prevalent in Hinduism. Since these vegetarians generally drink milk and may eat eggs, their diet may be nutritionally sound.

The second group of people are vegetarians for health reasons. They may believe that meat causes cancer or that there are harmful substances in meat or animal products including milk and eggs. Those vegetarians who do not consume any animal products or by-products are known as vegans. Their diets are often lacking in essential nutrients such as high quality protein, vitamin B12, vitamin D, calcium and iron.

It has been found recently that many vegans are developing nutritional deficiency diseases such as rickets, pellagra and scurvy. Medical records show irreversible physical and mental defects showing up in some children of such strict vegetarian parents.

Vegetarian diets that include milk or eggs can give proper nutrition if those animal proteins are taken in sufficient quantity. Cereal grains, beans and nuts can also help to make up the essential amino acid deficiencies. Generally, a vegan needs 50 percent more total protein than others. This is still not insurance that all of the essential amino acids will be consumed because the amino acids are found in far better proportions in meat and dairy products than they are in fruits and vegetables.

When vegetarians are careful about their dietary intakes, they may prove to be healthier than non-vegetarians. Because of the high need for complex carbohydrates and the poorer quality of protein in red meat, many athletes, particularly endurance athletes, have adopted a lacto-ove-vegetarian diet. Generally they will eat some fish and supplement with the B vitamins which may be lacking when red meat is reduced in their diets.

One study compared healthy vegetarians to non-vegetarians and found that healthy vegetarians had lower blood sugar and cholesterol levels than did their closely-matched non-vegetarian counterparts. Healthy vegetarians are still shown to be at a higher risk for deficiencies in vitamins B1, B6, B12, and D.[6]

Controlling Your Weight

Endurance sport athletes seldom have the problem of needing to reduce their weight. In fact the opposite is usually true — they don't eat enough. Pure skill sport athletes, such as softball players, may want to reduce excess fat in order to become quicker and faster.

The media have generally pushed the idea that "you can't be too thin or too rich." For those who have adopted this ideal of thinness, serious health problems, and even death, can wait at the end of the quest for thinness. While the problems of eating disorders and the female athlete triad were discussed in Chapter 12, they are so serious that we need to keep them in mind as we consider any weigh loss program.

Before beginning any weight loss program you will want sound medical advice on whether or not you are "overfat." The doctor, not the coach, should be the expert here. Some coaches, especially in gymnastics and diving, have caused their athletes severe problems by requiring them to lose weight. You can't tell from looking at the outside of the body what is under the skin. The best methods of determining the amount of fat a person has is through un-

Summary of Diet Ideas
1. Plan an eating change in which you reduce your daily calories by 500 in order to lose a pound a week.
2. Achieve this reduction by reducing fats and alcohol and eating smaller portions of food or eliminating some foods from some meals.
3. Add aerobic exercise to your life — swimming, walking, jogging, cycling at a level sufficient to expend at least 500 calories a week
4. Consider spreading your calories into several meals rather than the traditional three meals a day.

derwater weighing or through several skin caliper measures. The often used infra-red techniques to measure body fat are next to useless.[7]

If a weight loss program is medically suggested, it would be wisest to do it during the off season. The weakness which can result from a decreased calorie diet is not what you want during your sport season.

How To Lose Weight

The wisest approach to losing weight would be to find out why you are overweight. If it is genetic, perhaps medical help is needed. If you eat because of stresses, you should find another method to relieve the stresses, such as exercise or relaxation techniques or, if you must have something in your mouth, try gum or a low calorie food.

In all likelihood, if you adopt an aerobic exercise habit and a low fat and low alcohol eating pattern, the fat should drop off. Losing weight just for the sake of being thinner seldom works for very long. Consequently, you will have to determine whether you honestly want a healthier lifestyle or you just want to look better for the summer. A pattern of continually gaining and losing is frustrating and probably not worth the effort. But a true lifestyle change of healthy eating and effective exercise will pay many mental, physical, and social dividends.

We must recognize that the fat we wear comes primarily from the fat we eat.[8] Carbohydrates are used first for energy in the body because of the efficiency of conversion to glucose. Converting carbohydrates to fat requires about 23% of the food value to be used to make the conversion. Protein, if not used, will normally be converted into sugars and will be the second source of available energy. But the fat that you have consumed uses only 3% of its food value to convert it to body fat.[9]

So 25 grams of carbohydrate, which will yield 100 calories at 4 calories a gram, are reduced by 23% of the calories used to convert them to body fat. But fats consumed in your food are different. Eleven grams of fat at 9 calories per gram is 99 calories, but it only takes 3% of those calories to convert it all to body fat. Consequently, 96 calories of body fat can be deposited. So approximately 100 grams of carbohydrate, if not used for energy, will become 8.5 grams of body fat, but approximately 100 grams of fat from the diet will become 10.75 grams of body fat.

Yo-yo dieters are those who lose then gain, lose then gain, again and again. This type of dieting behavior will be at best discouraging, and at worst, harmful. Some researchers have found that if one's metabolism is continually decreased over time with repeated diets, it will be reduced permanently. People who have been on starvation diets may find that their metabolism drops. This was especially true in Nazi prison camps where the imprisoned Jews living on levels of calories far below starvation were still able to survive because their metabolism levels dropped. This drop seemed to be relatively permanent after they left the concentration camps. So, if you start out with a low metabolism and engage in yo-yo dieting, you run the risk of lowering your metabolism even further.

For people who continually diet, initially both fat and muscle are lost in about equal proportions. When the weight is allowed to return to pre-diet levels, the gain is almost all in fat. Then the next diet begins. Again both muscle and fat are lost. With the next weight gain more fat is put on. After a series of such diets, the person is fatter than before even though the weight is the same. In addition to the increase in fat, there is a corresponding decrease in lean body tissue, leading to an overall decrease in metabolism. It is your lean tissue that uses energy all the time, not your fat cells.

In order to make weight loss permanent, you must have a plan that will give you a lifelong change of habits. You will have to make certain that you have the proper amount of protein (about half of a gram for every pound of

In a study at the University of Tennessee, 10 active males (average age of 29) were tested in two types of equal calorie expenditure exercises to determine the differences in fat and carbohydrate use. On one day they pedaled an exercise bike at 33% of their VO2 max for 90 minutes. In the other test they pedaled at 66% of their VO2 max for 45 minutes.[10]		
	33% VO2 max for 90 minutes	**66% VO2 max for 45 minutes**
Calories used during exercise	Same	Same
Calories used during 2 hour recovery	Same	Same
Mount of protein used	Same	Same
Amount carbohydrate used	69 grams	106 grams
Amount fat used	42 grams	24 grams
Calories in fat and CHO	654	640

Caloric Expenditure Chart
Calories burned per pound per ten minute period
(Cal./Lb./ per 10 minutes)

Activity	10 min.
Archery	0.34
Softball (except pitcher)	0.3
Calisthenics	0.34
Classwork, lecture	0.12
Cross-country running	0.8
Dancing (vigorously)	0.12
Dressing	0.2
Driving	0.2
Eating	0.09
Football (American)	0.54
Gardening, weeding	0.4
Golf	0.34
Housekeeping	0.6
Mountain climbing	0.67
Table tennis (recreational)	0.26
Reading	0.06
Running: 7.0 mph	0.93
Running 8.7 mph	1.03
Running 11.6 mph	1.31
Sitting	0.09
Sleeping	0.06
Squash	0.7
Swimming: pleasure	0.7
Swimming: breaststroke	0.64
Swimming: crawl stroke	0. 56
Tennis	0.46
Volleyball	0.26
Writing	0.09

To reach the 8 calories per minute level (80 calories per 10 minutes), multiply your weight by the number of calories used per pound (above). Does your exercise reach the 80 calories per 10 minute period? If you do calisthenics at 0.34 calories per 10 minutes-you had better weigh 235 pounds to get in your exercise. But if you swim, you can get your minimum exercise if you weigh only 115 pounds. Remember to keep up your exercise for an hour if you are working only at the 80 calories per 10 minute level.

body weight), your fat consumption should be low (preferably in the 10%-20% range of fat calories as a percentage of total calories), and you should have an array of complex carbohydrates to give you the vitamins, minerals, and fiber that you need. You may want to add vitamin and mineral supplements to make certain that you have these nutrients at the optimal levels.

To aid in your pursuit of weight loss, you may decide to change your eating habits. It is a good idea to eat smaller, more frequent meals rather than infrequent, large meals. Every time you eat, you increase your metabolism because you put your digestive system to work. There is evidence that eating four or five small meals a day is better than eating two or three large ones. It also seems to reduce the cholesterol level of the blood.

Another approach to dieting is to eliminate some foods at some meals — instead of having potatoes every night, have them every other night. Or you may decide to have open-faced sandwiches instead of sandwiches with two slices of bread. (Some people use lettuce leaves instead of bread to make a sandwich.) Switching from red meat to poultry or fish and from regular ice cream to a "light" version can save you calories while maintaining your nutritional status.

For permanent weight loss, you want to lose about one pound of fat per week, no more than two pounds of body weight. The best way to lose weight permanently is to combine an aerobic exercise program (to burn fat and increase your metabolism) with a diet that is close to the diet you will maintain once you have reached your goal weight. It is also wise to begin a weight training program because you will want to increase muscle size so that you gain muscle while you lose fat. You must realize that permanent weight loss is a slow process — remember how long it took you to put on those extra pounds!

To lose one pound of fat per week, you must have a net deficit of 500 calories per day. This is because one pound of fat contains 3,500 calories. You may choose to achieve this solely by decreasing your food intake by 500 calories per day. However, if this is your approach, be warned: your metabolism will slowly decrease over time to accommodate for the decrease in food energy, thereby making it harder and harder for you to continue to lose fat.

You should also choose to increase your activity level to burn off 500 calories a day. Keep in mind that it takes a great deal of energy to achieve this goal, and it can be dangerous for you to embark on such a strenuous exercise program if you are currently not exercising. Therefore, it is best to combine both calorie reduction with exercise to achieve your goal. Aerobic exercise will keep your metabolism up as you lose the fat, and you won't have to restrict your calories to such an extreme because you will be burning off energy each time you exercise.

We now know that calories are used both during and after exercise. The longer and more vigorous the exercise, the longer one's metabolism is increased, and the more hours after the exercise is completed that the calorie expenditure will be increased over normal. While this increase in calories burned after one has finished exercising is not a large amount, it is still an increase over one's resting metabolism, and a calorie burned is a calorie burned!

Some people think that exercising will make them eat more. A quarter mile to a mile of jogging will have no measurable effect on the total intake of calories. In fact, by exercising just before a meal, you can dull your appetite and decrease your desire for more calories.

Behavior modification is another approach to weight loss. This approach is advocated by the behaviorist school of psychology. Several things can be done in an attempt to modify one's behavior. First, the person has to become aware of how much food is being eaten. It takes about 20 minutes for the stomach to inform the brain, by signals from the hypothalamus, that it has had enough food. If a person eats slowly for the first 20 minutes of a meal, the stomach has time to tell the brain it is full before a great deal of food is eaten. Secondly, a person may learn to savor the food differently by becoming conscious of the taste. Enjoy every bite, perhaps setting the fork down between bites. People can also learn to substitute food, such as a big salad and clear broth for sweets and fatty meats.

Before you can change your eating habits, you must be aware of exactly what you are doing. Behavior modification experts generally suggest that you keep a food diary for at least a week. The diary is to include of everything you eat and drink, the time you eat, what you were doing while eating, and the feelings you were experiencing at that time. You may find that you feel the urge to eat while you are studying, or when the television is on, or whenever you pass the refrigerator. Also, some require that you include who was near you at that time you eat.

After you have completed your food diary, look for patterns in your behavior. Do you like to eat in bed? Do you eat in your car or while you are in the kitchen? If so, you may have to modify your behavior to eliminate these places. You might make a rule that you will eat only while sitting at the dining room table with the TV turned off. Or maybe your rule would be that you will snack only in the hall. The idea of this is to make you aware of the behavior patterns you have established and to change them.

People who carry excess weight tend to be more subject to external cues in their eating habits. When presented with a fear situation, overly fat people ate about the same amount of food that they would normally eat, while

Often today in scientific research the term Metabolic rate at rest (MET) is used. Researchers use multiples of that resting rate to show how much more energy is being expended during the exercise. It is equal to about 80% of the number of calories (kilocalories).

For the average man 143 pounds (65 kg)

Exercise level	Number of kilocalories	METS per minute
Resting/sleeping	1.25	1
Light	2.0-4.9	1.6-3.9
Moderate	5.0-7.4	4.0-5.9
Heavy	7.5-9.9	6.0-7.9
Very heavy	10.0-12.4	8.0-9.9
Extremely heavy	12.5+	10.0+

For the average woman 121 pounds (55 kg)

	Kilocalories per minute	METS
Resting/sleeping	1.25	1
Light	1.5-3.4	1.2-2.7
Moderate	3.5-5.4	2.8-4.3
Heavy	5.5-7.4	4.4-5.9
Very heavy	7.5-9.4	6.0-7.5
Extremely heavy	9.5+	7.6+

those in the desirable weight range ate less food. When told it was past their dinner time, overly fat people would eat more than normal, while healthy weight people would not eat, or eat very little, unless they were hungry.

Another helpful hint may be to change your eating times. Instead of breakfast at 7, lunch at 12, and dinner at 6, you may try to fool your hypothalamus and stomach muscles. Let your stomach growl at 7, then eat something at 8. Then you might try having a small lunch at 11: 30. Your stomach muscles should be too embarrassed to growl at 12. You might sneak a snack at 5 and fool your hypothalamus again. Since we have been conditioned like Pavlov's dogs, to eat at certain times, we often need to unlearn these habits.

You can use other psychological cues when dieting. You might put up a chart to list your daily food intake and exercise program. You may also want to chart your weight every week. Remember, only you can be responsible for your weight loss, and it is up to you to take control of it. It is a good idea to set up both short- and long-term goals for yourself, and reward yourself every time you reach a goal. Keep in mind that a reward of a hot fudge sundae may not be the most effective reward!

A sensible weight loss diet requires that you maintain good nutrition. It is important to remember that, even when eating to lose weight, you must give your body the nutrients that it needs. It has been shown that mildly obese women who began a moderate exercise program decreased the amount of food energy they ingested. In addition, the food they did eat was of a lower nutritional quality when compared to sedentary dieters.[11] You must not compound your weight problem with inadequate nutrition while eating fewer calories, or your body will slip into starvation mode thereby lowering your metabolism in its attempt to store fat.

Usually reducing your intake of fat (which saves nine calories per gram), alcohol (which saves 7 calories per gram), and some carbohydrates (which

---

Evaluate your daily caloric expenditure on several days to get an idea of your activity level. The values below are in calories per pound per hour. Record your activity level below:

Activity (with value of calories use per pound per hour)
Multiplied by your weight in pounds
Multiplied by the number of hours (or the percent of an hour) spent in the activity
Equals the total calories used in the activity

How many calories do you expend in each of these activities?

	WT	Hours	Total calories used
Sleeping or lying in bed.	0.12 x _____	x _____	= _____
Sitting (reading, computer) bathing, eating, etc.)	0.17 x _____	x _____	= _____
Standing (washing, shaving, cooking, etc.)	0.26 x _____	x _____	= _____
Light work (housework, driving, mechanic, slow walking)	0.38 x _____	x _____	= _____
Faster work (table tennis, volleyball, sailing or canoeing, golf)	0.55 x _____	x _____	= _____
Heavier manual labor (carpenter, machine operation, plumbing, shoveling snow)	0.64 x _____	x _____	= _____
Active sports (downhill skiing, tennis, badminton, dancing, fast walking, slow jogging)	0.77 x _____	x _____	= _____
Very heavy exercise (cross country skiing, running fast, basketball, football, digging, sawing with hand saw)	0.90 x _____	x _____	= _____

What is your 24 hour total of calories used?_____

How many hours in the week did you use 480 calories (minimum for fitness) _____ saves four calories per gram) will result in successful weight loss. Alcohol is a major stumbling block to dieters who drink. Not only does it contribute 7 calories per gram, that's 170 calories for a bottle of beer, but because it is a depressant, it slows the body's metabolism. A person consuming 25% of his or her calories from alcohol reduces the body's ability to burn fat by 33%.[12]

Unfortunately, it is very easy to add calories. But if you know where to look, you'll be able to avoid many calorie traps. For example, a potato is not a bad thing to eat if it is baked or boiled by itself (100 calories). If it's mashed with whole milk, a serving increases to 150 calories. When butter and cream are added, the total calories shoot up to 250 (the same as French fries). For that same 100 calorie potato, hash browns jump your calories up to 400 to 500 calories per serving because of the oil used in frying. So, try to avoid fried foods as this skyrockets your fat intake. For most foods, choose those that are baked or broiled to help save yourself from those sneaky calories. Reducing sweets, while it may not be palatable, is one of the most effective ways of limiting calories.

Our old habits die hard, but often changes can be made. If you drink soft drinks, use the diet variety — even if it doesn't taste quite as good. Have your vegetable salad with a non fat dressing. Take the skin off of the chicken and save all of those fat calories. Forget the butter on the bread. Use nonfat products whenever possible. Eat more fruits and vegetables. Broil your meats. In other words, think about what is best — not what is usual — for you.

Exercise and Weight Loss

Gaining weight is a desire for some people. Shot putters, softball catchers, body builders and others may want to "bulk up" for their sport activity. When one focuses on weight gain, she is focused on increasing her lean body weight. This means that she wants to increase her weight by increasing muscle mass, not fat. To gain weight in muscle, the best method is to do resistance-type exercise, such as weight training. Second, you must ensure that you are eating enough protein in order to give your body the building blocks that it needs to make more muscle. It is not necessary to eat excessive protein, as this dietary practice brings with it its own set of health risks

Self Test

Place the appropriate number which best describes your answer to each question:

> 3—Almost always   2—Sometimes   1—Almost never

_____ 1. Do you eat 3 or more pieces of fruit per day? (Fruit juice counts as one piece.)

_____ 2. Do you eat a minimum of 3 servings of vegetables each day—including a green leafy or orange vegetable.)?

_____ 3. Do you eat 3 or 4 milk products per day? (such as milk, cheese, yogurt)

_____ 4. Do you eat a minimum of 6 servings of grain products each day? (breads, cereal, pasta)

_____ 5. Do you eat breakfast?

_____ 6. Do you eat fish at least three times per week?

_____ 7. Do you avoid fried foods? (including potato chips, fries)

_____ 8. Do you eat fast food four or more times per week?

_____ 9. Are the milk products you consume made from non-fat milk?

___ 10. Do you avoid high sugar foods and highly refined carbohydrates? (such as sweet rolls, cookies, non-diet sodas, candy, etc.)

If you score:
25-30 You are balancing your diet well.
18-24 Your diet can use improving.
10 - 17 your diet is unhealthy.

Low fat diet gourmet meals are possible. Send for the free "Metropolitan Cookbook" (Health and Welfare Department, Metropolitan Life Insurance Co., 1 Madison Avenue, New York, New York 10010). Or buy the American Heart Association's Cookbook. U.S. Dept. of Agriculture's Meat and Poultry Hotline 800-535-4555.

Notes:

1. J. Nutter, "Seasonal Changes in Female Athletes' Diets," *International Journal of Sports Nutrition* 1.4 (1991): 395-407.

2. E. Barrett-Connor, "Caffeine and Bone Fractures," *Journal of the American Medical Association* Jan. 26, (1994).

3. *University of California Wellness Letter,* Jan. (1992): 1-2.

4. Briggs, M. George and D. Calloway, *Bogert's Nutrition and Physi-*

cal Fitness (Philadelphia: W. B. Saunders, 1979): 246.

5. Briggs et al., 248.
6. Vudhivai et al., "Vitamin B1, B2 and B6 Status of Vegetarians," *Journal of the Medical Association of Thailand* 74 (1991): 465-701.
7. J. Clasey, "Body Composition: Bioelectrical Impedence Instruments — The Good, the Bad, and the Not Worth the Money," Presentation at the American Association for Health, Physical Education, Recreation and Dance, Orlando, FL, Mar. 21, 2000.
8. *Harvard Women's Health Watch*, Nov. (1994): 4.
9. E. Coleman, "Nutritional Update: Dietary Carbohydrate and Fat and Body Fat Accumulation," *Sports Medicine Digest* 10:7 (1988).
10. D.L. Thompson et al., "Substrate Use During and Following Moderate- and Low-Intensity Exercise: Implications for Weight Control," *European Journal of Applied Physiology* 78.1 (1998): 43-49.
11. Nieman, Onasch and Lee, 1990.
12. *Tufts Nutrition Letter*, 10:5, July 1992.

22

Ergogenics

*E*rgogenic means "work enhancing" or "energy producing." So ergogenic aids are whatever facilitates progress toward strength or bulk development or aerobic or anaerobic work. They can range from legal vitamin pills to illegal steroids.

Supplementation of legal substances can help improve performance, avoid fatigue, or prolong life. This supplementation is generally specific. One supplement may work on the fast twitch (type II) muscle fibers that are used in weight lifting and sprinting. Another may work on the slow twitch (type I) fibers that are used in endurance activities such as long distance running, dancing or soccer. Still another can provide the necessary building blocks for bones and other tissues. Another can make the blood more effective.

Contrary to some opinions, some pills may help you live longer and better. Vitamin and mineral supplements are often helpful, especially those that include the antioxidants. Aspirin is also a major health helper with only a few side effects.

For vitamin C and aspirin, the plusses definitely outnumber the minuses. But there are still factors to consider. If your mother died from gastric bleeding from taking an aspirin-like compound and your father died of a heart attack, what are your odds in taking aspirin? You will need medical tests to determine the best choice for you.

Another factor to consider is that a supplement may cost a great deal but do little or nothing. A recent study of a dietary supplement called SPORT found no beneficial effects on performance or recovery in trained athletes.[1] The scientific findings were quite different from the advertising claims.

Aids to Building Muscle

Of course, if you are going to build muscle you must work with resistance exercises effectively, but certain vitamins and minerals are also essential. Building muscle is done by making certain that your diet has sufficient amounts of high quality protein. Protein pills are generally a waste of money. Egg whites, skim or powdered milk, fish and chicken (without skin) have more and better protein for less money.

Extra meals can add more protein, carbohydrates, vitamins, and minerals to one's diet. An extra meal can vary from eggs, bananas and milk to commercially made high-protein "diet" drinks, to liquid meals specifically made for athletes and weight trainers. Some of the commercially available meals are made from soy protein, some from milk products. For those people with a milk allergy, the soy products are preferable. However, for those who can drink milk, the milk protein is a much higher quality than the soy protein because of its amino acid ratio.

Amino Acid Supplements

Before embarking on a high protein plan you should know what your protein intake is. If you take in more protein than your body can use, it merely breaks down the protein and converts it into sugars (glycogen) for energy or into fats to be deposited in your body. The excess nitrogen is then excreted in your urine.

Amino acid supplements are often used to make certain that there is enough protein in the body to develop the desired muscle bulk. The advantage of the amino acids over a high-protein meal is that the meal generally includes a great deal of fat, while the amino acids are fat-free. A cheaper and better source of high protein would be dry nonfat milk powder or low-fat cottage cheese.

The branched chain amino acids (BCAA) valine, leucine, isoleucine make up 30-40% of muscle protein. It has been thought that supplementing with them might help to build muscle protein and/or to increase endurance. While most amino acids are metabolized by the liver, the low levels of the necessary enzyme for breaking down BCAA in the liver force them into the skeletal muscles where more of the necessary enzyme is found. Exercise increases the amount of this enzyme in the muscle so more of the BCAA can be utilized. However, this does not increase one's endurance. There is also a question as to whether it can increase muscle size through the build up of muscle protein. [2] There is no strong evidence to support the hypothesis that BCAA supplements will help athletic performance. [3] Still there seems to be a great deal of interest in the amino acids which are branch chained.

Of the branched chain amino acids, leucine has been the most thoroughly investigated because its oxidation rate is higher than that of isoleucine or valine. Leucine also stimulates protein synthesis in muscle and is closely associated with the release of the factors which allow for the synthesis of glucose from molecules which are not carbohydrates (called gluconeogenic precursors), such as amino acids, lactates and the glycerol part of fat molecules. Leucine makes up about 5%-10% of body proteins.

The blood levels of leucine drop after exercise — from 11%-33% after aerobic exercise, from 5-8% after anaerobic exercise and by about 30% after strength exercises. A Finnish study used power-trained athletes on a diet including the generally recommended protein intake of 1.26 grams of protein per kilogram of body weight in a speed and strength program. After five weeks there was a 20% reduction of leucine. Leucine supplementation of 50 mg per kilogram of body weight per day, as a supplement to the daily protein intake of 1.26 grams per kilogram of body weight per day, appeared to prevent the decrease in the serum leucine levels in power-trained athletes. The investigators suggest that the current recommended dietary intake of leucine be increased from 14 mg/kg bodyweight/day to a minimum of 45 mg/kg bodyweight/day for sedentary individuals and more for those participating in intensive training in order to optimize rates of whole body protein synthesis.[4]

While consumption of BCAA, which are 30%-35% leucine before or during endurance exercise has been suggested as a way to prevent or decrease the rate of protein breakdown, the studies have not been conclusive relative to whether it will affect an athlete's performance. It might have a sparing effect on muscle glycogen degradation (muscle sugar breakdown) and the reduction of muscle glycogen stores. The studies are not unanimous in this possibility. In one study leucine supplementation (200 mg/kg bodyweight) 50 minutes before anaerobic running exercise had no effect on performance. However, in another study during 5 weeks of strength and speed training, dietary supplementation of the leucine metabolite beta-hydroxy-beta-methylbutyrate (HMB) 3 grams a day to athletes undertaking intensive resistance training exercise resulted in an increased deposit of fat-free mass (that is, more muscle) and an accompanying increase in strength. Muscle proteolysis (muscle protein breakdown) was also decreased with HMB. Additionally, there were lower blood levels of enzymes which would indicate muscle damage. and an average 50% decrease in plasma essential amino acid levels.

Most studies of leucine supplementation have included the other branched chain amino acids. There have been relatively few studies looking only at leucine. One study which included 76% leucine as part of a BCAA study indicated a reduction of fats in and around the organs and a higher level of performance by the athletes.

In a study of rats done at the University of Pennsylvania Medical School it was concluded that leucine stimulates protein synthesis in skeletal muscle.[5] In Scotland a study on pigs found that both BCAA and leucine alone reduced the use of the amino acid methionine, which is often at low levels in the human diet. [6]

Another amino acid, tryptophan, is associated with both fatigue and sleep. Either leucine alone or the three BCAA can reduce the amount of tryptophan in the blood and possibly reduce fatigue.[7] Still another amino acid, glutamine, has been considered to possibly have the potential to slow muscle protein loss.[8]

In spite of these isolated bits of research, one of the leading investigators in the world states that "in contrast to the claims made on sport nutrition products, branched-chain amino acids do not improve endurance performance, that the evidence that glutamine supplements may improve immune function is rather weak, and that the available commercial supplements contain too little arginine to increase growth hormone levels. No studies have been performed to investigate the claim that tyrosine supplements can improve explosive exercise." [9]

Those criticisms are amplified by another researcher who has written that:

Although current research suggests that individuals involved in either high-intensity resistance or endurance exercise may have an increased need for dietary protein, the available research is either equivocal or negative relative to the ergogenic effects of supplementation with individual amino acids. Although some research suggests that the induction of hyperaminoacidemia via intravenous infusion of a balanced amino acid mixture may induce an increased muscle protein synthesis after exercise, no data support the finding that oral supplementation with amino acids, in contrast to dietary protein, as the source of amino acids is more effective. Some well-controlled studies suggest that aspartate salt supplementation may enhance endurance performance, but other studies do not, meriting additional research. Current data, including results for several well-controlled studies, indicated that supplementation with arginine, ornithine, or lysine, either separately or in combination, does not enhance the effect of exercise stimulation on either hGH or various measures of muscular strength or power in experienced weightlifters. Plasma levels of BCAA and tryptophan may play important roles in the cause of central fatigue during exercise, but the effects of BCAA or tryptophan supplementation do not seem to be effective ergogenics for endurance exercise performance, particularly when compared with carbohydrate supplementation, a more natural choice. Although glutamine supplementation may increase plasma glutamine levels, its effect on enhancement of the immune system and prevention of adverse effects of the overtraining syndrome are equivocal. Glycine, a precursor for creatine, does not seem to possess the ergogenic potential of creatine supplementation. Research with metabolic by-products of amino acid metabolism is in its infancy, and current research findings are equivocal relative to ergogenic applications. In general, physically active individuals are advised to obtain necessary amino acids through consumption of natural, high-quality protein foods.[10]

So the jury is definitely out on the need for supplementation with specific amino acids. The more common advice is that if additional protein is needed in the diet, eat whole proteins such as egg whites, non-fat milk and fish as the best sources of complete proteins. Normally athletes on high-calorie, well-balanced diets get enough total protein. Those on low calorie diets or those who are vegans might profit from supplementation.

High Carbohydrates

High-carbohydrate foods can be taken before or after a workout to replace the glycogen stores in the muscles. Those products with simpler glucose molecules (short-chain glucose polymers) seem more effective in replacing muscle glycogen than the products that use table sugar as the carbohydrate source.

For years athletes have taken carbohydrates (dextrose, candy bars, high CHO drinks) to provide energy for endurance exercise SPACE and even for shorter aerobic sprints, they may not do what we have believed. A British study of well-trained cyclists in a 20 kilometer time trial discovered that whether taking a CHO drink or a similarly flavored placebo, the cyclists had the same power output, same heart rate and the same time. [11]

Vitamin and Mineral Supplements

Vitamin and mineral supplements are often used by weight trainers to make certain that they are getting enough of the necessary vitamins and minerals. The one-a-day time-release type is best. However, most athletes probably get enough vitamins and minerals in their basic diets with the exception of the antioxidants. Women also need more iron. They have a need for iron that is nearly double that of men. Calcium, to prevent osteoporosis, may also be necessary for some female athletes who may be endangered by the female athlete triad.

International Olympic Committee Medical Code Prohibited classes of substances and prohibited methods (January 31, 1997)

Doping consists of:
1. The administration of substances belonging to prohibited classes of pharmacological agents, and/or
2. The use of various prohibited methods.
 I. Prohibited Classes of Substances (International Olympic Committee)
   A. Stimulants
   B. Narcotics
   C. Anabolic Agents
   D. Diuretics
   E. Peptide and glycoprotein hormones and analogues
 II. Prohibited Methods
   A. Blood doping
   B. Pharmacological, chemical and physical manipulation
 III. Classes of Drugs Subject to Certain Restrictions
   A. Alcohol
   B. Marijuana
   C. Local anaesthetics
   D. Corticosteroids
   E. Beta-blockers

There are possible side effects from excess doses of some vitamins and minerals. The fat-soluble vitamins A and D are most likely to cause toxic effects, but some of the water-soluble B vitamins and vitamin C can also be taken at a toxic level.

Supplementing with the antioxidants is recommended. Since free oxygen radicals are produced continually by the body, and their production is increased by exercise, it is wise to take additional vitamin C, E, and beta carotene. Other antioxidants are found in grape skins and other fruits.

Increasing Muscle Size Through Strength Training

Testosterone, the male hormone, is primarily responsible for muscle growth. Most of the work on testosterone increase through strength training has been done on males. It has shown that strength work, in itself, increases testosterone. For example, heavy strength training responses increases the amount of total testosterone, free testosterone and for insulin-like growth factor. [12]

Illegal Substances

There are many types of steroids in the body. They are types of lipids with a particular type of chemical make up. The type of steroids we hear about in muscle development are those that are called anabolic steroids. These are synthetic derivatives of testosterone, the major male hormone, and they may speed up the processes which testosterone may affect, such as muscle development.

Anabolic/androgenic steroids are analogues of male hormone testosterone. Both types have a core 17-carbon steroid chemical structure that gives them anabolic (protein building) and androgenic (masculinizing) properties. Studies were developed to separate the anabolic from the adrogenic effects, but this has been only partially accomplished.

The various steroids may stimulate muscle growth for those who are working with heavy resistance exercises, but they have negative effects which may vary from drug to drug. Brittle bones which frequently break, high blood pressure, breast tenderness, liver damage, sperm count reduction, a reduction of the size of the testicles, and occasionally death are among the potential problems for men.

Women using these male hormones can develop the same problems as men. However, they may also encounter male pattern baldness, deeper voices and enlargement of the clitoris.

For athletes one of the major problems has been the damage to the connective tissues. Studies show that there is tendon damage every time, steroid-fed animals are made to exercise. Steroid users, who usually deny the possibility of heart damage through steroid use, will generally accept the fact of tendon damage. Steroids cause the body to make abnormal collagen, so they weaken tendons more than other body parts. Especially weakened is the muscle-tendon junction.

Pathological effects on collagen are also a big reason why steroid users wrinkle prematurely with their faces showing much more age than one would expect from their actual ages. It is because of all the abnormal collagen deposited in their skin. Look at some of the haggard faces of International Federation of Body Builders champions to see the effects. When you see the photos in magazines they don't show the obvious damage because the photos have been air brushed.

Teenage boys, who often take the drugs to develop bodies to impress girls, may speed up their secondary sex characteristic development. However, these drugs may make their bones harden too early. This would then stunt the growth of those boys. It goes without saying that the negative effects of the anabolic steroids far outweigh any benefits. That is why they are outlawed.

Among their many harmful side effects are leukemia (blood cancer), liver cancer and other liver problems, in addition to the following:

- Premature closing of the growth plates in the bones, stopping growth in height
- Bone brittleness, often resulting in breaks
- Decreasing testicle size (males) and reduced reproductive capacity
- Clitoral enlargement (females)
- Menstrual problems (females)
- Breast soreness and enlargement (males)
- Breast reduction (females)
- High blood pressure
- Lower amounts of high density lipoprotein (HDL) in the blood, which increases the possibility of hardening the arteries
- Increased blood clotting
- Abnormal enlargement of the heart
- Risk of sudden cardiac arrest
- Kidney damage
- Liver inflammation, which can result in cancer
- Impaired thyroid and pituitary functions
- Increase in nervous tension
- Problems with the prostate gland
- Impotence (males)
- Oily skin
- Skin rashes and acne
- Increased body hair
- Thinning hair on scalp
- Gastrointestinal problems
- Muscle cramps or muscle spasms
- Headaches
- Dizziness or drowsiness
- Nosebleeds
- Permanent hoarseness of voice (in females)

When steroids are taken the hypothalamus, the part of the brain that monitors and controls many body functions, will pick up the signal that there are too many male hormones in the body. It may then signal the pituitary gland, the adrenals, and the testicles to stop producing their hormones. When the steroid user stops using, the body may have difficulty adjusting to making its own hormones again. Many people who have been on steroids have also noted an increase in their aggressiveness. This is probably due to the androgens — such as testosterone and similar substances.

Steroids must be prescribed by a physician. Most, however, are obtained illegally on the black market. To compound the problem, many bodybuilders have taken 10 to 20 times the amount that would have given them maximum results. They have mistakenly assumed that if one is good, more is better, when in fact an excess sometimes slows the growth and strength — development process.

While there is no question that anabolic steroids add muscle bulk, there is a question as to just how much more one can gain with steroids rather than good food. The few studies done indicate very little difference. Anyone interested in strength and bulk gain should forget about steroids and instead work hard, eat properly, and get sufficient rest.

One wonders why any sensible person would attempt to build a strong, healthy muscular system with drugs that are harmful to other body organs. And why would any thinking person purposely take a substance that can shorten her life? The human growth hormone is considered by many to be the Cadillac of steroids. It has been shown to increase the size of genetically underdeveloped muscles in animals and humans. A Swedish study showed that in rats it increased both the number and the cross sectional hypertrophy of the muscles. [13]

On the other hand it may not work as well for humans. In some studies of people with genetically caused underdeveloped musculature, an increase in muscle size brings with it increased strength. In others, the size increase does not result in increased strength. A recent study on the growth hormone, done in Austria, indicates that for normal people who are working on resistance training, their strength was not improved by the administration of the growth hormone. It seemed that the increased size of the muscle belly was caused by fluid retention or an increase in the connective tissue, not an increase in the protein used in the contracting muscle fibers. These findings were similar in power athletes and weight lifters who did not increase their strength in concentric contraction of the biceps or quadriceps.[14]

For many years there were suspicions about the East German female athletes who won 160 Olympic gold medals and 410 silver and bronze Olympic medals along with 3,500 world and European championships in mainly swimming and track and field. As secret police records were disclosed, it was found that between 1974 and 1989 the girls and women had been given steroids and told they were vitamins. A number of negative effects have been found among 142 of these women, including miscarriages, damaged spinal cords from the increased musculature, birth defects to their babies and, in one, a loss of sexual identity that forced her to have an operation to change her sex. The men involved in the administration of the illegal drugs have been taken to court but have been released with very light or suspended sentences.

Increasing Anaerobic Capacity

The legal method of increasing one's ability to develop short term bursts of energy is by the administration of creatine. Short bursts of energy, which are used in weight lifting and sprinting, are examples of the use of anaerobic energy.

Creatine is an amino acid that plays a vital role as creatine phosphate (phosphocreatine) in regenerating adenosine triphosphate in skeletal muscle to energize muscle contraction. Oral administration increases muscle stores. During the past decade Creatine has assumed prominence as an ergogenic aid for professional and elite athletes. Safety issues of long-term use, however, have not been addressed satisfactorily. [15]

Creatine is a naturally occurring compound that is made in the body. It is synthesised from the amino acids glycine, arginine and methionine — primarily in the liver, but also in the kidneys and the pancreas. It is essential for muscle function. While it is naturally occurring and is found in good amounts in both meat and fish, most of it is destroyed in the cooking process. (A normal diet provides about a gram a day. Vegetarians have far less.) For this reason many researchers recommend that serious athletes in power events or events that require a surge of power supplement with this natural body substance. (At the time of this writing it has not been banned by the International Olympic Committee. However, the British Olympic medical authorities have taken a position against it for British athletes.)

Creatine is typically ingested as a monohydrate salt and is widely available for public purchase in supermarkets, nutrition stores, health food stores and the Internet and mail-order. Athletes currently use Creatine as a potential "safe and legal" alternative to increase performance, as compared to anabolic steroids. Research has clearly demonstrated that supplementation of 20-30 grams/day for several days can increase intramuscular creatine stores by 20-30% in most individuals; 20-40% of this increase will be in the form of phosphocreatine (PCr or CP). The precise cellular mechanism by which increased creatine and PCr concentrations produce ergogenic effects is unknown, but it has been hypothesized that any ergogenic effect is likely mediated by improved creatine and PCr availability to facilitate ATP resynthesis during short duration, high intensity activities. Clinical laboratory studies support this hypothesis.

Creatine is found in two forms. Approximately 40% is in the free creatine form (Crfree), while the remaining 60% is in the phosphorylated form, creatine phosphate (CP). The daily turnover rate of approximately 2 g per day is met by both food and supplementation and by the body's synthesis of the substance. While more creatine is found in the fast twitch muscles, the slow twitch fibers are able to resynthesize it because of their greater access to oxygen. The only side effect associated with creatine supplementation appears to be a small increase in body mass, which is most likely due to water retention but may be related to increased protein synthesis. [16]

In a Spanish study of elite soccer players with a group receiving creatine and another receiving a placebo, it was found that the intermittent sprinting and the jumping ability of the players was aided during play, but the endurance of the players between the sprints was not affected. [17] Most studies on creatine use have been short term. Researchers have been clear to state that they were unaware of long term problems with creatine supplementation. However a Belgian study has found no negative effect to the kidneys due to creatine usage even after five years of use. [18]

Creatine is one of the most popular supplements today. In strength sports it is probably the most popular. It helps to augment strength and power workouts and sport performance. [19] At Penn State University, a one week study comparing a creatine-using group with a placebo group showed that in the two exercises tested (squat jump and bench press), creatine supplementation resulted in a significant improvement in peak power output during all five sets of jump squats and a significant improvement in repetitions during all five sets of bench presses. [20] A study at the University of Southern Illinois, found significant increases in bicep curl strength for creatine users after six weeks of strength training. [21]

In a recent study of high school athletes between the ages of 14-18 (182 males and 146 females) it was found that 8.2% had used creatine. Only one of these was a female, and she was a volleyball player. Those who used it were in the older group (average age of 16.5 vs. 15). 20% experienced minor gastrointestinal side effects or muscle cramps. Most had learned about creatine from their friends and bought it at health food stores. [22]

Increasing Aerobic (Endurance) Capacity

Carbohydrate loading (glycogen supercompensation) has long been a method of increasing one's endurance potential in distance running and cycling and in soccer. It seems to work more effectively with cycling than with running. (It doesn't help in strength or speed events.) A typical older method would be to exercise to near exhaustion 3 or 4 days before the competition. This might include sprints to use the glycogen stores in the fast twitch (type II) muscles. This might be accompanied by a very low carbohydrate diet. Then two days before the competition the diet would switch to about 70% carbohdrates. Today with the change of diet, many athletes have a 60%-70% intake of carbohydrates so there is generally not as much need

Possible Side Effects of Steroids for the Liver
Cancer, jaundice, tumors, pelosis hepatitis
For the Cardiovascular System
High blood pressure, changes in cholesterol levels, heart disease, anaphylactic shock, septic shock, death.
For the Reproductive System
Atrophy of the genital organs, possible swelling of the genitals, sexual dysfunctions, sterility (which is reversible), menstrual irregularities, damage to a developing fetus. For men some major problems include impotence (inability for men to have an erection)and prostate enlargement.
Psychological Problems
Depression, listlessness, aggressive and combative behavior
Other
Acne, edema, hairiness in women, irreversible male pattern baldness in women, oily skin, stunted growth, abdominal pains, chills, diarrhea, changes in bowel and urinary habits, gall stones, hives, headache, excessive calcium, insomnia, kidney stones, kidney disease, muscle cramps, nausea or vomiting, purple or red spots on the body or in the mouth or nose, rash on skin, sore throat, unusual weight gain, unexplained weight loss, unpleasant breath odor, unusual bleeding.

for the emphasis on replenishing the depleted reserves. Still the concept of reduction of glycogen reserves through exhaustive exercise then the replenishment with complex carbohydrates still seems to work.

In a Canadian study comparing similarly trained male and female endurance athletes after a 4 day carbohydrate loading regime (increasing carbohydrates from 55 to 60% to 75% of the diet) then exercising at a 75% of their VO2 max for an hour. The CHO loading increased the amount of muscle glycogen in the men by 41% and increased their performance time, in an 85% VO2 max test, by 45%. The women, on the other hand, did not increase their muscle glycogen at all and their performance increased only 5%. It is common knowledge that women utilize more fat in their energy metabolism while men utilize more carbohydrate and protein. The study concluded that women did not store much glycogen during carbohydrate loading. [23]

For those who use carbohydrate loading there are a few things to remember. First, simple sugars such as syrups and candy enter the blood stream too quickly to give the type of endurance fuel needed. Complex carbohydrates such as whole grain breads, pastas, potatoes and starchy vegetables should be used. Pies, cakes, cookies and alcohol are out. Secondly, glycogen supercompensation increases the water retention. For every gram of glycogen stored 3 grams of water are necessary. This water retention would not be advisable in gymnastics or sprinting but would be very valuable for endurance activities.

Nasal dilators are used by many athletes to increase the area of the nostrils which can take in air. A study at the University of Alabama Medical School found that the dilator (Breathe Right) did increase the nasal area and decreased the amount of exertion which the subjects perceived. It also reduced the heart rates and the number of breaths per minute which the subjects needed. [24]

Stimulants can increase alertness and increase strength and endurance. Amphetamines and ephedrine were common stimulants but have been outlawed by the athletic community. Even caffeine is allowed only up to a certain level by the International Olympic Committee.

The only legal stimulant available is caffeine. It seems to increase strength by allowing more muscle fibers to be used in a single contraction. It seems to help endurance by increasing the amount of fuel available to the muscles. It has been thought to do this by allowing the use of the triglyceride blood fats for energy which thereby save the muscle sugars (glycogen) for later in the contest. However a recent study in the Netherlands casts some doubt on this possibility, while still finding that caffeine helped performance. [25]

Caffeine increases the arousal state because it is a central nervous system stimulant. Coffee, tea, and cola drinks all contain caffeine, as do some over-the-counter drugs. Caffeine has often been used by runners and cyclists. Some well-controlled studies suggest that aspartate salt supplementation may enhance endurance performance, but other studies do not. Further research is therefore needed. [26]

Ginseng may assist in reducing reaction time. In a study of 15 soccer players (7 taking ginseng and 8 taking a placebo) VO2 max and maximal heart rates were not different, but reaction time was reduced in the ginseng users. The authors, however, are suggesting that other studies should be done to verify or refute their findings. [27]

EPO and Blood Doping

Endurance activities depend on the capacity of oxygen transport to the exercising skeletal muscles. The ability to transmit oxygen through a greater number of red blood cells and an increase in hemoglobin can be done legally by living at a high altitude or illegally by blood doping (removing one's own blood then just prior to the activity, transfusing that blood back into one's body) or by injecting erythropoietin (EPO). Since the synthesis of EPO by bioengineering, doping with recombinant human EPO has become popular in some endurance sports particularly in cycling. This kind of doping might have been responsible for several sudden deaths in young athletes, primarily in racing cyclists.[28]

The deaths are most likely the result of the increased viscosity of the blood and thrombosis with potentially fatal results.[29] But another reason can be the narrowing of the arteries by an increase in the cell linings of the arteries which thereby narrow them.[30] This, with the possibility of increased clotting, can be lethal.

Altitude Housing

It has long been known that living at high altitudes increases one's red blood cells and increases the oxygen carrying capacity of the blood. This aids in endurance. Cross country skiers have traditionally either trained at high altitudes or slept in "altitude houses" in which the amount of oxygen is reduced as it would be at altitude. We now know that "sleeping high and training low" is an effective way to increase one's endurance.

A recent U.S. Olympic Committee study has also found that the amount of creatine produced is increased by merely living at a high altitude. It is further increased by training at that altitude. (In this case the altitude was 1860 meters or 6,100 feet.) Using 8 male and 8 female elite triathlon competitors in a five week study it was found that just being at the higher altitude increased the creatine by 300%. A week of training at that altitude increased it by another 70%.[31] So there is both an aerobic and an anaerobic benefit from living or training at altitude.

Supplementing Natural Body Substances

Dehydroepiandrosterone (DHEA) is a naturally occurring substance in the body. It is a precursor to both testosterone and estrogen. Its secretions are reduced as we age. Some have thought that supplementation with DHEA would increase testosterone in younger athletes. A study at Iowa State found that DHEA ingestion does not enhance serum testosterone concentrations or adaptations associated with resistance training in young men.[32]

Many sports organizations, such as the National College Athletic Association, the United States Olympic Committee and the National Football League have banned DHEA. Thus, for competitive athletes in these organizations, not only would it be unwise to take DHEA, it would be illegal. The risks of DHEA far outweigh any benefits.

Fluid-Replacement Drinks

Fluid replacement is essential for people who are sweating because of either their exercise or the outside temperature. The fluid can be replaced at the same time that the carbohydrates are replaced with a glucose polymer drink. Other popular drinks use dextrose or another sugar along with some of the minerals which are lost in perspiration. Sodium chloride (salt), magnesium, potassium and calcium are among the common additives to such sport drinks.

While several minerals are lost when one initially sweats, as the time goes on the sweat becomes more and more like pure water. Because of this, pure water is the major need. So if energy replacement is not your objective and cost is a problem, just drink water — lots of water. For some reason, even when we are very thirsty, we generally do not take in as much water as we lose during exercise. You should "force feed" yourself more water.

Fluid-replacement drinks to replace the water and electrolytes lost in perspiration have increased and decreased in popularity recently. First it was thought that only salt and water needed to be replaced after exercise. It was then recognized that there were other electrolytes (such as potassium) lost, so drinks such as Gatorade became prominent. Later it was recognized that the body tends to conserve its minerals, so athletes were told to drink only water. Now the pendulum has swung once again and sometimes electrolyte-replacement fluids are being recommended.

It has also been learned that simple sugars in the water (as many fluid-replacement drinks have) retard the absorption of the water from the intestines. However, drinks with glucose polymers (a more complicated type of sugar) are absorbed more quickly than plain water. You should also know that cool or cold water is absorbed more quickly than warm water.

Reducing Recovery Time

Shortening the recovery period after exercise is done immediately after a workout or a competition. Whether your workout is a weight training session or an endurance activity such as running, cycling or swimming, your maximum recovery cannot happen without an immediate replacement of the carbohydrates which had been lost during the exercise. While many weight trainers think that they need protein replacement — that is wrong. They need carbohydrates.

Muscle Recovery and Pain Reduction

Non-steroidal anti-inflammatory drugs (NAIDs), such as aspirin, can often reduce muscle soreness, but they increase one's susceptibility to heat and create a greater risk of heat stroke. Aspirin is probably the safest and it has other positive effects.

The 6 billion people in the world consume 50 billion doses of aspirin. Some, of course, are not eating their share! In the US aspirin is taken primarily to ward off a heart attack. Nearly 38% of aspirin doses are taken for this purpose. The recommended dose varies from 1/2 to 1 per day. Some people take an infant formula aspirin every day, some take a full aspirin every other day. Two major international studies have found that the risk of stroke is reduced by about 10% with the use of aspirin.

Reducing arthritis pain is the second most common use of the drug. A little over 23% of users take the drug for this reason. One famous sports physician with unbearable arthritis pain consumed a small bottle of aspirin daily to control his pain.

Controlling headache is the reason for another 14% of the population to take the drug. The remainder of users take it to reduce fever or to control pains in other parts of their bodies.

A reduced breast cancer risk has been shown in some large studies, but not all studies have found the same risk reduction. And some studies find that aspirin may increase the risk of colorectal cancer, but not all studies have found this. Since these drugs are known to be stomach and intestinal irritants it may be this negative quality which is responsible for irritations of the intestines and the possibility of developing a colorectal cancer. Of the NSAID type drugs low dose ibuprofen is least likely to cause gastrointestinal complications. Buffered aspirin does not seem to have this same protective ability.

Drugs such as aspirin, ibuprofen, indomethacin, naproxen and piroxicam are common types of anti-inflammatory drugs. They seem to have other functions as well.[33] But aspirin also has properties which reduce the clotting abilities of the blood platelets which reduces the risk of heart attack and strokes caused by clots. (But it can increase the incidence of strokes whose cause is hemorrhage.)

Notes:

1. B.W. Timmons et al., "The Efficacy of SPORT as a Dietary Supplement on Performance and Recovery in Trained Athletes," *Canadian Journal of Applied Physiology* 25.1 (2000): 55-67.
2. A.J.N. Wagenmakers and G. van Hall, "Branched Chain Amino Acids: Nutrition and Metabolism in Exercise," *Biochemistry of Exercise*, eds. R.J. Maughan and Shirreffs (Champaign, IL: Human Kinetics, 1996): 431-455.

3. P.M. Clarkson and M.M. Manore, "Nutritional and Pharmacological Ergogenic Aids," *Women and Sport*, ed. B. Drinkwater (Oxford: Blackwell Scientific, 2000): 321-323.

4. A. Mero, "Leucine Supplementation and Intensive Training," *Sports Medicine* 27.6 (1999): 347-358.

5. J.C. Anthony et al., "Orally Administered Leucine Stimulates Protein Synthesis in Skeletal Muscle of Postabsorptive Rats in Association with Increased eIF4F Formation," *Nutrition* 130.2 (2000): 139-145.

6. S. Langer et al., "Interactions Among the Branched-Chain Amino Acids and Their Effects on Methionine Utilization in Growing Pigs: Effects on Plasma Amino- and Keto-Acid Concentrations and Branched-Chain Keto-Acid Dehydrogenase Activity," *British Journal of Nutrition* 83.1 (2000): 49-58.

7. L.M. Castell et al., "The Role of Tryptophan in Fatigue in Different Conditions of Stress," *Adv Exp Med Biol* 467 (1999): 697-704.

8. D. Pearson, "The ABCs of Glutamine, BBAAs, and HMB," *Strength and Conditioning Journal* 21.4 (1999): 66.

9. A.J. Wagenmakers, "Amino Acid Supplements to Improve Athletic Performance," *Curr Opin Clin Nutr Metab Care* 2.6 (1999): 539-544.

10. M.H. Williams, "Facts and Fallacies of Purported Ergogenic Amino Acid Supplements," *Clinical Sports Medicine* 18.3 (1999): 633-649.

11. G.S. Palmer et al., "Carbohydrate Ingestion Immediately Before Exercise Does Not Improve 20 km Time Trial Performance in Well-Trained Cyclists," *International Journal of Sports Medicine* 19.6 (1998): 415-418.

12. W.J. Kraemer et al, "Effects of Heavy-Resistance Training on Hormonal Response Patterns in Younger vs. Older Men," *Journal of Applied Physiology* 87.3 (1999): 982-92.

13. M. Ullman and A. Oldfors, "Effects of Growth Hormone on Skeletal Muscle in Studies on Normal Adult Rats." *Acta Physiol Scand* 135.4 (1989): 531-536.

14. H. Frisch, "Growth Hormone and Body Composition in Athletes," *Journal of Endocrinol Invest* 22.5 Suppl (1999): 106-109.

15. E.B. Feldman "Creatine: A Dietary Supplement and Ergogenic Aid," *Nutrition Review* 57.2 (1999): 45-50.

16. T.W. Dermant and E.C. Rhodes, "Effects of Creatine Supplementation on Exercise Performance," *Sports Medicine* 28.1 (1999): 46-60

17. I. Mujika et al., "Creatine Supplementation and Sprint Performance in Soccer Players," *Medicine & Sport in Science & Exercise* 32.2 (2000): 518-525.

18. J.R. Poortmans and M. Francaux, "Long-Term Oral Creatine Supplementation Does not Impair Renal Function in Healthy Athletes." *Medicine & Sport in Science & Exercise* 31.8 (1999): 1108-1110.

19. W.J. Kraemer and J.S. Volek, "Creatine Supplementation: Its Role in Human Performance," *Clin Sports Med* 18.3 (1999): 651-666.

20. J.S. Volek et al., "Creatine Supplementation Enhances Muscular Performance During High-Intensity Resistance Exercise," *Journal Am Diet Association* 97.7 (1997): 765-770.

21. M.D. Becque, J.D. Lochmann and D.R. Melrose, "Effects of Oral Creatine Supplementation on Muscular Strength and Body Composition," *Medicine & Sport in Science & Exercise* 32.3 (2000): 654-658.

22. J. Smith and D. Dahm, "Creatine Use Among High School Athletes."

23. M.A. Tarnopolsky et al., "Carbohydrate Loading and Metabolism During Exercise in Men and Women," *Journal of Applied Physiology* 78.4 (1995): 1360-1368.

24. J.W. Griffin et al., "Physiologic Effects of an External Nasal Dilator," *Laryngoscope* 107.9 (1997): 1235-1238.

25. E.M.R. Kovacs, J.H.C.H. Stegen and F. Brouns, "Effect of Caffeinated Drinks on Substrate Metabolism, Caffeine Excretion, and Performance," *Journal of Applied Physiology* 85.2 (1998): 709-715.

26. M.H. Williams, "Facts and Fallacies of Purported Ergogenic Amino Acid Supplements," *Clin Sports Med* 18.3 (1999): 633-649.

27. A.W. Chmura et al, "Ginseng Treatment Improves Psychomotor Performance at Rest and During Graded Exercise in Young Adults," *International Journal of Sports Nutrition* 9 (1999): 371-377.

28. A.J. Scheen, "Doping with Erythropoietin or the Misuse of Therapeutic Advances," *Rev Med Liege* 53.8 (1998): 499-502.

29. D.J. Shaskey and G.A. Green, "Sports Haematology," *Sports Medicine* 29.1 (2000): 27-38.

30. N. Ikegaya et al., "Elevated Erythropoietin Receptor and Transforming Growth Factor-Beta1 Expression in Stenotic Arteriovenous Fistulae Used for Hemodialysis," *Journal Am Soc Nephrol*

11.5 (2000): 928.

31. R.L. Wilber et al., "Effect of Altitude Training on Serum Creatine Kinase Activity and Serum Cortisol Concentration in Triathletes," *European Journal of Applied Physiology* 81.1/2 (2000): 140-147.

32. G.A. Brown et al., "Effect of Oral DHEA on Serum Testosterone and Adaptations to Resistance Training in Young Men," *Journal of Applied Physiology* 87.6 (1999): 2274-2283.

33. M. Pahor and W.B. Applegate, "Recent Advances: Geriatric Medicine," *British Medical Journal* 315.7115: 1071.

23

Concerns for Fluid Replacement and Outdoor Exercising

We walk, run, play or compete in nearly all temperatures. Because of this we must be aware of the dangers of being too hot or too cold. We must also recognize the importance of replacing our body fluids before, during and after our workouts.

Heat

Excess heat not only negatively affects our performance, but it also can be a source of serious health problems. As the outside temperature increases it becomes less and less possible to get rid of the body heat exercise produces. For example, if exercising at 37 degrees Fahrenheit (3 degrees Celcius) you are 20% more effective in eliminating body heat than if you are exercising at 67 degrees F (20 degrees C) and 150% more effective than if you are exercising at 104 degrees Fahrenheit (40 degrees C). It is not uncommon for the body to reach a temperature of 104 to 106 degrees F (40 to 41 degrees C) when exercising. But normal resting body temperature is 98.6 degrees F (37 degrees C). The high heat makes it difficult, or impossible, for the perspiration to evaporate, so the body can't be effectively cooled.

The heat generated in the muscles is released by:
- Conduction—from the warmer muscles to the cooler skin.
- Convection—from the heat loss from the skin to the air.
- Evaporation—the perspiration being vaporized.

Conduction occurs through the body's liquids, such as the blood, absorbing the heat created by the contraction of the muscles and moving it to the cooler skin. Water can absorb many thousands of times more heat than the air can, so it is an excellent conductor of heat from the muscles.

Wind Speed MPH	What the Thermometer Reads (Degrees F)											
	50	40	30	20	10	0	-10	-20	-30	-40	-50	-60
	What it Equals on Exposed Flesh											
40	26	10	-6	-21	-37	-53	-69	-85	-100	-116	-132	-148
35	27	11	-4	-20	-35	-49	-67	-82	-98	-113	-129	-145
30	28	13	-2	-18	-33	-48	-63	-79	-94	-109	-125	-140
25	30	16	0	-15	-29	-44	-59	-74	-88	-104	-118	-133
20	32	18	4	-10	-25	-39	-53	-67	-82	-96	-110	-121
15	36	22	9	-5	-18	-36	-45	-58	-72	-85	-99	-112
10	40	28	76	4	-9	-21	-33	-46	-58	-70	-83	-95
5	48	37	27	16	6	-5	-15	-26	-36	-47	-57	-68
Calm	50	40	30	20	10	0	-10	-20	-30	-40	-50	-60

Little danger if properly clothed	Danger of freezing exposed flesh	Great danger of freezing exposed flesh

Convection occurs when the heat near the skin is absorbed into the atmosphere. For a swimmer in a cool pool, effective convection is very easy. For the runner it is more difficult. It is aided by a lower air temperature and by wind. A four mile an hour wind is twice as effective in cooling as is a one mile an hour wind. (This is the basis for the wind chill factor associated with winds in cool environments.)

Evaporation is the most effective method for cooling a body that is exercising in the air. Each liter of sweat that evaporates takes with it 580 kilocalories. This is enough heat to raise the temperature of 10 liters of water 58 degrees C (10 ½ quarts of water to 105 degrees F). As the skin is cooled by the evaporation of the sweat, the skin is able to take more of the heat from the blood and thereby cool the blood so that it can pick up more heat from the muscles. The humidity is the most important factor regulating the evaporation of one's sweat.

High humidity reduces the ability of your perspiration to be evaporated. It is the evaporation of the sweat that produces the cooling effect as the perspiration goes from liquid to gas. This amounts to a cooling effect of over a half a kilocalorie per gram of perspiration evaporated. Exercising in a rubber suit has similar effects to high humidity because the water cannot evaporate — it is not recommended.

Wind has the opposite effect. It affects the body temperature by cooling it faster than the registered temperature would warrant. We have all heard of the wind chill factor present on colder days. The wind makes the body experience more cold than would be expected by the actual temperature. *(See chart.)* But even on warmer days the wind will evaporate the perspiration and cool the body faster than might otherwise be expected. This may increase the need for fluids to continue the production of sweat.

Influence of the Menstrual Cycle

During the luteal phase (after ovulation) of the cycle, during moderate exercise, females' body temperature and heart rate tend to raise significantly.[1] Blood volume (plasma volume) seems to decrease during the follicular cycle (after menstrual flow). [2]

Fluid Replacement

The hyperthermia (high temperature) developed during exercise, particularly when the sweat cannot evaporate, is a major cause of fatigue. This is particularly true when the body has lost 2% of its water through perspiration. Since it is not uncommon to lose 1-5 liters of water when exercising it is not difficult to enter the stage of dehydration. The combination of dehydration and high body temperature can cause a number of physiological problems such as: a reduction of blood volume, an increase in the breakdown of liver and muscle glycogen (a sugar used for muscle energy), and the inability of the body to effectively pass certain electrolytes across the cells membranes.

While obviously it is recommended that people who exercise should replace 100% of the fluids lost, it is seldom done. The normal person will replace only about 50% during the exercise period. Dehydration of 4% of the body's weight will reduce one's endurance by 30% in temperate conditions but by as much as 50% when the weather is very warm.

Exercise in cold weather also requires adequate fluid intake. You must warm the air you breathe and your body is still producing heat. You will

---

Checklist for Reducing Heat-Related Problems

Preventing heat related problems requires that you:
- Recognize the temperature and humidity and take the required measures to reduce an injury.
- Drink a great deal of water and possibly some fluid replacement drinks during the practice, but don't take salt tablets. Drinks with a good deal of sugar may not be well tolerated by the body. Drink more than you think you need.
- Wear cool clothing that allows the perspiration to escape, white clothes will reflect the sun better.
- Exercise during the cooler part of the day, morning is better.

---

tend to produce more urine. These factors require you to take in more fluid. If you don't, your body will feel colder because your blood will not have sufficient volume to warm your skin effectively with the heat which it picks up from the exercising muscles.

Dehydration due to excessive heat and/or inadequate fluid intake can cause serious heat related illnesses. A sudden change in the heat or humidity where you practice or traveling to a warmer or more humid climate to compete can cause problems. If you were to travel to India, Egypt or the Caribbean to compete in a marathon, it would probably take 10 days to two weeks to acclimatize yourself to the warmer or more humid climate.

Among the changes which will probably occur in a high heat environment are: a reduced heart rate (due to less need for blood to heat the skin — resulting in less blood flow to the skin), an increase in the amount of blood plasma, increased sweating, perspiring earlier when exercising, increased salt losses, and the psychological adjustments made to the experience of greater heat and humidity.

Adequate fluid is essential to the functioning of an efficient body. When body fluids are reduced by sweating less fluid is available in the blood and other tissues. These make the body less efficient and, in some cases, can result in serious sickness or even death. To keep your body hydrated you should have frequent breaks for fluid intake. However, even frequent breaks seldom give an exerciser enough fluid. A person's thirst does not signal the true need for fluids.

The ingredients of sweat change as you exercise. At the beginning there are a number of salts excreted. Sodium chloride (common table salt) as well as potassium, calcium, chromium, zinc, and magnesium salts can be lost. The initial sweat contains most of these salts but as the exercise continues, the amount of salts in the sweat is reduced because some of the body's hormones come into play. Aldosterone, for example, conserves the sodium for the body. Consequently the longer we exercise the more that our sweat resembles pure water.

A comprehensive study of blood changes during a marathon has indicated that the sodium ions were not significantly reduced and potassium actually increased. This may make us question the need for these minerals in sports drinks. However the sugars and water in the sports drinks may be needed. The average marathon runner loses about 4 pounds during the race. Most of this is water with some of it coming from the use of sugars (glycogen) and body fats. (About 2900 kilocalories are used in a marathon run.) During the run the body creates some water as it uses the glycogen (stored sugar) for energy. About 36 ounces (1300 grams) is produced in this process.

Urination is also decreased thereby saving the body's water store. [3]

A normal diet replaces all of the necessary elements lost in sweat. Drinking a single glass of orange or tomato juice replaces all or most of the calcium, potassium and magnesium lost. Further, most of us have plenty of sodium in our daily diets.

Fluid replacement drinks on the market are not necessarily recommended. Water, the most needed element, is slowed in its absorption if the drink contains other elements such as salts and some forms of sugar. Water alone is therefore generally the recommended drink for fluid replacement — and it is certainly the least expensive. For those who want to replace water and sugars for energy the best drinks are those which contain glucose polymers (maltodextrins). So if you are using fluid replacement drinks, check the label then buy what you need — salts and/or sugars. Both caffeine (coffee, tea, and cola drinks) and alcohol dehydrate the body so should be avoided.

There is no question that adding carbohydrates, such as maltodextrins, is highly effective in replacing your body's fuel. In a study of marathon runners given either a high carbohydrate drink or a placebo every 15 minutes during a run, those receiving the high carbohydrate drink were able to keep the blood sugar glycogen much higher during and after the run. [4]

While water is generally recommended as the drink to replace lost perspiration, there are times when some electrolytes (sodium, potassium, etc.) must be replaced. People working in the heat in hard manual labor, marathon runners, soccer players playing under the summer sun in Texas or Arizona, and similar vocational or avocational warm weather pursuits will probably need extra electrolytes. In a study testing whether sodium or sugars (glucose) was more important in the body absorbing water, it was found that the sugars were more important in fluid replacement beverages. [5]

However, one study, with trained runners on a 2 hour treadmill run at 60% of VO2 max found that heat was controlled the same whether the runners received either 8% carbohydrate carbonated drinks, 8% non-carbonated drinks or water. [6] This study indicates that you can drink whatever you want — just drink. But it is the water, more than anything else, which is essential.

In the Commonwealth Games in Malaysia in September of 1998 Craig Barrett of New Zealand was leading the 50 kilometer walk by 6 minutes with a kilometer left in the race. He was a sure winner, but the heat of Kuala Lumpur was far greater than that in which he had been training in New Zealand. He had not taken in enough water and electrolytes and heat exhaustion overcame him. He fell, got up, fell again, then staggered to the side of the road and was taken to the hospital. He had not only become incapable of moving his legs but he was delirious and had no idea what was happening. When he regained consciousness in the hospital he thought he had won the race.

A British study using 12 male and 6 female well trained middle distance runners who ran six one hour runs, three indoor and three outdoor. In one indoor and one outdoor run no fluids were given. This gave an indication of the amount of fluid loss during the run. In one indoor and one outdoor run water sufficient to replace the fluid loss registered in the first run was given. In the third indoor and outdoor runs a sport drink was administered. The results showed that per pound of body weight, the men lost twice as much fluid as the women — about 1.9 kilograms for the men to 1 kilogram for the women. Both the water and the sport drink were equally effective in maintaining the blood volume, heart rate, body temperature and blood lactate levels. The sport drink, as should be expected, was superior in maintaining a higher blood glucose level. [7]

If you are exercising for more than 15 minutes or exercising in the heat you must be conscious of your need for fluid. In such situations it may be wise to eat a diet higher than normal in potassium and, depending on the amount of sweat, some extra sodium. You might consume a drink with extra electrolytes, such as V-8 juice or orange juice, or a sport drink with these elements. [8] Even a minimal level of dehydration (less than 2% loss of body weight due to perspiration) impairs the cardiovascular and the heat regulating abilities of the body. Even when exercising for less than an hour fluid replacement is essential. [9]

Problems Caused by Heat

Heat cramps are generally found in the cramping of the legs, arms or abdomen. The victim will be able to think clearly and will have a normal rectal temperature. The treatment is to give fluids with salt and possibly other minerals — as are found in most fluid replacement drinks. Heat cramps are particularly common among exercisers who are not yet in good physical condition and who are participating during warm days. There should be no problem in returning to activity the next day.

Heat exhaustion is generally caused by too little fluid or insufficient salts in the body. Water depletion heat exhaustion is caused by insufficient water intake or excessive sweating. The symptoms may include: intense thirst, weakness, chills, fast breathing, impaired judgment, nausea, a lack of muscular coordination and/or dizziness. If untreated it can develop into heat stroke — a rectal temperature of over 104 degrees F (40 C). The immediate treatment is to give water or an electrolyte replacement drink. When the case is severe it may require intravenous fluid replacement. The skin will generally feel cool and somewhat moist.

Salt depletion heat exhaustion appears to be similar to heat cramps. This can occur when large volumes of sweat are replaced only with water. If a great deal of salt was lost in the perspiration it can affect muscle function-ing. It is most likely to occur during the first 5-10 days of exercising in the heat. The symptoms may include: vomiting, nausea, inability to eat, diar-rhea, a headache (particularly in the front of the head), weakness, a lower body temperature and muscle cramps. Weight loss and thirst are not symp-toms of this problem.

Heat stroke can be caused by heavy exercise just as it can by high air temperature. It is a very serious condition which can affect many of the organs. It can occur when the interior organs of the body are heated above 106 degrees F (42 degrees C). At this temperature protein begins to break down. Enzymes are affected as are the cell walls. When the cells cannot function effectively, the organ functioning is impaired.

In addition to a body temperature in excess of 104 degrees F (40 degrees C) there can be a rapid pulse (100-120 beats per minute) and low blood pressure. There may also be confusion, weakness, fatigue, delirium, or the victim may lapse into a coma. The confusion which may be exhibited is often confused with a head injury in contact sports. The skin color is grayish indicating poor circulation, and it will be clammy. There may or may not be sweating. The pupils of the eyes may be very small.

Treatment requires the immediate cooling of the body. Don't wait for the hospital to treat the victim. It may be too late. Use ice packs to the neck, and groin. Full immersion in a tub of cold water is better. One who has experi-enced a heat stroke should not return to activity for at least a week or two.

Reducing the Risk of Heat Related Problems

To prevent these heat related problems athletic trainers often require that athletes regain 80% of their fluid loss before leaving the locker room. So if an athlete weighed 150 pounds before the practice and 146 pounds after-ward, the trainer could require that the athlete take in enough fluids to bring the weight back to slightly over 149 pounds before leaving the facility.

If you are concerned about overheating during your workouts it is rec-ommended that the temperature be taken with a rectal thermometer. The temperature during and immediately after exercise should be below 104 degrees. If you were to use another type of thermometer it would not give a true "core body" temperature because it would be affected by the cooling effects of sweating and other factors.

The best warm weather clothing is no clothes. But unless you are running in a nudist camp you had better wear something. Changing to dry clothes is not advised because the evaporation effect is maximized when the clothing is wet.

Cold Related Problems

Females exercising, at the same intensity as men in cold weather (24 degrees F or -5 degrees C) maintained about the same amount of heat production. But by the third hour the females' heat production dropped significantly below that of the men. Exercising in cold water (68 degrees F, 20 degrees C) men increased their metabolic activity while women did not. However the rate of body cooling was greater for males than females. This gives female swimmers an advantage in reducing complications from the cold water. [10]

Exercising in cold air may dry out the mucous membranes because cold air cannot hold as much water vapor as warmer air. Wearing a mask which traps the exhaled water vapor then can re-humidify the inhaled air can reduce this problem. However most problems relate to the effect of the cold temperature on the skin.

Frostnip occurs when the ends of the fingers, toes, ears or nose are chilled. The skin is very cold and somewhat stiffened. Warm the body part slowly. Using your hands to warm the affected area is best. The armpits may be used to warm chilled fingers.

Frostbite can begin with temperatures as high as 31 degrees (F) (-0.5 C). The most likely victims are people who have had the problem previously (a doubled rate), blacks, and of course those who work or play outdoors in cold temperatures. Frostbite can be superficial or deep and severe.

When frostbite has occurred, gently warm the area. Do not rub it to increase circulation because the rubbing can destroy the cells which have been frozen. A warm bath (104 to 108 degrees F (40-42 degrees C) is helpful. For severe frostbite the victim should be hospitalized where the rewarming can be done under proper supervision.

Proper protection is essential to avoid the problem and is doubly important to those who have already had one case of frostbite. Layers of wool clothing, vapor barrier clothing, adequate gloves, and a face mask if necessary. Outdoor practices and games are not recommended if the ambient temperature is -4 degrees Fahrenheit (-20 C) or the wind-chill factor is -40 F.

Hypothermia is a generalized body cooling. While the cooling is generally not as dangerous to body tissues as is heat, there is still a danger of death. It can occur quickly, such as when a person falls into very cold water, or slowly, when the person is exposed to low air temperatures.

Dehydration often occurs because the blood flow to the skin is reduced. This increases the volume of blood in the organs. The liver senses the increased blood volume so removes the excess water from the blood. This results in less total water in the body.

The people most susceptible to this type of problem are: older people (because of their reduced metabolic activity), young people with large skin surfaces but less body mass (ie. tall thin teenagers), hypoglycemic or diabetic people, and those with reduced glycogen stores (energy reserves) due to physical exertion or shivering.

Hypothermia can begin with outside temperatures of less than 64 degrees (F) (18 C) especially if it is wet. Long distance races and other endurance events in these low temperatures can cause problems. Swimmers, free divers, or scuba divers are particularly prone to the possibilities of hypothermia because water conducts heat away from the body 32 times more rapidly than does air.

The symptoms, in addition to feeling cold and shivering, may include: poor judgment, confusion, muscle stiffness and unconsciousness. If hypothermia is diagnosed get the person to the hospital as quickly as possible. The hospital can use special internal and external warming methods. Cold wet clothes can be removed and the body should be insulated against further cold. The body can be warmed with the victim's own body heat or in a warm room.

Prevention of cold injury is best done by dressing in wool or polypropylene clothing. (Cotton is not recommended because it holds perspiration and increases the heat loss through conduction.) The clothing should be in layers to reduce the body's heat loss and cold absorption through the better insulating qualities of the multiple layers and the trapped air between the layers. Effective gloves or mittens, a warm hat and/or ear muffs, wool socks, and possibly a woolen or other mask.

Air Pollution

The most common sites for air pollution are urban areas, especially near well traveled roads (carbon monoxide, lead, oxides of nitrogen and sulfuric acid), indoor ice rinks (oxides of nitrogen), and swimming pools (chlorine forming cancerogenic chloroform). Among the common air pollutants from autos and oil refineries are: carbon monoxide, sulfuric acid, carbon dioxide, oxides of nitrogen, and lead.

Runners in urban areas generally have high levels of lead in their blood. This is occurring while the levels of blood lead are being reduced in the general population because of the use of lead free gasoline.

Air is a limited resource. Normal air contains 21 per cent oxygen. When the percentage of oxygen in the air drops to 16 per cent, the brain is affected. Life cannot be supported if the oxygen level drops to six per cent. Vegetation takes in the carbon dioxide which we breathe out, then gives off the oxygen that we breathe in. This process is one aspect of the phenomenon called photosynthesis. An acre of beech trees in a forest consumes 2,000 pounds of carbon dioxide while giving out 1500 pounds of oxygen each day.

Motor vehicles burn more than 600 million gallons of gasoline each day in the U.S.. This burning increases nearly all the pollutants in the air. In a city such as Los Angeles. automobiles and trucks produce 45 tons of aerosols, 585 tons of nitrogen oxide, 35 tons of sulfur dioxide, and 9,775 tons of carbon monoxide daily. Aircraft add an additional 19 tons of nitrogen oxide and 190 tons of carbon monoxide to that city's air.

Sulfur compounds are a problem. Sulfur dioxide plus oxygen in the air becomes sulfur trioxide, which is more irritating than sulfur dioxide. The sulfur trioxide then combines with water vapor in the air to become sulfuric acid. (The chemical formula is $2SO_2 + O_2 = 2SO_3 + 2H_2O = 2H_2SO_4$). Coal, which is 1%-5% sulfur, is a major contributor to the sulfur dioxide content of the air. The sulfuric acid is bad enough on our lungs and on painted surfaces but it is then picked up through convection and becomes an ingredient in the acid rain which has become quite common in the northern latitudes. Sulfuric acid is the most destructive to lung tissue.

Carbon monoxide released by burning, especially burning gasoline, is picked up by the hemoglobin in the blood. The hemoglobin is then rendered useless in transporting necessary oxygen to the tissues. The heart must work harder and the blood pressure is increased. This strains the heart by making it work unnecessarily.

Carbon monoxide in the blood is increased while driving a car, standing on a busy road, or just living in the city. In downtown Los Angeles, carbon monoxide has been measured as high as 400 parts per million. At 600 parts per million, drowsiness occurs, and at 1,000 parts per million, a person could go into a coma. Exposure to carbon monoxide of one per cent in the air for five minutes could be fatal.

Among the symptoms of carbon monoxide poisoning (high carbo-oxi-hemoglobin) levels are: headache, nausea, dizziness, and a lack of muscular coordination. Such poisonings are most likely to occur to people who work near automobiles — mechanics, policemen, and parking-lot attendants.

Ozone is a type of molecule of oxygen which performs a necessary function of filtering out some of the harmful radiation of the sun. This occurs in the upper atmosphere 8-30 miles above the earth's surface. In the last ten years there has been a 5% loss of ozone in the stratosphere due to the use of chlorofluorocarbons CFCs) from spray cans and the freon used in air conditioning gases. Every drop of 1% in ozone is expected to increase the amount of ultra violet (UV) light which reaches the ground. This increases skin aging and serious skin cancer. It also increases cataracts, the hardening of the lens in the eye.

Closer to the ground ozone is an irritating element of smog. Rats exposed to ozone develop lesions in their bronchial tubes and lungs but do not seem to develop cancer. [11]

Various studies have indicated that some people may be able to build a tolerance to the negative effects of ozone. In general, residents of Los Angeles have developed some capacities for rebuilding lung tissues damaged by the pollutant. On the other hand, people with chronic emphysema, respiratory diseases, or people who have not been exposed to smog (such as many residents of Canada) do not have such abilities.

Lead in gasoline is another air pollution problem. Approximately three million tons of lead have been released into the atmosphere since it was added to gasoline in 1923. Poisoning begins when the level of lead in the body reaches 0.8 parts per million. Recent samples have shown that the average person in the U.S. has between 0.05 and 0.4 parts per million in the blood. The blood concentration is generally higher in areas near large numbers of automobiles. So far, no known deaths have occurred due to airborne lead poisoning.

The possible effects of air pollution are many. Lung cancer and emphysema are the most common that come to mind; but increased carbon monoxide levels could certainly increase heart attack rates by increasing blood pressure and making the cardiovascular system less effective. People living in urban areas have twice the lung cancer rate as those who live in rural areas.

Sulfuric acid has been found to be a constrictor of the bronchial tubes leading to the lungs. This is a particular problem for those with asthma but also affects many other people. With the bronchial tubes reduced in diameter it is more difficult to inhale and the necessary oxygen is decreased — thereby cutting one's endurance.

The oxides of nitrogen also reduce the ability of the respiratory organs (bronchial tubes and lungs) to function effectively. They also increase the risk of infection. Nitrogen is increased where propane (liquid nitrogen) is used as a fuel, such as in indoor ice rinks where the machines which clear and smooth the ice are generally propane powered.

Meteorological reports will generally give one the air pollution level for the next day. When it is high your workouts should be reduced or eliminated. Training is safer if it is done away from heavy traffic patterns and before or after rush hour.

Notes:

1. J. Pivarnik et al., "Menstrual Cycle Phase Affects Temperature Regulation During Endurance Exercise," *Journal Applied Physiology* 72 (1992): 543-548.
2. E. Haymes, "Environmental Challenges," *Women in Sport*, ed. B. Drinkwater (Oxford: Blackwell Science, 2000): 65.
3. J. Pastene et al., "Water Balance During and After Marathon Running," *European Journal of Applied Physiology*, 73 (1996): 49-55.
4. D.C. Nieman et al., "Carbohydrate Supplementation Affects Blood Granulocyte and Monocyte Trafficking but not Function After 2.5 Hours of Running," *American Journal of Clinical Nutrition* 66.1 (1997): 153-159.
5. C.V. Gisolfi et al., "Effect of Sodium Concentration in a Carbohydrate-Electrolyte Solution on Intestinal Absorption," *Medicine and Science in Sport and Exercise* 27.10 (1995): 1414-1420.
6. M.S. Hickey, D.L. Costill and S.W. Trappe, "Drinking Behavior and Exercise Thermal Stress: The Role of Drink Carbonation," *International Journal of Sport Nutrition* 4.1 (1994): 8-21.
7. J.A. White et al., "Fluid Replacement Needs of Well-Trained Male and Female Athletes During Indoor and Outdoor Steady State Running," *Journal Sci Med Sport* 1.3 (1998): 131-142.
8. M.J. Luetykemeier et al., "Dietary Sodium and Plasma Volume Levels with Exercise," *Sports Medicine (New Zealand)* 23.5 (1997): 279-286.
9. R. Murray, "Dehydration, Hypothermia, and Athletes: Science and Practice," *Journal of Athletic Training (Dallas, TX)* 31.3 (1996): 248-252.
10. E.M. Haymes, "Environmental Challenges," *Women in Sport*, ed. B. Drinkwater (Oxford: Blackwell Science, 2000): 67-68.
11. G.A. Boorman et al., "Toxicology and Carcinogenesis Studies of Ozone," *Toxicology and Pathology* 22:5 (1994): 545-554.

24

Sport Psychology and the Mental Approach to Conditioning

Sport psychology grew out of general psychology, particularly out of educational psychology and how we can learn more effectively. The first major study looking at mental skills in elite athletes was done as late as 1987.[1] In this chapter we will look at the benefits of exercise and sport and how one can improve her sport performance by effective mental techniques. We will also look at how top level athletes can become more effective. This is important for both the coaches and the athletes.

In a study of middle school athletes done at Northern Illinois University, it was found that the goals of the athletes changed over the season. The way the athletes perceived how well they had mastered their sports skills changed as they moved through the competitive season. The conclusion was that sport offers a different environment than is found in the academic or the "outside world" settings, so general psychology and education psychology principles may have to be adapted for the sport setting.[2]

Emotions also needed to be addressed by sport psychology. But some sport psychologists have recognized that top level athletes not only need to be able to control their emotions and concentrate on their techniques, they must also be geared to perfection. High level success is the aim of effective sport psychology. We are not looking at the "average" as we do in general psychology.

A study of the very top male and female elite athletes compared Olympic and world championship medal winners with elite college and top junior athletes. The study found that the highest level athletes were: [3]
- able to handle pre-competition anxiety better.
- more mentally balanced.
- able to concentrate better both before and during competition.

- more self-confident.
- better able to imagine themselves doing their event and were less affected by external (the coach's) motivational techniques.
- found more meaning in their sport.

The study also found that among the highest level elite athletes there were no gender differences, but among the college athletes, women had lower self esteem and they experienced more stress. These gender differences either reduced or disappeared when the female athlete believed that the activity was gender appropriate and the coaching feedback was clear. [4]

Fitness and Mental Health

Sport or exercise can have both positive and negative effects on our lives depending the extent and the level of our participation. Exercise is generally quite positive for our mental health. Among its benefits is the reduction of stress. But if we overtrain the effects on our psyches can be negative — stresses can be developed and depression can set in. On the other side of the coin, our mental efforts can increase our physical potentials.

The positive mental effects of exercise have been observed by athletes and physiologists of exercise. Athletes generally have shown higher than average levels of social maturity, self-confidence, and intellectual efficiency. The question is, did the athletic activity actually develop these qualities or were they already present in the person and perhaps were instrumental in the decision to become an athlete?

The circulation of blood to the brain during exercise aids in making one more alert. The physical activity during an exercise can also allow one to take out aggressions on inanimate objects, becoming more relaxed in the process. When people hit a tennis ball or pound the pavement while jogging, they may be unconsciously taking out frustrations that would otherwise be directed at a boss, teacher or parent.

There is a substance called catecholamine which is essential in several brain chemicals that help to transmit messages in the brain. One of the essential precursors for this brain chemical is called tyrosine hydroxylase (TH). TH decreases with age and may be a factor in mental changes and problems that can occur with age. The Geriatric Research, Education and Clinical Center of the Department of Veterans Affairs Medical Center in Gainesville, Florida has done a study with rats that showed exercise reduced the loss of TH. If this checks out with humans, we may have yet another mental benefit of endurance exercise. [5]

A study at Purdue University showed that untrained middle-aged university employees significantly improved their mental outlooks during the duration of a specially designed fitness program of calisthenics and jogging. Results of the study showed that statistically-significant positive changes occurred. The areas of self-assurance, stability, and imagination were all greatly improved in the test subjects. So whatever your age, from youth sport to masters level competition, there are positive results from your exercise.

Another reason for exercising aerobically is that we look better when we exercise effectively. And when we look good, we feel good. All of these benefits are generally found in athletes — especially those who are aerobically trained. Athletes are more likely to have a higher amount of self esteem, the major foundation for good mental health. Female athletes in schools have also been found to have fewer pregnancies. This seems to be because of their increased self esteem and the fact that there is more in their lives than just searching for an adequate social life.

The Mental Side of Competition

Whether you are competing with yourself in the weight room or competing against others on the practice court or the game field, your mental preparation is essential. Long before sport psychologists entered the scene, athletes were using the psychological technique of imagery -- mentally practicing before the competition. Goal setting, another essential of sport psychologists, has been implicit in every athlete's desire for higher-level performances. What sport psychologists have done, however, is to make us aware of how to do it better.

Mental Conditioning and Sports Psychology

There is an important side of our conditioning that is mental rather than physical. The mental aspects of conditioning include:

- Setting goals and developing the proper intensity of motivation.
- Taking advantage of the mental benefits that result from the release of endorphins (which produce a feeling of pleasure).
- Using mental imagery to increase the ability to perform our events or even to lift weights. Imagery can be used not only to learn a physical skill but also to control our sport-related anxieties.
- Learning to concentrate at certain times during the workout and at specific times during competition.
- Learning to relax between the segments of our practices, between practice sessions and even to relax during competition.
- Understanding the mental factors that are associated with athletic success. Many of these are specific to each individual athlete.

- Understanding and controlling our anxieties, both inside and outside of sport.
- Understanding our most efficient level of arousal for a sport performance.

Setting Goals

In any worthwhile area of our lives we should have well defined goals. The attainment of those goals should be measurable. If I say, "My goal is to run the 100 meters in 12 .2 seconds," it is a measurable goal. If I say "My goal is to be happy," it is not effectively measured. But if I break down what I mean by happiness, I should be able to make it more measurable. If I say, "To be happy I want 3 close friends, 10 close acquaintances, a B average in school, a varsity letter on the track team, to have a place of my own, "all of these goals are measurable.

Whatever your goal, it should be specific and attainable. So choose a goal which can be measured: I want to be able to improve my bench press by 2 pounds; I want to increase my long jump by 2 inches; or I want to be able to serve 8 of 10 American twists into a 2 foot square area in the right corner of the service court. Unless you are a top level athlete you would not place your goals as high as: I want to win the Olympic 800 meters; I want to win the Wimbledon singles championship next year; or I want to be an All-American in the individual medley.

Some goals are individual, some should be team oriented goals. The individual goals could be: I will be able to make 6 out of 10 free throws 90% of the time; I will bring my resting pulse to 55 beats per minute by June 1; I will be able to run the 400 meters in under 55 seconds by May 1. My individual goals relating to the team might be: I will speak to one new person each day at practice until I know everyone on the squad; I will invite 10 members of the team to my house for a barbecue; I will raise $50 in the team car wash. Team goals should be set by the team. They might include: our basketball team holding the other team's offense to under 50 points this week; 75% of the track squad will improve their best marks within two weeks; hold a jog-a-thon to raise $500 for new equipment.

In a study of Division One female college swimmers, those who set performance goals improved more and had less anxiety than the control group that did not set goals. Those setting goals also developed more self-confidence. [6]

The intensity and extent of one's desire to accomplish any of these goals is called motivation. The degree of motivation can be measured by how fervently the goal or goals are pursued. It has been said that a person isn't what she says but rather what she does. As a person successfully accomplishes goals in life, as in athletics, that person's self-confidence increases. And in sport, self-confidence is a major factor for success. This is a reason that coaches should not put down their athletes. While the coach may think that sarcasm stirs the athlete to achieve higher, in reality it generally is counterproductive. Encouragement is a far more effective psychological tool for helping people to succeed.

There is an old Irish proverb that says, "If you don't know where you're going you won't know if you get there." Goal setting is the absolute starting point for every athlete.

Imagery

Imagery, or visualization, is mental practice. Much of the early work in developing the technique was done in the United States, but it was the Eastern Block countries that refined and applied this knowledge. The basic principles, however, have been instinctively employed to some degree by many athletes for years.

In visualization the user can see the activity from the outside (external) or feel it from the inside (internal). Jack Nicklaus, the famous golfer, explains the external visualization process of himself as going to the movies. He just closes his eyes and sees himself performing his swing.

Greg Louganis, the Olympic champion diver, started his mental practice of a dive with the same kind of external visualization, then he felt himself doing the dive — internal visualization. He also found it helpful to play appropriate music while he mentally performed the dive.

You can apply these techniques to your individual skills. If you know that when batting you "step in the bucket," you can mentally see the pitch coming then step directly at the pitcher. If you are having trouble hitting your backhand drive, you can imagine a ball coming to your backhand, taking the proper steps and backswing, then watching the ball all the way to your racket. You can also apply imagery to your team responsibilities. A rebound has just been made and your team fast breaks. As the rebound is secured, you mentally take your proper path at full speed to the proper position. As a volleyball player you know that number five likes to hit cross court if she is on your left side. You mentally get ready for that shot — mentally putting yourself in different parts of the court then moving to the expected spot after mentally watching her arm and upper body through the entire hitting action.

Coaches should encourage their athletes to mentally practice their individual skills and their team responsibilities. When an upcoming opponent has been scouted and individual or team tendencies are learned, the coach should work the individual or the team through the desired skill or reaction pattern. The coach can have the players in a quiet room, eyes closed, then mentally take them through the skills, reactions or team play desired. Players get far more repetitions in doing an action mentally than they do on the field or court. Also, they can practice it perfectly. Once the players have learned this skill the coach can tell them what skills or reactions are most important to mentally practice. The athletes can then do this mental practicing at home.

Sport psychologist Bill Morgan from the University of Wisconsin, one of the very top people in the field, decided to test the physical effects of the two types of imagery. The sense of effort was greater in the subjects doing internal imagery than those doing external imagery and resulted in a significant increase in the breathing rate. However, both internal and external imagery produced significant elevations in systolic blood pressure (the pressure at the time the heart pumps) and this increase was identical to that experienced in actually performing the activity.

Oxygen consumption, breathing rate, heart rate and diastolic blood pressure (DBP) were similar between internal and external imagery. It was concluded that the psychophysiological responses to internal imagery resemble actual exercise more than external imagery.[7]

In any mental rehearsal, whether for a life goal, a conditioning goal or a sport specific goal, it is essential to think positively. Concentrating on failure will produce it. If you concentrate on success, you are, in effect, practicing to succeed. Successful golfers have long practiced this idea of positive visualization. They don't look at the water hazard or the sand trap, they visualize where they want to hit the ball and think positively.

Relaxation

Everyone can benefit from learning to relax more effectively. Hindu yogis have practiced the art of relaxation for thousands of years, and yoga continues to be regarded as a worthwhile pursuit today. A few years ago a Harvard University medical doctor, Herbert Benson, developed a simple technique of relaxation in which one simply sits in a chair, loosens one's clothes, closes the eyes, and breathes deeply while shutting out extraneous thoughts. [8]

Shutting out the thoughts while breathing deeply is the key element. Benson suggests repeating slowly a nonsense syllable with each breath. You might say "one, one, one" or "Om, om, om" as you inhale or exhale. Although other thoughts will come into your head, if you just keep repeating the nonsense syllable, those thoughts will leave. This type of relaxation has been shown to reduce stress and lower blood pressure.

Once you have become accomplished at the technique of relaxation, you can do it standing or sitting. In fact, many runners have learned to relax during their competition.

Since stress creates tension and uses energy, it will reduce your strength. For this reason it is important to be able to relax effectively during practice and before competition. If you get too nervous before a competition, relaxing techniques can reduce your arousal level to a point where you can be more effectively compete.

Concentration

When you concentrate, you narrow the focus of your thought power to one object or task, or even just one element of an object or task. Thus, a golfer may concentrate on just one small part of the golf ball before swinging to hit it. A weight trainer may concentrate on the pressure against the hands or on one muscle group before and during the exercise. A basketball player may concentrate on just the front rim of the basket when shooting, or a tennis player may just concentrate on seeing the ball hit the racquet. This kind of concentration is often called focusing.

When you are strength training you should concentrate on some area of every repetition, but you should concentrate more fully on the more important angle of movement. As a downhill skier in a slalom race you might concentrate on making your turn as quickly as possible while passing a gate. As a tennis player you might concentrate on the exact spot (height and position) that you want to toss the ball. As a shot putter you might concentrate on the last hard push of the fingers on the release. As a long jumper you might concentrate on getting height on leaving the board. As a dancer you can pick an imaginary spot to concentrate on while pirouetting.

The focus of concentration may change as a skill needs perfecting. A golfer may be told at one time to concentrate on a slow low takeaway, another time on a dimple of the ball, another time to keep the left arm straight, another time to keep the elbows close to the body, another time to take a divot. A good coach can help the athlete to pick a concentration point

Mental Training Works

Dr. Charles Garfield relates his experience as the subject of an experiment in the mental approach to weight lifting.[9] As a weightlifter who met Soviet psychologists at an international meeting, he doubted the validity of the results the Soviets had reported for mental training for weight lifting.

The Soviets asked him about his maximum bench press. He said it was 365 pounds, eight years earlier when he was in serious training. They asked his most recent bench press max, and he said 280. Then they asked how long he thought it would take to train to again reach his maximum. He said, "At least nine months." With this information the Soviets were ready to prove their position.

They asked him to attempt a 300-pound press. To his great surprise, he succeeded — barely. Then they directed his relaxation using advanced techniques and had him deeply relaxed for 40 minutes. They added 65 pounds to the bar and had him visualize lifting it. They had him mentally rehearse every aspect of the lift, from the feeling in the muscles to the sounds that he made while lifting. The process was repeated until he felt totally confident in what was about to happen. He concentrated on the lift and made it -- equaling his lifetime best.

Mental Control

Another aspect of the mental approach to sport is being in tune with your body. Being aware of your heart rate and your breathing frequency may help you if you are a long distance runner or swimmer. In a study of long distance runners, it was concluded that the improvements in running economy occurred as a result of the learning and using relaxation techniques. Their amount of oxygen used (VO2) was reduced by 7.3%, their heart rates were reduced by 2.5%, and their ventilation was reduced by 9.2% after six weeks of training. Based on other measurements, these changes did not occur because of the training but were accounted for by the mental effects of the biofeedback given during the six-week testing period. [10]

"The psychological skills in question, such as maintaining one's confidence and attentional focus, reducing unwanted stress, goal setting and the use of imagery are trainable."[11] To become a better athlete or a more effective team player, you can use these mental techniques to improve your skills and team play. What will help your sport the most? Pick out one or two areas for improvement then determine whether you need goal setting, imagery, concentration or relaxation — or what combination of these is needed. Practice what you need in the quiet of your home. Improving these mental skills will pay great dividends during your practices and competitions. As a coach you must recognize the importance of the mental side of your athletes and train them just as you do their bodies.

Notes:

1. M.J. Mahoney et al., "Psychological Skills and Exceptional Athletic Performance," *Sport Psychologist* 1 (2000): 181-199.
2. L. Williams, "Contextual Influences and Goal Perspectives Among Female Youth Sport Participants," *Research Quarterly of Exercise and Sport* 69.1 (1998): 47-579.
3. Williams.
4. D.L. Gill, "Psychological, Sociological and Cultural Issues Concerning the Female Athlete," *The Female Athlete*, ed. A.J. Pearl (Champaign, IL: Human Kinetics, 1993): 112-131.
5. N. Tumer, J.S. LaRochelle, and M. Yurekli, "Exercise Training Reverses the Age-Related Decline in Tyrosine Hydroxylase Expression in Rat Hypothalamus," *J Gerontol A Biol Sci Med Sci* 52.5 (1997): 255-259.
6. D. Burton, "Winning Isn't Everything: Examining the Impact of Performance Goals on Collegiate Swimmers' Cognitions and Performance," *Sport Psychologist* 3 (1989): 105-132.
7. Y. Wang and W.P. Morgan, "The Effect of Imagery Perspectives on the Psychophysiological Responses to Imagined Exercise," *Behav Brain Res* 31.52 (1992): 167-174.
8. Herbert Benson, *The Relaxation Response* (New York: William Morrow Company, 1975).
9. Charles Garfield, *Peak Performance* (Los Angeles: J. B. Tarcher, 1984).
10. S.J. Caird, A.D. McKenzie and G.G. Sleivert, "Biofeedback and Relaxation Techniques Improves Running Economy in Sub-Elite Long Distance Runners," *Medicine & Sport in Science & Exercise* 31.5 (1999): 717-722.
11. J.L. Duda, "Psychological Aspects of Training," *Women and Sport* ed. B. Drinkwater (Oxford: Blackwell Sciences, 2000): 117.

25

Sport Psychology and the Mental Aspects of Learning and Performance

Sport psychology is a relatively new kid on the block. The people in the field do not have exact definitions of what they mean when they say "anxiety," "stress," "arousal," "motivation" or other such psychological terms. Of course, in this regard they aren't much different from those involved in general psychology.

Here are some useful definitions that may clarify the terms for athletes and coaches:

- Motivation can be seen to be the underlying reasons for, and the strength of, one's desire to learn and/or to compete.
- Arousal is a state of excitement or stress in which the athlete feels mental excitement and physiological changes in which she prepares for an individual or team battle. Arousal can be experienced to any level — such as when an athlete is ready, is truly excited, or when the athlete has become overcome with the mental and physical tasks before her. It can therefore have a positive, highly positive or even a negative effect on the athlete.
- Stress is a mental state that results when the physical or mental demands that are placed on the individual require that person to use some form of coping behavior. Stress can be either positive or negative for an athlete, depending on the type and the amount.
- Anxiety results when the individual doubts her ability to cope with the situation and negative stress occurs.

Motivation

Motivation is a much more complicated factor in sport than is often assumed. The locker room pep talk is seen as potentially "motivating." Its real effect in psychological terms is "arousal." Real motivation is quite different from arousal. It includes the long-term goals to learn a sport skill and to become effectively conditioned for the sport. It also includes the desire to prepare for competitions.

An athlete's motivation is dependent on her goals. For example, a high school girl might go out for the track team to be with her friends, to lose weight, to achieve better fitness, to achieve status by being on a sport team, to win the league championship, to become all-state, to become an Olympian, to win the Olympics. It is also dependent on what she believes will bring success — hard work or luck.

Psychological Drives, Motivation and Coaching Styles

There are a large number of theories about what motivates people. In traditional psychology much of the early work centered around what motivates us. Freud believed it was a drive for pleasure, particularly sexual pleasure. Alfred Adler thought it was a drive for power. Erich Fromm thought that our main motivation was to be loved, and as civilized people, to love in the humanitarian sense. Victor Frankl found that the major human motivation was to find meaning in our lives. Abraham Maslow found a hierarchy of motivation depending on our needs, beginning with meeting our basic physical needs, then on to safety needs, then to the emotional needs of having one or a few people loving us, then to the level of having people like and respect us, then finally to the highest level such as self actualization by succeeding in needed human achievements such as justice, art, music, etc. Maslow put the other psychologists' need theories into an overall theory that found each earlier theorist right for a different level of maturity.

Sigmund Freud popularized the idea that we have unconscious drives that motivate us. We have our conscious minds, of which we are aware. "What's my name?" "Where was I last night?" The answers to these questions are in our conscious minds. "Why do I like sports?" "Why do I coach?" The answers to these questions may lie largely in our unconscious minds. Certainly we can give answers to these questions from our conscious minds, but they may not be totally accurate. Unconscious reasons are undoubtedly at work.

While Freud liked to find sexual reasons for most of our behavior, one of his early colleagues, Alfred Adler, thought that our most basic drives were for power. He believed that in our early years we developed inferiority complexes because as babies and children we didn't have much control over our world. Because of these deep feelings of inferiority we spend most of our lives trying to achieve power — power over ourselves and power over others. We also want other people to hold us in esteem. Both participating in sports and coaching help to fulfill this drive for power — especially if we are successful.

Another Austrian psychologist believed that being able to love was the most human thing we could do. Erich Fromm said that we learn to love by being loved. Love, in this sense, has nothing to do with sex. It has to do with caring for others. When Ashley Montagu, one of America's greatest social thinkers, was asked to write the section on love for the *Encyclopedia of Mental Health* he had to first define "love." His definition was, "Love is the communication to another human being of one's deep involvement in that person's welfare, of one's profound interest in him as a person, demonstrated by acts that support, stimulate and contribute to the realization of his potentials and the fulfillment of his personality." According to this definition Montagu said that mental health is the ability to love and the ability to work.

Some coaches coach because they want to help to bring out the best in their charges. It is the development of the minds and bodies of the athletes that is their primary goal. You can certainly see the value of this "loving" coach in youth sport — as well as sport in every level of education.

But what about the athletes? What motivates them? The major motivation for most athletes is the satisfaction of their power drives. With the exception of lower level sport where the only desired outcome is fun, some element of power is probably evident in most athletes. Sport participation at increasingly higher levels is more likely to satisfy the athlete because she has continued to improve (gaining power), has increased her success, and has gained the esteem of others.

Coaches should understand their own power drives and how an athlete who does not live up to her potential frustrates the coach's own power drives. This frustration can lead the coach to yell or to punish the athlete because the athlete didn't perform at a high enough level to satisfy the coach's power drive. But what is the effect on the athlete? Does it help her drive for power? Not much chance!

Achievement or Performance Goals

From about the age of 12, young people can differentiate the effect of "effort" versus "luck" in terms of success for difficult tasks. When this is recognized and a performance goal is set, the athlete's motivation can be seen in how hard she attempts to master the athletic task.

Achievement goals can be divided into task-oriented and ego-oriented goals. Those athletes who are task oriented are concerned with mastering an activity. How well they do in a competition is measured against how well they have mastered the task they have been practicing. The ego involved athlete is more concerned with beating the opponent. It doesn't matter whether winning is a result of poor opponents or of one's superior performance. So the ego-involved athlete is more concerned with the performances of others than herself.

Coaches and athletes often are so concerned with winning the next game or meet that they attempt to motivate through ego-involvement techniques. Yet in coaching we generally find that working to master the skill or skills needed in the competition will increase our performance level and increase our chances of winning the next competition. John Wooden, the former basketball coach at UCLA, is considered by many to have been the best coach of any team in any sport. His record of NCAA championships certainly shows that he was the best basketball coach of all time. Wooden's philosophy of coaching placed the emphasis on mastery of skills and team play. He said, "We don't worry about our opponents, we are only concerned with how well we play."

Anne-Metta Pensgaard is the sport psychologist for the highly successful Norwegian National Women's team in soccer. For her doctoral dissertation she was advised by Professor Glyn Roberts, thought by many to be the world's leading authority on motivation in sport. She analyzed both the situational factors and the individual differences which might create stress. The study was done on Norwegian winter sport athletes at the Olympics in Lillehammer, where the Norwegian team was the most successful. It was found that the athletes who felt they had less ability were more affected negatively by the coach and the team situation. Those who thought highly of their ability did not have this problem. The conclusion was that among elite athletes the coach should foster a "mastery" climate-mastering the tasks needed to compete.[1]

As Glyn Roberts has written: "If the person is task involved, then the conception of ability is undifferentiated and perceived ability is not relevant as the individual is trying to demonstrate mastery of the task rather than normative ability. ... On the other hand, if the individual is ego involved, then the conception of ability is differentiated and perceived ability is relevant as the individual is trying to demonstrate normative ability, and how his/her ability fares with comparative others becomes important."[2]

The people involved in the task of learning measure their success by whether they get better in their techniques and team play. If a girl improves her time in the mile run by 2 seconds but is last, she is happy. But an ego-involved athlete who improved her time in the mile by 5 seconds, but came in 4th and was behind people she had previously beaten, would be unhappy.

Athletes, as others, seem to have a basic leaning toward being either task- or ego-involved in terms of their motivation. This is probably due to the way they have been socialized by their families, teachers, friends, and coaches. When parents, teachers or coaches emphasize winning, the children will be more likely to be ego-oriented. When they are praised for their improvement, they are more likely to be task-oriented.

In sports the media are very much involved in making people think in an ego oriented way. We have been taught that the team losing the Super Bowl is just that, a loser — not the second best professional team in the country. The girl who "only got" the silver medal in Olympic skiing is a loser — not the second best skier in the world. Parents and coaches should be aware that fostering task-orientation and measuring success based on one's progress, rather than on the gold medal, is far better for the athlete. But how often do we see the parent who has never competed chastising his daughter because she didn't win?

Athletes, having chosen a competitive arena, are usually high in at least one of these motivational forces, but may be high in both. It is good to know what type of motivation is primary to you as an athlete. As a coach it is important to recognize the major sources of motivation for each of your athletes, then it is best to direct them toward the task goals — becoming better skilled and better team players.

Motivation to Master a Task

When people are task oriented, they are generally concerned with personal development and developing lifetime skills as purposes of sport.[3] They also see that their effort (motivation) is critical to their mastery of the tasks which they need to accomplish in order to be better athletes. Hard work, along with working with others, is the major motivation. As coaches we often assume that all athletes are motivated to work hard. It is probably our own motivation, so we assume that others are similarly motivated.

Task-motivated athletes are the kind that coaches expect. These athletes are concerned with getting better in the future by hard work today. Another advantage is that studies show these athletes enjoy the sport more than those who are ego involved. Their motivation is more intrinsic — coming from within the athlete.

When the coach or athlete emphasizes mastering the skill or the team strategy, there is more likely to be an increased effort in trying to do one's best. These athletes will practice harder. This is also positively correlated with the athlete feeling the "flow" of being caught up with the activity. Studies have shown that female athletes respond even better than males when the practices are task oriented and success is based on improvement.

Ego-Involved Motivation

When the coach emphasizes winning, particularly when there is a public performance or public reporting of the event, the athlete tends to become more ego involved. Her "self," rather than an effective high level performance, is more important. It is enhancement of one's status which is primary — the showing off of one's ability and beating of others.

The ego-involved physically competent athlete is inclined to use the least amount of effort in order to be successful against an opponent. Cheating will be resorted to if necessary. Trying to impress the coach is also found in the ego-involved athlete. This ego-motivated athlete is looking at "what's in it for me." Social status, career mobility and popularity are important for this person.

A poor athlete who is ego involved will not adjust well to competition. This athlete will tend to avoid challenges, to reduce her effort when faced with difficulties, and even to drop out of the sport. The ego-involved athlete is also likely to want to avoid practice, except where she can demonstrate her superiority to others. Feeling confident in her ability today is more important than working for success at a later date.

Despite these negatives regarding the intrinsic motivation, practice motivation and selfishness of the ego-involved athletes, ego-involvement is not necessarily bad. What is counterproductive is when the ego-involved person is not task oriented. Since a person can be high or low on scales for ego involvement or task motivation, the coach should be primarily concerned with increasing the motivation to perfect the tasks involved in becoming a better athlete. It is OK to have a high ego involvement if the task involvement is also high. But it is the task involvement level that is primary for developing an athlete or a team to her (their) fullest.

Readiness for Learning

A Norwegian study compared those who scored high with those who scored low on the Sport Competition Anxiety Test. Within these two groups some were given a novel task to complete either with or without mental practice. Those who scored low on the Sport Anxiety Test did significantly better at learning the new skill than those who scored high on the anxiety scale.[4] This strongly indicates that anxieties will impede our learning. Consequently, coaches and athletes must be concerned with reducing anxiety by minimizing or controlling the stresses relating to game and practice situations in which anxiety becomes a negative influence. Coping skills must therefore be learned to increase the athlete's potential.

Competition Related Anxiety

As competition approaches, anxiety should increase. While athletes relish the chance to compete, they can develop excessive stress from the anticipation of the competition. The ego oriented athlete going against easy competition shouldn't feel much stress. But when the competition is strong, and possibly better than she is, anxiety can be quite high. The task oriented athlete, being more concerned with an effective performance, should not be as stressed — especially if she is not expected to place in the event. But since most athletes have each type of motivation to some degree, we can expect the ego involvement to become higher even for the task-oriented person.

Reports over the years have indicated that the major reason for athletes to consult sport psychologists is their anxiety about a competition and how it may affect their performance. The ability to cope with pressure and anxiety is an integral part of sports, particularly among elite athletes.

Another important point that needs to be clarified is the difference between state and trait anxiety. While state anxiety can be considered to be more situational in nature and is often associated with arousal of the autonomic nervous system (such as the need to defecate, sweating, having a rapid heart rate), trait anxiety can be thought of as the general level of anxiety which a person has in her life. Trait anxiety influences performances because girls and women with high trait anxiety will react more to their perceptions of the competition — to their state anxiety.

If an athlete has trait anxiety (based on such things as hereditary propensities, problems at home, work or school), then the pressure from the competition (state anxiety) added to those other problems may be a difficult situation for the athlete. If the coach or athlete realizes the potential problems of the combined effects of the two types of anxieties a more effective approach to the competition anxiety or arousal can be made. A severely anxious athlete may need to be relaxed and calmed down. Another may need to be more focused on the event. There is no one answer to this problem, but being aware of these types of anxieties is the first step in learning to control them and making them work for the athlete.

Arousal and Readiness for Competition

Arousal can come from verbal challenges in a pep talk, but a deeper arousal can develop just because the athlete has worked very hard to prepare. It is seldom that a hard worker will come to the competition site not mentally ready to do her best. We know that we can't tell how aroused a person is by just looking at her. While some will obviously be tense, others will be jumping with excitement and anticipation. Still others will be sitting quietly imagining their perfect performance. It is really impossible for a coach to look inside her athletes and decide which ones need more arousal, which need to be relaxed and which are in a perfect state of psychological preparedness.

The Inverted U Theory of Arousal and Performance

One of the earliest models that attempted to explain the relationship between arousal and performance was the inverted-U hypothesis. It stated that as arousal increased performance would increase as well; but, if arousal became too great the athlete's performance would deteriorate. In other words, as stress began to build an individual could still feel confident in her ability to control it and her performance would improve. However, once a stressor became so great that the individual started to doubt her ability to cope with it, her performance would decline. Although this theory gave some explanation as to why performances deteriorated when individuals felt stress, it did not account for the differences in the performance of athletes who are exposed to the same stressor.

Individual Zones for Optimal Functioning

Researchers attempted to account for the differences in the performances of individuals through the concept of individualized zones of optimal functioning (IZOFs), a concept devised by the former Russian, now Finnish, sport psychologist Yuri Hanin — thought by many to be the top sport psychologist in the world. Yuri has developed and pioneered the study of how positive and negative feelings can increase or decrease sport performance in a number of sports.

According to this theory, each individual has an optimal level of preperformance anxiety which results in peak performances. However, if the pre-performance anxiety lies outside the area of the individual's zone of optimal functioning, whether too high or too low, then her performance will decrease. IZOFs can be determined by repeatedly measuring anxiety and performance or through the athlete's recall of anxiety levels prior to peak performances. Indeed, researchers found that IZOFs are better predictors of performance than the inverted U- hypothesis.

Hanin looks at several emotions such as anxiety, anger, or joy, and at the "global effect" of the general pleasantness or unpleasantness of those emotions and their effect on the athlete's sport performance. Subjective evaluations can be done daily as well as in the pre-competition days and after the competition. The athletes have been found to remember quite well how they felt prior to the competition in regards to the several emotions being measured.

While we might think that negative feelings would reduce our performance and positive feelings increase it, this is not always the case. There are times when negative feelings increase our performance level and positive feelings decrease it. Additionally each of these feelings can affect different athletes in quite different ways. Hanin's research spans a number of sports. He has worked to find the "individual zones for optimal functioning," or IZOF, for a number of top level athletes in a number of sports.

Both positive and negative feelings can have either positive or negative effects on an athlete's performance. Both the feeling (emotion) and its strength are important. In fact a strong feeling, positive or negative, for one athlete may have a different effect for that athlete if the feeling is weak. Or a strong feeling might be positive for one athlete but negative to another. Here is an example of what might be positive or negative for a hypothetical athlete. [5]

Among the possibly helpful feelings are: tension, dissatisfaction, being nervous, tight, uncertain, irritable, attacking. Among the feelings which often have a negative effect are: being tired, depressed, distressed, being exhausted, sorrowful.

It is not only the type of feeling but the intensity of that feeling which must be taken into account in predicting or evaluating the athlete's perfor-

Negative emotions having a positive effect	Positive feelings having a positive effect
Being scared Nervousness Being tense	Being determined Feeling confident Being motivated
Fearful Doubtful Distressed	Careful Quiet
Negative emotions having a negative effect	Positive feelings having a negative effect

mance. Hanin often uses the Borg Category Rating Scale. In this scale, as used by Hanin, the strength of the feelings can be subjectively rated by the athlete. The scale can be: 0=no feeling, 0.5=barely perceptible, 1= very light, 2= light, 3= moderately felt, 4= fairly heavy or fairly strong feeling, 5= heavy or strongly felt, 6 = more strongly felt, 7= very heavy or very strong, 8 and 9 are increasing grades of strength or perception, 10= extremely heavy or extremely uncomfortable to the level of being unendurable.

This type of scale can be used to measure not only how one feels about something, like "being anxious about the game" or "being concerned about one's homework or grades" or "being content at work" but can also be used in the physical realm to evaluate the fatigue being felt while strength training, running or practicing.

As a coach or athlete you may want to use a scale such as Borg has suggested or you might want to design a different scale on a 1 to 5 or 1 to 10 scale. You can use such a scale to measure the positive or the negative (pleasantness or discomfort) feelings of an athlete.

Borg type scale		
Negative ratings		*Positive ratings*
No perception of discomfort	0	Nothing positive felt
Slight perception	0.5	Slight positive feelings
Little perception of discomfort	1-2	More than slight
Moderate perception	3	Moderate positive
Fairly heavy perception	4	Fairly strong positive
Heavy	5	Strong positive
Heavier	6	Stronger positive
Very heavy	7	Very strong
Still heavier	8	Still stronger
Very, very heavy	9	Very, very strong
Extremely heavy (most I can endure)	10	Ecstatic

Using a simpler five level scale you could use:
0 – No feeling
1 – Some feeling
2 – Moderate (average) feeling
3 – Strong
4 – Unbelievably strong

In a study of Olympic level soccer players Hanin looked at the positive and negative effects of a number of feelings. He found that 23.1% of them predicted a good performance while 42.3% of them were related to negative performances. [6]

In the same study a difference was found between the successful and the less successful players. Two days before an important game the more successful players had more negative feelings which might make them ineffective than did the less successful players. The question then becomes how can you reduce these performance decreasing negative feelings by game time.

Hanin's most recent publication does a meta-analysis of all published studies of the varying levels of effects on the individual zones of optimal functioning.[7] "According to the individual zones of optimal functioning (IZOF) model, an athlete's performance is successful when his or her pre-competition anxiety is within or near the individually optimal zone. When anxiety falls outside the optimal zone, performance deteriorates." The IZOF model also assumes that high level athletes are aware of, and are able to accurately recall and anticipate, their pre-competition anxieties.

A meta-analysis of 19 studies from 1978 to 1997 (146 effect sizes based on 6387 participants) was conducted to examine the validity of the assumptions regarding the in-out of the zone notion and the accuracy of recalls and anticipatory measures of anxiety. The conclusion was that the performance of athletes who were in their previously determined optimal zones did significantly better than those who were not in their most effective zones.

A study of Harvard University track and field athletes compared the inverted U theory with the IZOF theory. To test the inverted U theory the athletes were evaluated an hour before the meet for their "task specific anxiety," that is, were they anxious about what they had to do in that meet, put the shot, start fast in the 100, etc. They were also evaluated on how they felt relative to the average amount of pre-competition anxiety they felt. Was it higher or lower than average. To evaluate their individual zones of optimal functioning (IZOF) they were asked to recall their best performances and how they felt prior to that performance.

The study showed that in terms of the inverted U theory, the athletes who had optimal levels of anxiety or arousal did no better than those who were not optimal. But in the IZOF evaluation, those who rated similar to their best performances did better. The conclusion was that IZOF was a significantly better predictor of performance than the inverted U approach. [8]

Another study which validated Hanin's IZOF idea was done on female high school swimmers. The swimmers completed the State Trait Anxiety

Inventory and the Body Awareness Scale at four different times: when there was no pre-competition worry; when they recalled how they felt prior to their best, average and worst performances; 24 hours before a meet and 1 hour before a meet. It was found that the better swimmers were more in tune with their feelings than were the average swimmers, and those feelings were more accurate for the important meets than the less important meets.[9]

Raglin then wanted to see if the IZOF theory also worked for teams. In a study of nine female volleyball team members the same State Trait Anxiety Inventory was used. It was administered three weeks before and two days before each match and evaluated how the each player thought she would feel an hour before each game. She was then evaluated on how she actually felt an hour before the game. Each athlete was also evaluated on how she felt before her best game. As was assumed by Hanin, there were considerable differences between athletes. The athletes were better able to predict their actual pre-competition anxiety for important than for the easy matches (78% vs. 22%). Their predictions taken three weeks before a match were not significant. Most important was that 55% of the players reported that they performed best when their anxiety was outside of the normal level, either at low or high levels of anxiety. [10]

As athletes this should make us conscious of what our own best level is. For coaches this should impress us with the fact that to have our teams function at the highest level, the anxiety or arousal levels of our athletes should not be the same — unless they are all the same. Even in team sports individuals function better or worse depending on whether they are in or out of their own optimal zone. So some athletes have to be calmed before a competition while others have to be aroused.

It is not only the actual anxiety being felt but also the way that the athlete handles the anxiety that is important. It has been found that, although the absolute level of pre-competition anxiety was similar between successful and unsuccessful Olympic gymnasts, there were differences in the way the athletes conceptualized the anxiety they were experiencing. The better performers viewed their anxiety as desirable, whereas anxiety was associated with self-doubts and negative thinking in the unsuccessful gymnasts. The same is true in school when people must take tests. Successful test takers enjoy the challenge while poor test takers are negatively affected by the stress. [11]

This research also focused on the location of an athletic event as well, finding that away games resulted in increased somatic anxiety and lower self-confidence. Age is also a factor. Adolescents, regardless of gender, ex-

Evaluate yourself daily on how you rate yourself in each of the "feelings" listed below, then rate yourself on how well you performed in the practice or in the competition.

Negative Feelings that are Often Positive for Performance

Very slight <   > Very strong

	1	2	3	4	5	6	7	8	9	10

Tension
Dissatisfaction
Being nervous
Feeling "tight"
Being uncertain
Feeling irritable
Wanting to attack someone
Other:

Negative Feelings that are Often Negative for Performance

Being tired
Feeling depressed
Being distressed
Feeling exhausted
Feeling sad for someone or something
Other:

Postive Emotions that may have Negative Effects

Careful
Quiet
Contented
Other:

Positive Emotions that may have Postive Effects

Confident
Determine
Motivated
Eager
Other:

perience significantly higher levels of cognitive and somatic anxiety and lower levels of self-confidence as the ability of opponents increased.

Gender is also a factor. Among males, cognitive and somatic anxiety is more strongly affected by their perception of opponent's ability and probability of winning. Females, on the other hand, experienced anxiety or self-confidence based on their own readiness to perform and the importance they personally placed on doing well. These gender differences are indicative of the need for coaches to develop interventions that are tailored to individual needs and the importance of considering all factors when developing an effective plan for pre-competition arousal and for controlling harmful anxieties.

So coaches and athletes who are looking for maximal performances must be aware of their motivations, their anxieties and their levels of arousal. Since they are keys to performance, they can be just as important as the type and extent of the physical conditioning of the athlete.

Rate how well you think you performed each day on a 1 to 10 scale.

As you become more aware of your own zone of optimal functioning you can better predict your performance and can possibly alter the negative feelings which you find hinder you.

Notes:
1. A.M. Pensgaard and G.C. Roberts, "The Relationship Between Motivational Climate, Perceived Ability and Sources of Distress Among Elite Athletes," *Journal of Sports Science* 18.3 (2000): 191-200.
2. G.C. Roberts, D.C. Treasure, and M. Kavussanu, "Motivation in Physical Activity Contexts: An Achievement Goal Perspective," unpublished manuscript (2000).
3. G.C. Roberts, D.C. Treasure, and M. Kavussanu, 12.
4. H. Halvari, "Effects of Mental Practice on Performance are Moderated by Cognitive Anxiety as Measured by the Sport Competition Anxiety Test," *Percept Mot Skills* 83.3 Pt 2 (1996): 1375-83.
5. Yuri Hanin, lecture by at the First International Conference on Skiing and Science, January 1998, St. Christoph, Austria.
6. Yuri Hanin and P. Syrja, "Performance Affect in Soccer Players: An Application of the IZOF Model," *International Journal of Sports Medicine* 16.4 (1995): 260-265.
7. M. Jokela and Y. Hanin, "Does the Individual Zones of Optimal Functioning Model Discriminate Between Successful and Less Successful Athletes? A Meta-Analysis," *Journal of Sports Science* 17.11 (1999): 873-887.

8. P.E. Turner and J.S. Raglin, "Variability in Precompetition Anxiety and Performance in College Track and Field Athletes," *Medicine & Sport in Science & Exercise* 28.3(1996): 378-385.

9. J.S. Raglin, W.P. Morgan and K.J. Wise, "Pre-Competition Anxiety and Performance in Female High School Swimmers: A Test of Optimal Function Theory," *International Journal of Sports Medicine* 11.3 (1990): 171-175.

10. J.S. Raglin, and M.J. Morris, "Pre-Competition Anxiety in Women Volleyball Players: A Test of ZOF Theory in a Team Sport," *British Journal of Sports Medicine* 28.1 (1994): 47-51.

11. J.S. Raglin, "Anxiety and Sport Performance," *Exerc Sport Sci Rev* 20 (1992): 243-274.

26

Handling and Reducing Stress

We all encounter stresses. They may be life-threatening or merely inconveniences. How we handle them can mean the difference between mental health and mental illness, and they can affect our success in terms of concentration and effort in practice and competition.

Stress is the response that the mind and body make when the psychological requirements are too high.[1] For example, reading a novel and reading a textbook in preparation for a test are both experiences in reading. But one may be quite stressful. Similarly, taking a test and writing a letter, both experiences in writing, will probably cause different levels of stress. And certainly running a 100 meter time trial in practice and running 100 meters in the Olympic finals will cause different levels of mental stress.

When you were a student, you might have been stressed by taking a test, interviewing for a job, balancing the work and study schedule with a social schedule, or doing a term paper. There can be financial problems, being unhappy living at home, having roommates who are discourteous, or having a professor who seems unfair. As we enter the workforce, become self-supporting, and start families, the cause of the stress may be different but the effects on our comfort are similar.

It is not the cause of the stress as much as the effect of that stress on the individual that is the major concern. Loud rock music may be pleasant for one person and a terrible noise to another. Studying for a test may be pleasant for one student and stressful for another. Giving a speech before an unknown group of people can be either stimulating or unpleasant depending on the situation. Serving for point match at Wimbledon can also be stressful or exhilarating.

Individuals with positive self concepts may experience less stress. Their positive ideas of themselves make them less likely to be overcome by the stressor, and they are more likely to feel in control rather than feeling the stressor is in control of them. Studies on humans at the International Centre for Health and Society at University College in London and studies on baboons in Kenya strongly indicate that the higher an individual is in the hierarchy of the society or job classification, the longer the individual lived. It seems that whether a lower class baboon or a lower class human, they had less control over their lives and therefore more life stress. This was true for humans even when other risk factors were controlled such as smoking, cholesterol level, and blood pressure. So self-esteem and the ability to control one's life are certainly positive factors and stress reducers.[2] Success in sport also can give us this increased feeling of self-esteem.

The Effects of Unhealthy Stress on the Person

The mind and body can react to stressors with anxiety, depression, or hostility.[3] These mental reactions can then be transformed into physical diseases such as heart attack, high blood pressure, ulcers, neck and back pains, and asthma. Now we find that even cancers and other illnesses are related to a lowering of the immune system — a possible result of stress.

A number of years ago the Holmes-Rahe scale was developed. It took into consideration a number of life events, both positive and negative, and correlated them with diseases. The more events a person experienced during a year the more likely it was that diseases would develop. How do you rate? (See box.)

Typically the causes and the effects of stress are different between men and women. Men's levels of stress-induced neurotransmitters increased much more during competitive and intellectual challenges. Women's levels increased more dramatically during stressful personal situations. Studies at the Karolinska Institute in Sweden and at Cornell Medical Center in the United State indicate that when husbands and wives have the same types of jobs the men's stress levels tend to drop as soon as they leave the office. Women's tend to stay high throughout the evening, probably because of the family responsibilities that continue into the evening.[4]

Good Stress and Bad Stress

Dr. Hans Selye, the Canadian researcher who was the pioneer of stress research, tells us that there is good stress (eustress, "eu" from the Greek word for "good") and bad stress (distress). We need stress in our lives, but we want to increase the eustress and decrease the distress. We want to have

Holmes-Rahe Social Readjustment Scale

Scoring for the Holmes-Rahe social readjustment scale
- Less than 150 life change units in a year resulted in a 30% chance of developing a stress-related illness.
- 150 TO 299 life change units in a year resulted in a 50% chance of illness
- Over 300 life change units in a year resulted in an 80% chance of illness

LIFE EVENT	SCORE
Death of spouse	100
Divorce	73
Marital separation from mate	65
Detention in jail, other institution	63
Death of a close family member	63
Major personal injury or illness	53
Marriage	50
Fired from work	47
Marital reconciliation	45
Retirement	45
Major change in the health or behavior of a family member	44
Pregnancy	40
Sexual difficulties	39
Gaining a new family member (e.g., through birth, adoption, etc.)	39
Major business re-adjustment (e.g., merger, reorganization, bankruptcy)	39
Major change in financial status	38
Death of close friend	37
Change to different line of work	36
Major change in the number of arguments with spouse	35
Taking out a mortgage or loan for a major purchase	31
Foreclosure on a mortgage or loan	30
Major change in responsibilities at work	29
Son or daughter leaving home (e.g., marriage, attending college)	29
Trouble with In-laws	29
Outstanding personal achievement	28
Spouse beginning or ceasing to work outside the home	26
Beginning or ceasing formal schooling	26
Major change in living conditions	25
Revision of personal habits (dress, manners, associations, etc.)	24
Trouble with boss	23
Major change in working hours or conditions	20
Change in residence	20
Change to a new school	20
Major change in usual type and/or amount of recreation	19
Major change in church activities (a lot more or less than usual)	19
Major change in social activities (clubs, dancing, movies, visiting)	18
Taking out a mortgage or loan for a lesser purchase (e.g., for a car, TV, freezer, etc.)	17
Major change in sleeping habits	16
Major change in the number of family get-togethers	15
Major change in eating habits	15
Vacation	13
Christmas season	12
Minor violations of the law (e.g., traffic tickets, etc.)	11

Shanelle parents expectations
her own self imposed pressures.
? mothers suicidals   cancer
  medical conditions = eating
                     car wreck killed her   father dying

the excitement of playing a tennis match, reading a stimulating novel, or traveling to a new destination. These are eustresses. We want to eliminate or control the distresses — the long drive to school or work, the hassles with the people at home, a harassing coach or teammate, the lack of challenge at our jobs.

Stress is natural for humans. Selye once observed that "Stress is the spice of life." [5] But as we encounter stress, we must be able to cope with it, then, if possible, eliminate the negative stresses.

Selye captured the importance of stress in our lives when he wrote, "... man's ultimate aim in life is to express himself as fully as possible, according to his own lights, and to achieve a sense of security. To accomplish this, you must first find your optimal stress level, and then use your adaptation energy at a rate and in a direction adjusted to your innate qualifications and preferences." [6]

Both the physical body and the mind can make adaptations to stresses. The body may adjust by a reduced immune function which can result in a lower resistance to diseases and more frequent colds. The person may develop allergies such as asthma, acne, skin rashes. The cardiovascular system may react with higher blood pressure, tightness in the chest, or a stronger or more rapidly beating heart. The blood vessels may react by increasing headaches or by slowing the blood flow to the hands and feet making them feel cold. The muscular system can respond with pains in the back, neck or jaw. The gastrointestinal system can show involvement by diarrhea, constipation, burping, excess gas, or ulcers. The nervous system may show signs such as dizziness, tics, menstrual irregularities, or sleep problems. Psychologically some people react by anger, boredom, depression, hopelessness, irritability, hostility, anxiety, panic, frustration or fear. The method of adjustment is likely to be inherited, although some people "learn" their adjustments by imitating others. Physical exercise counteracts nearly all of these negatives of stress.

Exercise is often overlooked as an effective method of stress reduction. But when one runs, swims, plays basketball or hits a tennis ball, there is some stress reduction. We often see only the physiological benefits of exercise without recognizing its mental effects. But it is known that forceful exercise, especially where hitting or kicking is involved, is an efficient way of reducing the effects of stress. "Kicking posts" have been used in some elementary schools so that students will have an outlet for their frustrations. Psychologists often use soft foam-filled bats or boxing gloves filled with air as vehicles by which people can take out their frustrations by hitting another person or an inanimate object.

Too often stress is handled by reaching for a tranquilizer, a sleeping pill or an alcoholic beverage. But "I need a drink" is often more of a problem than a solution. Pills and booze are not the effective solutions for which most people hope.

Coping With Stresses

While the ideal way to handle unwanted stresses is to eliminate them, this is not always possible. Consequently, we must often learn to handle the stresses with coping skills — relaxation techniques such as meditation, exercise techniques such as aerobic dance or swimming, or diversion techniques such as music or reading. - I will play positive upbeat motivational music

Coping techniques that may reduce the effects of distresses on us can be: 1) cognitive (from the mind to the body) such as meditation, 2) somatic (from the body to the mind) such as exercise, or 3) behavioral approaches (changing behaviors that are harmful) such as time management. [7]

Cognitive techniques begin with the mind. It is hoped that by correct thinking, or by "non-thinking," the body can be relaxed and the tensions of the distresses can be reduced. Among the cognitive techniques are meditation, the relaxation response, hypnosis, and thought stopping.

Somatic techniques begin with the body as the focus, but the mind relaxes as the body responds to the specific technique. Among the somatic techniques are: yoga, progressive relaxation, diaphragmatic breathing, massage, and physical exercise. Because this is a book on physical fitness we will emphasize the contributions of exercise to the reduction of stresses.

Physical exercise can help a person to relax in several ways. It can be a recreational pursuit, a rhythmic endurance exercise, or a pleasant physically fatiguing experience.

A recreational pursuit, such as a game of tennis or golf, a day of downhill skiing, or an afternoon of surfing or scuba diving can make a person forget about the problems that have created the stressful feelings in one's life.

A rhythmic activity such as distance swimming, running, walking, or cross country skiing can provide both the diversion of a recreational activity and the rhythmic breathing of a meditation session. But for such an exercise to have stress-reducing effects, several factors must be present. It should be enjoyable, it should be aerobic and not be competitive to the participant, and it should be of moderate intensity and last at least 20 minutes. [8]

While people generally report that they feel better after exercise, not all exercise is equally beneficial. In fact some exercise can create stress. A competitive runner or swimmer working to exhaustion so that a peak performance can be achieved in the championship meet is such an example. Similarly, recreational swimmers swimming in uncomfortably warm water showed an increase in stress. A golfer or tennis player under pressure to win would be another example.

People who are particularly competitive in life may carry that competitiveness into their recreational pursuits and negate the stress reducing benefits that would have accrued if the exercise had truly been recreational. It is important that if exercise is to be used to reduce stress, it must be pleasant — it must be play. Running may be play for one person but work for another. Shooting baskets may while playing for the recreational league championship may be distressful — especially if you are losing.

Many people have experienced a particularly high level of stress relief after 30-50 minutes of aerobic activity. This is often called the "exercise high" and is suspected to be related to the brain's reaction to increased endorphins — brain chemicals similar to opium.

If an exerciser, particularly an aerobic exerciser, has participated in the exercise several times a week for more than a year, the psychological benefits are greater. It has been found that for runners who had run at least 30 miles a week for two years, a single episode of high intensity work on a treadmill greatly reduced the anxiety level of that person and increased the alpha brain waves (the waves present during meditation). But this same level of exercise for people who were not long-time runners did not pro-

---

SELF TEST 1: What are the Major Stresses in my Life?

Rate 1 to 5 (with 1 meaning "little or no problem" and 5 being "the most severe and bothersome")

1. I don't have enough time to do what I need to do.____
2. Deadlines for assignments at school or at work are problems.___
3. My friends and family make too many demands on my time.___
4. I have at least one instructor who bothers me a lot.____
5. My roommates are problems for me.____
6. Taking tests is always a big worry for me.___
7. I don't know what I want to do with my life.____
8. I am having trouble with my relationship (or finding a relationship).____
9. My parents are problems for me.____
10. (Other problem[s])_____ bothers me a great deal.____

According to this evaluation the three major stresses in my life are:
1.
2.
3.

Self Test 2: Stress Symptoms
Rate 1 to 5 (1 being the least amount of problem) 1. I put off doing important things (procrastination).____ 2. I can't slow down my mind.____ 3. I don't sleep well (insomnia)____ 4. My moods change often.____ 5. I always have to be doing something.____ 6. I am tired a lot.____ 7. I get impatient often.____ 8. I avoid others as often as possible or I am very shy.____ 9. I am often angry.____ 10. I am often very sad.____
Which three adjustments do you make the most often? 1. 2. 3.

duce these same levels of relaxation.[9] These stress reduction benefits increased as the number of exercise sessions per week and the number of weeks increased. The benefits from the exercise seem to last 2-4 hours. [10]

It is obvious that a person who is physically fit will have a better self-concept than one who is out of shape. This is an important part of a person's total self-concept and their self-esteem. Since people with better self-concepts and higher self-esteem are more able to handle stressors, physically fit people should experience fewer negative effects from stressors than those who are unfit. [11]

Effective exercise has also been shown to reduce the illnesses that often accompany stressful events in our lives.[12] Exercisers also report a lower incidence of colon, breast, and prostate cancer. [13]

Exercise has been shown to be as effective as other stress management techniques in reducing depression, tension, and anger.[14] Since exercising aerobically (running, swimming, etc.) is inexpensive and takes the same amount of time as other techniques, while giving additional benefits of weight control and cardiovascular fitness, it should be high on everyone's list of necessary daily activities.

Choosing the Coping Technique

Each type of stress may be more effectively handled by the choice of an appropriate coping technique:
- When you are experiencing physical symptoms such as tense muscles, a rapid heart rate, or a lack of energy, a physical activity may help

Following is an outline of a few possible stressors. Each may cause great distress to some people and none to others.

Possible Stressors

PHYSICAL

- A lack of oxygen.
- Extreme fatigue or tiredness.
- Pain from pushing oneself hard in a workout or competition.
- An excess of lead or asbestos in the environment.
- Too much heat or cold.
- A strong wind.
- A loud noise, including loud music.
- Some chemicals (some acids or alkalis, alcohol.)

BIOLOGICAL

- An allergic reaction to poison ivy or oak.
- An upset stomach from the salmonella germ.
- Any disease, injury, or disability.
- Hunger or thirst.
- Physical problems of aging.

MENTAL

- A threat or a perceived threat.
- Boredom.
- Lack of success in sport or other areas of life.
- Lack of satisfaction of a basic drive (power, love, meaning).
- Failure at school or work.
- Mental problems of aging (each age may have its own problems).
- Being in a minority group (racial, ethnic, religious, etc.) if you feel discrimination.
- Experiencing a loss, such as death or the break-up of a relationship.

VALUES

- Doing something counter to what one's religion holds dear:
  - Having an abortion when it is considered wrong.
  - Lying.
  - Cheating on a test.

- Doing something counter to another type of value:
  - Ordering a second helping when on a diet.
  - Buying a coat that isn't needed when you are on a tight budget.

SOCIAL RELATIONSHIPS

- Not having a good friend.
- Unhappiness with parents or children (such as alcoholism or drug use).

ECONOMICS

- Not having enough money.
- Paying high taxes .

CAREER

- Unhappiness with one's career.
- Inability to obtain a job.
- Job pressures.
- Lack of control and authority on the job.

POLITICAL

- War or the threat of war.
- Injustices carried on by your government or another government.

GEOGRAPHICAL

- Living in a big city.
- Living in a ghetto.
- Living in a third world country.
- Living in an area which is negatively. prejudiced against you because of your sex, race, or religion.
- Living in a country which is very hot, very cold, or has long, dark winters.

SPORT

- Excessive fatigue.
- Harassment/abuse by a coach or teammate.
- Pressure to win.
- Time pressures of other activities interfering with practice time.
- Feeling burned out or overtrained.
- Reduced performance level.

Checklist for Choosing a Coping Method
If your stress symptoms are physical, choose a physical coping method (a sport, walking, jogging, weight workout).   If your stress symptoms are mental, choose a mental coping mechanism (meditation or hypnosis).   If your stresses are caused by too much to do and not enough time, think of a method such as time management or assertiveness training.

you to better handle the stress. Running, swimming, cycling, cross country skiing, massage, or yoga may be the best choices for your stress reduction.

- When your stress reactions are mental such as anxiety, worry, insomnia, and negative thinking about yourself, your better choices for coping may be: meditation, the relaxation response, or hypnosis.
- If your stresses are caused by a hectic schedule, having too many things to do and too much responsibility, your better coping mechanisms may be: assertiveness training (to be able to say "no" to some people who want more of your time), time management (to be better able to schedule the important activities), biofeedback, and psychological assistance to change your time pressured type A behavior to a more relaxed mode of living.

Handling Sport Stresses

As you well know, stresses can come from our sporting experiences and expectations and from our lives outside of our sport. To optimize our sport performances we must be able to understand the sources of our in-sport and out-of-sport stresses and how they are affecting our performances. Once we understand the sources and types of stresses we can make more intelligent attempts to either avoid or reduce the stresses.

Coping problems are more likely to occur with the less-experienced athletes and males and females tend to react differently. But as the athletes rise to the elite levels they tend to be much more effective in handling their stresses, and the males and females tend to react similarly. [15]

Notes:

1. Don Frankl, Paper delivered to the American Academy of Kinesiology, Washington, D.C., April, 1993.
2. "Why Workers Suffer Most from Stress," *Financial Times (London)* Feb. 26, 1995.

3. R.L. Repetti, "Short Term Effects of Occupational Stressors on Daily Mood and Health Complaints," *Health Psychology* 112 (1993): 125-131.

4. *Harvard Women's Health Watch* October (1994): 6.

5. H. Selye, *Stress Without Distress* (New York: Signet, 1975): 83.

6. Selye: 110.

7. Bonnie G. Berger, "Coping with Stress: The Effectiveness of Exercise and Other Techniques," Paper presented at the Annual Meeting of the American Academy of Kinesiology and Physical Education, March 24, 1993, Published in *Quest*, vol. 46, 1994.

8. Bonnie G. Berger, "Mood Alteration with Exercise: A Taxonomy to Maximize Benefits," Paper presented at the VIII World Congress of Sport Psychology, Lisbon, Portugal, June 23, 1993.

9. S.H. Boutcher and D.M. Landers, "The Effects of Vigorous Exercise on Anxiety, Heart Rate, and Alpha Activity of Runners and Non-Runners," *Psychophysiology* 25 (1988): 696-702.

10. J.S. Raglin and W.P. Morgan, "Influences of Exercise and Quiet Rest on State Anxiety and Blood Pressure," *Medicine and Science in Sports and Exercise* 19 (1987): 436-463.

11. L.A. Tucker, "Effect of Weight Training on Body Attitudes: Who Benefits Most?" *Journal of Sports Medicine and Physical Fitness* 27 (1987): 70-78.

12. J.D. Brown, "Staying Fit and Staying Well: Physical Fitness as a Moderator of Life Stress," *Journal of Personality and Social Psychology* 60 (1991): 555-561.

13. L.T. Mackinnon, *Exercise and Immunology: Current Issues in Exercise Science [Monograph No. 2]* (Champaign, IL: Human Kinetics, 1992).

14. B.G. Berger, E. Friedman, and M. Easton, "Comparison of Jogging, The Relaxation Response, and Group Interaction for Stress Reduction," *Journal of Sport and Exercise Psychology* 10(1988): 431-447.

15. J.L. Duda, "Psychological Aspects of Training," *Women and Sport* ed. B. Drinkwater (Oxford: Blackwell Sciences, 2000).

27

Harassment, Sexual Harassment and Abuse in Sport

Some might question the inclusion of this chapter in a book on conditioning, but harassment by a coach or other athletes can make the sport experience unpleasant and have severe consequences for the athlete. Harassing behavior by a coach can not only "destroy" individual athletes, but it can also hurt recruitment to teams. It is therefore important to create a sporting environment that protects against harassment.

Harassing behavior is unfortunately found everywhere in society, in the home, at school, in business, and in sport. It can be the parent or teacher calling a child "stupid." It can be a first grader making fun of another because of their big ears, skin color, thinness or size. It can be the bullies ganging up on a weaker classmate. It can be the older athletes putting down the younger or less successful teammates or opponents. Hazing, or team initiations, can single out a person or group of people and subject them to embarrassing, degrading or secretive behavior. When a coach either allows such behavior or participates in it, an athlete will feel uncomfortable and the sport experience will offer less to the participant. A coach who initiates or allows harassing behavior is reducing the cohesion of the team. It is one of the worst examples of a motivating climate and is definitely a negative influence on the victims. It also tears down the "team" feeling and allows for individual self-centeredness to emerge as the personality of the group.

Violence against girls and women is, in most countries, a large societal problem. Statistics from The United Nations concerning violence against women, reveals that: From 40%-60% of known sexual assaults have been found to be committed against girls 15 years of age and younger, regardless of the region or culture.[1] We also know that sexual abuse occurs in the home. Spousal abuse, child beating and incest are well documented. Since sport in many countries plays and important role in the society, it is logical that behind these figures there would be perpetrators and victims who are connected with sport. At this moment an English Olympic swimming coach is in prison for a number of years because of sexual abuse. An Irish swimming coach is facing similar punishment.

We can state that where harassment and abuse occurs in the society, we are going to find harassment and abuse in sport. We want coaches, athletes and parents to be aware of how the athletes can be used as subjects of harassment or abuse — and what can be done to minimize or eliminate the practice. We also believe that sport organizations can play a role in reducing harassment and abuse against women. First by developing policies to protect athletes in sport, but also by recruiting more girls and women into sport, because the self esteem gained from sport may act as protective factor against increased violence and harassment in society at large.

Harassing and abusive behavior can be done by both genders toward both women and men. Most commonly it is male coach to female athlete or male athlete to female athlete. Over the recent years it has also been verified that male athletes also have been victims of sexual abuse, primarily by male coaches. It is probably often even more difficult for a male athlete to report an incident of harassment or abuse than for a female. In a study from Canada of 537 athletes and 72 coaches, the reasons mentioned for why people were reluctant to report harassment were:[2]

Fear of being cut from the team	38%
Fear of not being believed	36%
Ashamed/embarrassed	51%
Loyalty to coach/team	29%
Don't know who to talk to	27%

The severe psychological damage that can be done to large numbers of female athletes makes this the most important chapter in the mental area of conditioning. For the athletes, you must understand what harassment is and how to avoid it, stop it, and report it. For coaches, it is important to understand the severe consequences of harassing behavior, both for your own coaching career and for the victim. It is also important that you, as a coach, report harassment or abusive behavior made by others if you see it. In the above mentioned study from Canada the athletes answered as follows on a question about who had initiated the harassment they had experienced:

Coach	25%
Official	14%
Teammate	30%

Spectator	22%
Parent	14%
Other	16%

These figures show that there are many other potential harassers in an athlete's environment than just the coach. And some of the abusive behavior by others, such as teammates or administrators, has left serious psychological scars on female athletes from which they may never recover.

What Is Harassment and Abuse?

We have already used the word harassment many times, so we had better define it. It is a difficult term to define, because any definition will contain a certain subjective, or interpretive element. This has been called the gray zone because not everyone perceives the same behavior in the same way. Hilary Findlay and Rachel Corbett, at the Centre for Sport and Law in Canada write that: "Harassment is a behavior, by one person toward another, which is insulting, intimidating, humiliating, malicious, degrading or offensive. It creates negative and uncomfortable feelings for the person, or group of persons, to whom it is directed. Such a person may feel anything from a discomfort or embarrassment in the presence of the person or group of people displaying the behavior, to a feeling of terror or even fear for her safety. [3]

Harassment can take many forms whether physical, verbal, sexual or emotional and most often involve a combination of these elements. At the extreme end of the harassment scale we can find both "abuse" and "neglect." The Canadian report defines abuse as: "Any form of physical, emotional and/or sexual mistreatment or lack of care which causes physical injury or emotional damage to a child."[4] Another definition of abuse is "invasion without consent," where invasion on the basis of sex is psychological, physical or both.[5]

Some people include abuse in their definition of harassment, and write often about "less severe" and "more severe" forms of harassment. Others point to the fact that there are stages along a continuum of sexual violence, which goe from sexual discrimination, involving various institutionalized oppressions (differential pay structures, unfair work practices or conditions), to sexual harassment (a combination of personal and institutional issues, such as jokes, lewd comments or sexual innuendoes, physical contact, fondling), to sexual abuse (such as forced sexual activity or rape).

It is important to know that the common characteristic of harassment and abuse against children and adults is an abuse of power or authority and/or a breach of trust. Since coaches normally have a lot of power and athletes often trust their coaches very much, we should all be aware of the potential for negative things to happen in the coach-athlete relationship. A sport team can be viewed as a surrogate family — with the coach as the unquestioned patriarchal figure. For this reason some researchers see the sexual demands of some male coaches as incestual.

One athlete observed, "I consider it incest — that's what this is all about. Because the time spent, the demands, the friendship, the opportunity they're giving you something no one else can. They're brother, uncle, father — the child feels safe and will do anything. That's why it's incest."[6]

Consequences of Sexual Harassment and Abuse in Sports

Research shows that the impact of sexual harassment can be severe for the athlete. It may have devastating effects that can include:

- Reduced ability to concentrate
- Sleeplessness
- Diminished ambitions and self confidence
- Poor performance at work
- Sick leave from work or sport
- Negative effects on family life and parenting
- Persistent feelings of shame and guilt
- Diminished athletic performance
- Depression
- A complete withdrawal from sport and social activities[7]

The Prevalence of Sexual Harassment and Abuse in Sport

Very few sport-specific data on the incidence and prevalence of harassment are available. It is suggested that approximately 40%-50% of sport participants have experienced a negative and uncomfortable environment.[8] This includes everything from mild harassment to abuse. A Danish pilot study of 250 sport students found that about 25% either knew about or had themselves experienced situations where a sport participant under the age of 18 had been sexually harassed by a coach.[9] In a survey of 1200 male and female elite athletes in Canada, of the 226 who replied, over 20% had experienced sexual intercourse with an authority figure in their sport, and 9% had experienced forced sexual intercourse.[10] Another Canadian study showed that there was far more evidence of harassment from peer athletes than from coaches.[11] A recent study in Norway found that 28% of the female elite athletes had experienced sexual harassment in sport either from an authority figure or from other athletes. This study compared female athletes to matched women outside of sport in work or educational settings. It concluded that elite athletes are not exposed to sexual harassment more than other groups in society. A difference between the athletes and non-athletes was found with regard to experiencing sexual harassment from an authority figure in sport compared with a supervisor or teacher. More athletes had experienced sexual harassment from an authority figure in sport (15%) than controls had done from supervisors or teachers (9%).[12] This indicates that authority figures in sports exhibit behavior toward athletes that is not tolerated or accepted at a workplace or in an educational institution. One reason for this may be that many Norwegian sports organizations have not developed the codes of conduct that have been required in business and educational settings. It should be noted that European sport is organized on a private club and national level, not in schools and colleges as is done in the U.S. Also the coaches and administrators in Europe don't need to be trained educators as is commonly true in the U.S.

The Coach-Athlete Relationship

" ... when he told me to swim an extra 1000 yards, I swam an extra 1000 yards. That's part of it, you're in a one down position to your coach. You do what they tell you to do. You don't say "no" when you're a child, you don't say no to an adult if they have a lot of authority and you're somewhat intimidated by them. ... Many of the top coaches are married to former athletes, so that's a way society sanctions this. As soon as she turns 23, they get married, and, you know, legally that's fine. He may retain all the power in that relationship, she may never be able to grow up and stand on her own."[13]

The first thing to remember is that, regretfully, there are some men who go into sport to get sexual access to children. A coach has power and authority over the children they're training. They have respect from the parents, respect from the community and, because often their lives are dedicated to children, it's hard to believe that a person in that position can be an abuser. All of that can be used as a cover by a man who has sexual arousal oriented feelings toward children.[14]

If men are going to abuse children, they have to form a relationship first.[15] Sport is a way of forming that relationship, and it is a way of turning that relationship into an abusive one. This process is called "grooming." This grooming process can go on for years without the individual who is being groomed realizing that there is an increasingly closer and stronger relationship between her and the perpetrator until she is unable to resist his sexual advances. The power afforded to the coach in his position of authority offers an effective camouflage for grooming and abuse. As the coach or sport authority figure moves psychologically and physically closer to the child athlete, the shift in boundaries tends to be unnoticed and is generally unreported. The athlete is usually bewildered by the sexual pressure and is afraid to report it because she risks the displeasure of her coach and teammates and may be punished by the coach by dropping her from the traveling team. Her athletic career can be ruined if she reports the behavior. Consequently, the more talented the athlete, the more likely it is that she will become the sexual victim. A recreational athlete can just quit, but the goals of the potential elite athlete may require that she submit to the sexual advances of the coach in order to stay in his good graces. Without the support of the coach, she cannot get the extra training and the higher levels of competition she craves. Some athletes may recognize the warning signs and resist the power of the coach as is shown in the following quote. It should be mentioned, though, that this athlete suffered later through being ostracized by all the squads coaches.

"When I got there, the team was in the reception, and I was told, 'There is no room for you.' ... The coach heard it and said, 'Don't worry, you can come in my room.' And something just didn't sound right. So I said, 'But I can't.' When you think, you know, if you're not allowed to bring a boy home, and you could certainly not bring him to your room ... how can you suddenly go into the coach's room? Now I think that the invitation wasn't innocent at all ... and no one helped me at all." [16]

A coach has power and authority over the children he is training, and it is hard to believe that a person in that position can be an abuser. Coaches also often have a lot of respect from both the community and from parents. Offenders are ordinary citizens who look and act normal in public and are often well-liked and charismatic.[17] "... many of these guys, like the guy who molested me, are very nice guys. They're successful, they're upstanding citizens in the community, according to male standards, so the don't look sleazy, they don't look like what we think of as a rapist, even though they are — it is statutory rape."[18]

Marg MacGregor writes that children are most at risk from someone they know and that offenders tend to put a lot of time and energy into creating situations in which they have access to children. In sexual abuse, the coach exploits his power. This power is sustained because he has the skills and abilities to develop, enhance and maintain success and a strong reputation for the sport. The athletes want skill, improvement and selections, the parents want success for themselves and their daughters, and the administrators need success in the sport for it to flourish and for their empires to survive. Because of these factors the coach is afforded the respect of authority and is in a position of power over athletes.[19]

331

Risk Factors

Here are some of the main findings from research studies that are particularly relevant for coaches and athletes:

- The risks of sexual harassment and abuse in sport are increased for particularly young girls, for whom the differences in age between perpetrator and victim leads to an unequal power relationship.
- The victims also are likely to have low self esteem in spite of being among the best on the team.
- If the child gets effective supervision from the parents, the perpetrator has less opportunity to abuse.
- Other "at risk" athletes are those with disabilities or learning difficulties and/or those for whom access to others is difficult, are also more vulnerable to abuse. The same is true for women athletes with eating disorders.

The research indicates that a distant relationship of the daughter with the parents, especially the father, may well also be a risk factor for sexual abuse in sport.

"We were just ripe for the picking ... everyone on our team was going through some personal family difficulty ... "[20]

In addition to parents, other people in the environment of the child are also important. Children who are isolated from other children seem to run a higher risk. Among athletes under 16 years of age the following four situations seem out to be particularly risky: attending national and international tournaments, being massaged by the coach, being at the coach's home, and when the coach drives the athlete home.

The sport context represents another set of potential risks of sexual abuse for the female athlete. Organizations which have no formal policies or procedures for recruiting, checking, inducting or monitoring employees, whether paid or volunteer, are easy targets for the pedophile. This is particularly the case in the lower ranks of a sport or at the recreational level where volunteer labor is often welcomed with little or no screening. Sports in which it is possible for individuals to be isolated either in or from the main training area, or where the athletes are taken on trips away from home, clearly have a responsibility to implement rigorous safety procedures.

Combating Sexual Harassment in Sport

A number of sports federations, schools, colleges, and countries have set, or are setting, standards for athletes, coaches and other authority figures. If you are an athlete, coach or parent, you should insist that a policy on sexual harassment and abuse be developed and implemented.

WomenSport International is an international organization whose aim is to bring about increased opportunities and positive changes for women and girls at all levels of involvement in sport and physical activity. WomenSport International has established a task force that has developed a brochure on sexual harassment in sport. Concerning prevention, WomenSport International encourages all sport organizations to:

- Prepare and implement codes of ethics and conduct for coaches, whether they work with adults or children.
- Foster a climate of open discussion about the issues of sexual harassment and abuse so that athletes with problems feel confident enough to speak out.
- Develop athlete autonomy wherever possible including adopting coaching styles which give optimum autonomy and responsibility to athletes.
- Become involved in coach education programs which inform and advise about the ethical and interpersonal issues of sexual harassment and abuse and about the technical aspects of physical touch in coaching the sport.
- Adopt athlete and parent education programs which inform and advise athletes on their rights and how to maintain their integrity and autonomy.
- Introduce and use reporting and mediation systems for both athletes and coaches, ideally with the assistance of trained social work or counseling professionals.
- Ensure that parents are fully informed of the whereabouts of their children at all times and are involved as fully as possible in supporting the work of coaches.
- Adopt rigorous screening procedures for the appointment of all personnel, whether coaching staff or voluntary workers.
- Be constantly vigilant and avoid complacency and expect and demand the highest standards of accountability at all levels of the sport.
- Celebrate the good work of athletes and coaches on a regular basis.

Coaches, as those closest to the athletes, have a duty to become aware of the high ethical standards of sport. They then need to not only be aware of their own potentially harassing behavior. but they should also teach their team members about harassment and abuse. In California a number of high schools and colleges have brought in experts on sexual harassment to talk to the athletes. The laws state that if a person makes a potentially degrading remark, especially calling someone a "fag" or "dyke," that person can be declared ineligible for the next game or even the sport season.

Below are some concrete examples of these different themes, which are used in the codes of conduct for coaches. Though these were identified as belonging to one of the above mentioned broader categories, they varied a lot in their specificity. Examples under each category will illustrate the types of behavior which should be considered.[22]

Responsibility of the Coach

1. Coaches must respect the rights, dignity and worth of every human being and their ultimate right to self-determination. Specifically, coaches must treat everyone equitably and sensitively, within the context of their activity and ability, regardless of gender, ethnic origin, cultural background, sexual orientation, religion or political affiliation.
2. Coaches have a duty and responsibility to take seriously all incidents or complaints of sexual harassment.
3. Sports massage should only be performed by trained personnel.

Intimate Relationships

1. Within the (professional) relationship between trainer and athlete, it is possible that either party will develop feelings which are not directly related to the practice of sport, such as fondness, love or a 'crush'. Sexual relations between the coach and athlete are strongly discouraged. It is advisable to bring one of the relationships to an end, whether this is the sporting or the sexual relationship.
2. No sexual activity/contact is allowed between athletes who are minors while on team trips, in sports facilities used by the team/organization, directly before, during or after team practices, games, training sessions or social activities conducted by the team or sports organization. No personnel shall have a sexual relationship with athletes in the same organization. When a person is in a position of trust or influence (such as a coach, league official, trainer), regardless of the fact that either or both persons may be of the legal age of consent.

Private Life

1. The coach will at all times during training sessions, matches and traveling, act in at reserved and respectful way toward the athletes and toward those spaces which the athlete occupies, such as changing rooms or hotel rooms. This requires that the coach will not intrude into the private life of the athletes — including asking questions about their outside lives or attempting to "date" the athlete.
2. A single coach or trainer should not be in the dressing room with athletes while they are showering or changing; two adults should be present together. If athletes are not comfortable showering or changing in the locker room then they should do so at home.
3. Staff members should not change or shower at the same time as athletes. Members of integrated teams should not shower or change in the same room at the same time. Comparable facilities should be provided for both sexes, or the athletes should alternate using the shower facilities.

Coach/Parent Relationship

1. When athletes are minors, the team should attempt to organize activities where parent/families can be included. Activities for "athletes only" should take place in a public facility; activities which take place in a private home should involve parents/guardians.

Venues and Meeting Places

1. Avoid unaccompanied and unobserved activities with athletes. This includes being alone in a room or vehicle.
2. No one other than the occupants of a given room will be permitted in the room unless the door is left open for visual access to outsiders.
3. The athlete will preferably not be received by the trainer at home without another adult present.

Language

1. The coach should refrain from using profane, insulting, harassing or otherwise offensive language; refrain from making sexual innuendoes about athletes.
2. Touching should never have a sexual nature, sexual undertones, or sexual jokes or innuendoes attached to it.
3. The trainer will refrain from all forms of sexually-charged verbal intimacies.

Touching

1. Where physical contact between coach and performer is a necessary part of the coaching process, coaches must ensure that no action on their part could be misconstrued and that any guidelines on this matter are followed.
2. Understand that coaches' intentions and athletes' interpretations of touching will be influenced by cultural differences and religious implications: by the age, sex and sexual orientation of the athlete, and the coach; and by their status as able-bodied, sick or disabled.
3. Be sensitive to the impact of different degrees of interpersonal proximity and be aware that unnecessary touching may offend. Be careful about which parts of the body are touched — different parts have varying social and sexual connotations. There is a difference between touching limbs and handling the torso. Touching areas close to erogenous zones is less acceptable than touching other parts of the body.
4. The coach may not touch a athlete in such a way that the contact can be reasonably interpreted by either party as being of a sexual or erotic nature, as would be the case in, for example, deliberately touching (or making someone else touch) genitals, buttocks or breasts.
5. All physical contact between athletes or between coaches and athletes should be for one of the following purposes:
   - to develop sport skills/techniques
   - to give sport massages
   - to treat an injury
   - to prevent an injury, e.g. spotting in gymnastics
   - to meet the requirements of the specific sport.

Coaches and athletes must also be aware of how remarks that athletes view as harassing, can reduce the athlete's performance and the performance of the team. It is well known in psychology that positive comments are far more motivating than negative remarks. The problem is that the "power drive" often makes it far more normal to degrade a person than to encourage and teach.

Codes of Conduct

A number of codes of conduct have been developed by sport and political organizations. More than 100 codes, policies, and other materials relating to ethical practice in sport and leisure have been analyzed by one study.[21] Many of these had been designed specifically with anti-harassment objectives in mind. In spite of the differences between cultures, the content analysis of the different national codes of conduct for coaches revealed many common areas, which are not sport specific. These central themes were:

- issues of responsibility of the coach
- issues concerning intimate relationships
- private life
- coach/parent relationship (cooperation with parents)
- venues and meeting places (being alone with an athlete)
- the language of the coach
- touching

Over the last few years, sport organizations seem to be more aware of the importance of trying to prevent sexual harassment and abuse. A logical consequence of what has been pointed out in this chapter is that awareness, information and education are very important and highly needed, whether it concerns coaches, parents or the athletes themselves. Sexual harassment and abuse in sport have probably gone on for as long as sport has existed. Lack of research and knowledge, the sensitivity of the theme, lack of policy and code of conduct and procedures may be some of the reasons why it has taken so long time before this theme has come into focus. In March, 2000, The International Olympic Committee (IOC) had its second world wide conference for women and sport. The conference adapted a resolution with the following item concerning sexual harassment:

"Urges the International Olympic Committee, the International Sports Federations, the National Olympic Committees and the National Federations to develop and implement a policy on sexual harassment including codes of conducts for athletes, coaches, sport leaders, and other Olympic parties to include this theme in all workshops and conferences organized by the International Federations and the National Olympic Committees."

If this resolution is followed up into practice one can hope for a world-wide consciousness raising concerning sexual harassment and abuse in sport, which in the end should lead to a more positive and enjoyable sport for girls and boys, women and men.

If you are being harassed or feel unsafe when you are training or playing sport, tell someone. Remember, it is not your fault.

Notes:
1. United Nations Development Fund for Women, "The Trust Fund in Support of Actions to Eliminate Violence against Women," Internet, February 2000.
2. *Speak Out ... Act Now. A Guide to Preventing and Responding to Abuse and Harassment for Sport Clubs and Associations*, (Sport Canada, 1998).
3. ibid.
4. ibid.
5. C. Brackenridge, "He Owned Me, Basically... Women's Experiences of Sexual Abuse in Sport," *International Review for the Sociology of Sport* 32.2 (1997): 115-130.
6. C. Brackenridge, loc. cit., Athlete survivor of sexual abuse in sport.
7. *Harassment in Sport: A Guide to Policies, Procedures and Resources* (Ottawa: Canadian Association for the Advancement of Women in Sport, 1994).
8. M. MacGregor, "Harassment and Abuse in Sport and Recreation," *CHAPERD Journal de L'Ascepld*, 64.2 (1998): 4-13.
9. Nilesen J. Toftegaard, "Den Forbudte Sone," Master Thesis, Department of Sport, University of Copenhagen, Denmark, 1998.
10. S. Kirby and L. Greaves, "Foul Play: Sexual Harassment in Sport," Paper presented at the Pre-Olympic Scientific Congress, Dallas, Texas, 1996.
11. M. Holman, "Sexual Harassment in Athletics: Listening to the Athletes for Solutions," Paper presented at the North American Society for the Sociology of Sport Conference, 1994.
12. K. Fasting, C. Brackenridge and J. Sundgot-Borgen, "2000 Females; Elite Sports and Sexual Harassment," The Norwegian Women's Project, Norwegian Olympic Committee and Confederation of Sports, Oslo, Norway.

13. C. Brackenridge, "Female Athlete Survivor of Sexual Abuse," Cited in *Spoil Sport* (London: Routledge, 2000).

14. C. Brackenridge, "Therapist of Male Sexual Abuser in Sport," Cited in *Spoil Sport* (London: Routledge, 2000).

15. ibid.

16. C. Brackenridge, "Female Athlete Survivor of Sexual Abuse," Cited in *Spoil Sport* (London: Routledge, 2000).

17. Marg MacGregor, loc. cit.

18. C. Brackenridge, "Female Athlete Survivor of Sexual Abuse," Cited in *Spoil Sport* (London: Routledge, 2000).

19. C. Brackenridge, "He Owned Me, Basically... Women's Experiences of Sexual Abuse in Sport," *International Review for the Sociology of Sport* 32.2 (1997): 115-130.

20. C. Brackenridge, "Female Athlete Survivor of Sexual Abuse," Cited in *Spoil Sport* (London: Routledge, 2000).

21. C. Brackenridge and K. Fasting, "An Analysis of Codes of Practice for Preventing Sexual Harassment and Abuse to Women and Children in Sport," Paper prepared for the Council of Europe Sports Division, 1999.

22. ibid.

Epilogue

*N*ow that we have looked at the best in scientific evidence relative to how our bodies work, what does it mean in terms of your own behavior as a coach or athlete?

Will you make the changes in your routines to adhere to what the sport scientists and other experts have recently found relative to conditioning effectively? Or will you continue to do what has been done for many years? It is difficult to change!

And remember that this book doesn't finalize the scientific contributions to effective conditioning. Nutritional knowledge doubles every three years. New findings on biomechanics, exercise physiology, sport psychology, sport sociology are being reported every month.

As a coach or athlete, you may be interested in keeping up with what is going on in the field of sports for women and girls. The recently published work *Women in Sport*, edited by Dr. Barbara Drinkwater, is a volume in the series titled *The Encyclopedia of Sports Medicine* that is sponsored by the International Olympic Committee's medical committee and the International Federation of Sports Medicine. It is essential for high-level coaches and sports medicine people who want to be current in the field of women in sport.

As a high school coach you can join your local or state coaches organizations. There are also national coaches associations for most sports.

WomenSport International is a worldwide group advocating the inclusion of more women into sport at every level-athlete, coach, administrator. For information contact:

Dr. Carole Oglesby, President
Pearson Hall, Temple University, Philadelphia, PA 19122

Dr. Barbara Drinkwater, Treasurer
Box 743, Vashon, WA 98070

Dr. Angela Schneider, Treasurer
University of Western Ontario
London, Ontario, Canada N6A 5CI

Womens' Sport Foundation is an American group with many of the same concerns nationally that WomenSport International has globally. Many coaches and researchers are members of both groups.

Women's Sports Foundation
Eisenhower Park, East Meadow, NY 11554

Index

— Frustration w/ Conditioning & Weightlifting.
- shoulder
- leg   } higher complaints
- shin injuries } since this class
- extremely sore   was started 3 years
  muscles   ago.

Weights — book helped, knowing
                what to tell the instructor.

105) Plyometric-
         bands — resistance.
         weight balls ; small - strengthen arms, drop & catch
                    larger - blocking   approach
                                                   drop ball
                                                   behind you.

Arm around fast :

Weights - lower back

Printed in the United States
213977BV00004B/2/A